S0-AVJ-915

Video Systems
in an IT Environment

The Essentials of Professional Networked Media

Video Systems
in an IT Environment

The Essentials of Professional
Networked Media

Author

Al Kovalick

AMSTERDAM • BOSTON • HEIDELBERG • LONDON
NEW YORK • OXFORD • PARIS • SAN DIEGO
SAN FRANCISCO • SINGAPORE • SYDNEY • TOKYO

Focal Press is an imprint of Elsevier

ELSEVIER

Acquisitions Editor: Angelina Ward
Project Manager: Carl M. Soares
Assistant Editor: Rachel Epstein
Design Manager: Cate Barr
Interior Design: Integra Software Services Pvt, Ltd

Focal Press is an imprint of Elsevier
30 Corporate Drive, Suite 400, Burlington, MA 01803, USA
Lincare House, Jordan Hill, Oxford OX2 8DP, UK

 Recognizing the importance of preserving what has been written, Elsevier prints its books on
acid-free paper whenever possible.

Library of Congress Cataloging-in-Publication Data
Application Submitted

British Library Cataloguing-in-Publication Data
A catalogue record for this book is available from the British Library.

ISBN 13: 978-0-240-80627-3
ISBN 10: 0-240-80627-1

For all information on all Elsevier Focal Press publications
visit our Web site at www.books.elsevier.com

Printed in the United States of America

05   06   07   08   09   10   10   9   8   7   6   5   4   3   2   1

Contents

Acknowledgments

This book would never have seen the light of day if it were not for many friends and colleagues who assisted me along the way. Some helped as technical reviewers, some as consultants, some as encouraging voices, and all as solid supporters. I am grateful to all of you. Thanks go to Frans De Jong, Santosh Doss, Brad Gilmer, Jacob Gsoedl, Mark Johnston, Greg Lowitz, Bill Moren, Harlan Neugeboren, Charles Poynton, Michel Proulx, John Schmitz, and Joanne Tracy.

This book is dedicated to my parents, Al and Virginia, and to my loving wife May, who provided constant support and encouragement during the entire project.

Introduction

There is a tide in the affairs of men,
which, taken at the flood, leads on to fortune,
omitted, all the voyage of their life
is bound in shallows and in miseries

—William Shakespeare

Astute sailors know the optimal time to catch the tidal flood toward the harbor. If missed, a ship may be caught in a storm or stranded at sea. An able captain and crew never pass up favorable currents. Today there is a different tidal flood that many captains of ship are seeking to ride to safe harbor. What is it? It is the tidal swell of information technology (IT)[1] that is being leveraged to create compelling video systems[2] and AV workflows for broadcasters and other professional operations. In the big picture, we are at the emergent stages of video systems designed from hybrid combinations of IT standard platforms (storage, servers, routers, networks, firewalls, middleware, software platforms, Internet, Web services, archives, etc.) and traditional AV methods and technology.

If you are only conversant in IT methods or only comfortable with traditional video techniques, then the hybrid combination may seem a bit

---

[1] The "IT" term is used throughout this book to refer to the standard platforms, systems, and methods that comprise information technology as used by business processes worldwide.

[2] In this book the term "video systems" includes audio systems and still graphics. As a composite, they are denoted by the term "AV" or "A/V" systems. The hybrid acronym AV/IT describes systems that use a combination of IT and traditional AV technologies.

strange and worrying. Will IT methods, systems, and techniques be responsive enough for the demands of real-time video? Can IT meet a 99.9999%
reliability goal? Can I run video over and through IT-based links and
switches? Will network congestion cause dropouts in my video? Will a virus
or worm take me off air? Can I upgrade my system while it is in use? Will the
short life spans of IT equipment lead to an unprofitable ROI and constant
retooling headaches? Is using IT too risky for my demanding operations?
Are the software components stable enough for mission critical applications?
Can I use IT + AV technologies and create a "Broadcast IT" system? These
and countless other concerns are discussed and resolved in this book. First,
let us look a bit deeper at the interesting cross section of IT plus AV.

Figure Intro.1 depicts the two domains of interest to us and their all
important overlap. As the workflows, methods, and technology of the IT
world and those of traditional video mix and combine, compelling new
formulations emerge. The IT sphere consists of domain experts plus all
the standard infrastructure and systems that make up IT. However, the
traditional time-based media sphere consists of domain experts, video-
specific links and routers, VTRs, cameras, A/V editors, on-air graphics,
effects processors, vision mixers, and much more. The overlap region

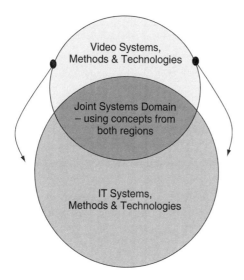

FIGURE   The joint systems domain of hybrid AV/IT systems.

INTRO.1

gathers selected components together from each domain, thereby creating IT-based media workflows.

Which domain has a greater gravitational pull on the other? In 2004, IT equipment and services was nearly a $1 trillion WW market (source: IDC) while the entire broadcast equipment market was $12.4 billion (source: DIS Consulting 2004). This is about a 100:1 ratio, and the smaller of the two is drawn to the larger to take advantage of the many levers that IT can provide for video system design. The arrows imply the gradual sliding on the AV domain onto the IT domain. Many of the biggest broadcasters have already embraced IT and have large deployments (see Chapter 10), whereas others are still waiting to put their toe into the water.

It is the compelling mix of IT + AV that is our focus. Our approach is judiciously biased toward the understanding of how AV systems can leverage IT techniques and tools. The chapters that follow cover IT in relation to the workflow needs of video systems. The intention is not to fully describe media technology but rather to explain IT in the light of video systems.

Figure Intro.2 illustrates a traditional AV system on the left and a hybrid AV + IT system on the right. Traditional is composed of custom AV components, specialized software, and exotic technologies—usually

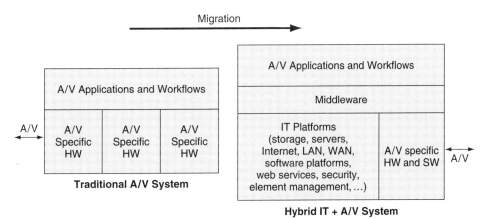

FIGURE

INTRO.2

The move to IT reduces the amount of custom A/V gear.

in small volumes. However, the hybrid mix leverages standard products from information technology and adds AV-specific elements only as needed by the workflow requirements. Some modern hybrid systems are 90% IT and 10% AV in terms of technology. Just a few years ago, the fabric of a typical AV system was 90% AV specific with just a pinch of IT. The next chapter outlines the solid business and technical motivations for the migration to hybrid systems.

SCOPE OF THE BOOK

Admittedly the world of video systems spans from the sophisticated workings of a CNN newsroom to a simple home video network. The coverage will not boil the ocean. Rather, the concentration is focused on the AV workflows used by professional broadcast, educational, government, business, and postproduction industries. There are thousands of TV stations and other video facilities WW that have not yet made the IT plunge so this is timely material.

Digital AV finds application in distribution (Web, satellite, digital cable, mobile, digital terrestrial) of content to home, business, and mobile. Home networks are catching fire too. However, our coverage focuses on production processes and not distribution or home networking. Nonetheless, many of the principles covered in these chapters are applicable to any digital AV network.

In addition to broadcasters, the discussions are relevant to media professionals in Fortune 1000 companies, government agencies, small business, cable MSOs, production facilities, and movie studios. Event videographers and prosumers are already seeing the gradual invasion of IT into their space.

So who are the target readers for this book?

◆ IT professionals—Domain experts, system administrators, directors, system engineers, security managers, CIOs, and support staff
◆ AV media professionals—Domain experts, chief engineers, VPS of Engineering, engineering managers, directors, systems integrators, design engineers, maintenance staff, technicians, facility planners, AV equipment vendors, AV sales personnel, and support staff

For media professionals, IT is framed in the context of AV systems, i.e., in what ways can IT help do my job better. For IT professionals, AV is framed in the context of IT systems, i.e., how can IT be used to create AV systems. The level of coverage is moderately technical, providing practical and actionable information for the following purposes.

◆ Understanding the forces causing the migration toward networked media

◆ Appreciating the basics of networked media

◆ Evaluating a video system's architectures, reliability, and scalability

◆ Understanding the fundamentals of networking, data servers, storage systems, data archive, and security as applied to networked media

◆ Comprehending the fundamental industry standards that apply to IT and AV infrastructures

◆ Evaluating the trends for networked media solutions and technology

◆ Providing insight into software platforms and their trade-offs

◆ Learning the support and maintenance themes for these hybrid systems

◆ Knowing what questions to ask of potential equipment suppliers

◆ Reducing the FUD[3] and social uneasiness that surround IT/AV systems

For sure, the information in this book concentrates more on IT in the context of AV than solely on traditional AV basics. However, Chapter 11 provides an overview of AV basics. If you are new to AV concepts, then it may be wise to review this chapter first.

IT means choice. Universal platforms, standards, and flexibility all embody IT. The focus of the chapters that follow is on the application of IT plus AV methods to build, operate, and support video systems in an IT-networked environment. If all this is alien to you, do not lose hope. Hang on and this book will turn alien to familiar. Do not become a prisoner of your point of view—widen out and explore the new vistas.

So, are you going with the flow? Are you catching the tidal wave that is changing AV systems forever? Let us ride this ship into safe harbors and enjoy the benefits of converged AV/IT systems. Yes, let us start on our journey of illuminating AV and IT systems in the light of each other's context.

---

[3] Acronyms are used throughout the book. Usually they are explained upon introduction, whereas in other cases, no definition is provided. When in doubt, check with the Glossary.

1 | Networked Media in an IT Environment

1.0   INTRODUCTION

Among his many great accomplishments, Sir Isaac Newton discovered three fundamental laws of physics. Law number one is often called the *law of inertia* and is stated as *Every object in a state of uniform motion remains in that state unless an external force is applied to it.*

By analogy, this law may be applied to the recent state of A/V system technology. The traditional methods (*state of uniform motion*) of moving video [serial digital interface (SDI), composite . . .] and storing video (tape, VTRs) assets are accepted and comfortable to the engineering and production staff, fit existing workflows, and are proven to work. Some facility managers feel, "If it's not broken don't fix it." Ah, but the second part of the law states ". . . *unless an external force is applied to it.*" So, what force is moving A/V systems today into a new direction—the direction of networked media? Well, it is the force of information technology (IT)[1] and all that is associated with it. Is this a benign force? Will its muscle be beneficial for the broadcast and professional AV production businesses? What are the advantages and trade-offs of this new direction? These issues and many more are investigated in the course of this book. First, what is networked media?

---

[1] IT storage and networking concepts are used universally in business systems worldwide. See the Introduction for background on IT.

1.1   WHAT IS NETWORKED MEDIA?

The term *network* in the context of our discussions is limited to a system of digital interconnections that communicate, move, or transfer information. This primarily includes traditional IT-based LAN (Ethernet in all forms), WAN (Telco provided links), and Fibre Channel network technologies. Some secondary linkages such as IEEE-1394, USB, and SCSI are used for very short haul connectivity. The secondary links have limited geographical reach and are not as fully routable and extensible as the primary links.

In contrast to traditional AV equipment,[2] networked media relies on technology and components supplied by IT equipment vendors to move, store, and manipulate A/V assets. With all respect to the stalwart SDI router, it is woefully lacking in terms of true networkability. Only by Herculean feats can SDI links be networked in similar ways to what Ethernet and IP (Internet Protocol) routing can offer.

The following fundamental methods and concepts are examples of networked media.

- ◆ Direct-to-storage media ingest, edit, playout, process . . .
- ◆ 100% reliable file transfer methods
- ◆ AV streaming over IT networks
- ◆ Media/data routing and distribution using Ethernet LAN connectivity, Fibre Channel, WAN, and other links with appropriate switching
- ◆ Networkable AV components (media clients): ingest ports, edit stations, data servers, caches, playout ports, proxy stations, controllers, AV process stations, and so on
- ◆ AV-as-data archive; not traditional video tape archive

The world of networked media spans from a simple home video network to large broadcast facilities. There are countless applications of the concepts in the list just given and many are described in the course of the book. We will concentrate on the subset that is the realm of the professional (and prosumer) media producer. Figure 1.1 illustrates the domain of the general professional video system whether digital or not.

---

[2] If you are not familiar with traditional AV techniques, consider reviewing Chapter 11 for a general overview.

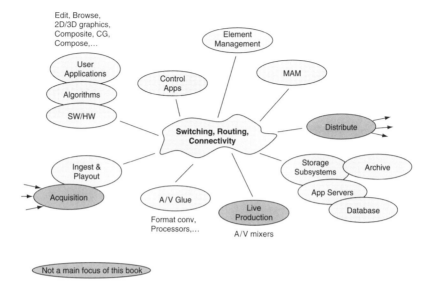

FIGURE

1.1
Professional video system components.

The components are connected via the routing domain to create an unlimited variety of systems to perform almost any desired workflow. Examples of these systems include the following.

1. Analog based (analog tape + AV processing + analog connectivity)
2. Digitally based (digital tape + AV processing + digital connectivity)
3. Networked based (Data servers + AV processing + networked connectivity)
4. Hybrid combinations of all the above

The distinction between digitally based and networked based may seem inconsequential, as networks are digital in nature. Think of it this way: all networks are digital but not all digital interconnectivity is networkable. The ubiquitous SDI link is certainly digital but it is not easily networkable. Over the course of discussions, our focus highlights #3 as primary with the others taking on supporting rolls. Items #1 and #2 are defined for our discussions as "traditional A/V" compared to item #3, which is referred to as "IT/AV or IT-based AV" throughout this book.

Again, looking at Figure 1.1, most of the components may be combined in various ways to make up an IT-based professional video system. However, three elements have extended applications beyond our consideration. The world of media acquisition and distribution is enormous and will not be considered in all its glory. Also, media distribution methods using terrestrial RF broadcast, cable TV networks, and satellite are beyond our scope. Additionally, live (sporting events, news . . .) production methods (field cameras, vision mixers) fall into a gray area in terms of the application of IT. More on this topic later in the chapter.

1.2   MOTIVATION TOWARD NETWORKED MEDIA

Over the last few years, there has been a gradual increase in new AV products that steal pages from the playbook of IT methods. Figure 1.2 shows the changing nature of video systems. At the core are untimed, asynchronous IT networks, data servers, and storage subsystems. At the edges are traditional timed (in the horizontal and vertical raster-scanning sense) AV circuits and links that interface to the core. The core is expanding rapidly and consuming many of the functionalities that were once performed solely by AV-specific devices. This picture likely raises many questions in your mind. How can not-designed-for-video equipment replace carefully designed video gear? How far can this trend continue before all notion of timed video has disappeared? What is fueling

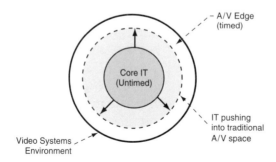

FIGURE

1.2

The expansion of the IT universe into A/V space.

the expansion? Will the trend reverse itself after poor experiences have accumulated? Our discussions will answer these questions.

There is no single motivational force responsible for the shift to IT media. There are at least two levels of motivational factors: business related and technology related. At the business level there is what may be called the *prime directive*. Simply put, owners and managers of video and broadcast facilities are demanding *"I want **more** and **better** but with **less**."* That is a tall order but this directive is driving many purchasing decisions everyday. More what? More compelling content, more distribution channels, more throughput. Better what? Better quality (HD, for example), more compelling imagery, better production value, better branding. Less what? Less capital spending, less ongoing operational costs, fewer maintenance headaches. All of these combine to create value and the real business driver—more profit. Of course there are many aspects to more/better/less but let us focus our attention on the technical side of the operations. In order to achieve more/better/less, the technology selection is key. The following sections examine this aspect.

Of course, there are issues with the transition to the IT/AV environment from the comfortable world of traditional A/V video. All is not peaches and cream. The so-called move to IT has lots of baggage. The following sections focus on the positive workflow-related benefits of the move to IT. However, in Chapter 10, there are several case studies that examine real world examples of those who took the bold step to create hybrid IT and AV environments. In that chapter you will feel the pains and joys of the implementers on the bleeding edge. In that consideration we examine the cultural, organizational, operational, and technical implications of the move to IT.

There are at least eight technical forces that are combining to create a resulting vector that is moving media systems in the direction of IT. Let us call the area enclosed by the boundary contour of Figure 1.3 the system IQ. This metric is synthetic but consider the area (bigger is better) as a measure of a system's "goodness" to meet or exceed a user's requirements. Each of the eight axes is labeled with one of the forces. Let us devote some time to each force and add insight into their individual significance. Also, for each force a measure of workflow improvement due to the force is described. After all, without an improvement in cost savings, quality, production value, resource utilization, or process delay, a force would be rather feeble. Although the forces are numbered, this is not meant to imply a priority to their importance.

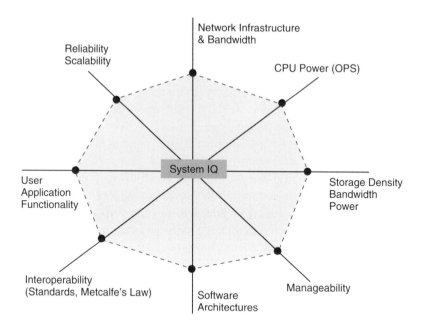

FIGURE

1.3
Eight forces enabling the new IT/AV infrastructure.

Snapshot

The Perfect Video System

The late itinerant Hungarian mathematician Paul Erdos developed the idea of "*The book of mathematical proofs*" written by God. In his spare time, God filled it with perfect mathematical proofs. For every imaginable mathematical problem or puzzle that one can posit, the book contains a correspondingly elegant and beautifully simple proof that cannot be improved upon. Erdos imagined that all the proofs developed by mere mortal mathematicians could only hope to equal those in the "book." We too can imagine a similar book filled with perfectly ideal video systems designed to match all the requirements of their users. Of the many architectural choices, of the many equipment preferences, and of the many design decisions, our book would contain a video system that could not be improved upon for a given set of user workflow requirements. True, such a book is a dream. However, many of the principles discussed in these chapters would make up the fabric and backbone of our book.

1.2.1   Force #1: Network Infrastructure and Bandwidth

The glue of any IT system is its routing and connectivity network. The faster and wider the interconnectivity, the more access any node has to another node. But of what benefit is this to a media producer? What are the work-flow improvements? Networks break the barrier of geography and allow for distributed workflows that are impossible using legacy A/V equipment. For example, imagine a joint production project with collaborating editors in Tokyo, New York City, and London (or among different editors in a campus environment). Over a WAN they can share a common pool of AV content, access the same archive, and creatively develop a project using a coordi-nated workflow management system. File transfer is also enabled by LANs and WANs. Does file transfer improve workflow efficiency? Consider the fol-lowing steps for a typical videotape-based copy and transfer cycle.

1. Create a tape dub of material—delay and cost
   a. Check quality of dub—delay and cost
   b. Separately package any closed caption files, audio descriptive nar-ration files (SAP channel), and ratings information
2. Deliver to recipient using land-based courier—delay and cost
3. Receive package, log it, and distribute to end user—delay mainly
   a. Integrate the closed caption and descriptive notation ready for playout
4. Ingest into archive or video server system (and enter any metadata)—delay and cost
   a. QA ingested material—delay and cost
5. Archive videotape—cost to manage and store it, format obsolescence worries

It is obvious that the steps are prone to error, are costly, and add delay. Let us look at the corresponding file transfer workflow.

1. Locate target file(s) to transfer
2. Initiate and transfer file(s) to end station—minimum delay for trans-fer (seconds to hours depending on desired transfer speed). Additionally, file-associated metadata are included in the transfer, thereby eliminating another cause or error—manual metadata log-ging. The transferred file integrity is 100% guaranteed accurate.

What are the advantages? No QA process steps—or very short ones—delay cut from days to minutes and guaranteed delivery (not lost or stuck in shipment) to end user. All in all, file transfer improves the workflow of making a copy and distribution of a program in meaningful ways. The walls of the traditional video facility are crumbling and the new virtual facility is an anywhere–anytime operation. So what are the technology trends for LANs and WANs?

Not all that long ago, Ethernet seemed stuck indefinitely at 100 Mb/s. Fortunately, there is a continual press forward to higher bandwidths and reach of networks. Today it is not uncommon to see 10-Gb/s Ethernet links and routers in high-end data centers.

Let us take a tangent for a moment and investigate the very high end of connectivity. Using wavelength division multiplexing on optical fiber, researchers at Lucent Technologies/Bell Labs have proven that a WDM optical transceiver is capable of delivering ~40,000 Gb/s of data on one strand of fiber. Using 1000 different wavelengths each carrying a 40-Gb/s (SONET/SDH OC-768) payload, they postulate that the astronomical rate of ~40 Tb/s is achievable per strand of fiber (see Appendix F).

Let us assume that we have encoded an immense collection of MPEG movies and programs each at 4 Mb/s. At this rate, one could transmit *10 million* different programs simultaneously on one single fiber. Since most fiber cables carry 200+ strands, one properly snaked cable could serve *2 billion* homes each accessing a unique program. Ah, so many channels, so few people. Amazing? Yes, but tomorrow promises even greater bandwidths. What is the point of this hyperbolic illustration? Video distribution and production workflows will be impacted greatly by these major advances in connectivity. Fasten your seat belt and hold on for a wild ride.

1.2.2   Force #2: CPU Compute Power

In a nutshell, it all follows from Moore's law. Simply put, Gordon Moore from Intel stated that integrated circuit density doubles every 18 months. The law had been in effect since 1965 and will likely continue for at least another 10 years according to Intel. Initially, the doubling occurred every

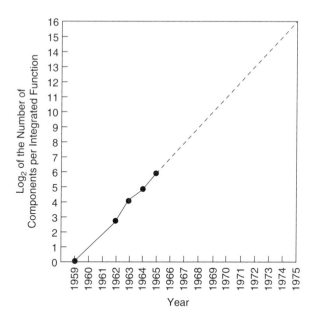

FIGURE

1.4

Moore's law: Graph from his original paper.

Source: Electronics, Volume 38, Number 8, April 19, 1965.

12 months so it has slowed a bit since then. Figure 1.4 is the famous diagram redrawn from Moore's original paper (*Cramming more components onto integrated circuits*) [Moore] and shows the doubling trend every 12 months. This diagram is the essence of Moore's law. Early among Intel's CPUs was the 8008 with 2500 transistors. As a graduate student at UC Berkeley, the author wrote an 8008 program to control elevator operations. In 2004 the Itanium 2 CPU (64 bits) had 120 M transistors—hence the prediction and power of Moore's law.

This law was not the first but the *fifth* paradigm to provide exponential growth of computing. Starting in 1900 with purely electromechanical systems, relays followed in the 1940s, then vacuum tubes, then transistors, and then integrated circuits. Since 1900, "computing power" has increased 10 trillion times. Our appetite for computing power is growing to consume all available power. Expect another factor of 8 (2004 base) by 2010.

Demonstrating one of the paradigms of computation, while a Lowell High School student, the author designed and built an eight-line,

Front view of Phone System   Rear view of Phone System

FIGURE   Eight-line, relay-based, automatic telephone system.
                From: May Kovalick.
1.5

relay-based, automatic telephone system for a San Francisco Science
Fair. Figure 1.5 shows the final 60 relay design. Relay logic was relatively
straightforward, and the sound of the relays completing a call was always
a kick. For a teenager, transistors were way too quiet. The top of the unit
is the power supply, the midsection has 40 of the 60 relays, and the lower
section has two dial-activated rotary relays and two line-finder rotary
relays. In the rear is the dial tone generator, batteries, and some additional relays. Not shown is a sound-proof box containing relays for generating the 20-Hz ringing voltage and various timing intervals.

Video processing needs a huge amount of computing power to perform real time or "human fast" operations. Once left to the domain of
purpose-built video circuits, CPUs are now performing three-dimensional

(3D) effects, noise filtering, compositing, compressing video (ala MPEG), and other mathematically intensive operations in real time or faster. It is only getting easier to manipulate digital video, which will consign traditional video circuits to a smaller and smaller part of the overall system.

Running CPUs in parallel, in one manner or another, increases the total processing power available to applications. The compute power of these systems is enormous and performance can exceed a trillion operations per second (TOPS). There are more details on this in Appendix C. On the memory front, the cost of one megabyte of RAM has dropped precipitously from $5000 in 1977 to $.1 in 2004 in constant dollars. This is a 50,000 factor decrease in only 27 years [HenPat]. At least one video server manufacturer in Japan offers a RAM-based server while eschewing the disk drive completely. Broadbus (www.broadbus.com) has introduced an all DRAM-based VOD server for distribution of on-demand programming to the home. All in all, CPU and memory price/performance is ever decreasing to the benefit of media system designers and their users. Incidentally, CPU clock speed has increased by a factor of $750\times$ from the introduction of the 8008 in 1972 until the Pentium4 in 2000.

Snapshot

What will you do with a 1 billion transistor, 20-GHz CPU?

Intel predicts that such a device will be available in 2009. The date may move but the eventuality will not; such a device is on the horizon. Is the device overkill? Consider some CPU-based software A/V applications:

- ◆ Encode and decode MPEG HD video in real time
- ◆ Perform 3D effects in real time much like dedicated graphics processors do today
- ◆ Format conversions, transcoding in faster than real time
- ◆ Three-dimensional animation rendering
- ◆ Real time image recognition
- ◆ Complex video processing
- ◆ Compressed domain processing

As processing power increases, there will be less dependence on special purpose hardware to manipulate video. It is possible that video processing HW will become a relic of the past—time will tell.

So what is the workflow improvement? Fewer devices are needed to accomplish a given set of operations. The end-to-end processing chain has fewer links. Many AV operations can be performed in real time using off-the-shelf commodity CPUs. There are, however, a few specialized processors that are optimized for certain tasks and application spaces.

In the area of specialized processors, the list includes

◆ Graphics processors (NVIDIA and ATI Technologies, for example)
◆ Embedded processors (Intel, Infineon, TI, and Motorola, for example)
◆ Media processors (TI, Analog Devices, and Philips, for example)
◆ Network processors (IBM, Intel, Xelerated, and a host of others)

In early 2005 IBM, Fujitsu, and Sony announced the Cell chip. This joint project has produced a supercomputer on a chip designed with graphics and AV processing in mind. Sony will use this as core to their PS3 game machine. IBM has created a demo stand-alone workstation using the Cell chip with an outstanding computing benchmark of 16 Teraflops. The Cell chip is configured as many smaller CPUs networked together on one substrate. No doubt we will learn more about this exciting new device as it goes into production. Sony and Fujitsu plan on using the Cell in their HD TVs. Compare this to the fastest, room size, supercomputer in 2005 IBM's Watson Blue Gene/L that clocks in at 91.3. Teraflops. See www.top500.org for a list of the top computing platforms.

Fast I/O is required to keep up with increasing CPU speeds. One of the new leaders in this area is the PCI Express bus. PCI Express (not to be confused with PCI-X) is an implementation of the PCI bus that uses existing PCI programming concepts and communications standards. However, it is based on serial connectivity, not parallel as with the PCI bus. The basic "×1" link has a peak data bandwidth of 2 Gbps. The link is bidirectional so the effective data transfer rate is 4 Gbps. Links may be bundled and are referred to as ×1, ×4, ×8, and ×16. A ×16 bus structure supports 64 Gb/s of throughput. All this is good news for AV systems. The link uses 8B/10B encoding (see Appendix E).

So there is every reason to be optimistic about the future of the "CPU," especially for A/V computing. But will it become the strong link in the computation chain of otherwise weak elements? Fortunately not, as the other forces grow in strength too.

1.2.3   Force #3: Storage Density, Bandwidth, and Power

At 3 o'clock on Figure 1.3 is the dimension of storage density (cost/GB), storage bandwidth[3] [cost/(Mb/s)], and power consumed (W/GB). For all metrics, smaller is better. Unless you have been living in a cave for the last 20 years, it is obvious that disk drive capacity per unit has been climbing at an astronomical rate. Much of the technology that makes up drives and other storage media also follow Moore's law, hence the capacity increase. The dimension of storage is a broad topic. The four main storage means are hard disk drives (HDD), optical disk, tape, and RAM/Flash. The application spaces for these are

1. HDD—video servers, file/database servers, Web servers, PCs of all types, personal video recorders, embedded products (portable music players)
2. Optical disk—DVD (4.7 GB single sided), CD (700 MB), Blu-ray (27 GB single sided), Advanced Optical Disc (HD-DVD, 15-, 20- and 30-GB versions), and other lesser known devices. Some sample applications are
   a. Consumer DVD—SD and HD
   b. Sony XDCAM using a variation of the Blu-ray format for field acquisition.
   c. Archive, backup
3. Tape—traditional video tape, archive, backup. Archive tape technology is discussed in Chapter 3A.
4. RAM/Flash—RAM is being used to replace disc and tape for select applications. The Panasonic P2 cam is a good example of a professional camera that has only removable Flash cards as the media store. With four removable memory cards at a total of 16 GB, ~80 min at DV25 rates may be stored; 32 GB is expected in 2006.

The hard disk is having an immense impact on the evolution of IT systems. Consider the implications of Figure 1.6 reprinted from an article by IBM researchers [Morris].

---

[3] The terms 'bandwidth' and 'data-rate' are equivalent in a colloquial sense.

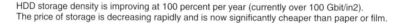

HDD storage density is improving at 100 percent per year (currently over 100 Gbit/in2).
The price of storage is decreasing rapidly and is now significantly cheaper than paper or film.

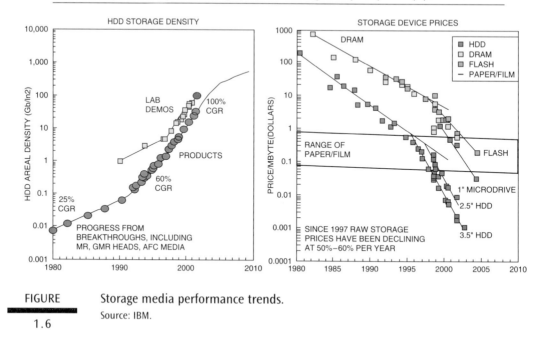

FIGURE   Storage media performance trends.

1.6   Source: IBM.

Storage density is currently over 100 Gbits/in.^{2} on the surface of the rotating platter. This is increasing at a compound growth rate (CGR) of 100% per year in 2005 and enabling 2.5″ form factor drives with capacities of 400 GB. This is expected to slow down modestly to about a 40% per year rate in 2010. HDD prices have decreased by about 5 orders of magnitude (100,000:1) since 1980, whereas storage systems' prices have decreased by a factor of 2.5 orders of magnitude. The faster fall in HDD prices compared to system prices implies that HDDs are a smaller overall part of storage systems. Chapter 3A discusses storage systems in detail. Raw HDD prices have been falling 50–60% a year since 1997.

It is enlightening to forecast the future of HDD performance, keeping in mind that fortune telling is risky business. So using Figure 1.6 and extrapolating to 2010, we should expect to see HDD capacities of around 1.5 TB per 2.5″ unit at a cost of $40 in constant dollars. Using the most advanced audio compression (64 Kb/s), a single HDD could store 1 million tracks of music (3 min average length). Imagine the world's collection of music on your personal computer or in your pocket. All this bodes well for professional video systems too. Video/file servers with 10 TB of combined storage (91 days worth of continuously playing content at SD-compressed rates) will be routine. Even at HD production rates of say 150 Mb/s, *one* 1.5 TB HDD will store 2.2 hr of material and at 19.3 Mb/s (ATSC payload rate) will store nearly 17 hr.

Storage pricing has been a major factor in the digital revolution. Consider some impressive storage metrics in 2005:

◆ 100 GB HDD is available for ~$65 and can store 100 hr of consumer-quality video
◆ 1 TB aggregated HDD is available for ~$550 and can store 500 movies
◆ 10 TB aggregated HDD is available for ~$5000 and can store 5000 movies

More storage for less is the trend and it will likely continue. Keep in mind that these metrics are for basic HDDs. When integrated into a full featured chassis with high-performance I/O, RAID protection and monitoring the system price per GB will be much more.

Storage Rule of Thumb

10 Mb/s compressed video consumes 4.5 GB/hr of storage.

Use this convenient data point to scale to other rates.

The development to higher capacities has other side benefits too. Note the following trends.

◆ Internal HDD R/W sustained rates are currently at 100 Mb/s and are increasing at 40% per year for SCSI class HDD units. The actual achieved I/O for normal transactional loads will be lower due to random head seek and latency delays.
◆ Power per GB for HDD units is dropping at a CGR of 60%. Today drives consume less than .1W/GB. This is crucial in large data centers that have hundreds of TB of storage. Storage systems consume an order of magnitude more power and 1W/GB is typical.

Are there any workflow improvements? Oh yes, and in spades. This force is single handedly driving IT into broadcast and other professional AV applications. Consider the case of the video server. In 1995, HP pioneered and introduced the world's first mission-critical MPEG-based video server (the MediaStream Server) for the broadcast TV market. Initially, the product used individual 9-GB hard drives in the storage arrays. In 2005, storage arrays support 400-GB drives. Now that is progress. Video servers enable hands-free, automated operations for many AV applications.

SCSI versus ATA Drives

Two different types of HDD have emerged: one is the so-called SCSI HDD and the other is the ATA (IDE) drive. In many ways the drives are similar. The SCSI drive is aimed at enterprise data centers where top notch performance was required. The ATA drive is aimed at the PC market where less performance is acceptable. Because of the different target markets, the common perception is that SCSI drives are the right choice for high-end applications and ATA drives are for home use and light business. A comparative summary follows.

◆ ATA drives are about one-third the price of SCSI drives
◆ SCSI drives have a top platter spin of 15,000 rpm whereas ATA tops at 7200
◆ ATA drives have a simpler and less flexible I/O interface than SCSI
◆ ATA consumes less power
◆ ATA drives sport 400-GB capacities in 2005
◆ Reliability at par

Because of the lower price of the ATA HDD, many video product manufacturers have found ways to use ATA drives in their RAID-based storage systems. The biggest deficit in the ATA drive is the R/W head access time, which is determined by the platter rotational speed. In the world of A/V storage, the faster SCSI platter rotation speed is not necessarily a big advantage. For the enterprise data center, the average HDD R/W transaction block size is 4–8 KB. However, for AV data transactions, several MB is a normal R/W block size (video files are huge). There is a complete discussion of this in Chapter 3A.

The ATA is on the ascension for AV systems. Working around the less than ideal specs of the ATA drive yields big cost savings. These drives are most always bundled with RAID, which improves overall reliability. Look for the ATA drive to become the centerpiece for AV storage systems. In addition, some drive manufactures specialize in ATA (and SATA) drives and offer specs that compete very favorably with SCSI on most fronts. See Chapter 5 for more on HDD reliability.

1.2.4   Force #4: IT Systems Manageability

Unmanaged equipment can quickly become the chaotic nightmare of searching for bad components and repairing them while trying to sustain service. Long ago, the IT community realized the necessity to actively manage the routers, switches, servers, LAN and WAN links, and even software applications that comprise an IT system. However, most legacy A/V-specific equipment has no standard way to report errors, warnings, or status messages. Ad hoc solutions from each vendor have been the norm compared to the standardized methods that the IT industry embraces.

Managed equipment yields savings with less downtime, faster diagnosis, and less staff to manage thousands of system components. Entire industries have risen to provide embedded software for element status and error reporting, management protocol software, and, most importantly, monitoring stations to view and notify of the status of all system components. This includes the configuration and performance of the system under scrutiny. There are sufficient standards to create a vendor plug-and-play environment so users have their choice of products when creating a management environment. However, there will always be vendor-specific aspects of element management for which only they will provide management applications.

No one doubts that the IT management wave will be adopted by many AV equipment manufacturers over the next few years. The IT momentum, coupled with the advantages of the approach, spells doom for unmanaged equipment. Of course the AV industry must standardize the AV-specific aspects of element management. See Chapter 9 for an extended discussion. Let us leave the topic at this juncture. Has this improved the workflow to produce or generate video programming? Well, only indirectly. With less downtime and more accessible resources, workflows will literally flow better.

1.2.5 Force #5: Software Architectures

There are two main forces in software systems today. They both have their adherents and detractors, and siding with one faction or the other can be a religious experience. It is obvious to almost anyone that Microsoft wields a mighty sword and that many professional application developers use their Windows OS and .NET software framework for design. The other camp is the Linux-based Open Source movement with backing by IBM, HP, and countless others who advocate open systems (see, for example, www.sourceforge.net, www.openoffice.org, www.linux.org). Closely associated with this is the J2EE Java centric framework (and several very good development platforms) as an alternative to the Microsoft .NET programming environment. Java is not open sourced and is controlled by Sun Microsystems. They do provide free user licensing, however. Many would like Sun to freely distribute the source code as the Linux community has done. The .NET and Java camps have built up a momentum of very credible solutions. Are there other alternatives? Yes, but they are niche players and the sum total of their influence will be small. Next, a little background on the status of the OS market.

The lion's share of the OS marketplace comes from two segments, namely enterprise servers (database servers, Web servers, file servers, and so on) and client based (desktop). After these two behemoths, many smaller segments follow, such as the embedded OS, PDAs, mobile phones, and more. Gartner Group analysts estimate that Microsoft Windows controls 96% of the desktop OS real estate in early 2005. Worldwide, Apple MacOS gets 2.8% and the Linux desktop is at 1% and growing.

In the WW server space, IDC states that UNIX commands a 39% share, Microsoft Windows a 32% share, and Linux a 9% share in early 2005. From all indications, Windows and Linux are growing at the expense of UNIX, Netware, and other platforms, which are shrinking. IDC predicts the Linux server to close in at a 15% share in 2008.

Does the selection of an OS and programming language development platform bring end user workflow improvements? Admittedly this is a complex question. The advantages are first felt by the equipment manufacturers. How? Using either Java or .NET programming paradigms produces efficiencies in product development, product enhancements, and change management. If the end user is given access to the code base or APIs for systems integration and enhancement purposes, then they will reap the advantages of these programming environments. Also, if the IT staff is trained and comfortable with these environments, then any needed upgrades or patches are more likely to be implemented without issue or anxiety.

Workflow improvements will come from the power of the software applications produced by either of these environments. Also, their flexibility (well-documented, open programming interfaces) will allow for software enhancements to be made to meet changing business needs. Software-based systems allow for great flexibility in creating and changing workflows. Older non-IT-based AV systems can be rigid in their topology. IT frees us to create almost any A/V/data workflow imaginable. Many video facilities already have one or more programmers on staff to effect software changes when business needs dictate. Look forward to a big leap in customer-developed solutions that work in harmony with vendor-provided equipment. The topic of programming environments is discussed in Chapter 4.

1.2.6   Force #6: Interoperability

Writer John Donne once said "No man is an island; every man is a piece of the continent." Much has been written for and against his proclamation of the dependent need for others. For our discussion, we will side with the affirmative but apply the sentiment to islands of IT. Gone are the days of isolated islands of operations. Gone are the days of proprietary connectivity. Today, end users of video gear expect access to the Internet, email, compatible file formats, easy access to storage, and workflows that meet their needs for flexibility and production value. "Give me the universe of access and only then am I satisfied" is the mantra.

Does this mean that operational "islands" are a bad idea? By no means. Whether for security, reliability, control, application focus, or some other reason, equipment islands defined by their operational characteristics will be a design choice.

Robert Metcalfe, the inventor of Ethernet [Gilder], once declared a decree now known as Metcalfe's law: "The value of a network of interconnected devices grows as the square of connected elements." What did he mean? Well, consider an email system of two members. Likely, boring, and limited. But a billion member population is much more interesting and useful. So too with media interconnectivity. As the number of connected elements and users grow, the power of productivity grows as the square of the connected devices. Collaborative works, file sharing, common metadata, and media are all powerfully leveraged when networked. Networking also adds layers of software complexity, which must be managed by the IT staff.

So Metcalfe's law is the response to the plea "Please, I want more productivity." Standards foster interconnectivity. SMPTE (Society of Motion Picture and Television Engineers), the EBU (European Broadcast Union), ARIB (Japan), the IEEE (Ethernet, for example), the ITU/ISO/IEC (MPEG, for example), and W3C (Web standards HTML and XML, for example) develop the standards that make Metcalfe's law a reality. There is more discussion on standards and user forums such as the AAF Association and the ProMPEG Forum in Chapter 2. Is there a demonstrative workflow improvement? Yes, in terms of nearly instant user/device access to AV content, processors, access to metadata, and user collaboration.

You may wonder why the synergy of a system is a function of the square of the number of attached nodes. Consider that most communication paths are between nodal pairs in a network. For example, node A may request a file from node Z, which is only one possible choice for A. With N nodes there are roughly N^2 number of combinations for 1:1 bidirectional communication; A can communicate with B or C or D, B can communicate with C or D, and so on until N^2 combinations are accumulated—hence Metcalfe's law.

Figure 1.7 shows some of the pairwise combinations in a population of $N = 6$. For this case, there are $2*(5 + 4 + 3 + 2 + 1) = 30$ pair-wise combinations (each bidirectional path is counted as two unidirectional paths, hence the factor of 2 multiplier). However, 36 would be the value based on 6^2. For $N = 25$, Metcalfe's law predicts 625 when there are 600 paths in actuality. The actual number of pairwise communication paths is $N^2 - N$ so as N trends to be large the $-N$ factor is a small correction as Metcalfe must have known.

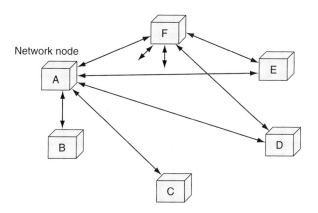

Network node

FIGURE

1.7
Metcalfe's law: Combinations of unidirectional pairwise communication paths tend toward N^2 as N (number of nodes) becomes large.

1.2.7   Force # 7: User Application Functionality

Application functionality is now largely defined and accessed via graphical user interfaces (GUIs) and APIs. Many of the hard surfaces of old have been replaced by more flexible soft interfaces. Oh sure, there is still a need for hard surface interfaces for applications such as live event production with camera switching, audio control, and video server control. Nonetheless, most user interfaces in a media production facility will be soft based, thereby allowing for change with a custom look and feel. A GUI as defined by a manufacture may also be augmented by end user-chosen "helper" applications such as media management, browsing, and so on. Using drag-and-drop functionality, a helper application can provide data objects to the main user application. In the end, soft interfaces are the ultimate in flexibility and customization.

Another hot area of interest is Web services. In brief, a Web service can be any business or data processing function that is made available over a network. Web services are components that accomplish a well-defined purpose and make their interfaces available via standard protocols and data formats. These services combine the best aspects of component-based development and Web infrastructure. Web services provide an ideal means to expose business (and A/V process) functions as automated and reusable interfaces. Web services offer a uniform mechanism for enterprise resources and applications to interface with one another. The promise of "utility computing" comes alive with these services. Imagine AV service operators (codecs, converters, renders, effects, compositors, searching engines, etc.) being sold as components that other components or user applications can access at will to do specific operations. Entire workflows may be composed of these services driven by a user application layer that controls the logic of execution. There are already standard methods and data structures to support these concepts. There is a deeper discussion of these ideas in Chapter 4.

1.2.8   Force # 8: Reliability and Scalability

The world's most mission-critical software systems run in an IT environment. Airline reservation systems, air traffic control, on-line banking, stock market transaction processing, and more all depend on IT systems. There are four basic methods to improve a system's reliability.

◆ Minimize the risk that a failure will occur

◆ Detect malfunctions quickly

◆ Quick repair time

◆ Limit impact of the failure

In Chapter 5 there is an extensive discussion of reliability, availability, and scalability. Also, enterprise and mission critical systems often need to scale from small to medium to large during their lifetime. Due to the critical nature of their operations, live upgrading is often needed so scalability is a crucial aspect of an IT system.

Many video systems (broadcast TV stations, for example) also run mission-critical operations and share the same reliability and scalability requirements as banking and stock market transaction processing but with the added constraint of real time response. IT-based AV solutions may have all or some of the following characteristics.

◆ A/V glitch-free, no single point of failure (NSPOF) fault tolerance

◆ Real time AV access, processing, and distribution

- Off-site mirrors for disaster recovery
- Nearly instantaneous failover under automatic detection of a failed component
- Live upgrades to storage, clients, critical software components, and failed components
- Storage redundancy using RAID and other strategies

These characteristics have a very positive impact on workflow. Keeping systems alive and well keeps users happy. True fault tolerant operations are practical and in use every day in facilities worldwide. As business and workflow requirements change, IT systems are able to keep pace by enabling changes of all critical components while in operation. All of these aspects are addressed in more detail in Chapter 5. The bottom line is this: IT can meet the most critical needs of mission critical video systems. Many systems offer better performance and reliability than purpose-built video equipment.

1.2.9   The Eight Forces: A Conclusion

The eight forces just described do indeed improve video system workflows by being more cost effective, reliable, higher performing, and flexible. The combined vector of all eight forces is moving video system design away from purpose-built, rigid, traditional A/V links toward an IT-based infrastructure. The remainder of this book delves deeper into each force and provides added information and insight. Several years ago, even the thought of building complex AV systems with IT components seemed a joke. Today, the maturity of IT and its far-reaching capability grants it an honored place in video systems design. During the course of this book, several case studies will show impressive evidence of real-world systems with an IT backbone.

Despite the positive forces described, there exists a lot of FUD surrounding AV/IT systems. Many of those well grounded in traditional AV methods may find stumbling blocks at every step. The chapters that follow will do their best in providing convincing evidence that AV/IT can indeed meet the challenges of mission critical small, medium, and large video system designs.

1.3   THREE FUNDAMENTAL METHODS OF MOVING AV DATA

There are three chief methods of moving AV assets between devices/ domains using IT. In Figure 1.8 the three means are shown connected to the central AV client. The means are:

1. **Direct-to-storage** real time (RT) or nonreal time (NRT) AV data access
   a. DAS, SAN, and NAS storage access
2. **Streaming** AV using LAN/WAN
   a. Included is AV streaming using traditional links
3. **File transfer** using LAN/WAN in NRT or pseudo RT

Storage access, streaming AV, and file transfer are all used in different ways to build video systems. The notion of an AV **stream** is common in the Web delivery of media programming. In practice, any AV data sent over a network or link in RT is a stream. For Figure 1.8, a client is some device that has a means to input/output AV information over a link of some sort. Some systems depend exclusively on one method, whereas another may use a hybrid mix of all three. Each of the methods has their strong and weak points, and selecting one over another requires a good knowledge of

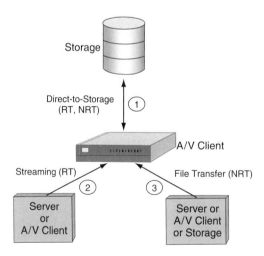

FIGURE   Three fundamental methods used to move A/V data.

1.8

the workflows that need to be supported. Chapters 3A and 3B review storage access, and Chapter 2 reviews streaming and file transfer.

Two acronyms, RT and NRT, are used repeatedly throughout the book so they deserve special mention. RT is used to represent an activity such as AV streaming or storage access that occurs in the sense of video or audio real time. NRT is, as expected, an activity that is not RT but slower (1/10 real time) or faster (5X real time). NRT-based systems are less demanding in terms of quality of service (QoS). These two concepts are intrinsic to many of the themes in this book.

In Figure 1.8, each of the three links represents one of the AV mover techniques. For example, one client may exchange files with another client or the central client may R/W to storage directly. The client in the center supports all three methods. The diagram represents the logical view of these concepts. The physical view may, in fact, consolidate the "links" into one or more actual links. For example, storage access, IP streaming, and file transfer can use a single LAN link. The flows are separated at higher levels by the application software running on the client.

A practical example of the three flow model is illustrated with the common video server (the AV client) in Figure 1.9. The I/O demonstrates streaming using IP LAN, traditional AV I/O, file transfer I/O, and storage access. The most basic video server only supports AV I/O with internal storage, whereas a more complete model would support all three modes. All modes may be used simultaneously or separately depending on the installed configuration. When evaluating a server, ask about all three modes to fully understand its capabilities.

Of course there are other ways to move AV assets (tape, optical disk manual transport) but these three are the focus of our discussions. Throughout the book these means are discussed and dissected to better appreciate the advantages/disadvantages of each method.

One of the characteristics that help define a video system is the notion of AV timing. Some systems have 100s (or 1000X more) of video links that need to be frame accurate, lip synced to audio, and aligned for switching between sources. The following section discusses the evolution from traditional A/V timing to that of a hybrid AV/IT system.

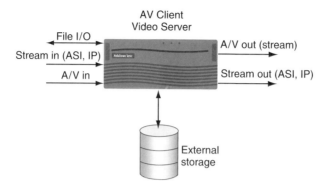

FIGURE   Video server with support for files, streams, and storage access.
                Image courtesy of Pinnacle Systems.
1.9

1.4   ISSUES WITH SYSTEM-WIDE TIMING

When IT and AV are mentioned in the same breath, many seasoned technical professionals express signs of worry. After all, is not video a special data type because of the precise horizontal and vertical timing relationships? It turns out that the needed timing can be preserved and still rely on IT at the *core* of the system. Figures 1.10, 1.11, and 1.12 show the migration from an all analog system to an AV/IT one. In Figure 1.10 every step of video processing and I/O needs to preserve the H/V timing. In Figure 1.11 the timing is easier to preserve due to the all digital

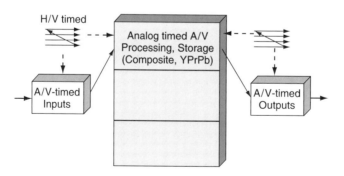

FIGURE   Traditional analog.

1.10

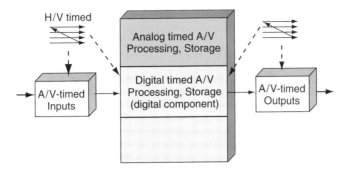

FIGURE   Traditional digital.

1.11

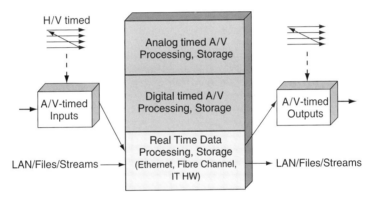

FIGURE   Hybrid AV + IT system.

1.12

nature of the processing. In Figure 1.12 the H/V timing is evident only at the edges for traditional I/O and display purposes. Figure 1.12 is the hybrid AV/IT model for much of the discussion in this book.

As discussed earlier, streaming using IT links is practical for some applications. If Figure 1.12 has no traditional AV I/O and only network links used for I/O, then the notion of H/V timing is lost at the edge of the system. In this case, there is a need for new timing methods that are IT based and frame accurate. In 2005, there are very few pure IT-only video systems. In a few years, pure IT-only systems may become popular; until then, let us pass on this particular special case for now, although it is revisited in Chapter 2. Next, let us see how well AV/IT configuration fares compared to its older cousins.

1.5   CAN 'IT' MEET THE DEMANDS OF A/V WORKFLOWS?

There are several important metrics when comparing traditional video to networked media system performance. These are the measures that the technical staff normally quantifies when calibrating or tuning a system. Figure 1.13 describes a simple AV system where **a perfectly aligned AV signal set** serves as an input along with a corresponding video reference signal and a time code (see Glossary) signal. The system may perform any process steps (delay, switch, process, route, store, replay, etc.) to the input signals and the output signals are always some function of the inputs. As a result, the outputs are referenced to the inputs in well-defined ways.

Under this group of conditions the output should be completely deterministic and measurable to a set of specifications. The question then becomes can a system composed of the hybrid mix of IT/AV work as well or better than a traditional AV-only system? Imagine the system in Figure 1.13 composed of a hybrid IT/AV mix and measured to a set of specs. Then convert the system to a traditional AV-only system and make the same measurements. How much—if any—would the measurements differ? Ideally, the IT/AV system would equal or exceed all measured specs. Is this the case? Are there some "sweet spots" for either system and, if so, what are they? Let us find out. The chief metrics (check Glossary if needed) of interest to us are as follow.

1. **A/V lip-sync**. This measures the amount of time delay between the audio signal and the video signal on the system output. Any deviation from zero shows the classic lip-sync characteristic. The input A/V alignment has exactly zero deviation.
2. **Video keying**. If an input key signal is present, does the keying operate without artifacts? Is it always frame aligned to the video fill signal?
3. **Frame accuracy**. Is the video output frame accurate to the output video reference (or input reference if desired)?
4. **Time code accuracy**. Is the time code output perfectly correlated (if needed) to the time code input value? Is the output time code perfectly correlated to the output video signal?
5. **Video reference accuracy**. If required, is the output video reference perfectly correlated to a video reference?

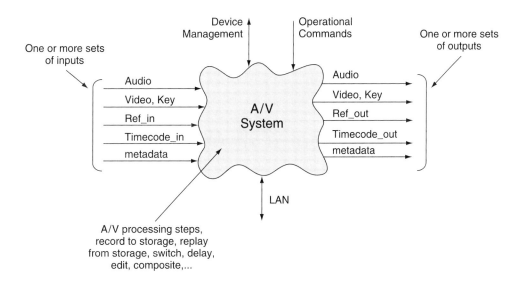

One or more sets of inputs

Device Management

Operational Commands

One or more sets of outputs

Audio
Video, Key
Ref_in
Timecode_in
metadata

A/V System

Audio
Video, Key
Ref_out
Timecode_out
metadata

LAN

A/V processing steps, record to storage, replay from storage, switch, delay, edit, composite,...

FIGURE

1.13

Traditional A/V system performance model.

6. **A/V delay**. Is the A/V delay (latency) through the system acceptable and constant? For some cases the acceptable delay should be less than a line of video ($<<62~\mu s$), whereas for others it may need to be several hours or more.

7. **Ancillary data**. If auxiliary information is present in the input signals (VBI, HANC, VANC, AES User Data, etc.), are they preserved as desired?

8. **Quality, noise, and artifacts**. Is there any noise or other undesired AV properties on the output signals? Are the output A/V quality and timing as desired?

9. **Glitching**. Are there any undesired interruptions (illegal A/V, dropouts, etc.) on the output signals? How well does the system perform when the input signals exhibit glitching or are disconnected?

10. **Deterministic control**. Are all system operations deterministic? Does every operational command (switch, route, play, record, etc.) consistently function as expected?

11. **Wide geographic environments**. Can systems be created cost effectively across large distances?

12. **A/V storage**. Can the input signals be recorded and replayed on command? What are the delays?

13. **A/V processing**. Can the input A/V signals be processed at will for any reasonable operation?

14. **Metric drifting**. Do any of the measured spec values drift over time?

15. **User metadata**. Are user metadata supported?

16. **Systems management**. How are A/V devices managed? What are methods for alarm reporting? How is the configuration determined and maintained?

17. **Live A/V switching**. Traditional A/V switching is very mature. Can an AV/IT system do as well for all functional requirements?

All of these metrics are indicative of system performance. If any one is not compliant the entire system may be unusable. A detailed analysis of each element is beyond our scope but the summary overview is appropriate. Table 1.1 provides a high-level overview of what features the different systems can provide and describes their "sweet spots." Note that traditional AV systems can and often are composed of a predominance of digital components (or analog + digital mix) but they lack the full featured networking and infrastructure of IT-based solutions.

System metric	Traditional A/V	Hybrid IT/AV
1. A/V lip-sync	Needs careful attention to keep A+V in sync	Needs careful attention to keep A+V in sync
2. Video keying	Needs careful attention to keep V+K in sync	Needs careful attention to keep V+K in sync
3. Frame accuracy (FA)	Requires careful design	Requires careful design. FA design requires new techniques when using IT

TABLE   Summary of Traditional A/V versus IT/AV Metrics

1.1

System metric	Traditional A/V	Hybrid IT/AV
4. Time code accuracy	Requires careful design	Requires careful design
5. Video Ref accuracy	Requires careful design	Requires careful design
6. A/V delay	May require occasional calibration. Long delays are difficult to achieve, short ones (one video frame) are easier	Deterministic delays are straightforward. Delays of <1 s may not be easy to achieve for some applications due to buffering delays
7. Ancillary data	Straightforward	Straightforward
8. Quality, noise, and artifacts	If analog based, may be subject to noise injection and subsequent artifacts	Digital systems less likely to add or be influenced by noise sources. Perfect, repeatable quality
9. Glitching	Careful design required to avoid glitching due to various anomalous conditions	Careful design required to avoid glitching due to various anomalous conditions
10. Deterministic control	Mature today. Traditional RS422 control link is not networkable	May be perfectly deterministic. Move toward all LAN based control underway
11. Wide geography	Difficult and expensive to preserve all the system specs	Straightforward and a sweet spot for IT
12. A/V storage	May be done with VTRs and robotics as needed. Expensive and impractical for some scenarios	May be done with disc or RAM storage arrays. Large, dropout-free storage. Tape free for most operations.
13. A/V processing	Straightforward if done with digital HW	Straightforward and networkable
14. Metric drifting	If any analog components, it is likely; if digital, unlikely	Unlikely
15. User metadata	No support for full featured metadata on VTRs and many other components	Metadata are of primary importance and support is common
16. Systems management	Not mature and lacking in standards and functionality	Very mature for general IT devices
17. Live AV switching (e.g., camera selection)	Commonly done to produce live sports, news, and drama events	Not common in 2005 due to the difficulty in live switching of a LAN frame accurately

TABLE   Summary of Traditional A/V versus IT/AV Metrics—(Continued)

1.1

1.6   ADVANTAGES AND DISADVANTAGES OF METHODS

Trade-off Discussion

Table 1.1 lists several "sweet spots" for IT/AV, namely No. 6, 8, 10, 11, 12, 13, 15, and 16.

- ◆ No. 6. Long delays are ideally implemented with IT storage systems. Long delays may be needed for time delay applications, censorship, or other needs.
- ◆ No. 8. Digital systems may be designed to be noise and artifact free with the highest level of repeatable quality.
- ◆ No. 10. See later.
- ◆ No. 11. Systems can span a campus, city, country, or the world without affecting video quality. There are countless such systems in use today.
- ◆ No. 12. IT storage methods are accepted for video servers and are in use daily in media production and distribution facilities. For all but deep archives, this means the demise of the VTR (tape free at last) for most record/replay operations. Tape is still in common use for field camera acquisition but even this is waning.
- ◆ No. 13. There are no geographic constraints on where the A/V processors may be located. Clusters of render farms, codecs, effects processors, format converters, and so on may be networked to form a virtual utility pool of A/V processing.
- ◆ No. 15. User descriptive metadata importing, storage, indexing, querying, and exporting are considered a cornerstone feature of IT systems. Chapter 7 investigates metadata standards and utilization in more detail.
- ◆ No. 16. IT systems management has a major advantage over the ad hoc methods in current use today (see Chapter 9).

Number 10 has the IT edge too for many applications. Traditional device control has relied on the sturdy RS422 serial link carrying device commands. Sure, it is trustworthy and reliable, but it is not networkable, is yet another link to manage and route, and has limited reach. LAN-based control is the natural replacement. There is one concern with LAN replacing RS422 serial linking—determinism. RS422 routing is normally a direct connection from controller to device under control and its QoS is excellent and proven. As has been the case, a video server with 10 I/O ports has 10 RS422 control ports! This is messy and inefficient in terms of control logic, but it is proven. However, a LAN may be routed through a shared network with at least some small delay. A *single* LAN connection to a device may control all aspects of its operation with virtually no geographic constraints. In fact, it is not uncommon to control distributed devices from a central location using LAN and WAN connectivity. This cannot be done using a purely RS422 control and reporting system. There are several ways to deal with the networking delay and jitter, which are covered in detail in Chapter 7.

Number 17 in Table 1.1 is one area where traditional AV methods are superior in 2005. This scenario assumes that event cameras have a LAN-like output that carries the live video signal. The signals are fed into a LAN-based switcher operated by a technical director where camera feeds are selected and processed for output. There are no accepted standards for frame-accurately aligning the isolated camera output signals over a LAN. Furthermore, there are no commercial LAN-based (for I/O) video switchers. Most professional cameras use a coax Triax link (or alternative fiber optic link for HD feeds) from camera to the production control room.

There are some promising new products in development that combine the best of traditional AV and IT. One is the Fusion AV router from ProBel. It combines ATM ports (AES 47 Audio over ATM spec) and standard AES/EBU audio ports in a single router. The ATM signals may be distributed over much wider areas (and point to multipoint too) than the AES/EBU signals.

Some researchers have built test systems for live event production that are almost entirely LAN/WAN and IT based. The European **Nuggets** [Nuggets] project (www.ist-nuggets.tv) in 2003 developed a proof of concept live production IT-based system. In their demo system, camera control, streaming AV over networks, metadata management, MXF, live proxies, and camera switching are all folded into one comprehensive demo. Their work is on the bleeding edge of using IT techniques for live production. The Nuggets effort is a good indicator of the promise of IT-based live production.

As technology matures, it seems likely that video systems for any set of user requirements can and will be implemented using IT methods. Admittedly, it may take many years for live event HD production to

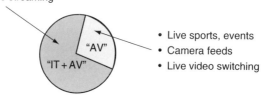

- A/V record/playout
- Media real-time processing
  – Effects, transitions, compositing,…
- Editing workstations, proxy browsing
- Storage systems, data archive
- Fault tolerant systems
- Non real time file transfers
- Non real time streaming

- Live sports, events
- Camera feeds
- Live video switching

"AV"

"IT + AV"

FIGURE   Sweet spots for traditional and hybrid A/V systems.

1.14

migrate to an all IT environment. Despite the latency drawback, most other video system application requirements are easily achieved today with IT/AV configurations. See Figure 1.14 for the production sweet spots for traditional AV versus AV/IT.

For a traditional TV station, 90% of daily operations have little need for live stream switching. Using nonreal time file transfers to move AV files can replace SDI in many cases. Sure, live news with field reporting requires video switching. In practice, most station operations can use a mix of AV + IT gear. However, ESPN's new HD Digital Center facility has 10 million A/V cross points in their router infrastructure. Their lifeblood is live events. In this case, because the need to switch streams under human control is great, traditional SDI is required in bulk. Still, the ESPN facility has its share of IT elements [Hobson].

Traditional A/V has one added benefit not sited in Table 1.1: familiarity. The engineers, technicians, and staff responsible for the care and feeding of the media infrastructure may have many years of experience. Moving to an IT/AV infrastructure requires new skills and changes in thinking. Some staff may resist or find the change uncomfortable. Others will welcome the change and embrace it as progress and improvement. Change management is always a challenge. We now have some track record of facilities that made the switch. Some are broadcasters who made the switch to an IT infrastructure while on air and others had the advantage of building a new "green field" facility where existing operations (if any) were not of concern. The challenges and rewards of building these new systems are reviewed in Chapter 10.

1.7   IT'S A WRAP: SOME FINAL WORDS

So can AV/IT meet the challenge of replacing (and improving) the traditional AV infrastructure? For all but a few areas of operations, the answer is a resounding yes! There is every reason to believe that IT methods will eventually become the bedrock of all media operations. True, there will always be a few cases where traditional AV still has an edge, but IT has a momentum that is difficult to derail. Do not let a corner case become the driving decision not to consider IT. The words of the brilliant Charles Kettering (GM research chief) seem truer today than when he spoke them in 1929: "*Advancing waves of other people's progress sweep over unchanging man and wash him out.*" Do not get washed out but seek to understand the waves of IT that are now crashing on the shores of traditional AV.

Now that we have established the beneficial aspects behind the move to IT, let us move to expand on the concepts outlined in this chapter. The next chapter reviews the basics of networked media as related to AV systems. The chapters that follow it will provide yet more insights and explanations for the major themes in IT as related to A/V systems. As Winston Churchill once said, "Now this is not the end. It is not even the beginning of the end. But it is, perhaps, the end of the beginning."

REFERENCES

[**Chen**] Xuemin Chen, *Transporting Compressed Digital Video*, Kluwer Academic Publishers, 2002, Chapter 4.

[**Gilder**] George Gilder, *Metcalfe's Law and Legacy*, Forbes ASAP, September 13, 1993.

[**HenPat**] John Hennessy, David Patterson, *Computer Architectures 3rd edition*, 2003, page 15, Morgan Kaufmann.

[**Hobson**] Ed Hobson, Ted Szypulski, *The Design and Construction of ESPN's HD Digital Center in Bristol, Conn.*, SMPTE Technical Conference 2004, Pasadena.

[**Moore**] Gorden Moore, Electronics, Volume 38, Number 8, April 19, 1965, *Cramming more components onto integrated circuits.*

[**Morris**] R. J. T. Morris and B. J. Truskowski, "*The Evolution of Storage Systems*" IBM Systems Journal, Volume 42, Number 2, July 2003.

[**Nuggets**] B. Devlin, H. Heber, J. P. Lacotte, U. Ritter, J. van Rooy, W. Ruppel, J. P. Viollet, "*Nuggets and MXF: Making the Networked Studio a Reality,*" SMPTE Motion Imaging Journal, July/August 2004.

2 | The Basics of Professional Networked Media

CHAPTER

2.0   INTRODUCTION

This chapter reviews the essential elements of networked media as they relate to the professional production of AV-based materials. Of course it is not possible to present a detailed explanation of each building block so let us call the coverage an "evaluation strength" treatment. What is this? If you need to evaluate various HW/SW architectures, system components, or systems issues, the coverage in this chapter (and others) provides you with the tutoring to ask the right questions. Rudyard Kipling said "*I keep six honest friends—what, why, when, how, where and who.*" In the end, you will be able to ask probing and intelligent questions when evaluating and specifying IT/AV systems.

This section does a broad-brush coverage while the remainder of the book dissects the same subjects to uncover their subtleties and deeper points. The following chapters probe deeper into select subjects;

♦ Chapter 3A and 3B—Storage systems
♦ Chapter 4—Software technology for AV systems
♦ Chapter 5—Reliability and scalability methods

◆ Chapter 6—Networking basics for AV

◆ Chapter 7—Media systems integration

◆ Chapter 8—Security for networked AV systems

◆ Chapter 9—Systems management and monitoring

◆ Chapter 10—The transition to IT: Issues and case studies

◆ Chapter 11—A review of AV basics

At the highest level is generic IT architecture. Figure 2.1 shows this six-tier architecture. It is deliberately abstract, as it can represent almost any process-oriented workflow. Networked media as defined for our purposes is more than pure networking. It encompasses all the stages in Figure 2.1. The diagram is split into two domains; the application specific one and the shared IT infrastructure. The application layers define the various applications needed to support a workflow. The lower layers provide the services and resources that the application logic calls upon. Next, let us peel back the onion on the bottom three layers in Figure 2.1. The higher layers are considered in other chapters.

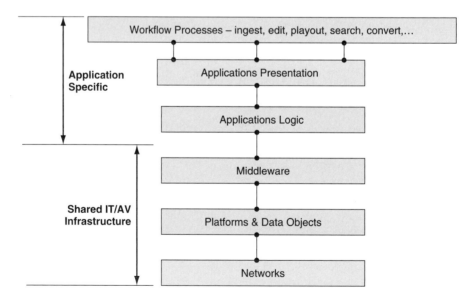

FIGURE   Generic six-layer IT architecture.

2.1

2.1   THE CORE ELEMENTS

Figure 2.2 provides a 5-mile high view of a generic IT architecture for the enterprise. This is the physical representation of the logical view of the three lower layers in Figure 2.1 along with the application clients. Also, most of the infrastructure in Figure 2.2 would be found in a typical hybrid AV/IT architecture. Missing from Figure 2.2 are miscellaneous AV links, video/audio routers, cameras, VTRs, logo inserters, video servers, and so on. IT architectures that are fine-tuned for AV are discussed in other chapters. Nonetheless, Figure 2.2 forms the foundational elements for our discussions throughout the book. The main elements to be discussed here are

◆ Application clients
◆ The router
◆ Ethernet switching
◆ The firewall and intrusion detection system
◆ Servers
◆ Storage subsystems
◆ Network infrastructure
◆ Software for all seasons

The Application Client

Clients come in all shapes and flavors. The application clients perform AV I/O, video editing and compositing, browsing, other media-related functions, or standard enterprise applications. This book uses the term "application client" in a general way, implying some device that accesses storage or servers or other system-wide resources. If the client does AV processing, then it may or may not have AV I/O ports. For example, a nonlinear editor (NLE) may have AV file access from a storage element in the network but it may not have physical AV I/O ports. Another client may only support AV I/O and not any human interface. This type of element is common for capturing content from live satellite feeds or as an AV playout device. The network attach may be an Ethernet port at 100 Mb/s, Gigabit Ethernet (Gig-E), or Fibre Channel. Why choose one over the other? These and other client-related aspects are discussed later in this chapter. See too the section entitled Networked Media Clients later in this chapter.

The Router

The router connects the facility to the outside world or to other company sites using IP routing. A router has three fundamental jobs. The first is to compute the best path that a packet should take through the network to its destination. This computation accounts for various policies and network constraints. The second job of the router is to forward packets received on an input interface to the appropriate output interface for transmission across the network. Routers offer a selection of WAN interfaces[1] (SONET, T1/E1, T3/E3, ATM, Frame Relay, ISDN, and more) and LAN (Ethernet with IP for our discussions) interfaces. The third major router function is to temporarily store packets in large buffer memories to absorb the bursts and temporary congestion that frequently occur and to queue the packets using a priority-weighted scheme for transmission. Some routers also support a virtual private network (VPN) function for the secure tunneling of packets over the public Internet.

The Ethernet Switch

Most campus networks are composed of a cascade of Ethernet switches. The switching may occur at the Ethernet level (layer 2) or the IP level (layer 3), although the distinction is not enforced here. Think of the switch as a *subset* of a full-fledged router; it is simpler and less costly than routers, although there are a host of technical differences too. More discussion of layer 2 and 3 switching and routing methods are covered in Chapter 6. Switches are the tissue of an enterprise network. Most switches can support "wire speed" packet forwarding at the Ethernet line rate (100 Mb/s or 1 Gb/s commonly). Small Ethernet switches (24 ports) are inexpensive with a per port cost of only $15.

Packet switches (and routers) have throughput latency that is ideally in the 1- to 20-μs range but can grow much bigger in the presence of

---

[1] See Appendix F for more information on WANs.

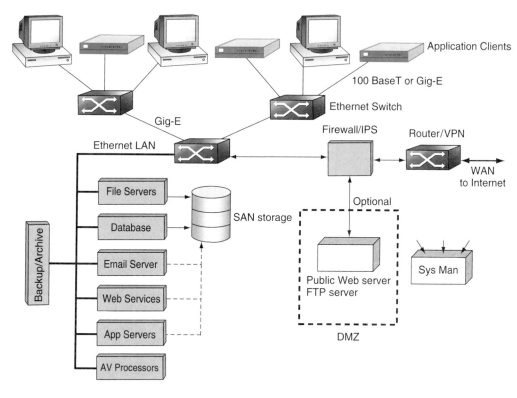

FIGURE

2.2

Simplified enterprise network architecture.

packet congestion. IP switches may be classed as asynchronous devices, whereas SDI AV routers are isochronous (equal timed) in nature with perfectly timed (fixed latency, very small jitter, and bit accurate timing) I/O ports. So it is apparent that routing AV packets is not exactly equivalent to SDI routing. It is precisely this issue that convinces some that IP switches cannot be used to route live AV signals. After all, if live video needs to be perfectly timed to within a nanosecond or so, then the IP switch is not fit for the job. This is addressed later in the chapter with the conclusion that switches (and routers) can indeed be used to switch live A/V packets.

The switch internal data routing structure is either shared memory or switch fabric and can reach speeds of 400 Gb/s nonblocking throughput for a carrier-class large size switch (200 ports). Terabit/s fabrics exist and are used in very high-end switches and routers. See www.avici.com and www.juniper.com for added insights. Like routers, they can support small I/O latencies in the 1- to 20-μs range, which is ideal for moving live AV streams.

A switch is deceptively simple from the connectivity point of view; it is just Ethernet I/O. Looking deeper we see that it must support 20 or more networking standards for efficient packet forwarding, Ethernet frame forwarding, secure device management, flow control, VLAN support, class of service, packet inspection, multicast, and a multitude of other protocols. Routers are more sophisticated and may support 35+ different protocols. There are many vendors to choose from and the price/performance ratio is improving with each generation thanks again to Moore's law.

The Firewall and Intrusion Prevention System

A computer firewall protects private networks and their internal nodes from malicious external intrusion resulting in a compromise of system or data integrity or a denial of service. It is usually a secure HW/SW device that acts to filter every packet that transits between a secure and unsecured network. It must have at least two network interfaces, one for the network it is intended to protect, and one for the risky network—such as the Internet. The earliest computer firewalls were simple routers. The term "firewall" comes from the fact that by segmenting a network into different parts, damage that could spread from one subnet to another is stopped—just as fire doors or firewalls stop a fire.

An Internet firewall examines all traffic routed between a private network and the Internet. Every packet must meet a preselected set of criteria or it is dropped. A network firewall filters both inbound and outbound traffic. Disallowing internal access to select external locations is vital in guaranteeing secure and legitimate business operations. It can log all attempts to enter the private network and trigger alarms when hostile or unauthorized entry is attempted. Firewalls can filter packets based on their source, destination addresses, or port numbers. This is known as address filtering. Firewalls can also filter based on application layer protocols such as HTTP, FTP, or Telnet.

The intrusion prevention system (IPS) is a sort of super firewall. They filter at the content layer. For example, they may look for and prevent attacks from incoming worms, ill-formed protocols, and other higher layer tricks. A more detailed coverage is outlined in Chapter 8.

Servers

Servers come in many forms and are a common element in an IT infrastructure. Their basic function is to host software applications that clients can access over the network. These functions may be done in an AV real time sense or in nonreal time. The common functions are shown in Figure 2.2. For the purposes of AV functions, the following are of interest.

- File server—Store/retrieve AV files for access by clients. Normally, the delivery of files over the network would be in nonreal time. The server usually appears as a networked drive (//K: or//MyServer:) to the client. Files can be moved to and from application clients.

- A/V processor—This is a networked resource for processing AV essence. Typical functions are compressing/decompressing, file format conversion (DV to MPEG), 3D effects, proxy file video generation, and more. Most often the processing is not in real time but live streams may also be supported.

- File gateway—This is the boundary point for transferring files to and from external sources. A gateway may do file conversion, proxy video file generation, bandwidth management, and more.

- Control and scheduling, media asset management (MAM), element management, and other services offered on a server platform.

See Chapter 3A for more details on servers and their architecture.

Storage Subsystems

Many enterprises use SAN-based storage to reduce the number of independent storage systems. A SAN provides for a *single storage pool* to be shared by different nodes. For media centric IT systems, there is often the need for huge amounts of high availability, *real time* storage. Terabytes of online storage (thousands of hours of standard definition video) with aggregate bandwidths of gigabits per second are not uncommon for large installations. The *real time* spec is a frequent requirement for systems that read/write live AV to storage. SAN and NAS storage system are discussed in Chapter 3B. Additionally, there is discussion about nonreal time and real time storage QoS and their application spaces.

Networking Infrastructure

The Ethernet LANs in Figure 2.2 connect to create networks of virtually any size. These systems are mature with powerful features, such as

◆ Scalability from a few networked elements to thousands.

◆ Scalable to any required data throughput.

◆ Reliability "to the budget"; i.e., the reliability will be only as good as you can afford.

◆ LANs can be configured with virtually 100% uptime for the core routing and switching components. QoS per link can be defined offering an overall media-friendly infrastructure.

◆ LAN segmentation for building virtual network islands for media production intelligently isolated from the normal IT company operations.

◆ Network management of all components. Faults, warnings, status, and systems configuration information readily available from intuitive GUIs.

◆ WAN connectivity for wide area distribution of streams and files.

Of course a LAN is more than Ethernet connectivity. A smorgasbord of protocols run on the Ethernet links, such as IP, TCP, UDP, HTTP, IPSec, and many more. They are mature and used universally in a variety of real world environments. These are discussed in Chapter 6.

Throughout the book networks are used as transport for AV streams and files. Figure 2.3 illustrates how many simultaneous, real time video streams of different rates can fit into the listed pipes. At the top of Figure 2.3 is uncompressed 1080i HD (see Glossary) at 1.194 Gb/s image payload data rate. Standard gigabit Ethernet cannot carry even one stream of this format. The bottom of Figure 2.3 shows that SONET OC-192 can carry ~10,000 streams of Web video (see Appendix F). The packing densities are ideal, and a realistic packing may be 70% of these values due to a variety of link, transport, and format overheads.

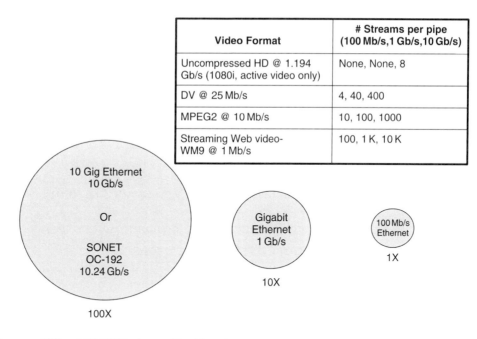

Video Format	# Streams per pipe (100 Mb/s,1 Gb/s,10 Gb/s)
Uncompressed HD @ 1.194 Gb/s (1080i, active video only)	None, None, 8
DV @ 25 Mb/s	4, 40, 400
MPEG2 @ 10 Mb/s	10, 100, 1000
Streaming Web video- WM9 @ 1 Mb/s	100, 1 K, 10 K

10 Gig Ethernet
10 Gb/s

Or

SONET
OC-192
10.24 Gb/s

100X

Gigabit
Ethernet
1 Gb/s

10X

100 Mb/s
Ethernet

1X

FIGURE

2.3

Filling LAN/WAN pipes with video streams.

Not to scale, ideal, no overhead.

Compression increases packing density greatly. Fully uncompressed digital cinema at so-called 4 K resolution reaches ~9.6 Gb/s, and some vendors use exotic InfiniBand links to move the images. Using MPEG2 compression, the same program can fit nicely into a 19.3-Mb/s ATSC pipe. Newer HD compression methods can squeeze even more, reaching ~8 Mb/s—a whopping 1200:1 bit savings, albeit with a loss of the pristine quality.

Software for All Seasons

At every layer in Figure 2.2, software plays a major role. The software may be classified into the following domains:

◆ Application and services related
◆ Operating systems (OS) for clients, servers, and other devices

◆ Middleware protocols for client and server communications
◆ Programming frameworks

These technologies work hand in hand to complete a solution. These domains are discussed in Chapter 4. See [Britton] for more information too.

2.2   STANDARDS

It has been said that the nice thing about standards is that there are so many to choose from. So true—and for good reason. Without standards—and lots of them—interoperability would be hopeless. Figure 2.2 could never exist (with heterogeneous components) without standards. From personal experience, sitting through hundreds of hours of debates and the due diligence of standards development, the pain is worth the gain. Figure 2.4 outlines a short list of standards bodies, user groups, and industry associations that are active in both IT and AV spaces.

The mother of all standards bodies for AV (broadcast, post, and cinema) is the Society of Motion Picture and Television Engineers (www.smpte.org). The Audio Engineering Society (AES) also contributes a significant effort. The International Telecommunications Union (ITU) is the world's largest telecoms body, and the ISO/IEC (two separate bodies that cooperate) has developed many standards with MPEG (and JPEG) being the most significant for our space. The European Telecommunications Standards Institute (ETSI) works in fields that are germane to European interests, such as the DVB broadcast standards in association with the EBU. The IEEE and Internet Engineering Task Force (IETF) have developed thousands of standards (request for comments, RFCs) for networking interoperability. The W3C contributes important recommendations, such as XML, HTML, SVG, MathML, SMIL, Timed Text, and Web services. Among user groups, the ProMPEG Forum and the Advanced Authoring Format Association (AAFA) contributed to interoperability for file transfer using MXF and AAF, respectively.

Many of these bodies have liaison connections to other bodies, and the dashed lines in Figure 2.4 indicate these relationships. For example, every SMPTE standard may have a corresponding ANSI (US master

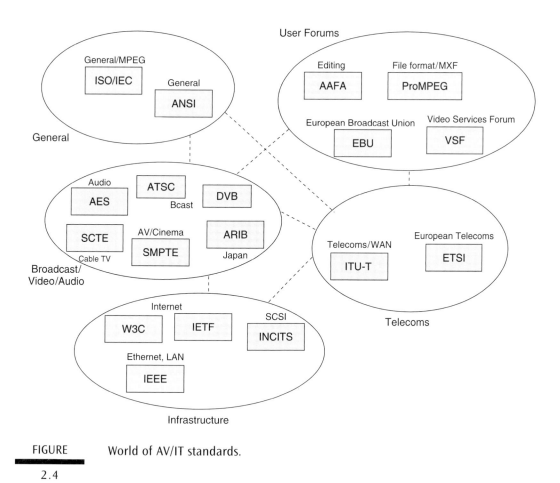

FIGURE

2.4

World of AV/IT standards.

body) standard. The ProMPEG Forum's 4 year development of MXF was officially standardized by SMPTE in 2004. Normally, user groups have no power to set standards but they can make recommendations that sometimes become de facto standards, much like what AAF has become for edit decision list exchange. Not all liaison connections are shown in Figure 2.4.

There will be no end to the development of standards to provide for interoperability and a consistent user experience. When standards do not exist, the market votes for the winner(s) with their pocketbooks. This can be frustrating for end users, but due to commercial pressures, this is often the only way a technology can rise above the crowd. The VHS tape "standard" was decided by market vote and the newer HD-DVD format will likely fight it out with the Blu-ray Disc to see who wins the living room for the next generation of DVD.

Standards are the fabric that holds modern IT systems together. If you want to know more, most of the standards bodies have Web sites in the form of www.NAME.org. Some of the standard documents are free for the asking (such as the IETF; learn about TCP, for example, by downloading RFC 793), whereas others require payment (such as SMPTE and the ITU) per document. Many professionals in the broadcast and cinema industry subscribe to the SMPTE CD-ROM, a collection of all their standards for easy access. The price is about $250. See [SMPTE].

Of all the standards groups, SMPTE is the most active in video systems standardization. The following is a summary of the work efforts (obtained from SMPTE documents) of the technology committees that develop standards. Only the committees that are developing AV/IT-relevant standards are listed.

General Scope of Technology Committees

To develop SMPTE engineering documents; review existing documents to ensure that they are current with established engineering practices and are compatible with international engineering documents where possible; recommend and develop test specifications, methods, and materials; and prepare tutorial material on engineering subjects for publication in the SMPTE Journal or for other means of dissemination benefiting the Society and the industry.

The following standards groups are sponsored by SMPTE. This is a subset of the total number that also includes film technology.

Technology Committees (AV Focus)

◆ Television Recording and Reproduction Technology (V16): The application of the general scope as it pertains to all phases of the recording and reproduction of television image, audio, and ancillary signals, including editing and signal processing within the recorder.

◆ Television Systems Technology (S22): The application of the general scope as it pertains to the design, management, and control of systems based on the integration of the technologies of video, audio, data essence, compression, recording, metadata, wrappers, file formats, and transfer protocols.

◆ Television Image Technology (I23): The application of the general scope as it pertains to the generation, acquisition, form, function, processing, interconnection, and presentation of video signals when those signals represent conventional images.

◆ Video Compression Technology (C24): The application of the general scope as it pertains to the encoding, processing, switching, and decoding of video signals to, in, and from the compressed domain.

◆ Metadata and Wrapper Technology (W25): The application of the general scope as it pertains to the definition of metadata and wrapper types and their structures for storage, transmission, and use.

◆ File Management and Networking Technology (N26): The application of the general scope as it pertains to the definition of file management and transfer protocols, their structures for storage, transmission, and use, and the physical networks that carry them.

◆ Data Essence Technology (D27): The application of the general scope as it pertains to the definition, coding, function, and application of data mechanisms other than those of video data, audio data, and metadata.

◆ Digital Cinema Technology (DC28): The application of the general scope as it pertains to providing an industry technical forum for digital cinema; identifying key systems and technology issues; developing and recommending an approach to digital cinema; identifying, establishing, and coordinating necessary working groups to achieve overall digital cinema objectives; and providing standards and recommendations to ensure interoperability, compatibility, performance, and support for future innovation.

◆ Television Audio Technology (A29): The application of the general scope as it pertains to the mechanisms and practices used in the production, processing, recording, reproduction, distribution, and presentation of sound records for television systems.

◆ Registration and Identification Technology (R30): The application of the general scope as it pertains to the definition, content, transport, storage, and registration of data structures for identification of digital assets and associated rights, for identification of storage, transport, processing, and similar systems, and as it pertains to operations of the SMPTE Registration Authority.

2.3   AV MEDIA CLIENTS

Looking again at Figure 2.2, let us morph it slightly to give it a more media centric personality. Without changing anything in Figure 2.2 we can add the notion of AV by defining the *AV application client*. So, consider the top level to be a mix of AV clients and non-AV clients. The necessary traditional A/V routing infrastructure is not shown in Figure 2.2 and is left out to simplify the overall diagram. See Chapter 10 for a discussion of a more dedicated, full-featured, AV/IT system based on the principles developed in this book.

Broadly, there are four different classes of AV client. Figure 2.5 shows their general I/O characteristics. The I/O notation is abbreviated, as

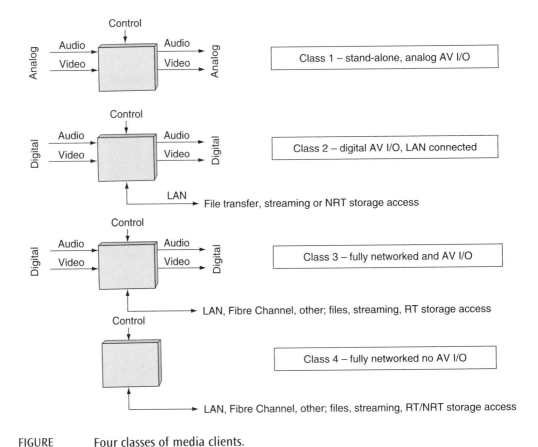

FIGURE   Four classes of media clients.

2.5

time code signals and video reference inputs are omitted because they are not relevant to our immediate discussion. Also, the definitions are not meant to be rigid. Other hybrid combinations will exist. For example, clients with digital A/V inputs but no outputs or visa versa (ingest stations, cameras, etc.) are not specifically shown. The point of the four classifications is to discern the major client types and their characteristics. Let us consider each class and its applications. Also, no one class is superior to another class. Each has its strengths and weaknesses depending on the intended application. Some clients also have management interfaces but these are not shown to simplify the diagrams.

2.3.1 Class 1 Media Client

This is the simplest class and is shown for completeness. It is all analog I/O (composite, component video), stand alone with no network connection. It is the legacy class of AV client and includes VTRs, analog amplifiers, linear switchers for edit suites, master control stations, special effects devices, and so on. This class has become out of favor; it does not take advantage of digital or networked advantages. Still, there are many facilities with rooms filled with these devices in legacy AV systems.

2.3.2 Class 2 Media Client

This class is distinguished with the inclusion of coax-based serial digital interface (SDI) I/O for AV connectivity and LAN connectivity. The LAN port may be used for file exchange and AV streaming but *not* access to net-workable, RT storage by definition. Support for device-internal storage is common. Audio I/O is also included using the AES/EBU interface.

A sample of this class of client is the Sony IMX eVTR, which is an MPEG-based, tape deck with SDI I/O and a LAN for MXF file export. Another example is the Panasonic P2 Camera with LAN (and removable memory card) for exporting stored clips. Consider too the stalwart video server. Doremi Lab's V1 server, Leitch's Neo, Pinnacle's Thunder, and Thomson GVG's M-Series iVDR are all class 2 devices with internal (or bundled) storage. Graphics devices such as Chyron's Duet family,

Inscriber's Inca family, and Pinnacle's Deko family are also examples of class 2 devices. True, some of them may also be optionally attached to external real time storage. In this case, these devices are considered a class 3 device (see Appendix J for more information on the workhorse video server).

Other examples of class 2 devices are the countless models of stand-alone nonlinear editors (NLE) from many vendors. These normally have digital I/O and LAN to access files over a network. Most AV test equipment is of class 2 but may not have any AV output ports. The class 2 device was the first to bridge the traditional AV and IT worlds back in the mid 1990s. At the time, it was ground-breaking AV technology.

2.3.3   Class 3 Media Client

This class is a fully networked device; it is a turbocharged class 2. Not only does it have SDI I/O, but it has real time access to external networkable storage. Of course, it also has LAN access for file exchange and streaming. The access to real time external storage is the major differentiating characteristic of this class compared to class 2. Storage connectivity may use one or more of the following methods with current top data rates.

1. Fibre Channel (up to 2/4 Gb/s per link)—SAN related.
2. LAN using Ethernet (up to 10 Gb/s)—NAS and SAN related.
3. IEEE 1394 and USB 2.0 for connecting to small, local storage systems. This mode offers limited network access to storage.

These methods are discussed in greater detail in Chapter 3A. Methods 1 and 2 are in heavy use in the IT infrastructure and are crucial to building any IT/AV system. IEEE 1394 and USB 2.0 are limited in their range and networkability, but they find niche applications for low-cost clients.

In theory, networked clients can access storage from any location. This is a powerful feature and it enables AV I/O to be placed in the most convenient location independent of storage location. This freeness of location has its trade-offs: an excellent link QoS is required to connect the client with the storage. Nonetheless, some systems will take advantage of this leverage point and more so as technology matures. Some class 3 devices also have internal HDD storage.

AV data storage systems are core to the new media facility. There are many ways to construct these systems, they come in a variety of forms, and they allow for whole new workflows that were impossible just a few years ago. These aspects are discussed in Chapters 3A, 3B, and 7. Of course, relying on data storage systems to keep all AV digital assets represents a major shift in operations; no more video tapes to manage and no more lost digital assets (if managed properly). There are several schools of thought regarding storage access by a client or server. Some of the methods are

A. Networkable RT storage pool available to all authorized attached clients. Classes 3 and 4 use this.

B. Networkable NRT storage pool available to all authorized attached clients. NRT storage has a relaxed QoS compared to RT storage. Classes 2 and 4 use this.

C. Islands of NRT storage. This is like B except there is not one consolidated pool of storage.

Method A is used with class 3/4 clients. Methods B/C are more appropriate for class 2/4 devices but may also apply to class 3. In Method C, files may reside on various file servers or arrays throughout a facility. If this occurs, then the asset management may become a serious nightmare due to the balkanization of resources. In fact, most modern systems use either A or B for their design methodology.

The distinction between RT and NRT is important in several regards. RT storage is used by clients for streaming AV processes such as recording and playout. NRT is used by clients for file transfer, off-line AV processing, metadata access, database access, and so on.

Examples of class 3 clients are Avid's AirSpeed, Leitch's VR and Nexio series of networked server, Omneon's Spectrum Media Server, Pinnacle Systems' MediaStream 8000 with Palladium Storage, the SeaChange Media Client attached to their Broadcast Media Library, and Thomson/ GVG's K2 media client/server system. For comparison reasons, all these are video server products.

Other examples are networked nonlinear editors: Avid's Media Composer family of editors with Unity storage, Quantel's family of editors with sQ Server storage, Pinnacle's Liquid Edit family and others. This class of media client offers the most flexibility compared to the other classes.

2.3.4   Class 4 Media Client

This is a class 3 or 2 device without any AV digital I/O. This client type is a fully networked station that does not have a need to ingest or playout AV materials. Some class 4 stations may use NRT file transfer for importing/exporting files. Other stations may access RT storage pool, whereas others may support streaming.

Examples of this client type include visual content browsers (low-rez normally), reduced functionality NLE stations, graphics authoring (Adobe Illustrator and Photoshop, for example) QA stations, asset managers, file gateways, file format converters, some storage, DRM authoring stations, file distribution schedulers, AV processors, and displays. One special version of this client type is a control device that sends operational commands to other clients to record, play, route, convert, retrieve, and so on. Importantly, no AV data pass through a control-type media client. Automation vendors offer a variety of media client control devices.

2.3.5   The Classes in Perspective

Figure 2.6 is a simple chart showing the value of networked clients. The class 3 client is the most useful due to its fully digital nature and networkability. The price/performance ratio, however, will always be a selection criteria so all client classes will find ample use in video systems as designers seek to drive down the total cost. In general, class 4 is the least expensive from a hardware point of view, and class 3 is the most expensive. Of course the software costs per device can range from insignificant to very expensive so there is no simple way to classify the price/performance across all classes of clients. In the final analysis, classes 2–4 will find ample use across a wide range of new video system designs.

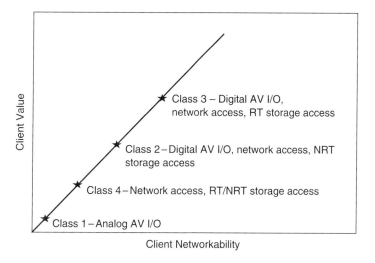

FIGURE
2.6

The relative value of media clients.

2.4   FILE TRANSFER, STREAMING, AND DIRECT-TO-STORAGE CONCEPTS

As mentioned in Chapter 1, three methods are key to moving A/V information in a video system. Most client types may use combinations of these methods. Figure 2.7 shows a system that has all three types of A/V data-moving means. When considering the three, they may be compared against each other in three pairs or considered separately by their own stand-alone merits. Analyzing the methods by direct 1:1 comparisons (files versus streaming, files versus direct to storage, direct to storage versus streaming) is a bit tedious and somewhat obscures the overall trade-offs. To complicate things even more, because direct to storage may be NRT or RT access, our classification will analyze each method separately with some 1:1 for the most important characteristics.

In summary, the high-level characteristics of each method are

◆ **File transfer**—Move files from one device to another (or point to multipoint). NRT transfers are easy to implement using FTP or HTTP, have no geographic limitations, and have 100% guarantee file transfer.

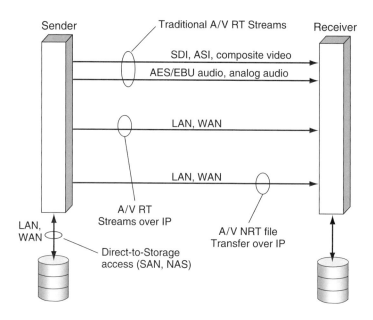

FIGURE

2.7

Streams, file transfer, and storage access.

- ◆ **Streaming AV**—Stream data from one element to another (or point to multipoint), usually in real time. Traditional A/V streaming (SDI, composite) is common in video systems. IT-based streaming is mature as well but is used mainly for content distribution to end users. Voice over IP (VOIP) is a form of audio streaming.

- ◆ **Direct to storage**—Random read/write data access by a storage attached client. Attached clients may have access to a clustered file system for a full view of all stored files. Storage access may be NRT or RT. Of course, RT access is more demanding on the connect infrastructure.

When transferring, steaming, or storing, it is good to know the storage and data rate appetite of the A/V data structures. Table 2.1 outlines some popular formats and their vital statistics. See Chapter 11 for a discussion of A/V formats.

It is always good to have a rule of thumb when computing storage requirements. The best metric to memorize is the one in row 3 of Table 2.1. By knowing that 10-Mb/s video requires 4.5 GB/hr, it is easy to scale for other values because of the convenient factor of 10 scaling.

A/V format	Byte rate per hour	Comments
64-Kb/s compressed audio for an iPOD	28.8 MB/hr	1000 hr is ~29 GB, a small-capacity HDD
2-Mb/s MPEG video for a PVR	900 MB/hr	100, 2-hr movies is ~180 GB, one ATA disc
10-Mb/s MPEG video	4.5 GB/hr	Typical rate for video servers storing SD commercials for TV
25-Mb/s DV video or HDV video, or ~28 Mb/s with audio and overhead	11.25-GB/hr video only, or ~12.65 GB/hr with audio	One 180-GB HDD can store 16 hr of DV or HDV video
166-Mb/s uncompressed 4:2:2 SD video, 8 bit (720H × 480V × 30 FPS)	75.4 GB/hr	Uncompressed A/V has a huge appetite
995.3 Mb/s for uncompressed 4:2:2 HD 1920 × 1080 × 30 imaging	448 GB/hr	The ATSC/DTV standard compresses video to 19.3 Mb/s, shaving off 98%
384 Mb/s per frame for 4K H by 2K V uncompressed (4:4:4, 16 bits per RGB pixel) digital cinema	4.145 TB/hr (24 FPS) 9.216 Gb/s	Requires massive storage and I/O bandwidth for pristine quality

TABLE   A/V Storage and Data Rate Appetites

2.1

So 1 hr of DV requires 28/10 * 4.5 = 12.65 GB/hr. Many of the chapters in this book refer to A/V storage and bandwidth requirements so it is a good idea to become familiar with these stats. Please note that *Mb/s* means megabits per second and *MB/s* means megabytes per second. A small b represents bits and a capital B represents bytes—8 bits.

When building an AV/IT system, which method is best to achieve the most flexible workflows—file transfer, streaming, direct to storage, or some hybrid combination? What are the trade-offs among the methods? Let us consider these questions.

2.4.1   File Transfer Concepts

Figure 2.8 is used as the basis for our discussion. Clients A/B/C/D can all send and receive files. Frankly, each of these devices may also be a server but let us use the client name for now. The file mover

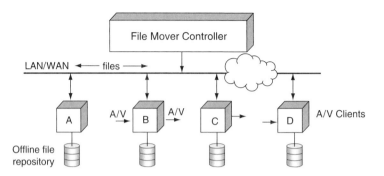

FIGURE   NRT file transfer topology example.

2.8

block is some sort of external control logic (automation system) that directs NRT file movement from a sender to a receiver(s). Additionally, individual clients can pull or push files from/to other clients in a peer-to-peer arrangement or using FTP or Web protocols such as HTTP. Files can be transferred in a point-to-point or point-to-multipoint fashion. Each client has local storage of various capacities. File transfer between a source and a destination is often referred to as "store and forward," although the moniker is losing favor. The file mover has the master database of the location of all files (or can locate a file using queries as needed). Client A may be the master file repository, but this is not a requirement for a file-based architecture.

Table 2.2 lists the general characteristics of a file transfer. Although not cited, many of the features of file transfer are different from either streaming or direct to storage methods. If you had to deliver a 5-s summary of file transfer, the top three points would be: 100% error-free delivery is possible, NRT delivery normally, point-to-point is the most common mode.

Table 2.3 (in reference to Figure 2.8) outlines the foremost advantages/disadvantages of the file transfer method. One acronym needs explaining: just in time file transfer (JITFT). In a file centric system, a client may need a file for a critical operation at a certain time of day. The file mover, for example, may schedule the file transfer (move

- Move files between sender and receiver. Support for reading files (pull a file from a remote host) and writing files (push a file to a remote host)
- Point-to-point or point-to-multipoint support
- Guaranteed delivery of files or best effort
- Faster, approximately equal, or slower than real time transfer speeds
- Files are moved entirely or partial transfers
- Files protected by password, user name, and access groups
- LAN and WAN support
- Large file support (100 + GB class)

TABLE	Feature Set for General-Purpose File Transfer
2.2	

file from client D to client B) such that a needy client receives the file in question "just in time" as a worst case. There is a delicate balance between sending files too soon (hogs client's local storage) and too late (may miss a deadline due to the NRT nature of file transfer). JITFT is a way to think about these issues.

Snapshot

Moving files – it is time versus money

When transferring an HD or SD file, a low rate link may be chosen to save money. Slow links result in long delivery times—possibly many hours. However, an improved QoS (more money) can reduce the delivery time— several seconds is achievable. So as with many things in life, money saves time.

The NRT moniker is a bit vague in terms of the actual file transfer time. For some systems, a $1/10$ file transfer speed (1 min of program material takes 10 min to move) is sufficient, whereas other system designs may require an $\times 10$ file transfer speed. The rated speed of transfer and the infrastructure performance are intimately connected. This will not be studied in detail, but it should be obvious that an $\times 10$ file transfer speed requires a storage and link QoS approaching RT if not much better. Aspects such as component failover during a fast transfer need to be accounted for to guarantee JITFT performance. The analysis in Table 2.3 assumes that NRT < RT in terms of speeds. If NRT is defined as >>RT, then many of the advantages/disadvantages are inaccurate. Of course a

NRT file transfer advantages	NRT file transfer disadvantages
100% error-free delivery possible or best effort with FEC	Media management can be complex due to files being scattered among many clients. Who owns the master file copy? Where is the master file? How many copies are floating around? Who has delete privileges?
No need for instant failover in case transfer link or network switch fails. Easy to assure fault tolerance using alternate path diversity	Delivery latency can be an enemy in a JITFT system. This can be a major issue for nondeterministic AV requirements; example, *play file ABC now*
Uses standard IT-based file servers and JITFT logic to deliver files	An NLE client may need hundreds of files for an edit session. It can be very slow to move files from external storage to an edit client; lost productivity
Delivery rate may be set from much less than RT to much more than RT	Cannot implement streaming workflows easily
No reliance on RT storage QoS, less expensive $/GB of storage	Partial file transfers not common

TABLE   Advantages and Disadvantages of NRT Transfers

2.3

JITFT-based design can also use a wide mix of NRT speeds, making the system design more difficult in terms of QoS and failover requirements.

The advantages/disadvantages comments in Table 2.3 are not meant to be row aligned, i.e., there is not necessarily a correlation between the advantage and the disadvantage on the same row.

2.4.1.1   *Reliable File Transfer Techniques*

The bedrock protocols for file transfer over networks use the TCP, UDP, and IP families. TCP is a packet-reliable protocol and is widely used. UDP is a "send-and-hope" methodology and also finds wide use. Table 2.4 outlines the chief methods used to transfer files using both TCP and UDP. Most of the entries support multiparty transfers. Some are best-effort delivery using an FEC and some offer 100% error-free delivery. Please refer to Chapter 6 for more information on IP, TCP, and UDP.

Let us consider the first four methods in Table 2.4. FTP (RFC 969) is the granddaddy of all file transfer methods and is used daily to move

Applications	Transport layer	Significant aspects
FTP/browser HTTP/browser	Bidirectional TCP/IP Other TCP-like protocols	Very common TCP acknowledges every packet and provides poor throughput over long-fat-pipes 100% reliable transfer
FLUTE	Unidirectional using IP Multicast	Massive point-to-multipoint file transfer using FEC to correct for errors. New
GridFTP	Bidirectional TCP/IP	Multipoint distribution and partial file transfer. Specialized
Desktop Drag-Drop file transfer	TCP/IP supporting CIFS, NFS, or AFP	These are general file access protocols that may be used to move entire or partial files. Ubiquitous
ATSC, DVB use for sending program guides and related data	Unidirectional UDP data wheel based on ISO/IEC 13818-6 DSM-CC spec	Data sent as a repeating wheel with a simple FEC Possibly long delay to get 100% reliable file since no back channel. Good for point-to-multipoint
Solutions from Kencast, Aspera Software, and others. With FTP-like support too	Unidirectional UDP with sophisticated FEC	Data sent once with sophisticated FEC for 5–30% (typically) data loss recovery Good for point-multipoint satellite distribution and lossy networks with 100% reliable transfers within FEC limits. Excellent throughput
Solutions from Kencast, Aspera Software, and others. With FTP-like support too	Unidirectional UDP with sophisticated FEC and backchannel using TCP or other protocol	As above but with back channel to request packet resend once FEC correct limit is reached 100% reliable over very lossy channels with excellent throughput
Telestream and others	Unidirectional UDP, no FEC, with backchannel signaling	Simple, very fast, works well in low loss channels

TABLE   File Transfer Method Classifications

2.4

millions of files. In practice, FTP does not formally support partial file transfer (start–end points within a file) or point-to-multipoint transfers. To reduce the deficiencies of FTP, the IETF is developing FLUTE – RFC 3926. This is a new file transfer protocol for doing point-to-multipoint transfers and supports a massive number of simultaneous receivers over unidirectional IP channels. Because there is no back channel, each receiver uses FEC methods to recover modest amounts of data lost (if any) during transmission.

The third row in Table 2.4 outlines GridFTP (www.globus.org). This is a protocol for use in grid computing (Appendix C). It extends the standard FTP protocol with facilities, such as multistreamed transfer and partial file transfer. The effort is currently not under the sponsorship of the IETF. Fourth, files may also be transferred using the desktop drag-and-drop method common to many computer applications. In this case, the underlying protocol is not FTP but usually CIFS, NFS, AFP, or another remote file access protocol (see Chapter 3B). It is apparent that there are a variety of file transfer methods in use, but garden-variety FTP does the lion's share of work today for simple point-to-point applications.

The Ubiquitous FTP/TCP Method

Developed in the 1970s at UC Berkeley, the file transfer protocol (FTP) is a wonderful tool for point-to-point file transfers using bidirectional links. Figure 2.9 shows the basic client–server FTP arrangement. Separate logical control and data connections are shown. In general, the client establishes a TCP control connection over a LAN/WAN with the server side. The server may accept more than one client connection (sometimes hundreds). Commands are sent to request the server to transfer files or accept files.

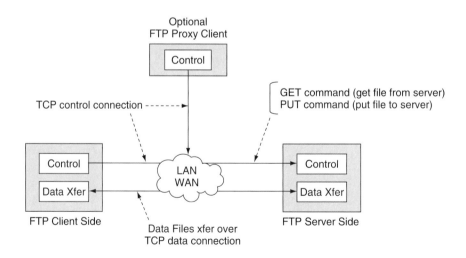

FIGURE   FTP client and server with control and data logical connections.

2.9

Typical commands are GET_File to request a file transfer (server to client) and PUT_File to send a file (client to server). The server responds by pushing or pulling files over the data connection. No file data move over the control connection. Of course, using TCP guarantees a 100% correct file transfer even over congested networks. FTP works quite well over a confined LAN and transfer speeds can be exceptional. Transferring large files (gigabytes) is always a challenge if the link is slow (or long), as the transfer time can take many hours.

For long-distance transfers, TCP is not ideal and, in fact, can be as much as *100 times slower* than alternative transport means. Why is this? Simply put, TCP's reliability scheme limits its data throughput inversely with network latency and packet loss. When packet loss is detected, TCP reduces its "congestion window" size exponentially. The window size defines the maximum number of bytes in the transmission pipeline before the receiving end acknowledges receipt to the sender. After recovering from a packet loss, TCP increases the window linearly and slowly. Hence, aggressive back-off and slow ramp up limit the TCP throughput considerably. See Chapter 6 for a discussion of how and why this limits throughput.

Another important aspect of FTP is a supported mode called "proxy client." Many everyday FTP transactions involve the client and server as discussed. But what if a third party (the proxy; for example, an automation system) needs to initiate a file transfer between the client and the server? How is this done and does the proxy receive any file data? In Figure 2.9 the proxy client is shown with only a control connection.

Consider an automation system (the proxy client) requesting an archive system (the FTP server) to send a file to an on-air video server (the FTP client). The proxy client initiates the transaction and file data move between the two end points. From the standpoint of the FTP server, it is blind to where the request originated. It could have come from the proxy or the standard FTP client. See (RFC 959, Figure 2.9) for more information on FTP and the proxy client.

Formally, FTP does not support partial file transfer say from a mark-in point to a mark-out point in the file. This hobbles applications that want to transfer 1 min out of a 60-min program, for example. Sony has used the optional FTP SITE command for this purpose in their eVTR. This method is being copied by others and it may become a de facto standard.

One FTP application vendor that supports the proxy client mode and the SITE command is FlashFXP (www.flashfxp.com), but there are others.

Stepping away from TCP and its cousins, let us consider the bottom four rows in Table 2.4.

Data Wheel File Transfer Method

Consider the case of transferring a single file to thousands (or millions) of set-top boxes and televisions over a satellite or cable system. This is the case for the distribution of the electronic program guides. It is not practical to use a packet-reliable protocol such as TCP, so DAVIC (Digital Audio Video Council, active in 1994–1997) invented the data carousel as a repeating data stream. Data are sent in packets (UDP in functionality and concept) to all end points with a modest forward error correction (FEC) to correct some errors at the receiver point. Data repeat as a wheel, so if say 5% of the data file was not received on the first pass, then the missing packets will likely be recovered on the next or subsequent passes. The data transfer rate may be very slow but the patient receiver will be rewarded with a 100% data file given sufficient passes of the data wheel. DVB and the ATSC standards specify this method for sending "files" to set-top box receivers. This protocol is an example of a hybrid file transfer and data stream. Figure 2.10 shows the features of a transport means that is part pure file transfer and part streaming. Given the limited

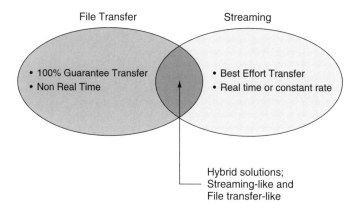

FIGURE

2.10

File transfer and streaming domains.

use of this protocol, other more efficient means have been invented as referenced in the last three rows of Table 2.4.

IP Multicast

Snapshot

IP Multicast is a bandwidth-efficient method (and set of standards) for moving data across a network to multiple locations simultaneously. Multicast requires that all the IP switches in the network cooperate. See http://www.answers.com/topic/multicast for a tutorial on the subject. It is not commonly implemented for professional AV applications and is slowly gaining maturity.

Sophisticated FEC Methods

Forward error correction is a general means to correct for a fixed percentage (say 10%) of packet loss at the received end of a file transfer without needing to contact the sending site for retransmission. Files may be sent over unidirectional links (UDP in concept) at much greater rates than TCP will allow, but UDP lacks the reliability layer of TCP. Also, UDP naturally supports point-to-multipoint transfers. Figure 2.11 outlines a general system that relies on UDP for file transmission and FEC to correct receive errors. All errors within the correctable range will be repaired with 100% reliability. A return channel may be used to augment the FEC for requesting packet resends when the loss exceeds the correctable range (>10%, for example).

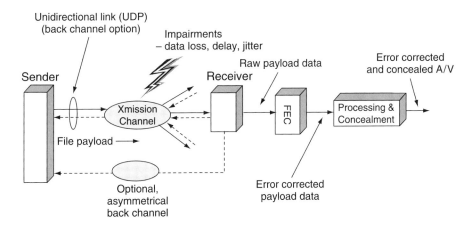

FIGURE   File transfer delivery chain over unidirectional links with FEC.

2.11

There is no free lunch, however. To correct for say 20% data loss the FEC overhead is at least 20% and usually more. The FEC overhead may be located at the end of every packet/data block or distributed throughout the data stream. Algorithm designers choose from a variety of methods to correct for errors. The common audio CD uses a data-recording method called EFM (eight to fourteen modulation). When this is coupled with Reed–Solomon coding, burst errors of 4 KB (a scratch) may be corrected. Even a horribly scratched audio CD (or video DVD) will likely play with 100% fidelity thanks to Mr. Reed and Mr. Solomon.

There are several methods that provide for error correction: Hamming codes, Fire codes, Reed–Solomon, BCH codes, Tornado codes, and countless proprietary codes like the ones from Kencast (www.kencast.com) and Aspera (www.asperasoft.com), for example [Morelos]. See Chapter 5 for examples of how RAID works to correct for errors from disk drives. The overall winner in terms of efficiency for burst error correction is the Reed–Solomon coding scheme, although other coding schemes may be more efficient under a variety of operating modes. These methods often support the common FTP programming interface semantics (GET, PUT, etc.), although not the FTP protocol layer.

Just how good is the Reed–Solomon FEC? In the R/S world, N total data symbols with K user message symbols have an FEC overhead of $N - K$ data symbols. So if $N = 204$ and $K = 188$, then 16 "overhead" symbols are needed to perform the FEC correction. It turns out that $(N - K)/2$ symbols may be corrected by the RS algorithm. If each symbol is a byte, then for this case 8 bytes may be corrected with an overhead of 16 bytes. True it is not 100% efficient (one bit overhead per corrected bit would be ideal), but it is relatively easy to compute, good at large block error recovery, and well understood.

Looking at Figure 2.12, a 16-byte electronic correction code (ECC) is appended to the end of a 188-byte data payload for this example. This is an example of the ubiquitous DVB-ASI transport stream format. The 16-byte overhead can correct for up to 8 corrupted payload bytes as applied by the FEC algorithm. Using more ECC bits corrects for more corrupt payload bits. But what if not all the errors can be corrected? Of course if the receiver can ask for a resend then the bad bits may be recovered. This raises issues such as the latency for the resend, the logic to do this over a field of say thousands of receivers, the requirement for a back channel,

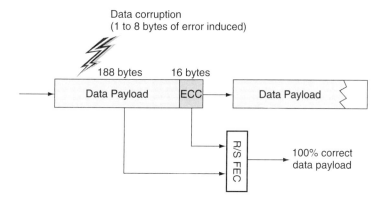

Using FEC to correct errors: An example using R/S.

and so on. Under some circumstances, it may be better to *conceal* an error when the FEC has run out of stream rather than request a resend of data.

An example of this is to silence a portion of an audio track during the period of corrupt data samples. Another case is to replicate the previous video frame when the next frame is corrupt. Muting, duplicating information, or estimating has its limits naturally but it works remarkably well when the method is not overused. The audio CD format uses a combination of FEC and error concealment to reconstruct errors in the audio stream. Of course it is not feasible to conceal some data errors any more then it is practical to estimate the missing digits in a corrupt phone number (or metadata or compressed coefficients and so on). As with all methods to recover data, the designer needs to use prudence in applying the right mix of FEC, resend, and concealment. Concealment can only be applied after A/V decompression has occurred (if any), as it is nearly impossible to conceal errors in the compressed domain.

File Transfers Using UDP without FEC

The last row in Table 2.4 includes methods using UDP without any FEC for reliable data payload transfers. During the course of the file transfer, the receiver acknowledges only bad or missing packets using a separate TCP-based (or UDP) message sent to the sender. The sender responds by retransmitting the requested packets. The HyperMAP protocol from Telestream (www.telestream.net) is an example of such a protocol. UDP payloads with negative acknowledgments can be very efficient, especially over a channel with low loss or in a point-to-mulitpoint transfer. A channel with 3% packet errors can achieve ~97% of the throughput of the raw link. HyperMAP has some added A/V-friendly features too, such as resume-interrupted transfers, resume a transfer from a different location, and pause/resume a transfer. It beats FTP/TCP in terms of performance at the cost of being a proprietary protocol. There are many variations on this theme in use today.

Another way to speed up data transfers is to use a **WAN accelerator**. These are small appliances placed at each end of a WAN link and use protocol tricks to increase date transfer rates. How is this done? One method is to replace any TCP streams (as used by FTP) with UDP streams and appropriate error recovery methods. The protocol remapping techniques are non-standard but the appliances hide this fact from all upper-level user applications. It is not unusual to get a 30 to 100X improvement in data transfer speeds across a long distance WAN connection.

This class of product falls under the umbrella of wide area file services (WAFS). Besides TCP speed up, WAFS appliances also increase the performance of storage access over a WAN. See Chapter 3B, section 3B.3.2 for more insights on WAFS.

Snapshot

Swarms of Files

It is likely that you have heard of iMesh, Kazaa, Morpheus, or other applications for file transfer across the Web. These are used commonly to transfer A/V files using peer-to-peer transfer—often illegally. The reference to them is provided as an example only and not as an endorsement. Still, these programs are commonly used for legal file exchange as well.

There is no file mover equivalent for these programs and clients initiate and exchange files with other clients. One novel peer-to-peer transfer method is from BitTorrent. Using the BitTorrent software, a client downloads pieces of a file from several clients simultaneously until all the pieces are collected. A *swarm* is a collection of clients all connected to share a given file. By each client sharing only pieces of a file, more clients can share and receive a given file simultaneously. See bittorrent.com for more information and links on swarming.

Choosing the Best Method

So which of the methods in Table 2.4 is the best? Well, it depends on your needs. FTP/TCP works quite well for short hops (Round_trip_delay < than 20 Ms) within a campus environment. Very large FTP/TCP through-puts on the order of 350 Mb/s and greater may be achieved over Ethernet-based LANs. FTP is the de facto standard for file transfer and most equipment vendors support it. For wide area file distribution, FEC methods work very well and have wide industry acceptance. The proven fact that non-TCP transport layers can deliver files up to 100X faster is a huge impetus to use TCP alternatives such as UDP coupled with a pow-erful FEC (or with negative acknowledgments) or WAN accelerators.

2.4.1.2   QoS Concepts

Quality of service is a concept crucial to many aspects of A/V—both traditional and IT based. Typically, QoS metrics define the quality of transmission on any link that connects two points. An Internet con-nection, a video link from a sports venue, or a satellite stream may all be classified by their QoS metrics. Of course QoS concepts can be applied to just about any process, such as application serving or storage access. Specific metrics are applied as appropriate.

The **big four** QoS link and network parameters are *data rate, loss, delay, and jitter (variation in delay)*. These metrics apply to digital paths only. Ideally, a 270-Mb/s multihop SDI path QoS is 270 Mb/s rate guar-anteed, loss is near zero, delay is approximately wire speed, and jitter is near zero. The QoS of a consumer's Internet[2] end-to-end connection is more relaxed with variable data rates (DSL or cable rates), some packet loss (.2% for traffic is typical), modest delay (~5 Ms for intracity end points), and some jitter expected (~20% of delay average). Aiming for an ideal QoS may be a waste of money if a relaxed QoS will meet your needs. After all, the tighter the QoS, the more expensive the link. Regardless of the QoS for any practical link, an error can occur in the received video stream. Despite SDI's well-defined QoS, it always offers *best effort* delivery. Receive errors may be concealed in some manner.

---

[2] These values are point-in-time averages and your mileage will vary.

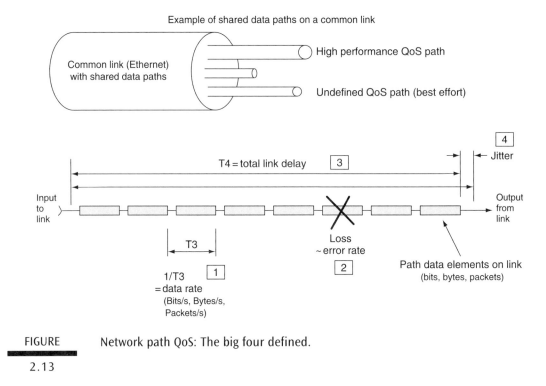

FIGURE   Network path QoS: The big four defined.

2.13

Figure 2.13 illustrates the four key QoS metrics for an end-to-end network path.

Figure 2.13 shows how each metric is measured in principle. Also, some links (such as Ethernet) may carry many different unrelated connections simultaneously—each with its own QoS requirements. Whenever paths share a common carrier, attention is needed to keep them separate and with no cointerference. Isolating paths is not easy, as one rogue path (data bursting over its assigned limit, for example) can ruin the QoS of the entire link. It is normally left to the end point transmitting gear to meter data and set the QoS rate. Many WAN links meter data rates, usually at the edges, and will throttle data to its assigned range.

The required QoS of an AV-related link depends on whether the link is used for file transfer or streaming video. These two methods are compared in the following section.

2.4.2   Streaming Concepts

In addition to file transfer, streaming is a second popular method used to move digital media between two or more devices. There are five main characteristics that highlight the differences between streaming and file transfer (see Table 2.5). Examples of streaming abound: digital TV broadcast over terrestrial and satellite links, traditional SMPTE 259M SDI and composite links, Intranet (campus) AV streaming, and popular Web media as distributed by radio stations, news organizations, and other sources of streaming AV.

Some links are designed to natively carry real time streaming, such as the ubiquitous SDI, and, in the WAN sense, T1/E1, SONET, and other Telco links. Digital broadcast standards ATSC and DVB support streaming. Still others such as asynchronous Ethernet can be made to carry streams using appropriate IP-based protocols. There are more variations on the streaming theme discussed later.

Each streaming method uses completely different means but achieves the same end result; namely, the best effort (usually) delivery of real time AV materials to one or more receivers. In some applications, streaming may do the job of a file transfer and visa versa so it is prudent to compare these two methods. Figure 2.14 shows a simple example of a point-to-multipoint streaming configuration. Let us consider each row of Table 2.5 [Kovalick].

Streaming	File transfer
Best effort quality (typically), unidirectional link normally	Guaranteed 100% delivery (typically), bidirectional link normally
Synchronous, isochronous, or asynchronous delivery choices	Asynchronous delivery advantage
Delivery time pacing 1X, 4X . . .	Any desired delivery time
Point to multipoint is natural	Point to multipoint requires complex logic
Tight QoS desired	Relaxed QoS

TABLE   Streaming versus File Transfer

2.5

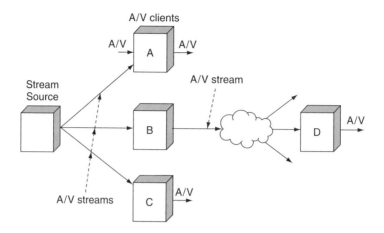

FIGURE

2.14

Real time streaming topology example.

Normally, streamed content is delivered in a *best-effort* fashion. If there is no back channel and only a modest FEC is used, then there is no way to guarantee reliability. Of course with a back channel the quality can be outstanding, but streaming is implemented most efficiently without a return channel. If the packet loss is overwhelming, then the efficiency of FEC is lost. A streaming application with a heavy FEC or back channel use may indeed be considered a file transfer method as Figure 2.10 indicates in the overlap area. Most practical streaming applications in use today provide for best-effort delivery.

Row 2 of Table 2.5 outlines the different timing relationships that a delivery link may use. Digital video streams can be isochronous, synchronous, or even asynchronous. These timing relationships are covered later in this section. Isochronous and synchronous connectivity put strict requirements on the QoS for the link.

Another important aspect of comparison is the delivery timing as listed in row 3 of Table 2.5. For live events, a RT-streamed link may be the only practical choice. But for many other applications (copies, distribution, archive, etc.), a NRT file transfer is preferred. In fact, choosing the delivery time adds a degree of flexibility not always available in streamed video. It may be prudent to do a program dub at 100X without loss of quality or, to conserve resources, distribute a program at 1/10 real time. Of course one can use streaming to mimic a file transfer but the *best-effort* delivery of most streaming methods results in file transfer having the quality edge.

The point-to-multipoint nature of most simple streaming methods is difficult to match using file transfer (row 4 of Table 2.5). True, as shown in the section on file transfer, there are methods to do multipoint transfers but they are sophisticated and not as simply implemented as streaming for the most part. Take the case of the traditional SDI link. To send a SDI-based signal, to say 10 receivers, is a snap. Merely run the source SDI signal through a 1:10 distribution amplifier or use an SDI router with multiple ganged output ports. See Appendix I for insights into a novel multipoint streaming method.

Finally (row 5 of Table 2.5), the cost of networking infrastructure is dropping much faster than that of video-specific infrastructure. Networking components are following price curves that are tied directly to Internet infrastructure costs as discussed in Chapter 1. In general, file transfer has the cost edge for NRT applications, as the associated QoS can be very poor and still achieve a 100% reliable file reception. Of course, a loose QoS may be used for RT streaming, but the rate, loss, delay, and latency specs must be accounted for. One example of this is Internet telephony or voice over IP (VOIP). VOIP is a RT streaming operation using modest QoS and therefore some long-distance telephone calls have less than desired quality.

If you have followed the discussion to this point then it should be apparent that file transfer and streaming both have a place in video systems design. File transfer has an overall edge in terms of guaranteed quality compared to streaming for NRT content distribution, but RT streaming beats file transfer when live programming is sent from a source to one or more simultaneous receivers. LAN-based streaming for professional applications is rare despite its everyday use over the Internet and business Intranets. WAN-based streaming (point-to-point trunking) has found some niche applications. MXF has support for streaming and some early tests show promise. See [Devlin] for more on using MXF for steaming applications.

2.4.2.1   Streaming Delivery and Timing Methods

A streaming receiver should be able to "view/process" the received stream in real time. The notion of clocking is usually associated with a stream, as the receiver normally needs knowledge of the sender's time references to recreate the target signal. A good example of a timed stream is a typical NTSC/PAL broadcast TV signal. Another example is that of video moving over an SDI or composite link. Many Telcos offer A/V streaming wide area connectivity using the analog TV-1 service, a digital 45-Mb/s compressed video service or a 270-Mb/s uncompressed service. Accessing Web video on a PC is normally a streaming operation (or progressive down load). Streams can be sent over just about any kind of link if the appropriate (rate, loss, delay, and jitter) considerations are met. A stream may be sent over a path using the following forms of connectivity.

- **Isochronous (equally timed bits) links**. In this case the medium (SDI and AES/EBU links) has an inherent bit clock to guarantee precise timing relationships. The clock is embedded into the on-the-wire format. The transmit clock may be recovered directly at the receiver from the link's data bit stream. In a well-provisioned link, there is zero data loss, very low jitter, and low delay. This link was designed with RT streaming as the goal.

- **Synchronous (with time) links**. With synchronous links, end-to-end timing coordination is accomplished using a system-wide common clock. SONET and SDH are good examples of synchronous links. See Appendix F for more information on telecoms links. Streaming AV over a synchronous link requires extra effort compared to using SDI alone but low data loss, jitter, and delay can be achieved.

- **Plesiochronous (almost synchronous) links**. In this case the sender clock and receiver clock are not 100% locked, but are very closely in sync. Two plesiochronous signals are arbitrarily close in frequency to some defined precision. These signals are not sourced from the same clock and, after a time, they become skewed. Their relative closeness allows a switch to cross-connect, switch, or in some way process the signals. The inaccuracy of timing may force a receiver to repeat or delete data (video) in order to handle buffer underflow or overflows. Examples of these links are the ubiquitous T1/T3, E1/E3 telecom links. The clock drift specs are a function of the timing hierarchy as defined and used in the telecoms world. If time stamp clock recovery methods are used in association with these links, true loss free AV streaming is possible.

♦ **Asynchronous data links**. Ethernet is a typical asynchronous link. True, it has a notion of clocking (100BaseT has a nominal clock of 100 Mb/s), but the timing is loose and there is no concept (normal use) of clocking coherence between Ethernet links. Streamed AV may be carried over asynchronous links if the time stamp methods described for synchronous communications (see later) are applied. With error correction or using TCP/IP, excellent low loss and jitter characteristics may be obtained. One trade-off is typically long delays compared to the other links discussed.

It is possible to achieve outstanding A/V streaming quality using asynchronous or plesiochronous links if attention is given to coordinating the end point timing relationships. Let us call this technique *synchronous communications*.

Synchronous Communications

With synchronous communications, the timing coordination is accomplished by synchronizing the transmitting and receiving devices to a common clock signal by some means. The links may be tightly clocked (SONET/ATM), loosely clocked (Ethernet), or not clocked at all (Internet connectivity). Methods for a receiver to recover a sender's clock are as follow.

♦ **The sender and receiver use the same clock**. GPS-based global clock, for example or use independent Cesium clocks such that any frequency drift is inconsequential. Another method is to use the network time protocol (NTP, RFC 1305) at both ends. SONET is an example of a WAN link using common clocks. Alternatively, IEEE-1588 precision time protocol (PTP) provides timing signals over IP/Ethernet and can achieve 10- to 100-μs microsecond accuracy in campus networks. This accuracy is about one horizontal line of video (see **ieee1588.nist.gov.**).

♦ **Derive a clock from received embedded time stamps**. This is commonly used for Web A/V streaming, MPEG broadcast (DVB, ATSC, and satellite) for home TV, and other applications.

♦ **Derive signal timing from the received signal stream**. A PAL or NTSC signal is designed so that a receiver may recover the sender's "clock." The common video composite signal also supports receiver timing recovery. A receiver uses the embedded horizontal and vertical timing information to recreate the sender's notion of the same timing. If designed properly, a receiver can stay locked indefinitely to the sender's clock references.

Note that synchronous end-to-end communications are *not* necessarily dependent on some sort of synchronous link. True, the tighter the link clocking the easier it may be to stream AV. But think of *synchronous links* and *synchronous communications* as different concepts. That is why it is possible to achieve respectable AV live streaming over the Web—one of the most egregious examples of a nonsynchronous network.

Figure 2.15 shows a segmentation of methods to achieve end-to-end streaming over links of various sorts. For most real time streams, the receiver needs to recover the transmitter's original sense of timing before the AV can be viewed or otherwise processed live.

The SDI link has a special place in the heart of the video systems designer. It is possible to create a complete AV system with thousands of SDI links all completely lock stepped in sync (video line and video frame synced). As a result, live frame accurate switching (camera choice or other source choice) between the various SDI links is a relatively trivial matter. It is not so easy when it comes to using the other links

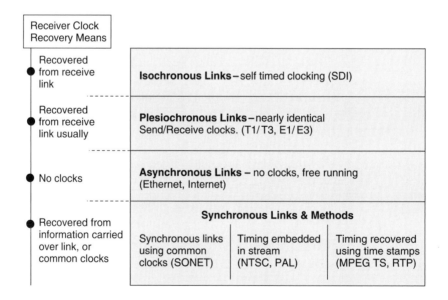

FIGURE   End-to-end communication methods for AV streaming.

2.15

in Figure 2.15. See Appendix B for some insight into synchronizing multiple independent A/V signals from nonisochronous sources. Still, IT links can be used for many typical AV streaming applications with proper care.

Push-and-Pull Streaming

There is one more aspect of streaming to contemplate before we leave the subject: stream flow control. There are two general methods to move a stream from a sender to a receiver: push it out from the sender without regard for the receiver or pull it from the sender under control of the receiver. A broadcast TV station operates using the *push* scenario. No end point receiver can throttle the incoming stream—take it or leave it. The sender must push the output stream with the exact flow rate that the receiver will consume it. In the second method, the receiver *pulls* data from the sender. A viewing PC asks for, say, the next 5 s of video and the sender complies by sending it. When the receiver has consumed 4 s, it asks the sender for more and so on. This method allows for the receiver to control the stream precisely according to its needs (display video, for example). Frankly, push streaming is used most commonly. In fact, most Web-based consumer A/V streaming is UDP push based. One special use of pull streaming permits the receiver to pause, fast forward, or rewind a stream by commanding the sender to act like a virtual VTR. Of course, physics will not allow a receiver to fast forward a live stream.

Interactive Streaming

Interactive Web-based streaming (start, stop, pause, fast forward, rewind, etc.) requires a client feedback mechanism to control the source server. In Web applications, the real time streaming protocol (RTSP, RFC 2326) may be used for this purpose. No AV data are transported over RTSP—it is a stream control method. Rather, the real time transport protocol (RTP, RFC 1889, 3550, and 3497) is used for streaming transport. RTP provides end-to-end network transport functions suitable for applications transmitting real time AV over multicast or unicast network services. RTP does not address resource reservation and does not guarantee QoS for real time services. These protocols will find some use in professional, high-quality applications, especially for point-to-point trunking applications.

High-Quality, High-Rate Streaming

Many streaming applications are for low data rate, end-user needs. However, there is an application class for very high-rate professional "trunking" over IP networks. Point-to-point links between AV facilities (sports, news, and campus events) have been provided for years using T3/E3, SONET/SDH, and other connectivity. These links can be very expensive and often require compressed AV to reduce the data rate. With the advent of available IP access, several vendors offer SDI extenders over IP.

One such product is from Path 1 Networks (www.path1.com). The Cx1000 IP Video Gateway delivers uncompressed RT SDI (270 Mb/s) over IP networks. The unit maps the SDI data input onto a 1-Gb Ethernet link and a second remote unit unwraps IP data and outputs it on an SDI link, resulting in transparent trunking. The Ethernet link may be WAN connected for even greater reach. Using clock recovery and FEC methods, the gateway provides excellent QoS in the presence of link jitter (250 Ms) and packet loss. A 2003 report by the respected market research firm of In-Stat/MDR predicts that IP streaming for professional use (one way and two way) will be a $2.2B ww, world wide business segment at the end of 2007.

Well, that is it for the coverage of streaming. These concepts are referenced throughout the book and are fundamental to AV/IT systems. For more information on professional streaming methods and applications, refer to the Video Services Forum. This is an industry group that specializes in streaming AV transport technology (www.videoservicesforum.org).

2.4.3   Direct-to-Storage Concepts

Figure 2.16 shows a simplified plan of a shared storage model for attached clients. In this case, clients A/B/C/D all have RT read/write access to a single storage system. NRT access will not be analyzed in as much detail because NRT is a relaxed form of the RT case. In the RT case, external storage *appears* as local to each client. All files are stored in the same repository and there is no requisite for files to be moved (file transfer) between clients or from the storage to a client. Individual clients may have local physical storage but this is not a requirement. Individual clients may also be restricted from accessing all the available storage and from deleting files. User access rights and permissions may be set for any client to

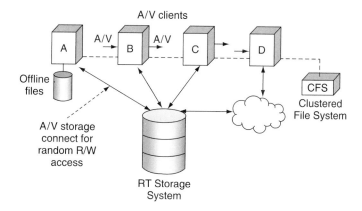

FIGURE   Real time direct to storage topology example.

2.16

guarantee a well-managed storage system. With direct access to storage, clients have the ability to random access read/write data into any stored "file" in real time. For the shared storage model to be most effective, all clients also need to share a common file system. Let us assume this exists for our analysis. Clustered file systems (CFS) are discussed in detail in Chapter 3A and provide for a true file-sharing environment among attached clients. Without a CFS, only the storage hardware may be shared.

Regarding the RT aspect of storage, it can also come in different flavors. By strict definition, RT storage allows for AV-stored data to be read/write in *AV real time* without exceeding the loss, delay, and reliability specs for the system. Playing a Super Bowl or World Cup commercial ($2.2 million for 30 s) to air from RT storage will require a higher level of QoS than say supporting the QoS needs of a five station edit system. As a result, the overall QoS of either a RT or a NRT system is a strong factor of system requirements.

Table 2.6 lists the advantages/disadvantages of the shared storage model. An advantage in a row is not necessarily aligned with a corresponding disadvantage in the same row. Treat the columns as independent evaluations. To gain more insight, compare Table 2.6 to Table 2.3 and Table 2.5 on file transfer and streaming.

The biggest plus of the shared storage model is the fact that all clients have immediate RT read/write random access to all storage. This is not a

Advantages	Disadvantages
Storage is immediately available to all clients/users (with permission) all the time for random R/W access	Demanding QoS to support all client access in RT
Media management is simplified by having all content in one repository. No versions of files in unknown places	High-availability RT storage is more difficult to design and test than for NRT. A CFS is needed for true file sharing, as only storage hardware is shared
No JITFT file mover logic or prequeuing is needed. Files only need to be transferred when importing/exporting to external devices	Single storage system for all A/V data puts content at risk if there is a total failure. Use of mirrored storage or RAID methods mitigates this
Streaming workflows are a natural fit; ◆ Ingest to store ◆ Edit while ingesting from store ◆ Playout while editing from store	Not trivial to perform hot upgrades; adding more storage, updating storage controller software, and so on. NRT storage may relax this slightly
This is a common workflow for sports highlight packages, for example	

TABLE   Real Time Shared Storage Access

2.6

feature of streaming or file transfer. Also, workflows may be designed in almost any form, as files do not need to be moved before AV operations can start. A general conclusion is that shared storage trumps file transfer and file transfer trumps streaming for the majority of operational needs in an AV/IT facility. This conclusion must be taken in context. Sure there are sweet spots for each method. If the application is live production, then streaming using SDI is required. In practice, facility SDI links are routed to provide access and reach. Also, file transfer is more appropriate than streaming for delivering files in NRT over unreliable links or long distance. Each method needs to be considered on its own merits and in relation to a particular target workflow. Examples of all methods are to be found in facilities worldwide.

2.4.3.1   Using File Transfer to Create a Virtual Shared Storage Model

Figure 2.8 shows each client with individual storage. Figure 2.16 shows a similar configuration but in a shared storage model. If the individual storage pools in Figure 2.8 all had identical file content, then each client would see the same files. At times, there is a design advantage for individual storage to act like shared storage. To put it another way, if Figure 2.8 smells and feels like Figure 2.16, then some aspects of data management and control are simplified.

How can the two figures be made to act as equals from the client perspective? One way is to mirror all file content on all storage in Figure 2.8. This way each client sees the same storage as the others. Of course, there is a waste of $N - 1$ times the individual storage for N clients. Also, there is a time delay to copy content from say D to A, B, and C. Then too there is the extra bandwidth needed to make the $N - 1$ copies. For example, if a video clip is ingested into client D (Figure 2.8), it needs to be copied (faster the better or JITFT) to A, B, and C so they each have access to the file. Ideally, A/B/C/D always have identical files. File copying is one way to make Figure 2.8 look like Figure 2.16 from a data access view. Of course if client B modifies a file, the others need to get a fresh copy. This is not an issue for playout centric systems but would be for editing centric systems, for example.

However, is the price of wasted bandwidth and storage worth it? With disc drive capacity approaching 500 GB and bandwidth getting less expensive, some designers are working with this model. Its most virtuous aspect is no need for a sophisticated clustered file system. The price to manage file movement, deal with deletes and file changes, support the needed copy bandwidth, and have sufficient mirror storage is worth the effort and cost to eliminate the need for a CFS for some workflows. This reasoning is especially valid when only a few clients are needed but may break down if say five or more clients are needed. There are many ways to look at this problem and using JITFT reduces some of the constraints if the workflow allows for it. Also, because many systems do not require a complete file mirror on all clients, this decreases the need for $N - 1$ times the storage. With proper knowledge of what files are needed for use, copying is reduced greatly at the cost of precise knowledge of how the files will be used. This is not always well known at the time of file creation so a brute force copy is often simpler to do.

Overall reliability is a strong suit for this method (Figure 2.8). If client A dies, D can take over. Relying on small "edge servers," each with its own storage, simplifies the system design, albeit at the cost of file management. As with most engineering choices, the trade-offs are critical and will work for some applications but not for others. A strong case may be made for the clustered file system and eliminating all the file movements. Most large broadcast TV server systems for on-air playout (say five or more clients supporting 16+ channels of A/V) use the CFS method, whereas some smaller systems (two or three clients) use the file mirror method.

2.5   THE THREE PLANES

Is there a unified way to visualize all the disparate elements in Figure 2.2 (with AV media clients)? The diagram has the inherent traits of **data flow, control, and systems management** even though the concepts may not be apparent from a high level. Figure 2.17 is a pictorial of these three planes or layers. Each one has an associated protocol stack. Consider the following.

◆ **Data or user layer**—AV data moving across links in RT or NRT. The data types may be all manner of audio, video, metadata, and general user data. This plane is alternatively called data or user. One term describes the *data* aspects of the plane, whereas the *user* handle denotes the applications-related aspects.

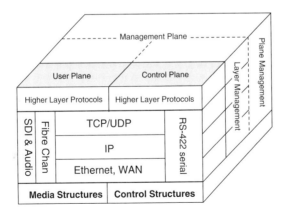

FIGURE 2.17   The three planes: Data/user, control, and management.

◆ **Control layer**—This is the control aspect of a video system and may include automation protocols for devices (AV clients, VTRs, data servers, etc.), live status, configuration settings, and other control aspects.

◆ **Management layer**—Element management for alarms, warnings, status, diagnostics, self test, parameter measurements, remote access, and other functions.

This model has been used for years in the Telecom's world with mature stacks across all three domains. In this case, the data plane is the actual data/protocols related to a telephone conversation, the control plane is the logic/protocols needed to establish and manage a call, and the management plane manages switching systems and configures them for subscriber-calling features. The famous Signaling System (SS7) protocol is used worldwide as the control protocol. SS7 is an architecture for performing out-of-band signaling in support of the call-establishment, billing, routing, and information-exchange functions of the public-switched telephone network (PSTN). The legacy of Telecom's logical view of the three planes is being applied to IT systems and hence AV/IT systems. Of course the three stacks are completely different for our needs, but the overall concepts are still valid.

The detailed examination of the three layers and their implications is left to Chapter 7.

2.6   INTEROPERABILITY DOMAINS

This section outlines the seven chief domains that contribute to interoperability between an AV system and external access. Each of these seven interface points is data/user (five of the seven), control (one), or management plane related (one) in terms of the three-plane model. The seven numbered interop domains are shown in Figure 2.18. Frankly, older non-AV/IT systems had more interoperable functionality because there were fewer data formats, control protocols, and interfaces. There was a time when a video system could be built using one VTR control protocol and links for composite video (SD only) and analog audio. Today there is more of everything; more formats, more interfaces, and more protocols so the move to AV/IT provides more choice with the associated headaches of more chance of interoperability problems between vendors'

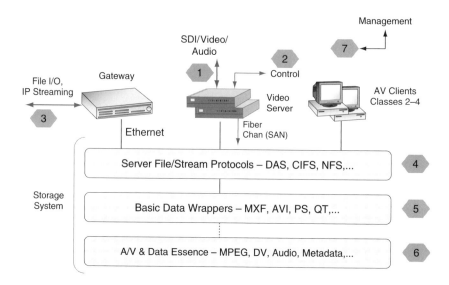

The seven interoperability domains.

gear. To be fair, even without the IT component, advanced AV interfaces and data structures are more complex then just a few years ago.

Think of Figure 2.18 as representing a combination of client types 2–4 discussed earlier plus an external storage subsystem. Each client type may have some combination of the interfaces shown in Figure 2.18. Some of the concepts discussed in this section are discussed in more detail in Chapters 7 and 9. However, this section is useful for studying interoperability issues in the context of each other. Viewing all seven at once also provides a higher level view of how to realize cross-product interoperability across a range of system components.

Domains 1 and 2: Traditional A/V and Control Points

Interface point 1 consists of traditional AV streaming interfaces such as SDI, composite, ASI, AES/EBU audio, and so on. These standards are well documented and supported on most equipment. If a vendor supports one of these interfaces, there is little that can go wrong. This interface point is likely in the first place in terms of interoperability and maturity. In the context of the three planes, this is a data plane element.

The control interface (2) is also vital for automated operations. Some, but not all, elements have a control interface point. For now, let us postpone a discussion of this plane until Chapter 7.

Domain 3: File Transfer and Streaming

This domain has several dimensions, including file and streaming protocols and file formats. FTP has become de facto for file transfer but there are other choices as Table 2.4 outlines. However, file incompatibility can be a cause of grief. A gateway performs file format translation as needed by the storage formats at layers 5 and 6 (see later).

Streaming using IT means (LAN/WAN) is not well established for professional AV systems, despite its common use in the Web space. Oh sure, IP streaming is used for low-bit rate proxy browsing, but high data rate, IP-based streaming is not common except for some AV trunking applications. Streaming AV over say SDI is well established and is represented by interop point (1). This is not to imply that there are no standards for IT streaming; there are many. However, there is precious little consensus for AV LAN-based streaming interoperability at the professional level. This may change over the next few years.

Domain 4: Storage Subsystem Interfacing

Clients can connect to storage using several mature protocols. There are two classes of storage interface:

◆ DAS (direct attached storage) using SCSI, Fibre Channel, USB2, IEEE 1394, or other interface.
◆ Networked-attached clients using SAN and NAS technologies.

If you have ever connected a disk array to a PC or server, you have implemented DAS. When a client is outfitted with a Fibre Channel I/O card and connects to a common storage array, a SAN is being implemented. Whenever a client accesses stored files on a networked file server, NAS protocols are being put to work. NAS is a client/server file level access protocol that provides transparent networked file access. NAS-connected clients are more common than SAN connected due to the popularity of high bandwidth file servers and Ethernet/IP networking.

Chapter 3B is dedicated to the coverage of DAS, SAN, and NAS. The bottom line is this: for client interoperable connectivity to storage, standards should be used. Always ask your providing vendor what protocols they use for client to storage connectivity.

Domains 5 and 6: Wrappers and Essence Formats

The next pieces in the interop puzzle are the file wrapper and essence formats. A wrapper format (interface point 5) is not the same as a compression format. A wrapper is often a content neutral format that carries various lower-level AV data structures. The simplest wrapper may only provide for multiplexing of A + V. The ubiquitous AVI file type is a wrapper and can carry MPEG, DV, Motion-JPEG, audio, and other formats. These are often called AV essence formats (layer 6). Another wrapper format is MXF. This is a professional wrapper format standardized by SMPTE and has profiles for carrying many different video, audio, and metadata formats. Interface point 5 only exists if the stored files are wrapped by AVI, MXF, QT, or similar.

Also at layer 6 are metadata schemas. These are the rules for defining and packaging metadata values usually within XML but not exclusively. There are currently several SMPTE efforts to standardize metadata for a variety of AV system operational needs.

File format translation between external types and internal formats may be required. For example, an external AVI file may enter (or exit) via point #3 but the internal format only supports MXF. So the format converter remaps the AV formats as needed. Several companies sell file conversion gateways, among which are Telestream's FlipFactory, Front Porch Digital's BitScream, products from Masstech, and others. Despite having some new format standards for file exchange, such as MXF, there are boatloads of older formats that cannot be ignored. File conversion has some trade-offs, such as speed of conversion, potential loss of AV quality, testing format conversions, and handling metadata properly. Chapter 7 covers format conversion in more detail.

Domain 7: Device Management

This interface normally supports SNMP, the ubiquitous IT-based protocol for retrieving device metrics on the health, status, and configuration of the product. But just because a product supports SNMP does not imply that all of its measured metrics are easily usable. External management consoles can only make sense of the data structures returned by SNMP if they are well defined and standardized and this is not yet commonly done by AV vendors. This is a hot topic in product development. There is much more on this in Chapter 9.

Interop Conclusions

The seven interface points are crucial in achieving interoperability with external users and interfaces. Successful interfacing is founded on standards and commonly used protocols and formats. For sure, there are other interface points such as vendor-supplied APIs, but these seven form the core for most AV systems. In complex systems there will likely be some interface incompatibility but these issues can be managed. For the most part, SMPTE, the IETF, and ITU/ISO/IEC are the organizations responsible for standardizing data, control, and management planes. As we continue to move from the purely traditional AV world to one of merged AV/IT, there will be growing pains. Progress is good and new standards are being developed to improve the level of interoperability.

2.7 TRICKS FOR MAKING IT ELEMENTS WORK IN REAL TIME

For many years, purpose-built gear was needed to acquire, move, process, and output AV signals. When some early adopter equipment companies decided to use a mix of AV and IT elements, there were objections from many quarters. Some classic objections to using IT components are as follow.

- They are not designed to pass frame accurate, RT video, and audio.
- There will be too much packet loss, jitter, and delay.
- Ethernet is asynchronous and SDI is isochronous so the two cannot interoperate.

◆ Available data rate is not well defined in an IT network.

◆ Building frame-accurate systems is impossible.

Then too there are objections about security threats such as viruses, worms, spyware, and other network-related pests. Security-related issues are covered in Chapter 8. But what about these other objections? Let us find out.

Figure 2.19 serves as the landscape for the basis of our discussion. The configuration shows NAS-attached clients, an Ethernet IP switch, and a file server (NAS storage). The clients access storage using the TCP/IP protocol suite. There are several areas where latency, jitter, and loss can accumulate if not managed properly. The trick to realizing excellent client performance is in the judicious use of the I/O buffer. Each client has a small buffer of a few seconds and they may be described as follows.

◆ *Look ahead* buffer as used in the ingest client.

◆ *Look around* buffer as used in the NLE client.

◆ *Look behind* buffer as used in the playout client.

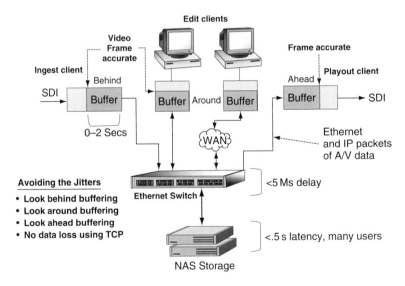

FIGURE

2.19

Making IT components work in real time.

Buffering is a way to smooth out IT component I/O irregularities. Of course buffering also adds delay and at times this may induce workflow problems or cause a client to appear as sluggish in response to a command. Generally, the more buffering that is used, the more irregularities and network problems may be hidden. So in a way, **more buffering solves everything** (related to data jitter smoothing), yet **time delay is evil** (related to response times). So indeed, the careful use of buffering can balance the needs of response time and smoothing needs. Hence, the art of buffering.

The general idea of buffering to smooth out irregularities is seen in Figure 2.20. A bucket is filled with an irregular flow of water. The input flow has an *average rate* that is constant but the instantaneous rate will vary. A valve is adjusted randomly to represent irregular filling from uneven data delivery mechanisms inherent in the network switching, routing, lost packet recovery, storage delivery latency, and so forth. At times the bucket is nearly full, at other times nearly empty, but it never overflows or underflows. A regulator at the base of the bucket adjusts the output flow to be exactly even with no variations of flow rate regardless of

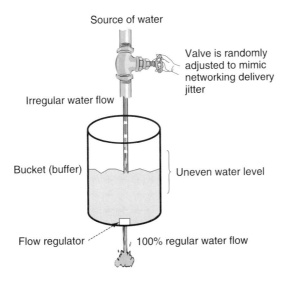

Source of water

Valve is randomly adjusted to mimic networking delivery jitter

Irregular water flow

Bucket (buffer)

Uneven water level

Flow regulator

100% regular water flow

FIGURE

2.20

Using a buffer to smooth out irregularities.

the level of water in the bucket. As a result, the bucket acts like a buffer to smooth out any input irregularities and allows for a smooth output flow. The average input flow must equal the output flow for the method to work. Also, when the source of liquid changes, the bucket may need to be purged so as not to mix sourced data flows. Using this analogy, let us apply it to Figure 2.19.

The *look behind buffer* in the ingest client receives a regular flow of streaming AV and sends it to storage over the network. The buffer has video stored from the past—hence the look behind name. With a second or so of buffering, most IT-caused irregularities can be smoothed out as data are written to the storage. There may be occasions where a much bigger buffer is needed. Consider the case where the storage array is off-line for minutes longer. Under this condition the ingest client can cache long periods of incoming video and write it to storage when the storage connectivity resumes. See the section on caching in Chapter 3B.

The *look around buffer* in the NLE client smoothes out I/O requests to storage. This buffer lets a user look around a point in the time line with a human-fast response. Again, using bigger buffers (caching) yields even more advantages. Finally, there is the *look ahead buffer*. This one is located in the playout client and queues A/V data for frame accurate playout. In many video applications, there is ample time to queue a file into the buffer space before playout starts. In some cases, prequeuing is done faster than RT rates so there is almost no delay from when the buffer starts to fill with new data and when playout starts. In the final analysis, buffering is the magic needed to coerce an IT infrastructure to behave in an AV-civilized manner.

2.8   USING IT METHODS TO ROUTE TRADITIONAL A/V SIGNALS

One of most common operations in a facility is to route streamed AV signals. Figure 2.21 illustrates a traditional AV routing structure using SDI links. Three SDI routers switch the AV signals. Two key features of this configuration are very small in/out latency (on the order of tens of nanoseconds) and H/V timing is easy to establish at any point in the chain. Another feature is easy splitting of a signal for more than one output. In this case, AV1 is fed to two outputs, one for signal monitoring.

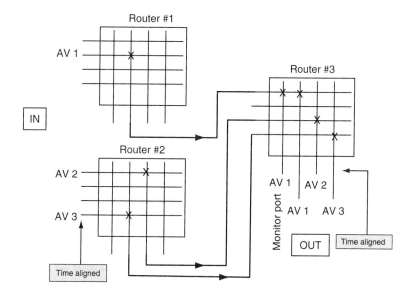

FIGURE

2.21

Traditional A/V router example.

What is the IT-based counterpart? Figure 2.22 shows an example. Ideally the in-to-out relationships should be the same as in Figure 2.21. The router layer may be IP or ATM switching or other non-video specific means. Today there are no IT-based routing means to duplicate the configuration specs found in Figure 2.21. Why not? The following summarizes the issues.

- IP/ATM networks have latency on the order of microseconds to many milliseconds for campus size routes.
- H/V timing is lost during network routing. H/V timing must be reestablished at the output ports. Protocols such as RTP support time-stamped streaming over IP/ATM networks but even this does not guarantee recovery of the input H/V timing.
- Point to multipoint (splitting an input signal into one or more outputs) is difficult to achieve. ATM supports this mode; IP multicast supports it too but neither is used commonly within an AV facility.

The reality is that traditional AV routing is a marvel and will not be replaced soon by IT means for those applications that demand it.

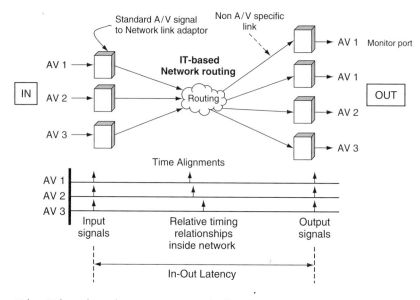

Using IT-based routing to transport A/V signals.

Duplicating the features of SDI routing is not easy, but over time methods will be developed as IT pushes deeper into all aspects of AV. Converting SDI signals to go over a WAN was mentioned earlier in this chapter, but this is normally for point-to-point video trunking and is an *extender* of SDI and not a replacement for it.

Importantly, the culture of using SDI and AES/EBU for all linking misses opportunities to use alternate non-real time means such as file transfer. As a result, IT-based networking will replace timed AV networks where it makes economic sense coupled with workflow efficiencies.

2.9   IT'S A WRAP: A FEW FINAL WORDS

This chapter has outlined the essential elements of an AV/IT system. It is the basis of the remaining chapters in this book. Despite the fast-changing world of IT technology and products, the ideas in this chapter will not soon become stale with age. The comparisons among file transfer, streaming, and direct to storage are time-honored methods that will transcend any particular vendor's products. The interoperability domains will only become more mature as industry experience accumulates. In the end, the information in these sections is a good foundation for understanding the essentials of networked media systems.

REFERENCES

[**Britton**] Britton, Chris, *IT Architectures and Middleware*, Addison-Wesley, 2000.

[**Devlin**] Devlin, Bruce, et al., *Nuggets and MXF—Making the Networked Studio a Reality*, IBC 2003 Technical Conference Proceedings, page 94.

[**Kovalick**] Kovalick, Al, *A Reference Architecture for Digital A/V*, SMPTE Journal, August 1998.

[**Morelos**] Morelos-Zaragoza, Robert H., *The Art of Error Correcting Coding*, Wiley & Sons, 1991.

[**SMPTE**] For an excellent table summary of professional digital tape and compression standards, visit www.smpte.org/smpte_store/standards.

3A | Storage System Basics

CHAPTER

3A.0 INTRODUCTION TO STORAGE SYSTEMS

The core of any AV/IT system is its ***storage and file server*** infrastructure. After all, that is where the crown jewels are stored—the AV and meta-data content. This chapter discusses the basics of storage systems: networked architecture, virtualization, file systems, transaction types, HDD performance, transaction optimization, RAIDs, clustering, and hierarchical storage, among other topics. The next chapter analyzes storage access methods (DAS, SAN, and NAS). Between these two chapters, the essentials of storage with focused attention on AV requirements are covered. You may need to bounce between the two chapters, as many of the concepts discussed are so intimately related.

The landscape is first described using Figure 3A.1. This gives a high level view of the domain of focus. There are five horizontal layers in this model. Each layer is briefly studied with more detail added during the course of this chapter and the next. There are many real world products and systems that have their roots in this configuration. Consider

◆ AV edit cluster of *N* clients (craft editors and browsers), NAS or SAN attached. They may connect to one or more servers over a network. The servers in turn have access to storage. Clients may edit directly off

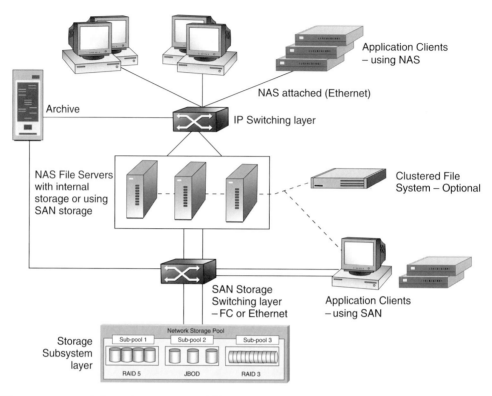

FIGURE   General view of a storage and file server infrastructure.

3A.1

the storage (direct to RT storage model) or use file transfer methods to load projects directly to the edit client.

◆ Ingest and playout system. In this case the clients are ingest and/or playout nodes. Under control of a scheduler/automaton program or manual trigger, each of the clients will perform the record/playout operation on command. Some commercially available distributed video servers use the NAS method for client connectivity and some use the SAN method. Most large-scale video servers from the major vendors are based on either of these two methods. See, for example, server products and systems from Avid, EVS, GVG, Leitch, Quantel, Pinnacle Systems, Omneon, SeaChange, Sony, and others. Small, stand-alone servers are often self-contained with no SAN or NAS storage connectivity, although they usually have a LAN port for file transfer support.

◆ Clients may be A/V processors that are programmed to do effects, coding, or conversions of all kinds. One commercial example of this is the file FlipFactory file conversion gateway from TeleStream.

Incidentally, Media Asset Management (MAM), automation control, systems management, and A/V Proxy servers are not shown in Figure 3A.1. These elements are not relevant to the discussion at hand. Nevertheless, these elements are vital to any real world A/V system and their contributions are discussed in other chapters. Also not shown are any traditional (non-IT based) A/V links. These links may always be added as needed.

The Client and IP Switching Layers

The first (top) layer is the application client. The client types are discussed in detail in Chapter 2. Each client can access the NAS file server over a network. Technically, a NAS-attached client accesses the storage layer via the file servers. In some cases, however, the server layer will also provide application services, such as file format conversion, encoding/decoding of the stored essence, caching, bandwidth regulation, and more.

The second layer is IP switching. This can be as simple as a $100 switch or a complex campus-wide mesh of switches. The reliability can be minimal or extend all the way to a fault resilient network with various strategies of failover. Although Ethernet is the most common link, other less common links exist but are not the subject of this discussion. It is possible to design and operate this layer with excellent QoS with support for RT client access to the servers. See Chapter 6 for more information on switching.

The Server Layer

The third layer is the server subsystem. Servers may be located anywhere across the network. In general they may be storage servers or application servers that execute application code. The simplest configuration is a single NAS file server attached to storage. Microsoft offers the Windows Storage Server; many vendors use this as the core file system for their

NAS products. At the other end of the spectrum is cluster computing with a mesh of servers working together as one. Cluster computing strategies range from a few independent servers that are load balanced to hundreds that appear as one virtual server. Fault tolerance and scalability are paramount in a cluster.

Grid computing is another technique that is differentiated from cluster computing (see Appendix C). The key distinction between clusters and grids is mainly in the way resources are managed. In the case of clusters, the resource allocation is performed by a centralized resource manager and all nodes work together cooperatively as a single unified resource. In case of grids, each node has its own resource manager and overall there is no single server view as with clustering.

The big five players in the enterprise hardware server market are listed in Table 3A.1. The revenue includes any loaded OS software if present. The worldwide server market was about $46 billion in 2004.

One unique incarnation of a server is called a blade. Compared to a stand-alone rack-mounted server, a blade is a server on a card that mounts into a multicard enclosure. The packing density, cost, and efficiency (shares power supplies, enclosure, and other elements) are outstanding. Blade servers accounted for only 3% of all servers sold in 2003

Vendor	Q3 2004 revenue	Market share
IBM	$3659	31.7%
Hewlett-Packard	$3094	26.8%
Sun Microsystems	$1176	10.2%
Dell	$1170	10.1%
Fujitsu/Fujitsu Siemens	$714	6.2%
Others	$1733	15.0%
All vendors	$11,547	100.0%

[a] From IDC's Worldwide Quarterly Server Tracker, November 2004. Revenues are in millions.

TABLE   Worldwide Server Market[a]

3A.1

but IDC expects them to account for 29% by 2008 (see Appendix K). Also, IBM recently opened up their blade design so others may copy it freely. The IBM design for the PC is legendary and it is possible that history may repeat itself. It so, their blade design may become the de facto server of choice. Time will tell.

The Storage Switching Layer

Layer four (Figure 3A.1) is the storage switching layer. In the simplest of cases, a server connects to a single storage array with barely a hint of switching or none at all. At the other end of the scale, the storage switching layer is a complex Fibre[1] Channel switching fabric (SAN) with failover mechanisms built in. More recently, some storage arrays support native Ethernet SAN connectivity based on iSCSI (SCSI protocol over TCP/IP). Fibre Channel has owned this space for the last 10 years so the migration to new methods will take some time. Note too that SAN clients connect directly to storage over Fibre Channel bypassing the server layer. A SAN-connected client (1 Gb/s FC link, for example) has access to ~800 Mb/s of storage bandwidth. Until recently, this type of performance has only been available using Fibre Channel.

Ethernet has won the war of enterprise connectivity and is pushing Fibre Channel lower in the value chain, although the two will coexist for many years to come. The trends to Ethernet/IP are very interesting but legacy Fibre Channel SANs will not be replaced overnight. It is possible to build all five layers of Figure 3A.1 with only Ethernet/IP connectivity. During this transition, companies such as Cicso, HP, and McData provide gateways that link IP and Fibre Channel to create hybrid SANs. As a result, the modern SAN is composed of pure Fibre Channel at one end of the scale, a hybrid of IP and FC in the middle, and iSCSI at the all-Ethernet end of the spectrum. Replacing FC with Ethernet/IP has many implications, which are discussed in this chapter.

---

[1] The spelling of fibre has always been with the British spelling rather than the american fiber. This is a legacy of the standard body's efforts to differentiate it from older *fiber* optic cabling schemes.

The Storage Layer

Layer five, at the bottom, is the user storage layer. Storage systems range from a simple external USB2-connected array up to many terabytes of Fiber Channel (or Ethernet) connected arrays. At the high end, the arrays are complex systems of many drives (hundreds) with RAID protection and mirrored components to provide for the ultimate in reliability. There are a variety of very clever architectures from different vendors all claiming some unique advantage in performance (access bandwidth + storage capacity + low access latency), reliability or packing density or usability (connectivity + management + backup + support) or price, or some combination of all of these. Storage is big business.

IDC reports the 2004 worldwide disc storage systems[2] factory revenue as approximately $20.8 billion (see Table 3A.2).

The storage subsystem shown in Figure 3A.1 is a mix of various types ranging from RAM-based to disc-based RAID systems of various flavors.

Vendor	2004 revenue	Market share
HP	$4922	23.6%
IBM	$4298	20.6%
EMC	$2987	14.3%
Dell	$1507	7.2%
Hitachi	$1259	6.0%
Sun Microsystems	$1238	5.9%
Others	$4650	22.3%
All vendors	$20,862	100.0%

[a] From IDC, March 4, 2005. Revenues are in millions.

TABLE   Worldwide Disc Storage Systems Factory Revenue[a]

3A.2

---

[2] IDC defines a disc storage system as a set of storage elements, including controllers, cables, and host bus adapters, associated with three or more disc drives [direct attach storage device (DASD)/hard disc drive (HDD)]. A system may be located outside of or within a server cabinet. The average cost of the disc storage systems does not include infrastructure storage hardware (i.e., switches) and nonbundled storage software.

If managed properly, a distributed storage system may appear as one array. Using the methods of storage virtualization and/or clustered file systems (discussed next), just about any mix of storage technologies may be combined into a homogeneous whole. While it is true that the storage system may be built from optical, holographic, or tape media, these are considered as archive or backup formats due to their slow access times.

Long-Term Archive

The last piece of the puzzle in Figure 3A.1 is long-term archive. This component may connect into layer two (NAS attach), layer four (SAN attach), or be accessed via FTP depending on the design of the overall system. Archives are normally based on long-term storage with removable tape or optical media. Most commercial archives have access times considerably slower than HDD arrays but offer much greater storage density. For most AV applications, it is possible to find a content balance among on-line storage (HDD based), near-line, and off-line storage. For more on this topic, see the section on Hierarchical Storage later in this chapter.

3A.1   STORAGE VIRTUALIZATION AND FILE SYSTEM METHODS

With so many different devices connecting to the same storage system in Figure 3A.1, who is the traffic cop that regulates access? How does any one server or SAN client manage its storage pool? Who assigns access rights? What prevents a client from writing over the data space of another client? Who owns the directory tree? Well, there are two general ways to solve these sticky problems: storage virtualization and use of a clustered file system. Storage virtualization is considered first.

3A.1.1   Storage Virtualization (SV)

This method partitions the entire array or collection of arrays into blocks that are individually assigned to select servers or SAN clients. It insulates the requesting devices from the physical storage by providing a layer of indirection (filtering, mapping, aliasing) between the request for stored data and the physical address of that data. This process is often called storage virtualization and there are a variety of ways to accomplish it. In effect, the available storage is carved up into virtual pools that act as independent storage arrays. There is no common view of *all* storage from the client's perspective but only the portions they are allowed to see.

For example, in Figure 3A.2 server A can only see files X, Y, and Z, client B can only access files A, B, and C, and server C has access to files P, Q, and R. The respective files reside in sections of memory that are assigned to the attached clients and servers. There is no shared file system view—rather, memory is carved up and apportioned as needed. Dividing up the memory this way guarantees access rights; server A cannot mess with files that belong to server C and so on. However, attached

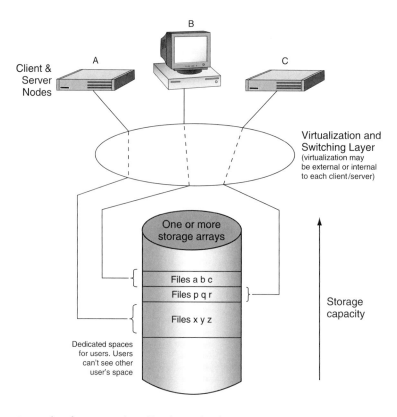

FIGURE   Example of storage virtualization: Sharing storage HW.

3A.2

devices cannot share files easily, as they are walled off from each other. Sometimes this is an advantage and other times it is not. So why do it? Here are a few of the main reasons to use virtualization [Veritas]:

♦ Manage all storage with a centralized application: Reduces labor costs to manage heterogeneous storage systems.

♦ Users and applications have better access to storage: User access to storage is not limited by geography or the capacity of an isolated storage module.

♦ IT administrators can manage more storage: Gartner Group estimates that managers can increase the amount they can administer by at least a factor of six if storage is consolidated.

♦ Lower physical costs of consolidated storage: Existing storage is used more efficiently because one pool (a SAN) is apportioned rather than managing DAS islands. In effect, it is more efficient to manage one pool with N straws drawing from it than N pools each with one straw (see Figure 3A.3).

♦ Scale with more reliability compared to DAS pools: Scale by adding arrays and then map their access as needed to multiple requesters. Allocate capacity on demand.

Virtualization is accomplished in several ways. The most popular is to map each node's assigned storage space to a physical address. This is done using the mapping, aliasing, and filtering of requested addresses.

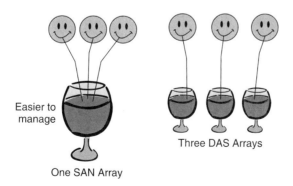

FIGURE   A SAN is easier and less costly to manage than islands of DAS.

3A.3

Figure 3A.4 shows a diagram of the concept. Node A has a storage address range from 0 to 500, which maps onto array A's physical address 500 to 1000. Node C has an address range from 0 to 2000, which maps into two different arrays, each contributing a 1000 and 1001 address respectively. Mapping is implemented in various ways, and logical unit number (LUN) masking is a popular choice. If done in the storage array controller, then they do the mapping based on the identity of the requesting node. Some vendors support the virtualization operation at the node level, switch, or storage array level so the virtualization layer in Figure 3A.2 is a logical view, not a physical one.

The debate about where to locate the virtualization logic is an interesting one. The ANSI/INCITS group has released the fabric application interface standard (FAIS). This standardized API facilitates LUN masking, storage pooling, mirroring, and other advanced functions at the fabric switch level. As a result, FAIS enables advanced storage services, which adds value to the storage system and reduces the need for proprietary solutions.

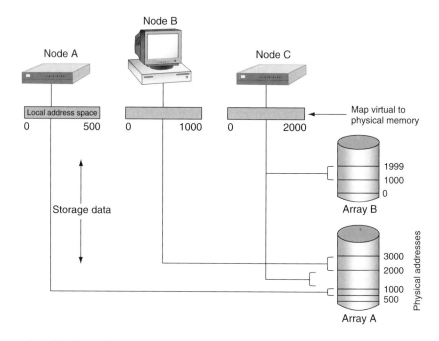

FIGURE
3A.4

Virtualization using address mapping.

The main public companies that support storage virtualization are the names in Table 3A.2 plus Brocade Communications Systems, Cisco Systems, McData, and Veritas Software. There are many other smaller vendors offering hardware and software virtualization solutions.

3A.1.2 Clustered File Systems (CFS)

A second method for managing a storage pool is to provide every attached node (SAN clients and NAS servers) with a single, universal view of file storage. A CFS allows multiple attached devices to have read and write access via a single file system for all available storage. Using storage virtualization, only the physical storage is shared. With a CFS, however, storage *and* files are shared. File sharing is complex, as clients/servers may R/W to any file (with permissions), thereby creating potential for multiple users to write over the same portion of data. So file-locking mechanisms are needed to assure that files are reliably opened, modified, and closed. A full-featured, fault-tolerant CFS is a thing of beauty. Incidentally, no actual user data passes through the CFS controller, only file system metadata is managed.

In Figure 3A.5, the CFS is made available to all nodes. In Figure 3A.5, it is not important how the nodes connect to storage, only that they do and all see a shared file system. In reality, each node has an installable file system (IFS) software component for redirecting all user application file calls to the remote CFS controller instead of the local file system. In Figure 3A.5, node B may only access files a, b, and c whereas node C has access to all the files. This is markedly different from virtualization. With a CFS, any node has potential access to any file in storage given the preassigned access rights. There are no inherent walls as with virtualization—all storage is accessible from any node in principle.

There are three main methods for a node to access a file system.

◆ Node only uses its internal file system. For example, a Windows 2K/XP server or client is based on Microsoft's NTFS file system. This file system manages any directly attached storage (DAS or SAN based).

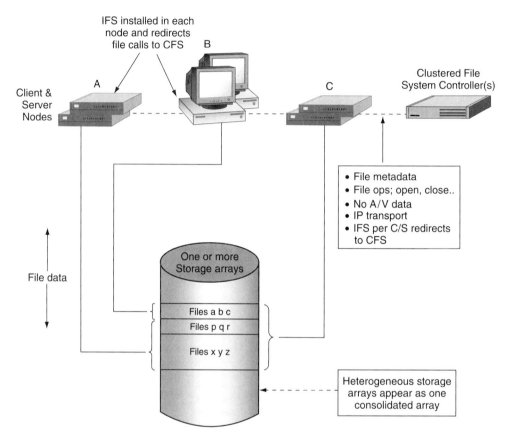

FIGURE 3A.5 Example of using a CFS: Sharing storage HW *and* files.

- ◆ Node connects to remote server (NAS attach) and sees that server's FS (as in \\Company_Server\your_files format).
- ◆ Node has an installable file system software component to access an external CFS view of the storage. Each node can be part of a SAN or NAS. A node (or user of the node) selects the CFS view of the file system as it would select the CD ROM drive or external file server (as in X: drive). The nodal platforms may be of any type (Linux, Windows, Mac, etc.) and a corresponding IFS is needed for each platform.

There is little magic in implementing the first two choices; they are commonly used. However, implementing a CFS is nontrivial. Why? Some of the common features are

♦ Negotiate all R/W access to a heterogeneous pool of storage from a heterogeneous pool (Windows, UNIX, Linux, Mac) of requesting nodes. Not all CFS implementations support all node types.

♦ Simultaneous users (hundreds or more) accessing up to millions of files.

♦ Data striping across storage arrays to increase access bandwidth.

♦ Data block locking, file locking, and directory locking.

♦ Bandwidth control to support QoS demands.

♦ Fault-tolerant operation using dual auto failover CFS metadata controllers. It may also implement a journaled FS (JFS) for supporting CFS failure with graceful recovery by performing a rollback to some stable FS state.

♦ Access control settings per user/group/campus.

The CFS must be a responsible citizen; it is a single point of file metadata for all member nodes. If it faults in some way, everyone is unhappy.

The CFS is a masterful administrator. It manages all the metadata that define a typical hierarchical FS: the storage access rights and permissions per user/group, address maps that associate physical user memory with directory/file names, and tools to create/read/write/delete files. Each node has a low bandwidth TCP/IP (or even UDP) connection to the CFS and over this channel all CFS requests/responses are made. The CFS must potentially support hundreds of simultaneous requests across the entire FS spectrum of operations. Indeed, creating and testing a CFS is a massive undertaking.

3A.1.3 Volume Management

Whether a system is configured for virtualization or a CFS, the concept of volume management is important. Many practical systems combine a pool of disc arrays into one or more volumes for user access. By hiding individual arrays and mapping them into volumes, it is much easier to allocate array storage to individual users or groups. Figure 3A.6 illustrates a small system with four arrays. Array set A has three arrays, each with individual drives. The AV files are striped across all three arrays. Striping provides for improved nonblocking access to files. Striping is discussed later in this chapter. Array set B is only one array. All four are virtually combined to be one 5 TB volume V:. Users do not know if their files are stored on arrays A or B and should not care in most cases.

In some systems, volume V: can be further divided into user or group space. By using a volume manager application, virtual volumes V1, V2, and V3 may be created and assigned as needed to the user community. The amount of assigned storage may be changed as needed for business processes. In advanced systems, user utilization and department billing are included. Volume management conceals the details of array configurations and provides simple volumes (V1:, V2:, V3:, etc.) for user access. For a simple example of a volume manager under Windows XP, access Control Panel, Admin Tools, Computer Management, and Storage.

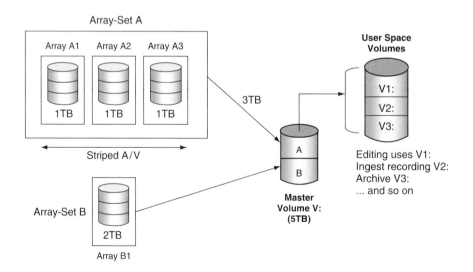

FIGURE   Example of volume organization.

3A.6

3A.1.4   Distributed File Systems (DFS)

A DFS is differentiated from a CFS in how the FS is implemented. Both attempt to create a single file system image for all storage but they do so in different ways. With a CFS, file metadata reside on a separate and dedicated FS controller (or more than one for fault tolerance). With a DFS, the FS is distributed among the nodes (servers normally) such that the FS function spans servers and is a part of each server node. Think of a DFS as a way to repackage a CFS by folding its functionality into the servers that access storage. Since a DFS spans, say N servers, they must all cooperate together to create the single FS image. It is easy to imagine that this is complex in terms of guaranteeing reliability, stability, and scalability. DFS success stories are rare but the Andrew File System (AFS) is probably the most successful. It was developed by Carnegie Mellon University and is now available through open source as OpenAFS (www.openafs.org). AFS is supported by Linux as well.

Unfortunately, the term DFS is a bit overloaded. Indeed, even Microsoft offers a form of one but it is not a DFS in the true sense. To make matters worse, many authors refer to a DFS as a CFS and visa versa because they are so intimately related. However, Microsoft's use of DFS is limited.

With Microsoft DFS,[3] users no longer need to know the actual physical location of files in order to access them. For example, if marketing places files on multiple servers in a domain, DFS makes it appear as though all of the marketing files are on a single server. This ability eliminates the need for users to go to multiple locations on the network to find the information they need. DFS also provides many other benefits, including fault tolerance and load-sharing capabilities, making it ideal for all types of organizations. As a result, DFS locates the actual files across a domain of servers and *consolidates their appearance* for easy browsing. The actual files remain on desperate servers and storage systems, but the view of these appears as consolidated to a user searching for files. Microsoft uses DFS in this limited way. It is not the same as a true CFS or its derivatives.

---

[3] This paragraph is paraphrased from Microsoft's description of their DFS. See www.microsoft.com/dfs.

3A.1.5   Virtualization or CFS: How to Choose

So when would a facility use virtualization and when would a CFS (or true DFS) be more appropriate? Figure 3A.7 shows that the selection of one versus the other is based on how users operate. With AV applications, because users tend to share files, work in collaboration, and use the same types of tools, a CFS is appropriate. In a business setting (running SAP, ERP, CRM), users rarely collaborate between applications so virtualization suits the usage patterns. In fact, both are used in organizations worldwide.

In the technical and general business computing arena, there are several CFS vendors that offer general purpose (COTS) products.

◆ SGI's CXFS (Clustered eXtended File System) 64-bit FS for Irix, Linux, and Windows access to storage (SAN) or servers (NAS). Supports up to 9 million TB of storage (9 Exabytes). This was designed to support AV applications.

◆ IBM's GPFS (General Parallel File System) for heterogeneous node access to a massive clustered server system. This CFS (actually a DFS)

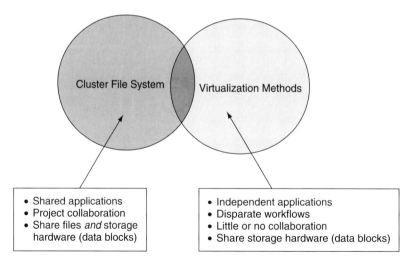

FIGURE   Individual benefits for CFS and virtualization.

3A.7

is not sold separately but only in conjunction with GPFS clustered servers. IBM also offers the SANergy FS as a stand-alone product.

◆ Veritas' Storage Foundation CFS. This is used in general enterprise applications. The Veritas CFS delivers a cohesive solution that provides direct access to shared disks and files from all heterogeneous nodes in the cluster.

◆ ADIC's StorNext FS for heterogeneous node access to storage.

◆ Rorke's ImageSAN CFS for Windows NTFS nodes.

◆ Cluster File System's Luster FS. In recent testing on production super-computing clusters with 1000 clients, Lustre achieves an aggregate parallel I/O throughput of 11.1 GB/s utilizing in excess of 90% of the available raw I/O bandwidth. It is Linux based.

◆ Red Hat's Global File System (GFS) for Linux server clusters. This is a direct competitor to Luster.

◆ Sanbolic's Melio FS for heterogeneous node access to storage.

In addition to general-purpose CFS solutions, there are captive CFS solutions that are bundled with AV SAN/NAS systems. These CFS products are included as part of a vendor's overall storage solution. In some cases the CFS is buried in the infrastructure and is not called out as a CFS, but it is. Most of the systems support NLE, video server I/O, and other nodal functions for news production, transmission, and general edit applications. Basically, if an AV workflow requires file sharing among collaborators, then a CFS is an enabler. Some of the leading AV systems that include a bundled CFS are as follow.

◆ Avid's Unity storage for editing and news production applications. Their Open Media File System (OMFS, a CFS) is used by Avid and third-party AV clients.

◆ Leitch ICE (Integrated Content Environment) using RaidSoft-shared storage and server clustering software with a CFS.

◆ Omneon MediaServer System with the Windows compliant EFS (Extended File System, a CFS).

◆ Pinnacle Systems' Palladium Storage. This is a SAN/NAS storage system supported by the Palladium File System (a CFS) and supports Windows-based and MediaStream nodal clients.

◆ Quantel uses the ADIC StorNext CFS alongside their sQServer storage system. This is a COTS CFS integrated into an A/V environment.

- SeaChange Broadcast MediaCluster play-to-air video server with a custom-embedded CFS (actually a DFS) configured to work with each of the nodes in the cluster.
- Thomson/GVG K2 client/server with support for Windows-based transmission servers and news production nodes. This system uses the StorNext CFS from ADIC.

For the most part, these AV vendors chose to build their own CFS and not use a COTS version. Why? There are several reasons. One is for total control in mission critical environments. Another is based on a make-versus-buy analysis. Still another is performance related to reliability, failover speed (not all COTS versions are optimized for AV applications), and integration with embedded client operating systems (non-Microsoft). Time will tell if the COTS versions will beat out the custom versions in the market. The COTS versions have massive engineering behind them and are feature rich. The AV-specialized ones are niche products and may well get sidelined as the industry matures. Some of the COTS versions are A/V friendly and this trend will most likely continue.

3A.2   CLIENT TRANSACTION TYPES AND STORAGE PERFORMANCE

Client applications conduct exchanges with servers and storage using a wide range of transaction types. Figure 3A.8 shows three of the most typical.

- Complex transaction. An example is to obtain the rights to edit a valuable piece of content. This may require exchanging user name, password, condition information, purpose, and granting a use token. Note that the storage may be accessed several times during the transaction. A database (SQL Server, Oracle, MySQL, etc.) may be involved with this type of transaction.
- Simple transaction. An example is a NAS-attached client asking the server layer to read a block of video MPEG data from the storage array.
- Direct R/W transaction. An example is a direct R/W to storage using a DAS or SAN connection.

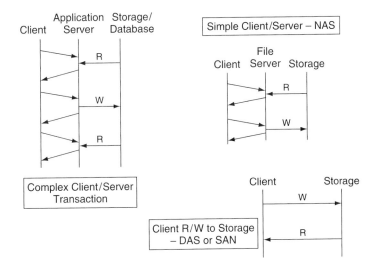

FIGURE   Storage transaction types.

3A.8

For each of these transactions, the storage system (HDD based for this analysis) is accessed and its efficiency of performance depends on the access patterns. There are four main aspects that contribute to the overall performance of a storage system.

1. R/W patterns: Size of R/W block *and* random or sequential access to the HDD surface
2. Mix of reads versus writes from 100% read (0% write) to 100% write (0% read)
3. Utilization of the array from 0 to 100% usage
4. Capacity remaining from 0 to 100%

Each of these factors impacts various performance metrics. Figure 3A.9 shows a "billiard table" diagram with each side being one of the four factors just described. It is assumed that the array is not laboring under any failure modes (RAID data recovery in use). The purpose of the diagram is to encapsulate all four of the metrics into one visual imprint. Starting at the bottom left and moving clockwise around the outside, the left axis is a measure of user data access patterns (strong influencer of access bandwidth), the top is a measure of the mix of R/W transactions

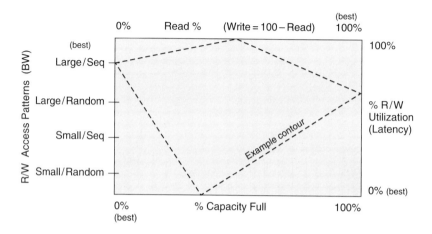

FIGURE

3A.9

Storage system performance billiard table diagram.

(influencer of access bandwidth), the right axis is the total throughput utilization (measure of latency), and the bottom axes is a measure of the remaining capacity of the array. For *each* of the four axes, moving clockwise is an improving metric. For example, the top of the right axis indicates 100% utilization of the array. For this case, the R/W requests form a deep queue and therefore transaction latency is inevitable due to the heavy loading. However, the lower portion of the right axis is 0% utilization so the occasional R/W request gets immediate response because there are no other requests to compete for storage resources. These four elements are developed in the next sections.

3A.2.1   Optimizing Storage Array Data Throughput

Considering #1 from the previous list, the two most important metrics that influence individual disc performance are block size and data seek method.

♦ Large R/W blocks (.5- to 2-MB block), medium R/W blocks, or small R/W blocks (4- to 64-KB blocks).

♦ Random or sequential R/W data access. Random: The next R/W may be at any physical address on the disc causing the HDD head to seek to a new track. Sequential: The next R/W address follows in order so that the R/W head of the disc does not have to seek a new track.

These factors are not relevant if the storage system is RAM based, as RAM has no concept of rotating surfaces or R/W head movement. When using a HDD-based array, however, the **seek time and rotational latency** are very important. These are illustrated in Figure 3A.10. **Seek time** is the time it takes for a disc drive's read/write head to move to a specific track on the disc platter. Seek time does not include latency nor the time it takes for the controller to send signals to the read/write head. **Rotational latency** is the delay between when the controller starts looking for a specific block of data on a track (under the head) and when that block rotates around to where it can be read by the read/write head. On average, it is half the time needed for a full rotation (which depends on the rotational speed, or rpm, of the disc). It is because of the seek time and rotational latency that the block size (large/small) and random/sequential access methods have such a big impact on drive R/W performance. As we shall see, the rpm of the platter (spans 7.5 to 15 K usually) is not a key factor in the average data throughput for large A/V data blocks. First, here is an illustration to better appreciate these issues.

Let us say that you plan to go to Maui, Hawaii for vacation. The airplane trip is analogous to the seek and latency times before you arrive. Once you arrive on Maui you likely want to stay as long as possible. The longer you stay the less bearing the initial air travel delay has on your

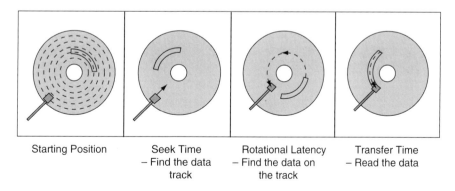

| Starting Position | Seek Time
– Find the data
track | Rotational Latency
– Find the data on
the track | Transfer Time
– Read the data |

FIGURE   Key access metrics for HDD performance.

3A.10

overall journey. If it takes 5 hr to reach the island and you stay 2 weeks, then the one-way travel time is only 1.5% of your total vacation time. However, if you only stay for 5 hr and then hop on the red eye to return home, then the one-way travel time was a huge part of the overall journey (50%). What a waste! This is the same as when doing a R/W transaction to a HDD. The bigger the data block, the more time is spent reading/writing and with less travel time to get there. As a result, the average R/W bandwidth is strongly related to block size; bigger blocks yield higher data rates on average.

What about random versus sequential access? When planning your tour of Maui's best beaches you could randomly visit five different beaches (Wailea, Hamoa, Kapalua, etc.) or plan to visit them by the most direct route, thereby saving travel time. This is the same as when doing a R/W access to a disc. If the R/W head does not seek to a new track (a sequential access) for each R/W transaction, then the overall through-put is increased compared to random R/W access. It is not always easy to place data sequentially (due to disc data layout strategies controlled by the OS), but AV data lend themselves to this type of placement due to their large size and typical sequential access for a read. So let us celebrate long vacations with plenty of beach time.

These factors may be logically grouped into four specific access patterns.

1. Large blocks/sequential access (best AV access rates)
2. Large blocks/random access
3. Small blocks/sequential access
4. Small blocks/random access (worst AV access rates)

As per the reasoning thus far, the access bandwidth progressively improves from the worst case (bottom) item to the best case (top) item. It is arguable if items number 2 and 3 are always positioned this way. For some cases they may in fact be reversed. There is a considerable per-formance gain between the top and the bottom items. Figure 3A.11 shows the actual measured access bandwidth versus the block size for random R/W transactions.

The test configuration is four data drives plus one parity drive in two RAID-3 sets. So in all, there are eight data drives and two parity

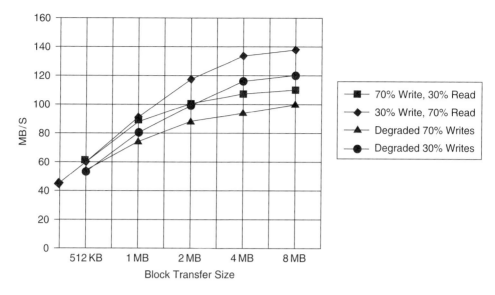

FIGURE

3A.11
Array performance versus block size.

Source: Pinnacle Systems.

drives. RAID is fully explained in Chapter 5, but suffice for now that it is a reliability mechanism to recover all the data from one (or more) faulty drive. All user data are striped across all eight data drives (RAID 0) so an 8-MB user block is split into eight, 1-MB blocks—one per data disc. In Figure 3A.11, the aggregate R/W bandwidth for the multidrive array is 140 MB/s with a mix of 70% reads and 30% writes and a block size of 8 MB. The same R/W mix reaches only 60 MB/s with a block size of 512 KB and much less for a 16-KB block that is common in many non-A/V transaction applications.

Notice that the mix of reads versus writes has a profound effect on the array throughput. The top axis in Figure 3A.9 is a measure of the R/W mix. For a 30% read and 70% write mix, the bandwidth is about 110 MB/s. Why is this? In a RAIDed configuration a write has a penalty, as the parity disc needs updating for every write to the four data drives. If user data are not striped across all data drives but are written to only one, then the write penalty is much worse. The reasons for this are developed in Chapter 5. A read does not need to access the parity drive unless there is a faulty data drive that needs restoration. Some vendor's solutions activate RAID when a drive is late in returning read data, as this improves latency performance. Figure 3A.11 also shows data access rates under a "degraded mode." This is the case where one of the data drives is being rebuilt (RAID node) in the background during R/W transactions. Rebuilding a drive steals valuable bandwidth from user R/W activity.

The right axis of Figure 3A.9 is a measure of array utilization. As mentioned, the more array transactions per second, the longer the delay to complete a transaction. Because transaction delay is never good, many systems are designed to operate at less than ~80% utilization for a given latency. One more issue that can affect throughput is data fragmentation.

3A.2.2   Fragmentation, OS Caching, and Command Reordering

The image of the storage array data layout starts looking like Swiss cheese if the R/W and delete block sizes are small. The result is called fragmentation. There are two types of fragmentation: *file fragmentation* and *free space fragmentation*. File fragmentation refers to files that are not contiguous but rather are broken into scattered parts on the disc. Free space fragmentation refers to the empty space that is scattered about rather than being consolidated into one area of the disc. File fragmentation reduces read throughput, whereas free space fragmentation reduces write throughput. Interestingly, if data are formatted in large blocks, then the fragmentation is a nonissue. In fact, sequential AV files and fragmented AV (random access) files have about the same access performance if the R/W block size is large according to the reasoning that has been developed. As a result, in many AV systems, there is no need to defrag the arrays. This is good news because the defrag process is slow and might cause marked array performance problems for systems that operate 24 × 7.

In practice, it is the AV equipment vendor's choice to fine-tune drive access and improve array throughput and latency. Many OS's decide when (waiting adds latency for reads/writes) and with what block size (may be very small, 16 KB) an array is accessed. For maximum performance, some AV centric applications bypass the OS services for managing the disc array access and rely on custom caching and R/W access timing.

The ideal model is for all access to be sequential (or random), large block transactions. However, it is often difficult to guarantee this, as small block transactions (metadata, proxy files, edit projects, etc.) and large AV transactions are mixed for most applications. A mix of small and large block accesses can reduce the overall data throughput by up to 50%. For this reason, some vendors offer two different storage arrays for large AV systems; one for large block A/V data and one for standard small block transactions.

HDD sequential R/W access has improved performance compared to purely random access for small block access. All modern drives have an internal cache for R/W queuing. So when a drive has, say, 10 random read commands in queue, then it can choose to reorder the access to optimize the read rate. A random command sequence of reads (or writes) is turned into a nearly sequential (approximates it) access operation. While it is true that read data may be returned out of order, the performance can be noticeably improved over the pure random access case. For most AV applications, out-of-order returned data are resequenced easily by the application or other element. The extra logic needed to accomplish reordering is well worth the effort for the gains in performance.

The next section outlines common benchmarks for measuring storage system performance. Much of the reasoning that was developed in the previous sections is related to benchmarking. Figure 3A.9 is a way to visualize the factors that contribute to a performance benchmark.

Storage System Benchmarks

Comparing storage system (SAN, DAS) performance and metrics can be a daunting task. By analyzing vendor data sheets and comparing specs, a reviewer may find a true apples-to-apples assessment to be nearly unattainable. This was the case until the Storage Performance Council (www.storageperformance.org) published their SPC-1 benchmark metric. The SPC-1 metric is a composite value of real world environmental characteristics made up of the following:

◆ Demanding total I/O throughput requirements
◆ Sensitive I/O response times

- Dynamic workload behaviors
- Storage capacity requirements
- Diverse user populations and needs

SPC-1 is designed to demonstrate the performance and price/performance of storage systems in a server environment. The SPC-1 value is a measurement of IOPS (I/Os per second) that is typified by OLTP, email, and other business operations using random data requests to the system. The metric was designed to measure virtually any type of storage system from a single disk attached to a server to a massive SAN storage system.

Two classes of environments are dependent on storage system performance. The first is *systems based* with many users or simultaneous execution threads saturating the I/O request processing potential of the storage system. This type is typical of transaction processing applications such as airline reservations or Internet commerce. This spec is documented by SPC-1 IOPS. The second environment is one where wall-clock time must be minimized (application based) for best performance. One such application is a massive backup of an array of data. In this case the total time needed to do the operation is crucial so a minimum latency per I/O is crucial. This spec is documented by SPC-1 LRT (least response time) and is measured in milliseconds.

Of course a storage system's performance is not the same as the performance of an individual HDD. It is good to review the basic performance metrics for a single HDD. As with an array, the key measures are access bandwidth, seek/latency, and capacity. A typical high-end HDD drive has the following specs:[4]

- 400-GB capacity (ATA and SCSI) with a maximum sustained read transfer rate of 60 MB/s. Maximum sustained rates are rarely achieved in the real world, as they are measured on the outer tracks of the disc only. The inner track sustained data rate is about 70% of the maximum

---

[4] Note that MB/s indicates Megabytes per second whereas Mb/s indicates megabits per second. The B/b nomenclature is commonly misused in the technical literature so beware.

value. A sustained transfer requires a large file, continuously available without seeks or latency delays.

◆ Burst I/O rates >1 Gb/s. This is the HDD internal buffer to/from the external bus transfer rate.

These are truly amazing specs and drive vendors keep pushing the speeds and capacity higher and higher. The useable, average transfer rates for large files may be 70% of the maximum value. Of course for many AV applications, system design demands specifying the worst case transfer rate, not the best or even average case. The HDD seek/latency spec is almost frozen in time (does not follow Moore's law), which affects the number of transactions per second that a drive can support.

Snapshot

Access Density

Disk drive **performance** is improving at ~10% annually despite storage **density** growing 50–60% annually. Raw disk drive performance is normally measured in total random I/Os per second and can surpass 100 I/Os per second.

Access density is the imbalance between storage density and performance. Access density is the ratio of performance, measured in I/Os per second, to the capacity of the drive, usually measured in Gigabytes. Access density = I/Os per second per Gigabyte. For streaming video, I/Os per second is not always an important metric, as long as I/Os are common.

3A.3   STORAGE SUBSYSTEMS

This section outlines several modern storage architectures. The following technologies are core to the modern AV/IT architecture. The following storage methods are discussed:

1. JBODs and RAID arrays
2. NAS servers
3. SAN storage
4. Object storage devices

In each case the technologies are examined in the light of AV work-flows. To fully appreciate storage requirements, check out the storage appetite for various video formats in Chapter 2. Before investigating the four main storage types, let us cover some basic concepts that apply to most storage systems.

3A.3.1   HDD Capacity and Access Data Rate

Every HDD provides storage capacity and an I/O delivery rate. They are both important and often misunderstood. We tend to think of a HDD as being defined by its capacity as in, "I just bought a 250-GB hard drive at Fry's Electronics." That may be true but that same drive also has an I/O spec. However, it is just as valid to say, "I just bought a 160-Mb/s drive at Fry's." Disc bit density has increased about 60% annually since 1992, but storage device performance (random I/Os per second) is improving at only 10% per year. See the Snapshot on Access Density.

Drive vendors are focused on capacity more than increasing the I/Os per second or raw R/W rates. Some applications need capacity (a PVR) whereas some need I/Os per second (Web server with thousands of simultaneous clients). Here are some practical requirements for a few applications.

◆ Centralized VOD server with the top 30 movies serving 1000 individual viewers (Cable TV premium service) each with PVR-like capabilities. Thirty, 2-hr movies require only 135 GB at 5 Mb/s (one drive). The aggregate read access rate is 1000 times 5 Mb/s = 5 Gb/s. If a single HDD has a spec of 15 MB/s, then it takes 42 drives (all movies replicated on all drives) to meet the read access rates. For this case it is wise to use RAM storage. For 10,000 viewers, things get messy and clever combinations of RAM and HDD are sometimes needed and/or some restrictions on PVR capability.

◆ At the other end of the scale is the case of 100,000 hr of .25 Mb/s proxy video. Any of the content may be viewed by 200 desktop clients at once. To store the proxy files requires 11.25 TB total. If each HDD has a capacity of 250 GB (at 15 MB/s), then it requires 45 drives to store 11.25 TB. The read bandwidth needs can be met with one drive (6.25 MB/s total for 200 viewing clients).

So it is obvious that storage capacity is not the only HDD spec of importance when doing an AV system design. The examples prove that the HDD disparity between required capacity and delivery rates can reach a factor of 50 or more for some designs. There are raging debates in the VOD design community over the best way to store the content. Some vendors only use HDDs, others use RAM only, and some offer a hybrid of HDD/RAM to meet the demanding needs of capacity and bandwidth.

Snapshot

The Case of the Missing 90 GB

In computing it is standard to use KB as representing 1024B. Likewise a MB is 1024 KB and a GB is 1024 MB. This is thinking[5] in a power of 2. So KB = 2^{10} bytes, MB = 2^{20}B, GB = 2^{30}B, and TB = 2^{40}B. Disc drive manufactures, however, use KB to represent 1000B, MB = 10^6, and so on. A 300-GB capacity HDD is exactly 300×10^9 bytes, but when the drive is installed in most computer systems (Windows based, for example), its capacity is expressed using a K, M, or G based on 1024B. Just a tad confusing.

For example, a 1-TB HDD would show an installed capacity of .91 TB (.91 * 2^{40}, = ~10^{12}) so a 1-TB (1000B reference) HDD is the same as .91 TB (1024B reference). There is about a 90-GB difference between the two methods. The "error" (~9%) is not trivial but not an actual loss either. Do not confuse this with the difference between raw and formatted capacity—that is a true loss of useful capacity.

3A.3.2   Aggregate Array I/O Rates

An array filled with say N identical drives will deliver N times the storage capacity of one drive but the aggregate I/O rate will not always be N times the I/O rate of one drive. Why? Drive I/O rate depends on how the I/O controller manages drive access. Is there an individual link from each HDD to the controller or are all HDDs connected together on a common

---

[5] See Appendix A for some 2^N computing tricks.

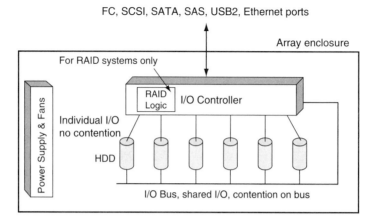

FC, SCSI, SATA, SAS, USB2, Ethernet ports

Array enclosure

For RAID systems only

RAID Logic   I/O Controller

Power Supply & Fans

Individual I/O
no contention

HDD

I/O Bus, shared I/O, contention on bus

Each HDD has a dedicated
or shared path to the I/O
Controller – not both.
This is for illustration only.

FIGURE   A simple JBOD or RAID arrray.

3A.12

bus or arbitrated loop? Both methods are shown in Figure 3A.12. In the first case the drives have individual access to the I/O controller so there is no contention among drives. In the second, all drives will share I/O bus resources and hence simultaneous HDD access is impossible. Aggregate access rates depend on several factors and file striping is one of them.

File Striping and Array Performance

File striping increases access bandwidth by distributing the files across all drives in an array (or even across arrays). Figure 3A.13 shows one method of file striping to increase the aggregate access bandwidth. Because the file is divided among N drives, ideally, the file access rate is N times the case of the file being stored on one drive on average. Distributing a file across N drives allows more simultaneous clients to access the same file. One downside of this scheme is the vulnerability to file loss in the event

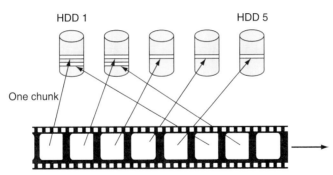

File ABC divided into chunks for striping (~1 MB per chunk, varies)

FIGURE   File striping example across 5 discs.

3A.13

of a HDD failure. If any one unprotected drive fails out of N, then the entire file is lost in practice. This increases the need to provide fault resilient methods to store data (see Chapter 5). When several users need simultaneous retrieval of the same file, accessing the discs out of order reduces HDD queuing delays. The methods used to avoid queuing delays are varied and beyond the scope of our discussion but they can be managed to achieve good performance. Also, if the HDD I/O bus burst rate is much faster than its R/W platter rate, then some of the contention will be reduced.

Generally, if there is HDD I/O contention (I/O bus connection in Figure 3A.12), an array offers an access rate profile as shown in Figure 3A.14. Figure 3A.14 is derived from measured results and shows a 25% reduction (75% of ideal) in aggregate I/O when there are eight drives sharing a common I/O bus. This phenomenon is also seen when files are striped across multiple arrays each with N internal discs. Your mileage may vary since the rate reduction is a result of contention mechanisms that will differ among storage subsystems.

Optimizing and managing capacity and access rate at the HDD or array level are not child's play. Most AV vendors tackle these issues in different ways. When evaluating a storage system, ask the right questions to fully comprehend what the real world performance is.

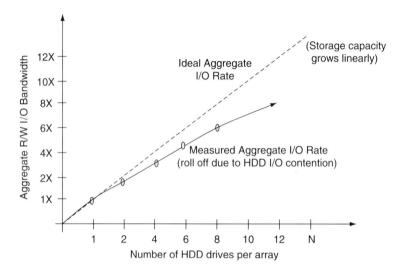

FIGURE   Storage array aggregate I/O bandwith versus number of drives.

3A.14

The following summarizes the main points when adding capacity and/or I/O bandwidth to a system.

♦ Adding arrays or discs to an existing system adds storage capacity. However, the new capacity is made available to clients based on the configuration settings of SAN virtualization or a CFS if present.

♦ Adding arrays or discs to an existing system adds I/O capacity. However, the amount of R/W bandwidth available to clients depends on the presence of striping techniques and configuration of any SAN virtualization or CFS if present.

3A.3.3   General Storage Requirements

There are several factors to consider when selecting or defining a storage system.

♦ Usable capacity after accounting for redundancy (reliability) overhead.

♦ Usable R/W bandwidth considering the usage patterns: sequential, big block I/O, random or small block I/O. Remember, accessing small audio or proxy files (small block size usually) is markedly different from accessing high bit rate (large block rate usually) video files.

◆ Usable R/W bandwidth after accounting for RAID HDD rebuild methods.

◆ Reliability methods.

◆ Failover methods—done in A/V real time or not.

◆ Management methods—faults, warnings, alarms, configuration modes.

◆ A host of other features that may be significant depending on special needs.

When selecting a storage system, it is good policy to ask questions about these factors. There is no list that covers all user needs so take the time and investigate to really understand the ins and outs of any system under investigation.

Many AV facility owners/operators desire to use COTS storage (read cheaper) when configuring NLEs and video server nodes on shared storage. In general, however, these systems require AV vendor specified and tested storage systems (read expensive) to meet a demanding QoS. COTS storage vendors are happy to provide a generic product, but when it fails to meet the required QoS, they often will not make the needed upgrades. However, AV vendors guarantee that their provided storage works well in demanding QoS environments. The bottom line is that COTS storage may work for some AV workflows—if the shoe fits wear it—but AV vendor-provided storage should always function as advertised. Next, let us overview the five basic storage subsystems found in various forms in most IT infrastructures: JBOD and RAID arrays, SAN, NAS, and object storage.

3A.4   JBOD AND RAID ARRAYS

There is nothing sophisticated about Just a Bunch Of Discs (JBOD) but you've got to love the name. It is the simplest form of a collection of disc drives in a single enclosure. Figure 3A.12 shows an example of a JBOD with either individual HDD links or a common I/O bus approach. It is really just an enclosure with power supplies, fans, drives, and an optional I/O controller board. The I/O controller may act as a gateway between the I/O ports (FC, SCSI, SATA, SAS, USB2, Ethernet ports) and the internal drive I/O. By definition there are no RAID functions. Advanced array features such as iSCSI I/O using Ethernet are possible but more often are found on RAID arrays. Admittedly there is no precise definition of a JBOD, but simplicity and low cost reign. Pure JBODs lack the drive reliability that is often demanded so their use is confined to areas where reliability is not of prime importance.

When JBODs grow up they become RAIDs. No, it is not bug spray. RAID—Redundant Arrays of Inexpensive (or Independent) Discs— describes a family of techniques for improving the reliability and performance of a JBOD array. A RAIDed array can allow one (or two in some cases) of N discs to fail without affecting the storage availability, although the R/W performance may degrade. This concept is now accepted as de rigueur and many hard disc arrays offer RAID functionality. See Chapter 5 for a detailed discussion on RAID techniques and categories.

3A.5   NAS AND SAN STORAGE

Networked attached storage (NAS) and storage area networking (SAN) are discussed in Chapter 3B—a chapter dedicated to these technologies. In a nutshell, both technologies are used to provide storage to network attached nodes. A NAS provides remote resources for both sharing storage and sharing files. A SAN, in its most native configuration, provides only shared storage resources. With the use of a CFS, discussed earlier, a SAN may be configured to share files among attached nodes. Clients attach to a NAS using Ethernet usually. Clients and servers attach to SAN storage using Fibre Channel and, more recently, Ethernet. General-purpose servers (including NAS servers) often use SAN storage. They both can offer excellent AV performance and are the bedrock of many AV/IT systems.

3A.6   OBJECT STORAGE

A new class of storage is on the horizon; it is object storage. It differs from traditional file (NAS) or block based (SAN) storage in several ways. Object storage devices (OSDs) store data not as files or hard-addressed blocks but as objects. For example, an object could be a single database record or table—or the entire database itself. An object may contain a file or just a portion of a file. An OSD is a content-addressable memory; provide it with an identifier (metadata fingerprint) and it will return the content represented by the ID. The fingerprint is formed using a hashing algorithm for generating a unique 128B (or similar) value that is used to identify and retrieve data.

Imagine that a 30-s video program has a fingerprint ID of value X and that this value uniquely represents it. If only one bit changes anywhere in the video, say due to a pixel change, the value of X changes. In practice, a requesting client asks for file ABC, which translates to a pointer of value X, and the OSD locates file ABC using this pointer. Depending on the implementation, clients may access the storage using CIFS/NFS (discussed in the next chapter) or via a custom API provided by the OSD storage vendor. OSDs are finding application as near-line or secondary storage so they will not be replacing traditional high-performance RT storage any time soon.

Objects are stored on OSDs that contain processors, RAID logic, network interfaces, and storage hardware. Each OSD manages the objects as they deem necessary. The OSD hides the "file" layout, addressing, partitioning, and caching from a requesting client. Objects may reside on one OSD or be partitioned across a network of OSDs. This abstraction is practical for some file types such as X-rays, images, videos, email archives, and a myriad of documents that are normally recovered whole. Partial access is also allowed. Using metadata to track and manage files adds flexibility in scalability, performance, location independence, authenticity, and reliability compared to traditional addressable storage. The value of the metadata fingerprint also maintains the integrity of the file against changes.

Linux server clusters are one means to implement OSD systems. Among the vendors in this space are Cluster File Systems (www.clusterfs.com), Panasas (www.panasas.com), and Permabit (www.permabit.com). Other companies are attacking the market with stand-alone storage systems (not based on Linux clusters). For example, EMC (www.emc.com) offers Centera (object based) and Network Appliance (www.netapp.com) offers NearStore Appliance (not object based). NearStore is going after the same market segments (near line, secondary storage) as Centera but without using object storage.

Object storage is a new model and will find some niche applications over time. AV data types are ideal candidates to be treated as objects. Example systems that may use OSDs are a post house or film studio with thousands of hours of digital content. Each piece of material (or any derivatives) will have a unique fingerprint that may be used for asset tracking. Because OSD systems can scale to >100 TB with NSPOF reliability, they are also ideally suited for mission critical near-line storage.

3A.7   HIERARCHICAL AND ARCHIVAL STORAGE

Installed digital storage is expected to grow 50–70% per year for the foreseeable future. In 2002 alone, 5 Exabytes of new digital information were produced. Of this, 92% was stored on magnetic media for the most part (see Appendix D). The economics of storing all this on RAM or even hard disc is untenable. As a result, IT has developed a hierarchy or pyramid of storage to balance the needs of users and owners of digital data. Each step in the hierarchy trades off access rates, capacity, and cost/GB. These three metrics are the key drivers behind the idea of tiered storage. Next, a brief analysis of the trends in tiered storage is considered.

Figure 3A.15 presents a simple view of a three-tier storage system. In fact, some ranks may not be present in all systems (no near-line, for example), but our analysis considers the full featured case. At the top are the application clients and servers that demand fast data access times with unlimited access to stored data. On-line SAN or NAS storage is typical with speedy access times (in the AV real time sense) but with limited storage. Lower in the chain is second-tier storage. The trade-off here is giving up low access times for less expensive ($/GB) storage with more capacity. Second-tier may not guarantee RT access under all conditions. At the bottom is the archive layer or near-line storage. Here, excellent capacity and lower $/GB are the key metrics, with access times being very slow compared to HDD arrays.

In addition to the economic needs of trading off access rates, capacity, and cost, there are several business uses of tiered storage.

◆ Long-term archive
◆ Daily server backup/restore

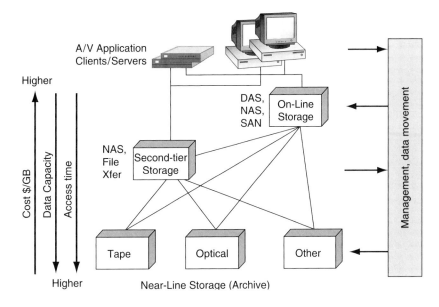

The hierarchy of storage.

◆ Disaster recovery copies

◆ Snapshots creating a point-in-time copy of data for quick recovery

◆ Data mirrors for regional access or improved reliability

◆ Replication—like mirroring but writes are asynchronous

Most of these factors are discussed in Chapter 5.

3A.7.1   Data Flows across Tiered Storage

The flow of data between the different storage elements is outlined in Figure 3A.16, the storage onion. Four example flows are identified. Flow "A" is the common client to DAS/NAS/SAN storage connection. In most cases the client controls access to the on-line storage pools. In case "B," data move between the archive and a second-tier store. The client layer is unaffected by the transfer of content when it occurs. However, some director (controller) moved the files, perhaps based on a JITFT schedule, for later use by a client/server or transfer across a WAN.

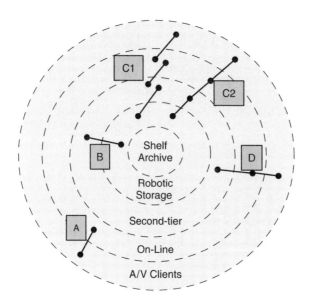

The storage onion—sample data movement paths.

In flow "C," data are moved from archive to client (or in the opposite direction) in either separately completed steps (C1) or as part of a continuous data flow (C2). In the first case, a director moves data between stores in steps as needed by schedules or other requests. There may be a wait period (minutes to days) between steps in the chain. In the second case (C2), a director moves data from the archive to second-tier to on-line in one continuous step for use by the A/V client. One example of this second case is a request for an ASAP A/V playback of some archived material. The playback file is located on the archive and moved to the second-tier store. As the second-tier store is being loaded, the target file is moved to the RT on-line store. As the on-line store is being loaded, playout of the file may commence. Sure, it may be more logical to move the file from archive directly to on-line, but let us use the C2 flow as an example only.

Now, the C2 flow is tricky but it can be implemented with proper attention to data streaming rates. Compared to C1, C2 requires a high-performance QoS for each element in the chain and strict attention to the timing of the flow. From request to client playback start may take 15s to several minutes depending on the archive type (optical or tape). The flow of data along the C2 path must be continuous and never "get behind" the playout consumption data rate; if so, the playout data will dry up. The data flow across all devices in the chain must, on average, meet

RT playback (or record) goals. Frankly, the continuous C2 flow is an unlikely workflow in the real world. The stepped version C1 is practical and done everyday in workflows like those at Turner Entertainment's Cartoon Network (see Chapter 10). Of course, C1 may require ~15 min (or less with fast transfers) to transfer a 5-min file along the path. It is more likely to see an archive to on-line continuous transfer (skip the second-tier stage) if there is pressure to playout ASAP. The bottom line is that both C1- and C2-like flows are practical in the real world.

The last flow is task "D." This is a traditional two-stage file transfer from second-tier to on-line to playout. Typically, automation software schedules the transfers (JITFT mode) between near-line and on-line and initiates the playout at the client. D may be either of types D1 or D2 as with the C flow. If D is implemented, D1 is the more common flow.

Some AV/IT workflows use all of these methods (A–D) in harmony. However, not all AV facilities have need for an archive but some do. For example, Turner Entertainment uses a StorageTek PowderHorn tape archive just to store its 6000 cartoon library. Turner uses a true three-tier storage approach (C1) for the Cartoon Network and a two-tier approach (D1) for other networks.

The cost to manage data can be enormous and it is one of the biggest issues in IT today. AV workflows do not escape the management burden. Despite the nearly 70% increase in data annually, there is only a 30% increase in the ability to manage these data. So what are the best practices to manage data?

3A.7.2   Managing Storage

Over the years different strategies have emerged to manage storage. For many years hierarchical storage management (HSM) has been the mainstay for large enterprise data management. The most current thinking is centered on information life cycle management (ILM). ILM is the process of managing the placement and movement of data on storage devices as they are generated, replicated, distributed, protected, archived, and eventually retired. ILM seeks to understand the value of data and migrates them across storage systems for the most cost-effective access strategy. A report from Horison Information Strategies [Horison] states that enterprises need to "understand how data should be managed and where data should reside. In particular, the probability of reuse of data has historically been one of the most meaningful metrics for understanding optimal data placement. Understanding what happens to data throughout its lifetime is becoming an increasingly important aspect of effective data management." The concepts behind ILM are useful for any AV facility design, expansion, or rethinking of current storage strategy (see [Glass]).

Implementing an ILM strategy requires a combination of process and technology. Some process oriented questions are as follow.

♦ What is the value of data as they age?

♦ Do data become more or less valuable?

♦ How long should we keep data?

♦ What storage policies can we apply to our data?

♦ What is the right balance of our data across the hierarchy to optimize ROI and user experience?

♦ Do we understand the different data types that drive our business?

Figure 3A.17 posits one possible scenario of data reuse as they age. Figure 3A.17 is general, and various data types exhibit different access signatures. Knowing that access rates decline over the life of data allows automation logic to migrate data to less costly storage. AV data typically fall into a similar pattern.

Several companies specialize in managing the AV data archiving process. EMC (AVALONidm), Front Porch Digital (DIVArchive), Masstech Group (MassStore), SGL (Flashnet Archive Manager), and SGT are among the few who cater to the special needs of the AV industry. They provide software to manage the migration across the hierarchy and to control storage robotics. What makes managing storage special in AV facilities? A few aspects are AV data flows involving very big files (15-GB movies), unusual AV gear compared to enterprise devices, and time-critical delivery. Some traditional AV equipment automation companies manage data movement between near-line and on-line storage as well. Most large-scale facilities need both storage management and control automation software solutions to meet all their AV data flow needs. As on-line and off-line storage capacity increases and prices drop, fewer designs demand a full three-tier solution.

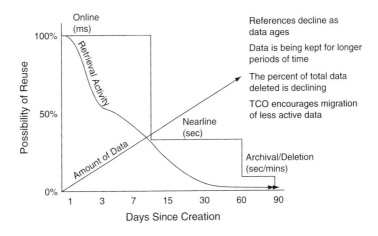

FIGURE

3A.17

Data access rates decline with age of data.
Source: Horison.

Many large broadcasters use tape archive systems. Sometimes the content is owned by the broadcaster (movies, dramas, for example) and they expect very long-term storage. Alternatively, the archive may cache materials for several months or years for reuse later. One example of programming reuse is at KQED in San Francisco, a PBS member station. They store up to 12,000 hr of PBS programming locally in an ADIC archive for reuse as needed. See Chapter 10 for a case study on KQED.

3A.7.3   Archive Storage Choices

Off-line archive devices can be complex and usually involve some or all of the following:

1. Tape and/or optical removable media
2. Drives to control and R/W the media
3. Robotics to insert/remove media from drives
4. Housing for controllers, media, drives, and robotics

There has been a debate about what is a true archive media format. Some vendors tout 7–15 years media life as an archive format, whereas another will say that true archive needs a 35+-year media life. Although a worthwhile discussion, let us bypass this argument and treat any data tape or optical media as an archive format.

Archive devices are divided into at least three different camps: tape (helical and linear heads), optical disc, and holographic. In the main-stream, tape is the most popular followed by optical. Some vendors manufacture all the components in the value chain, whereas others only offer pieces. For example:

◆ Sony manufactures media, robotics, and enclosure for the PetaSite tape storage system. The PetaSite supports up to 1.2 Petabytes (10^{15} bytes is one Petabyte). One Petabyte of capacity can store ~100,000 movies at a 10-Mb/s compressed rate.

◆ Spectra Logic manufactures the Spectra 20K tape robotic system. It uses the Sony AIT tape drives and AIT media. This low-end system can store 20 TB using 200 cartridges. ADIC, another vendor, also focuses on robotics, not media or drives, and supports AIT, LTO, SDLT, and other choices with storage to 30.6 PB.

◆ Imation manufactures tape media, including format support for DLT, Ultrium (LTO), AIT media, and 9×40 series and optical discs.

Magnetic Tape Systems

The magnetic tape industry produces more than 10 different recording formats with nearly 15 automated tape robotic suppliers. Cartridge capacities are expected to approach 4 Terabytes in 6 years based on planned improvements in recording density. The automated tape market is expected to grow as archive and disaster recovery requirements increase due to all things going digital [Moore].

There are four main contenders in archival tape formats. Sony offers AIT/SAIT (Super Advanced Intelligent Tape). A consortium of several vendors created the LTO (Linear Tape Open) format branded as Ultrium. Quantum offers the DLT/SDLT (Super Digital Linear Tape) format. StorageTek offers the 9×40 tape format family. These four formats and their respective storage systems battle it out for various market shares.

The current cartridge capacity leader is the Sony SAIT-1 format with 500 GB native capacity at 30MB/s R/W rates. The road map for the SAIT family shows 4 TB/240 MB/s cartridges in 2009 (SAIT-4). The LTO group is following closely behind with their road map. Figure 3A.18 shows the respective road maps for both these formats.

Of special note is the new Quantum SDLT 600A with DLTxchange. It uses standard DLT technology and tapes but adds some features that fit agreeably into AV/IT workflows. The drive works stand alone or in a robotic library, has a Gigabit Ethernet port, and appears as an FTP server on the network. Each tape has its own file system and directory. There are restrictions; it does not allow for random writes (appends only) but does allow random reads. It is an amalgam of a tape archive and FTP server with its associated directory of stored files. The file system is MXF aware and provides for quick metadata access per file. Also, partial file requests with mark_in and mark_out time codes return a new MXF file with only the requested content. It is the first AV-friendly and networked tape-based store to enter the AV/IT space.

In closing, a complete analysis of storage system performance involves metrics beyond tape formats. Other metrics include storage capacity per

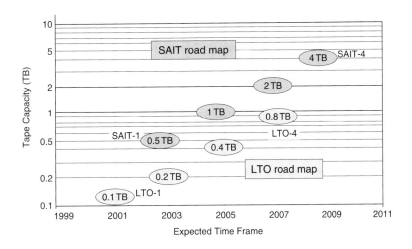

FIGURE   SAIT and LTO tape road maps.

3A.18

square foot and cubic foot of enclosure space, aggregate R/W through-put, tape retrieval time, search time, overall capacity, cost per TB (or per MB/s), and line power needed per TB. Depending on your workflow, space, and power needs, these metrics have varying value.

Optical Systems

Optical has always lagged magnetic tape in capacity and data rate but recent products show promise for low-cost archives. Optical discs come in several flavors, including

◆ DVD with a single-sided, dual-layer capacity of 8.5 GB (single layer is 4.7 GB).

◆ Blu-ray Disc is a potential DVD successor format. Blu-ray's data-only format is called ProDATA (Professional Disc) and has a capacity of 23.3 GB at 11 MB/s. In 2005 the format extends to 50 GB at 22 MB/s and in 2007 to 100 GB at 43 MB/s using four layers of data. Sometime after 2008 a single disc will support 200 GB using eight layers. This format is backed by Sony and others and uses blue light laser R/W technology. The ProDATA specs and the Blu-ray AV specs for home use differ in capacity and rate.

◆ Toshiba/NEC has introduced the advanced optical disc format sup-porting a dual-layer, single-sided read-only disc to 30 GB in 2004. This format also uses blue wavelength lasers and has been selected by the DVD Forum as the HD-DVD format. It will compete with Blu-ray, although there are intense talks to merge parts of the two competing technologies for the everlasting good of the end consumer.

Figure 3A.19 compares these two formats and their key specs for consumer AV use.

Optical R/W rates are much less than for tape but their access times are a factor of 10 or more better. Also, the robotics for managing optical discs tends to be less expensive than tape robotics, as the disc is very light and easy to maneuver. The optical-based archive is finding applications in A/V facilities worldwide.

One example of an optical storage system is the TeraCart from Asaca Corp. It supports SAN and NAS connectivity and ProDATA discs with an

		Blu-ray Disc	HD-DVD
Data Capacities [GB]	Single-Layer	25	15 (pre-recorded) 20 (rewritable)
	Dual-Layer	50	30 (pre-recorded) 32 (rewritable)
Maximum Recording Time, HDTV	Single-Layer	2 hours	2 hours
	Dual-Layer	4 hours	4 hours
Maximum Data Rate [Mbps]		36.5	36.5
Video Encoding		MPEG-2 MPEG4/AVC VC-1	MPEG-2 MPEG4/AVC VC-1
Laser Wavelength [nm]		405	405

FIGURE   Key parameters of the Blu-ray Disc and HD-DVD formats.

3A.19

enclosure capacity of 9.8 TB in only 4 square feet of footprint. More than 2000 hrs of 10-Mb/s programming can be stored in one relatively small unit. Up to eight libraries may be connected to act as one unit. Figure 3A.20 shows this unit, the AM420PD.

Other Archive Devices

This section reviews some new and promising methods to archive data. One that is starting to gain momentum is Massive Array of Inactive Discs (MAID). The concept behind MAID is HDD-based storage designed specifically for WORO (write once, read occasionally) applications, where the focus is on infrequent access rather than I/Os per second. Applications that only occasionally access data permit the majority of discs not to spin, thereby conserving power, improving reliability, and simplifying data access. A typical MAID architecture may have only 1% of data spinning at any one time. Data access is measured in milliseconds to seconds—the time it takes to spin up a drive. MAID will have

Asaca TeraCart using ProDATA storage (9.8 TB).

application in broadcast facilities where archived data are only accessed occasionally, say to load a day's playlist. MAID is not used for long-term, deep archive.

Holographic storage has been a promising technology for years. Until recently, it seemed as though it would languish forever in the laboratory. At last, a few companies are producing commercial versions. Aprilis Technology (www.aprilisinc.com) offers a small unit with a 3-in. rotating platter that stores 200 GB. This is unprecedented performance in such a small device. It uses single-write, read-many (WORM) removable media. Another vendor of holographic storage is InPhase Technologies (www.inphase-technologies.com). They are developing a similar unit with 300 GB of capacity at 20-MB/s transfer rates with a road map to 1.2 TB/ (160 MB/s) on a single platter. It will be released in 2006. Several of the value propositions for holographic storage are leaders in density per cubic foot (32 TB/cubic foot), 50-year media life (magnetic tape is 8 to 20 years), and reading rates faster than ProDATA optical (factor of 2X in 2005). Not to be ignored is the cost of the media itself. Holographic discs promise to be the low-cost leader compared to tape or other optical. Of course, holographic storage is immature and needs industry experience before it takes any appreciable market share from tape or optical.

On the bleeding edge, IBM is doing laboratory work on a project called Millipede. Using nanotechnology, they have demonstrated a data storage density of a trillion bits per square inch—20 times higher than the densest magnetic storage available today.

3A.8   IT'S A WRAP: SOME FINAL WORDS

Storage technology is at the heart of all AV/IT systems. A good understanding of these concepts will help you better evaluate vendor's products. Plus, you will be able to decipher vendor speak when it comes to their storage offerings and connectivity. Expect to see the "pocket server" in a few years as HDD density continues to head into the stratosphere. Storing 500 hr of content on one drive is not far off and small AV media clients scattered throughout a facility may become commonplace. It is not hard to imagine an AV infrastructure with centralized storage (a mix of on-line and near-line) and media clients located across the LAN and WAN.

The next chapter outlines three common methods for clients and servers to connect to storage. The trilogy of DAS, SAN, and NAS are the basis of modern storage connectivity. By aggregating the information in this chapter with the next, you will develop a good foundation of the essentials of storage systems.

REFERENCES

[**Glass**] GlassHouse Technologies, White Paper, *Uncovering Best Practices for Storage Management*, www.glasshousetech.com, 2002.

[**Horison**] *Information Lifecycle Management*, Horison Information Strategies, 2003, www.horison.com.

[**Moore**] Fred Moore, *Storage Manifesto*, Spectra Logic Inc., 2002.

[**Veritas**] www.veritas.com has several white papers on virtualization of storage.

3B | Storage Access Methods

CHAPTER

3B.0   STORAGE CONNECTIVITY: DAS, SAN, AND NAS

This chapter studies the three common methods for servers and clients[1] to connect to a storage subsystem. The previous chapter outlined the basics of storage systems and this one adds the dimension of connectivity between clients/servers and storage. You may need to bounce between the two chapters, as many of the concepts discussed are so intimately related. Common ways to illustrate the three key methods are shown in Figure 3B.1. This illustration is a bit poetic, as in reality some of the layers are very thin. But that is okay; it is a great place to start our discussion. In the final section of this chapter, Figure 3B.1 is revisited with some flesh added to more fully compare the three methods.

Of the three, direct attached storage (DAS) is the simplest but least flexible. It provides block-based storage access to a directly attached client/server. DAS is a common choice for applications that require high-performance, local storage. The storage area network (SAN) replaces the simple connectivity of DAS with a switched fabric. Both clients and servers are connected to a fabric, allowing for scalable performance and capacity. It too provides native, block-oriented access to storage. Third, network attached storage (NAS) uses networking to attach clients to file

---

[1] Clients and servers are often collectively called the host computer when connecting to storage.

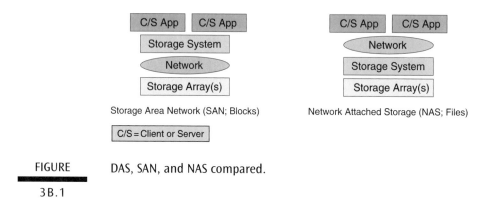

Direct Attached Storage (DAS; Blocks)

Storage Area Network (SAN; Blocks)   Network Attached Storage (NAS; Files)

C/S = Client or Server

FIGURE   DAS, SAN, and NAS compared.

3B.1

servers. NAS provides remote storage with an included file system. In NAS architecture, multiple hosts can share files. The distinction between SAN and NAS can be confusing at times so the differences are clearly outlined in this chapter. The analysis emphasizes the features and aspects that are especially relevant to A/V systems. Let us start with DAS.

3B.1   DIRECT ATTACHED STORAGE

This section provides a moderately detailed overview of DAS interface technology. Depending on your interest level, it may be more than you need. If your goal is to understand DAS buzz words and what is behind them, then this section is for you; if not, skip ahead to Section 3B.2 on SAN technology.

DAS is the most common form of external storage connectivity. Until recently, the venerable SCSI connection was the most poplar DAS method, and many servers and workstations have SCSI ports for connecting to external storage. A host computer connects directly to an array enclosure over a DAS link with little or no networking in between—it is a direct attach model as the DAS name implies.

The traditional SCSI interface was introduced as a method of connecting multiple peripherals to computers. It was developed by the T10/11 working groups of the InterNational Committee for Information Technology (INCITS). It is based on a parallel bus structure, with each attached device having a unique ID (or address). The SCSI bus will support up to 15 devices plus the host controller and can transfer data at burst speeds of up to 320 MB/s (Ultra 320). Because of the multiple device support, extended cable length (up to 6 m), and excellent transfer rate, the SCSI interface has been used to connect external devices such as scanners, CD duplicators, and HDD storage enclosures. USB2 and IEEE-1394 have replaced SCSI as an external interface of choice for many peripherals.

SCSI started life (1986) as a single parallel interface that included three closely connected elements: physical, protocol, and command specifications. Since then it has matured into a family of standards, including specs for each of these independent levels. Figure 3B.2 outlines the essentials of the standards. At the top level are the command structures, including device specific commands such as SBC (SCSI block commands) and SSC (SCSI stream commands) and the more generic SPC (SCSI primary commands). The midlevel contains protocols (that carry the upper layer commands) for a variety of physical links. The bottom level lists the common physical links. Notice that Fibre Channel carries

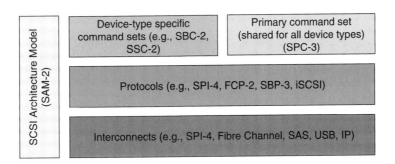

FIGURE   SCSI standards structure.

3B.2

Source: SCSI Trade Association.

SCSI commands, as does USB. Note too that the physical level is mapped to select upper layer protocols. As a result, Fibre Channel carries FCP and USB carries SPB and so on.

Protocol Soup

The bulleted list below outlines three legacy and three newer protocols that are key to the IT infrastructure. The first three are mature technologies with many vendors offering products for the market. The bottom three are newly defined standards, and only some vendors (2005) provide compliant products. However, it is expected that SAS (serial attached SCSI) and iSCSI (IP SCSI) will become the market leaders over the long run for enterprise applications.

◆ SCSI parallel interface (SPI-4 is the latest for support of Ultra 320)
◆ SBP-3 (serial bus protocol) for use over IEEE-1394 and USB-2 links (personal and small office use)
◆ Fibre Channel Protocol (FCP) over Fibre Channel physical (more on this later in the chapter)
◆ iSCSI over Ethernet/IP physical (SAN)
◆ Serial attached SCSI (SAS), which is defined at the command, protocol, and physical layers
◆ SCSI RDMA protocol over InfiniBand (RDMA = Remote DMA)

In some cases, the physical links are defined by the SCSI standards group as with traditional parallel SCSI or the newer serial attach SCSI links. In other cases the physical link is defined by others (Ethernet, USB-2, IEEE-1394), but the protocol and command layers are SCSI standards. So when someone says that a link is *SCSI compatible*, you need to ask questions to confirm what is actually meant. Is it at the command, protocol, and physical level or some subset of these?

The older parallel SCSI interface is losing favor due to several factors: short distance span, bulky cable/connectors, connector reliability, not networkable, cable cross talk, and limited data throughput. SAS is replacing legacy SCSI links. Other links will coexist with SAS. For example, FC and InfiniBand have found a niche, iSCSI is universally networkable, and USB is ubiquitous in PCs. Selection is normally predicated on price/performance. At the high end, InfiniBand was developed primarily as a server-to-server link (more on this later in the chapter), and the RDMA function is widely used in that environment. RDMA mapping is not a SCSI command set in the traditional sense. DMA is a method of transferring data from one memory system to another without passing through a host (or server) CPU. Bypassing the device-CPU speeds up transfers by a factor of five or more. With the strong emergence of iSCSI and SAS, RDMA will likely become a corner case for any DAS applications.

Figure 3B.3 shows the universe of DAS connectivity. In fact, there are more choices available (IBM offers several captive alternatives) but these will be the most common ones moving forward. A variety of vendors sell storage arrays with support for these link types. Some announced serial DAS offerings are

◆ Fibre Channel arrays (mature): Most major storage vendors
◆ SAS arrays (newly developed): Most vendors will follow

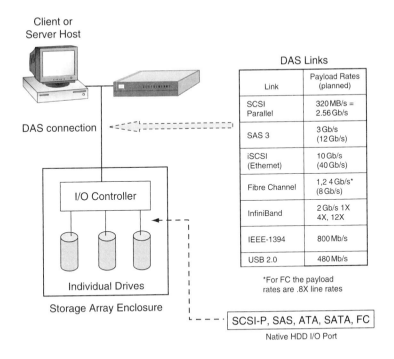

Link	Payload Rates (planned)
SCSI Parallel	320 MB/s = 2.56 Gb/s
SAS 3	3 Gb/s (12 Gb/s)
iSCSI (Ethernet)	10 Gb/s (40 Gb/s)
Fibre Channel	1,2 4 Gb/s* (8 Gb/s)
InfiniBand	2 Gb/s 1X 4X, 12X
IEEE-1394	800 Mb/s
USB 2.0	480 Mb/s

*For FC the payload rates are .8X line rates

FIGURE   DAS connectivity examples.

3B.3

FIGURE

3B.4

Example of USB DAS attached storage appliance.
Image courtesy of Maxtor.

- ◆ iSCSI arrays (newly developed): Adaptec, EMC, EqualLogic, FalconStor, HP, IBM, Network Appliance, Nimbus, others. This is a small sample only; expect consolidation.
- ◆ IEEE-1394, USB storage appliances (mature): Maxtor, Seagate, Sony, NEC, LaCie, Iomega, and many more
- ◆ InfiniBand: No vendors announced (for storage products)

Let us examine some sample products. Figure 3B.4 shows a USB, ATA-based personal storage array from Maxtor. Using USB-2 connectivity, up to 129 drives enclosures may be DAS attached to the USB serial path (needs bridges). This model is the OneTouch II.

At the other end of the scale, Figure 3B.5 shows a DataDirect Networks S2A3000 HDD-based storage array. It has four Fibre Channel I/O ports (optional eight), has slots for 200 SATA or FC drives, 60TB capacity, and 700 MB/s sustained throughput. This unit may be DAS attached, but for most applications is is shared with several servers and/or clients using SAN technology.

3B.1.1   HDD I/O Connectivity and Drive Types

Closely allied with DAS connectivity is the native HDD I/O interface port. This section outlines the common HDD ports and drive types. The native HDD I/O port type is not necessarily the same as the DAS link type as seen from Figure 3B.3. Table 3B.1 outlines common native HDD I/O connectivity choices.

ATA (parallel form) and SATA are dedicated for HDD I/O only and are not normally deployed outside a storage array enclosure. The other

Example of large disk array for DAS or SAN attach.

Image courtesy DataDirect Networks.

three link types are used for native HDD I/O *and* DAS connectivity. An HDD I/O type and its array enclosure I/O type do not need to match in any way. It is possible to have internal ATA drives with Fibre Channel connectivity on the array enclosure. Of course the I/O controller needs to translate across command, protocol, and physical domains for this scenario so matching up the HDD I/O type and the enclosure I/O type is a simplifying advantage. Figure 3B.6 shows comparisons for the three serial drive I/O specs.

HDD I/O port type	Comments
SCSI-P	Also used as a DAS link <6 m
Serial attached SCSI (SAS)	Serial replacement for SCSI-P Also a DAS link—10 m
ATA-P (ATA commands)	Only for HDD I/O— <1 m
Serial ATA (SATA)	Serial replacement for ATA-P Only for HDD I/O— <1 m
Fibre Channel (SCSI commands)	Also used as a DAS link— <10 km optical

Native HDD I/O Interface Connectivity

	Serial ATA	Serial Attached SCSI	Fibre Channel AL
Performance	Half-duplex	Full-duplex	Full-duplex
	1.5 Gb/sec (3.0 Gb/s announced)	3.0 Gb/sec (at intro.) 12 Gb/s announced	2.0 Gb/sec 8 Gb/s announced
Connectivity	1 m internal cable	>6 m external cable	>15 m external cable
	One device	>128 devices	127 devices Loop or loop switch
	SATA only	SAS and SATA	Fibre Channel only
Availability	Single port HDDs	Dual-port HDDs	Dual-port HDDs
	Single-host Point-to-point	Multi-initiator Point-to-point	Multi-initiator Shared media or point-to-point
Drive Model	Software transparent with Parallel ATA	Software transparent with SCSI	Software transparent with SCSI

FIGURE

3B.6

HDD I/O: Comparing three serial port types.
Source: SNIA.

ATA versus SCSI Drives

In general, ATA (started life as IDE) connectivity is the alternative to SCSI based connectivity. ATA drives have been used in PCs for many years. Because they offer lower performance than SCSI drives, ATA rules at the low end and SCSI at the high end. The commands, protocols, and physical connectors are completely different between SCSI-P and ATA-P. SATA is the serial equivalent of ATA-P just as SAS is the serial equivalent to SCSI-P. Fortunately, due to excellent cooperation among industry groups, there is now only one backplane connector type for both SATA and SAS drives. This allows storage array manufacturers to build one array enclosure and it can be populated with either ATA or SCSI drives or a mix (if supported). Finally, SCSI and ATA are converging along parallel lines.

Some of the salient differences between SCSI and ATA drive types are

1. Drive MTBF (SCSI has the lead):
   a. SCSI HDD MTBF is factory measured 24×7 for 3 months or more for new designs.
   b. ATA is tested stop/start and thermal cycling. As a result, ATA is not tested as thoroughly as SCSI. A shorter test cycle saves money.

2. Drive performance (SCSI has the lead)
   a. SCSI head seek times are generally smaller and rotational latency is less because SCSI rotates at 10/15 K rpm and ATA at 5400/7200 rpm.
3. ATA drives have higher capacity than SCSI due to lower rotational speeds.
4. ATA drives can be a factor of three to six *less expensive* than an equivalent capacity SCSI drive. ATA volume shipments are ~10X of SCSI shipments so pricing will be better.

At first glance the SCSI drive appears to lead in performance and reliability but at the penalty of much higher prices. In practice, the reliability of an ATA drive and a SCSI drive are about the same, although the specs may seem to indicate otherwise. See Chapter 5 for some enlightening analysis on HDD reliability. Second, the performance is indeed better with SCSI for small block R/W transactions. However, as discussed in Chapter 3A, for large block R/W transactions the rotational latency has marginal impact on R/W access rates. For AV applications the ATA drive provides a big advantage due to its superior pricing, with all other aspects being about equal. SCSI drives are marketed as the high-end choice so drive vendors receive more profit margin than on lower-end ATA drives.

In general, IT server farms tend to use SCSI drives while desktop and low-end servers tend to use ATA drives. Figure 3B.7 shows a suggested

	Desktop PCs	Entry Servers	Mid-range Servers	High-end Servers
Fibre Channel RAID				•
Ultra320 SCSI RAID			•	•
Ultra160 SCSI		•	•	
Serial ATA RAID	•	•		
Parallel ATA RAID	•			

SAS alternative since 2004

FIGURE 3B.7   Positioning of FC, SCSI, SATA, SAS, and ATA HDD application areas.

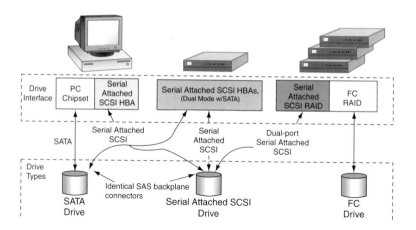

Drive Interface | PC Chipset | Serial Attached SCSI HBA | Serial Attached SCSI HBAs, (Dual Mode w/SATA) | Serial Attached SCSI RAID | FC RAID

FIGURE

3B.8

SATA, SAS, and FC for low-, mid-, and high-end systems.
Source: Adaptec.

positioning of FC, SCSI-P, SAS, SATA, and ATA discs across a range of computing needs. Again, for AV centric applications, ATA drives are an excellent choice even for the most demanding applications (uncompressed e-cinema at 7-Gb/s rates). Figure 3B.8 illustrates drive connectivity for low-, mid-, and high-end systems for general use. For the low end, SATA drives; for the mid range SATA or SAS; and for the high end SAS or FC SAN connectivity are employed.

3B.1.2   ATA and SCSI I/O Convergence

As mentioned, the SCSI and ATA special interest groups have collaborated and agreed on a common backplane connector and protocol for the serial versions of both ATA and SCSI. This was a formidable task because there is little in common between traditional SCSI and ATA parallel standards. The drive types will remain separate, but the serial I/O for each drive will converge. SAS standardizes a combination of three protocols, each of which transports different information types over the serial interface:

◆ Serial SCSI protocol
◆ Serial ATA tunneling protocol (STP) passes through ATA commands

♦ SCSI management protocol (SMP) provides HDD management information

The SAS connector is form factor compatible with the SATA connector. SATA signals are a subset of SAS signals, enabling the compatibility of SATA devices and SAS controllers. SCSI/SAS drives will not operate on a SATA controller and are keyed to prevent any chance of plugging them in incorrectly.

In addition, the similar SAS and SATA physical interfaces enable a new universal SAS backplane that provides connectivity to both SAS drives and SATA drives, eliminating the need for separate SCSI and ATA drive backplanes. This consolidation of designs greatly benefits both backplane manufacturers and end users by reducing inventory and design costs.

Some of the benefits of this converged approach are:

♦ Only one HDD I/O connector type for both serial SCSI and serial ATA drives
♦ A storage enclosure may support both ATA and SCSI drives
♦ Host software drivers can include bundled support for SCSI and ATA if desired
♦ Common management commands and responses

A SATA drive can plug into a SAS backplane connector or a serial SCSI drive can plug into the same connector (Figure 3B.8). How does a host computer know what type of drive is installed and which protocol to use for communications? The SAS standard defines a method by which a host can identify the drive type and then correspond only with that drive type. Incidentally, the physical layer electrical signals (voltages, clocking) are different between SAS drives and SATA drives. Although the SAS spec defines maximum clocking speeds, the values are different for each drive type. The drives will evolve differently but the interface spec will remain a common feature of each drive type.

SAS connectivity has a bright future and therefore so do SAS and SATA drives. Figure 3B.9 shows a road map for the SAS standard with link speeds of 12 Gb/s in 2010. Small enclosures with gigabits per second of data flow and Terabytes of capacity are just around the corner.

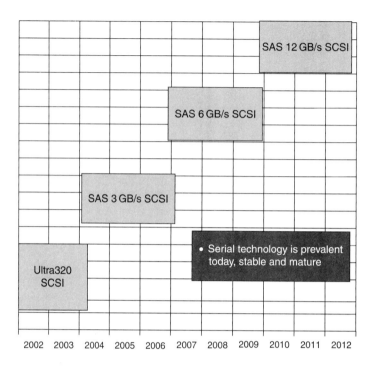

FIGURE

3B.9

Serial technology has a bright future.

Source: Adaptec.

3B.1.3   Remote DMA: The Next Frontier

Designers are always looking for faster methods to move data across networks. In this light, emergence of the remote DMA technique is interesting. A DMA (direct memory access) operation is commonly used within a PC or server for internal memory-to-memory data transfers without the involvement of the CPU. It is always beneficial when the CPU is removed from the data transfer path. A DMA operation provides very low latency and super high transfer rates. The "memory" in a DMA operation is typically DRAM with HDD on the horizon. RDMA extends the idea to memory-to-memory data transfers across a network. Several techniques have been developed to this end. InfiniBand is the leading technology to implement RDMA.

InfiniBand is a 10/30-Gb/s ultralow latency, non-IP, communication, storage, and embedded interconnect. InfiniBand, based on an industry standard, provides a robust data center interconnect. With 30-Gb/s products currently shipping, InfiniBand is at least a generation ahead of competing fabric technologies today. It was developed to cluster servers in data centers. It is considered exotic technology and is only found at the high end of computing configurations. One of the leaders in Infiniband-based products is Mellanox (www.mellanox.com). They offer a 144-port switch with a throughput of 2.88 terabits/s.

A competing RDMA method was defined by the RDMA Consortium (www.rdmaconsortium.org) and uses TCP/IP (not InfiniBand) as the transport means over a variety of physical networks. 10 Gb/s Ethernet will likely be the most common physical layer. Why invent yet another RDMA method when InfiniBand seems to do the job? Because InfiniBand is not IP networkable, it will never find the wide acceptance of Ethernet/ IP. Although new, some storage vendors offer products with RDMA/ Ethernet support. The RDMA/IP method bypasses the traditional CPU and TCP/IP software stack (TCP/IP is processed in the HBA card) and utilizes zero copies of data packets during the transfer of data. It is the ultimate in efficiency for moving data between two memory locations over IP. It remains to be seen how, if at all, RDMA technology will be used by AV vendors. The first application may be film related projects with uncompressed rates ~7 Gb/s.

3B.2   STORAGE AREA NETWORKS

SAN is a mature technology and accepted way for multiple clients and/or servers to access storage pools over a network. SAN architectures are often chosen for applications that need highly scalable performance from storage. Fibre Channel SANs are installed today in 62% of companies showing $1 billion or more in annual revenues [Chudnow]. According to Art Edmonds, Chair of the FCIA in 2004 [FCIA], "Fibre Channel technology continues to be the technology at the heart of SANs installed around the world. Conservative estimates place the number of SAN installations at 100,000 worldwide." SANs are universally accepted as the preferred way to access storage in big deployments. This section studies SAN methods with emphasis on components, benefits, architectural requirements, protocols, and futures.

SAN replaces the link-based architecture of DAS with a switched fabric. Administering DAS islands is more expensive and complex than managing a SAN. Managing say 10 independent islands of servers connected to individual DAS storage is more costly than managing one shared pool. In effect, it is more efficient to allow N straws to draw from one huge pool (SAN) than to have N pools each with only one straw (DAS). See Figure 3A.3 in Chapter 3A for an illustration of this concept. In one McKinsey study (ca. 2001), the cost of administration for a collection of DAS devices was $.84/MB compared to $.38/MB for a SAN of equivalent storage (your mileage will vary). According to one famous study by the Gartner Group, the cost to acquire a storage system is only 20% of the total cost of ownership (TCO) over its useful life.

As a result, there is a big motivation to concentrate a storage pool of homogeneous or heterogeneous devices. A SAN accomplishes this and hence the deployments of it in IT worldwide. However, the storage concentration also requires some way to manage and assign portions of the storage to the attached devices. One method is to use a clustered file system (CFS) and another method is to use virtualization. It is good to note that a SAN provides blocks of storage to attached clients, whereas a NAS provides direct file access. See Chapter 3A for a refresher on these concepts.

Let us use Figure 3B.10 as the basis of the SAN study. On the far left top are Fibre Channel (FC)-attached AV clients (Ingest, Playout, NLE, processors, and other nodes) that connect through a FC switch fabric to access storage. In the middle are NAS-attached servers. The servers access storage through the SAN switching fabric. On the far right is a remote archive that accesses the main SAN through an IP network. In this case the archive FC traffic is tunneled over TCP/IP and is converted back to FC to enter the switch fabric. This particular view of a SAN is Fibre Channel centric but FC could be replaced with Ethernet and iSCSI, as discussed later. All the components inside the dotted box constitute the SAN. Note that virtualization and caching are optionally included in the network storage pool at the bottom of the diagram. There are of course many different ways to build a SAN, but the common defining high level traits are as follow.

◆ Servers and other nodes access storage via Fibre Channel or Ethernet. Every attached node sees the storage as though it is local.

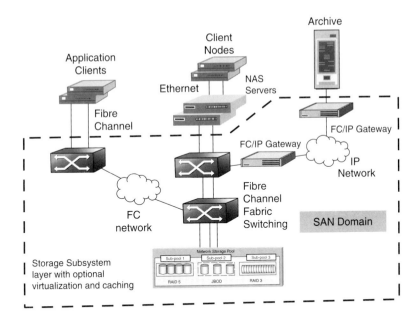

FIGURE

3B.10

General view of FC-based SAN architecture.

♦ The switching fabric allows any attached initiator to access homogeneous or heterogeneous block storage—not files. However, virtualization or CFS policies can partition the storage.

♦ Storage management methods for one pool of storage.

These SAN personality traits are not sufficiently specific to define the
design. Other criteria are needed. The design should match the functional requirements. So what are these functions? Let us see.

3B.2.1   Form Follows Function

The famous architect Louis Sullivan is considered the inventor of the
modern skyscraper. The Chicago buildings produced by Sullivan (and
Dankmar Adler, his structural engineer) were at the leading edge of
skyscraper design and were known for their gorgeous and tasteful

architecture. One of his dictums was *form follows function*. When designing a storage system, be it SAN or NAS, the form of the architecture should follow its intended function. In a simple minded view, the function of a SAN is to access data. However, looking deeper there are at least eight guiding principles [Glass] for defining the function of storage.

1. Availability and performance—information access needs
2. Scalability—expected growth in capacity, access nodes, and transfer rates
3. Reliability—may span from basic to mirrored with ~100% up time
4. Utilization—percentage of usage per population of attached nodes
5. Security—access rights and intrusion prevention
6. Connectivity—accessibility of the storage system
7. Backup and archive—various strategies to meet business needs
8. Cost (TCO)—does it meet budgetary needs over time

The form or architecture of a SAN (or NAS) should be a strong factor of these eight functional requirements. Of these eight, performance, scalability, reliability, utilization, and connectivity are tied to the physical nature of a SAN. It is the protocols and configurations that define how to meet these needs. The next section considers these aspects of a SAN.

3B.2.2   The Fibre Channel-Based SAN

The three most important elements in legacy SANs are the Fibre Channel link, FC switches, and storage. Most installed SANs are FC based; however, Ethernet/IP is used in newer SANs. For now let us concentrate on Fibre Channel; IP SANs are considered in the next section. What is Fibre Channel, what are its sweet spots, what are the defining configurations, and what is its future?

Fibre Channel is a serial, gigabit link technology designed to connect nodes to storage or to transfer data between nodes. Its speed ranges from 1 Gb/s to 4 Gb/s. In April of 2004, the members of the FCIA [FCIA] ratified the extension of the Fibre Channel road map to include 8-Gb/s Fibre Channel (8G FC) for copper backplanes and copper cable storage device interconnects. This ensures that Fibre Channel continues to provide the highest performance available for storage interconnects.

Fibre Channel is not a network link in the Ethernet sense so its use is confined to local configurations. It may be configured in three ways: point to point, routed via a switch (or a mesh of switches), or in a serial arbitrated loop. Despite its name, it comes in both copper and optical flavors. The copper version is limited to about 20 m (2G FC) but can reach 80 km using single mode optical fiber. See [SNIA] and [FCIA] for more details on FC. Additional features of importance are as follow.

◆ Guaranteed data delivery using hardware-related protocol handshakes. This is a key feature of FC, as data reliability is assured by hardware on the host bus adaptor (HBA) card and not by a software stack running on the host CPU. Off-loading data delivery to hardware operations rather than software can increase the throughput by an order of magnitude, plus it frees the main CPU for other more important tasks. TCP/IP has traditionally been very host CPU intensive so FC has gained the edge. This is changing, as will be seen when iSCSI is discussed.

◆ Very efficient data packaging with 2K frame sizes.

◆ Connection oriented virtual circuits for excellent QoS.

The Fibre Channel protocol stack is shown in Figure 3B.11. The Fibre Channel standard defines a multilayered architecture for moving data. There are five hierarchical layers defined, named FC-0 to FC-4, with FC-4 being the highest layer. The layers are defined as

◆ FC-0—The interface to physical media.

◆ FC-1—The encoding and decoding of data (8b/10b) and out-of-band physical link control information for transmission over the physical media. See Appendix E.

◆ FC-2—The transfer of frames, sequences, and exchanges comprising protocol information units.

◆ FC-3—Common services required for advanced features, such as striping, hunt group, and multicast.

◆ FC-4—This layer describes the interface between Fibre Channel and various upper level protocols. A number of different protocols are supported as ULPs, including SCSI, IP, and high-performance protocols such as HIPPI and ATM. These protocols are encapsulated and carried over FC. In 2005, SCSI command mapping is the most widespread, with the others used sparingly or not at all. SCSI mapping over FC is called FCP.

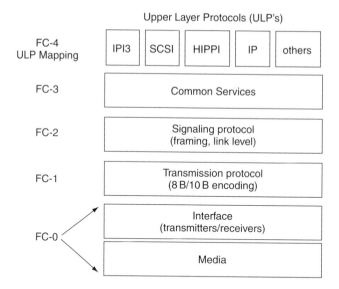

Upper Layer Protocols (ULP's)

FC-4
ULP Mapping

| IPI3 | SCSI | HIPPI | IP | others |

FC-3 — Common Services

FC-2 — Signaling protocol (framing, link level)

FC-1 — Transmission protocol (8 B/10 B encoding)

FC-0 — Interface (transmitters/receivers)

Media

FIGURE   Fibre Channel protocol stack.

3B.11

Fibre Channel may be configured in three different ways as Figure 3B.12 shows. Point to point is the most straightforward. Many FC systems used the arbitrated loop (FC-AL) method to move data. FC-AL is a topology in which nodes are connected together in series and share the aggregate bandwidth of a single FC link. Of course the serial configuration is not ideal due to the obvious problems with a daisy chain; however it is efficient for connecting together a few FC disc drives on the same link. Hubs eliminate some of the daisy chain problems but switches are the preferred way to route FC frames.

From personal experience, hub-based FC-AL is problematic for mission critical real time AV applications. Processing errors, disc failures, intermittent links, or simply rebooting a device can all incur a "LIP storm" (loop initialization primitive). LIP storms can cause multiple devices to send nonstop streams of initialization commands, requiring a great deal of hands-on attention by IT personnel until the problem is located and the loop stabilized.

With FC-AL, the available Fibre Channel bandwidth of 800 Mb/s (1G FC) is shared among all loop members. If four nodes are communicating with four separate storage devices on the loop, each connection

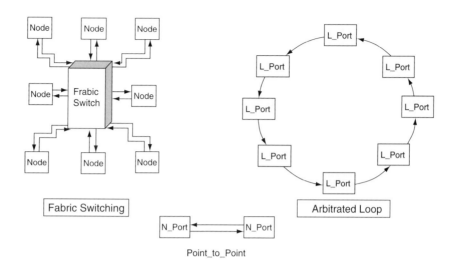

Fibre Channel connectivity choices.

pair would be able to sustain approximately 200 Mb/s. Because of this sharing, devices must arbitrate for access with the loop before sending data.

The alternative to the loop is switching fabric. A fabric requires one or more switches to interconnect host computers with storage devices. With a fabric, the bandwidth is not shared. Each connection between two ports on the switch has a dedicated 800 Mb/s so a 16-port FC switch can support 8 paths (8 in, 8 out) and each path can support 800 Mb/s of payload (1G FC). The switch's internal engine needs to handle at least 8 × 800 Mb/s = 6.4 Gb/s in one direction and 6.4 Gb/s in the other (FC is a full duplex). Also, switches are very resilient to problem nodes. Bad citizen nodes (intermittent, LIP storms, etc.) do not disturb the traffic on the other ports. This is another reason why a switch is the preferred interconnect (compared to FC-AL) when building a real time AV centric FC network.

Fabric switches are reasonable in price compared to a few years ago when they were considered exotic devices. Several companies sell them with \$400/port (1 G) being common in 2005. Of course for bigger switches (such as the Brocade SilkWorm 12000 Director) with 128 ports the cost/port is more because it is a high-end product with loads of extra features. Blade-based FC switches have now been made available (see Appendix K). In the final analysis, using switch fabrics offers better fault tolerance and QoS compared to hubs with FC-AL for demanding AV applications.

At the high end is the so-called Fibre Channel director. This is a glorified switch by another name. There is no industry-wide definition of a director, but the common traits as seen from a survey of several FC directors by different vendors are as follow.

- ◆ Hot upgradeable firmware
- ◆ Dual elements: power supplies and control modules
- ◆ Hot pluggable elements (backplane is an exception): Boards, Power supplies, control modules, and GBIC I/O ports
- ◆ At least 64 ports

A FC director switch fits an enterprise that has the following needs:

- ◆ very high SAN reliability
- ◆ downtime for upgrades is very small
- ◆ a large port count
- ◆ limited personnel for managing many small switches

As you evaluate FC switches versus directors the differences will center on brute force switching versus sophistication. The legacy SAN is built out of FC-based elements. Does IP have a place in a SAN architecture? This is considered in the following section.

3B.2.3   Hybrid SANs: Merging FC and IP

Within the last few years there has been a lot of work to move SANs to TCP/IP based networking. Why? FC-based SANs require specialized hardware and FC is an expertise not common in many IT departments. Without a doubt, Ethernet/IP has won the networking wars. Managing

Ethernet/IP is common knowledge and already a part of the day-to-day operations in most companies. To many IT managers, the move away from FC to all Ethernet would be welcome if the price/performance goals could be met, but Ethernet/IP is far from a shoe in. The cost of deploying Fibre Channel, particularly the cost of the switches, has come down dramatically. Top-notch performance is still easier to achieve with FC. There is a huge engagement of deployed FC-based SANs and these will not be converted to IP SANs overnight. Also, any scaling up of existing SANs will demand FC-compatible technology, not forklift upgrades. That being said, there is a strong case for IP SANs as this section will show. Table 3B.2 outlines [SNIA] some of the benefits when using IP to extend a SAN.

3B.2.4   IP SAN Technology Choices

There are three relatively new technologies that have been invented to meet the needs of the IP SAN coexisting with the FC SAN. These are iSCSI, iFCP, and FCIP. Each has a definite purpose and application area. In practice, there are three types of SAN: all FC (today's legacy), hybrid FC and TCP/IP, and all TCP/IP. iFCP and FCIP are designed for hybrid FC/IP SANs and iSCSI is designed to be a full FC replacement technology. See Figure 3B.13 for a view of the migration from legacy FC to IP SANs. Fibre Channel will survive the onslaught of IP but its market position will diminish for sure. Time will tell if IP completely swamps FC or FC holds its ground.

IP networks	FC networks
Global scale	Local data centers
Many switching nodes (1000s)	Few switching nodes
Heterogeneous link support	Excellent QoS, high data rates
QoS a strong function of TCP and network reach	Homogeneous links/switches
Built-in recovery means routing around bad links or switches	Automatic rerouting not easy
Well understood by the IT staff	Less familiar to IT staff

TABLE   Comparing IP versus Fibre Channel

3B.2

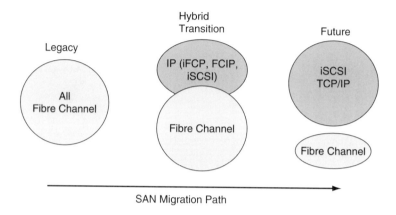

FIGURE   The migration of SAN to all IP.

3B.13

The definitions of these three new protocols are

◆ iSCSI—A TCP/IP-based standard for accessing data storage devices over an IP network using SCSI as the storage access protocol. In relation to a traditional SAN, TCP (usually over Ethernet) carries the SCSI commands rather than Fibre Channel. There are no FC-related protocol layers. iSCSI is a native way to map SCSI over IP. An iSCSI storage array should behave similarly to a FC array in terms of LUN masking and so on.

◆ iFCP—The iFCP specification (Internet FCP) is a gateway-to-gateway protocol for the implementation of the FCP layer (FC-4 SCSI layer) using TCP/IP switching and routing elements instead of Fibre Channel components. The transport, link, and physical layers (FC-0 to FC-3) in FC are replaced with a TCP/IP network and underlying physical link (usually Ethernet). Using TCP guarantees reliability over IP networks and it replaces the reliability functionality inherent in FC's lower layers. iFCP's primary advantage is as a SAN gateway protocol that bridges both FC and IP domains yet has the SCSI FC-4 layer in common.

◆ FCIP—This protocol (FC over IP) standardizes a complete wrapping of all but the physical layers into TCP/IP packets. The IETF has defined similar encapsulations of FC over ATM and SONET. The primary function of FCIP is to forward FC frames. Think of FCIP as a FC extender protocol using IP. Two geographically separated FC SANs may be linked over an IP link using FCIP. This protocol is best used in point-to-point connections between SANs with no FC address routing.

These three similar yet different protocols are often a source of confusion. They all allow a sender to communicate with a receiver over IP using SCSI as the command language. Figure 3B.14 shows the three protocol stacks. TCP/IP maps SCSI commands in all three cases. For another view of the three protocols, consider Figure 3B.15. Some of the key features are

- iSCSI can be used to create a complete TCP/IP SAN with no FC needed. Given the presence of iSCSI ported storage arrays, a SAN may be built without any FC technology. The possibility of a global SAN is enabled.
- iFCP is used to bridge existing FC systems across TCP/IP networks. The IP packets may be routed and managed using FC target addresses. This is a key feature and iSNS is used to associate FC addresses with IP addresses.
- FCIP is used to extend a FC link over an Ethernet/IP link with no routing based on FC addressing. This will find limited use.

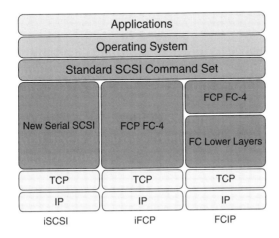

FIGURE   iSCSI, iFCP, and FCIP protocol stacks.

3B.14

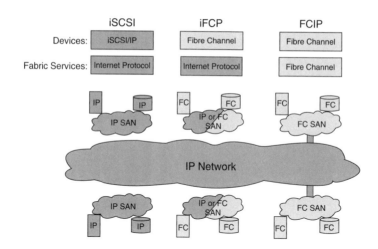

iSCSI, iFCP, and FCIP networking configurations.

iSNS

Snapshot   The Internet Storage Naming Service (iSNS) protocol is designed to facilitate the automated discovery, management, and configuration of iSCSI and Fibre Channel (iFCP) devices on a TCP/IP network. iSNS provides intelligent storage discovery and management services comparable to those found in pure Fibre Channel networks, allowing a commodity IP network to function in a similar capacity as a SAN.

3B.2.5   TCP/IP SAN Performance

How will these protocols be used over the next few years? For upgrades to existing FC SANs, iFCP and FCIP will be used. Performance should be excellent and in line with pure FC configurations if the traffic engineering is modeled correctly. For new SAN installs, designers will choose between FC-based or IP (iSCSI)-based configurations. Given the super performance of FC solutions, will IP/Ethernet be able to equal it? Here are some of the considerations that limit iSCSI SAN performance.

1. TCP guarantees data delivery. In the general case, the host (and target) TCP stack is implemented in the CPU, which uses valuable CPU cycles and may limit the throughput under high data rates.

2. Congestion in the IP network can seriously throttle throughput.

3. Long pipes between host and target can throttle throughput if the round trip delay time (RTT) exceeds some critical values.

4. Large data rates can "choke" the pipe and cause the data delivery to back off.

As it turns out, because all four of these can be optimized for top performance, it is possible to achieve FC-like speeds and reliability in an IP environment. Chapter 6 covers each of these four points in detail under the heading "*TCP/IP Performance.*" A discussion of iSCSI accelerators using TCP off-load engines (TOEs) is also covered there.

To whet your iSCSI appetite, current "low-end" iSCSI storage systems (12 HDD, RAID 50[2]) have benchmarked at ~500 Mb/s read throughput per attached client (single Xeon CPU, no TOE card) with support for six clients pulling ~3 Gb/s aggregate. Write performance is about 60% less than read. Under HDD failure the R/W performance will drop by 30% or more. RAID 10 is a good compromise with more balanced R/W specs but with less total bandwidth available. iSCSI storage with 2.5-Gb/s throughput can support ~50 dual-stream playout clients, each decoding 25-Mb/s DV files.

With the proper care and feeding of TCP/IP, many new SAN installs will use Ethernet/TCP/IP instead of Fibre Channel. It will take years for iSCSI to replace FCP but the road maps to IP are the clear future for main-line applications. In the meantime, hybrid solutions of IP and FC will coexist. Fibre Channel is not dead by any means but it is stepping aside as the grand old man of SAN in favor of the new kid on the block, iSCSI.

Snapshot

iSCSI Terminology

A host needs iSCSI *initiator* software to start an iSCSI transaction. Each transaction terminates at some iSCSI *target* in a storage system. The iSCSI initiator is analogous to an NFS client or an FCP initiator in an FC SAN. iSCSI software initiators/targets are available from vendors for Windows or Linux and other operating systems. iSCSI storage devices are sold stand alone but it is also possible to roll your own by installing the iSCSI target onto a server unit with attached storage.

---

[2] RAID 50 is a RAID 5 with striped data across (RAID 0) all data drives. RAID 10 is a mirror (RAID 1) with striped data across all drives.

3B.2.6   SAN with Virtualization and Cluster File Systems

So far the discussion on SAN technology has focused on connectivity and networking. Two other important aspects are virtualization and the cluster file system. These are discussed in detail in Chapter 3A. Virtualization is a method to carve up the storage into separate volumes assigned to clients and servers as part of the storage management process. However, the CFS gives SAN clients and servers access to a shared file system. Both may be applied to a SAN environment. Figure 3B.16 illustrates how SAN clients and servers can share files (not just storage hardware) by including the CFS. It is good to remember that a SAN does not require a CFS—it is always optional. A SAN provides block-based storage in its most native form. However, if an AV workflow demands file sharing as in a news production or a file playout scenario, then a CFS is often included. Many AV vendors provide a SAN storage with a CFS for editing clusters, AV recording, and playout. In most cases, the CFS should be fault tolerant as well as the storage subsystem. Next, let us review the SAN vendor landscape and then focus on the third item in our trilogy—NAS storage.

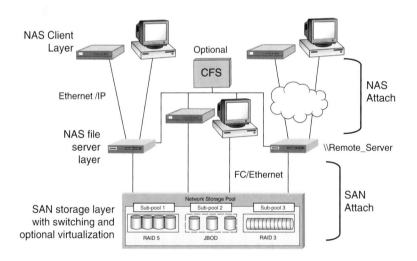

FIGURE   SAN and NAS connectivity.

3B.16

3B.2.7   SAN Vendor Overview

There are many vendors of SAN storage systems from low to high end. Traditional SAN systems are composed of Fibre Channel switches, directors, RAID storage, storage management software, and optional clustered file systems. Some vendors provide for a complete turnkey solution, whereas others provide select pieces of the total puzzle. Some of the top SAN players are Brocade, Cisco, EMC, Hitachi Data Systems, HP, IBM, and SUN. Apple is competing with their Xsan product for the Mac. There are countless others too but studying these vendor's products will give you a good flavor of the landscape. Of special note are the several AV-specific vendors who offer SAN storage in support of their NLEs and video server nodes. There are also several new players entering the iSCSI SAN race. These will compete with the incumbents for this new storage space.

3B.3   NETWORKED ATTACHED STORAGE

NAS storage appears as a remote file server (X: drive or \\Remote_Server) to any attached clients. NAS is a category of storage device that appears as a node on the IP network. A NAS file server does not provide any of the functions that an application server typically provides, such as email or Web page serving. However, the NAS server always provides a file system view of its storage with optional services such as file conversion, bandwidth management, automatic backup, synchronized mirroring (for transparent redundancy), and caching. A typical NAS environment is shown in Figure 3B.16.

For many server installations, the NAS server uses SAN-attached storage. In the simplest case, there is only one NAS server with DAS storage and no SAN. At the other end of the spectrum, there may be many NAS servers sharing storage or using separate storage. The servers may also use clustering technology to create a huge virtual server. As part of a SAN, the servers may be configured with virtualization or a clustered file system, depending on functional needs.

3B.3.1   NAS Attach Protocols

Figure 3B.17 outlines the I/O and basic structure of a NAS server. The server may have SAN, DAS, or internal storage and offer one or more NAS attach protocols, such as NFS, CIFS/SMB, HTTP, or AFP. In a nutshell, a NAS server is a remote file server with all the features that a file system offers. Additionally, some vendors will offer a general-purpose product that includes SAN (FC and/or iSCSI) or even RDMA attach points to create a one-size-fits-all product. Concentrating on the most general-purpose case, a NAS server is the storage and file system for a remote file server transaction. Clients communicate with the server using Ethernet and TCP/IP with an associated file access protocol. In general, the protocols enable a client to establish a session with a remote device, open/close files, R/W files, create and delete directories and files, search for files, and more. There are many more similarities than differences among the various NAS attach protocols.

One of the most common access protocols is the network file system (NFS) and was invented by Sun Microsystems in the 1980s. It was

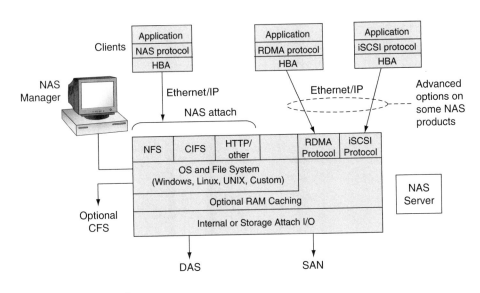

FIGURE   Inside a NAS device.

3B.17

originally designed for file sharing between UNIX systems. Today, NFS is used primarily with machines running some variant of the UNIX OS. Common Internet file system (CIFS) is the nearest neighbor to NFS. It was invented by Microsoft and IBM in 1985 and started life as the server message block (SMB). Starting as a DOS networked file exchange, it has become a worldwide standard for client–server data sharing. SAMBA is the moniker for an open-source implementation of the CIFS/SMB protocol and a Brazilian dance introduced in 1917. The nondance version permits Linux/UNIX systems to masquerade as a Window server, thereby enabling cross platform file exchange. Most NAS servers also support the hypertext transfer protocol (HTTP). This is used for Web-based administrative needs and file download to Web browsers. Finally, some NAS servers support Apple filing protocol (AFP), which is Apple's version of a file-sharing protocol. These protocols tend to coexist peacefully and each has found their niche in the NAS world.

Snapshot

CIFS, NFS, and HTTP: Duct Tape for Networks

Whenever a client connects to a remote server for storage access or Web content, one of these three protocols is commonly used. Without universally accepted access methods, a network (the Internet in particular) would be like a telephone system where every phone used its own brand of touchtone dialing—no one could connect to anyone. NFS and CIFS are more general purpose than HTTP, which was designed to retrieve Web pages. The minimal requirements for CIFS/NFS connectivity are

◆ Mount remote storage as an X: drive (or \\Remote_Server) or equivalent at local client
◆ Remote storage file open, close, R/W, delete, create directories, and so on
◆ File access restriction rights per client/user
◆ Support TCP/IP (some use UDP) for network routing and reliably data transport

Most legacy NFS connectivity uses version 2 or 3. Version 4 was recently approved as an IETF standard (RFC 3010) and includes improved access security and byte level locking (needed when multiple clients are writing to the same file).

3B.3.2   NAS Vendors and Product Features

NAS servers fall into several categories; small appliances, midsize, and enterprise size systems. The following is a representational list of vendors in this space, ordered from low end to high end. It is by no means exhaustive.

◆ Low end: Dell's PowerVault, Iomega's 400M/1TB, Snap Appliance's Snap Server

◆ Midtier: IBM's TotalStorage family, INLINE's FileStorm series, HP's StorageWorks NAS

◆ High end: BluArc's Silicon Server, EMC's Celerra, Exavio's ExaMax 3000, Isilon's IQ series, Network Appliance's FAS series

There are countless others, but studying these vendor's products will give you a good flavor of the landscape. Each of the vendors has a value proposition that attempts to differentiate it from the others. The appliances and midsize servers are often a single server with embedded storage. The high-end enterprise units are built with scalability and load balancing and may include multiple servers clustered to appear as one. One way to cluster a NAS is with a CFS/DFS as described in Chapter 3A. The NAS servers from BluArc use hardware acceleration to speed up all critical paths, such as TCP/IP, CIFS/NFS processing, read/write operations, replication, snapshots, and other storage management tasks. The products from Isilon are AV friendly and support fine grain storage/throughput scaling using server clustering with excellent reliability and load balancing. Exavio also designed their NAS product with media storage in mind and offers a huge storage density (120 TB in one 7-ft. rack) and clever caching algorithms to increase the usable throughput. There is no doubt that NAS storage is mature and well accepted in the modern enterprise and AV facility.

The operating system of a NAS server may be a key selling point. Microsoft's storage server is a big draw because of its familiarity and features. It is an optimized OS for NAS servers. Some NAS vendors, such as Network Appliance, have designed proprietary file systems to add features and performance over nonspecialized operating systems. In addition, the Linux OS has a major market share in this space. Remember, a NAS server is dedicated to behaving like a storage device, whereas a general-purpose server may run applications programs of all types. However, most COTS NAS servers also offer auto-backup, restore, fault tolerance methods (RAID and more), specialized management, and more. To improve access performance as measured by latency and data throughput, some high-end systems support heavy caching. For some applications, a cache can improve the average storage access performance markedly. Even apparently random I/O performance can be improved using clever prediction with caching. See Section 3B.4 for more on caching.

NAS Acceleration over WANs

At times, storage consolidation among disparate facilities or remote storage access is required to improve AV workflows and/or a system's management efficiency. Under these scenarios, WAN data throughput can become the weak link in the operational chain. CIFS and NFS were designed for LAN networks and are chatty protocols with resulting poor performance over WANs. Wide area file services (WAFS) appliances are a new category of product to remedy this problem. These devices are protocol accelerators and use prediction and caching to dramatically improve CIFS and NFS performance. For example, the local appliance will return acknowledgments for routine session creation instead of waiting for a delayed remote machine response.

The performance improvements can be striking. Figure 3B.18 shows an example of a test case using a T1 line at ~1.54 Mb/s from San Francisco to Houston with a round trip delay of 60 Ms. Opening and downloading a 5-MB file takes only 11 s using WAFS, whereas the same file takes 122 s without the appliance. In fact, the data transfer takes only 3 s if the file is in the appliance cache.

For more insight, study the product offerings and white papers from FineGround Networks (owned by Cisco), Peribit Networks (owned by Juniper Networks) or Tacit Networks. These are but a few of several WAFS product vendors.

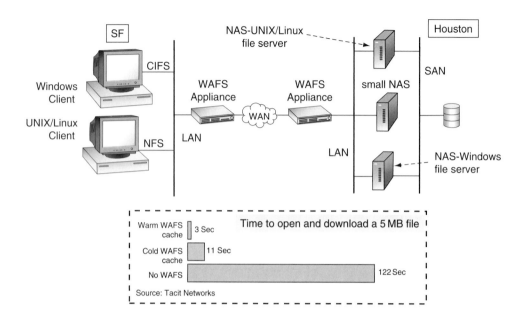

FIGURE   WAFS performance acceleration example.

3B.18

3B.3.3   AV-Friendly NAS Connectivity

The goal of NAS protocols is to provide for easy, reliable remote storage access with low latency and scalable bandwidth. They were designed for the general-purpose computing environment. It is not surprising that they lack some features needed for high-performance AV applications, such as guaranteed access bandwidth QoS and large block ($>>$ 64 KB) R/W to storage. A NAS connection without guaranteed QoS may result in AV glitching when the stream is throttled due to server congestion. Also, NFS and CIFS have associated caching strategies for optimizing small block R/W storage access. Unfortunately, they do not optimize large block R/W access and the caching algorithms leave a lot to be desired in terms of disk access performance.

Because of the potentially poor performance of NFS/CIFS in the large block access AV setting, some vendors have developed proprietary NAS protocols to meet their needs. Avid and Pinnacle Systems are among a few that provide their own protocols. By way of example, the Pinnacle version is called Media Access Server Protocol (MASP) and is used in conjunction with CIFS. There is a MASP software installable agent for the client and server side. Think of MASP as providing the AV client *data path* for all media-related transactions with a NAS server and CIFS as the *control path* (file open, close, R/W, delete, etc.) for the connection. Because MASP bypasses CIFS's data caching methods, it optimizes both small and large data block storage access, thereby guaranteeing a ~2X improvement compared to CIFS alone. Also, it meters every data packet so that a maximum R/W rate may be set per client. This is crucial when many clients connect to the same NAS server. Each client must be an excellent network citizen or mayhem will rule. A single rogue client can ruin the neighborhood if it tries to hog all the bandwidth it can. Shame on bandwidth hogs! Unfortunately, there are no standards in this area so each vendor has been forced to fend for itself. This does not mean that NFS/CIFS cannot be used for AV applications, only that they may compromise performance due to their caching methods.

3B.3.4   NAS and Server Clustering

It is possible to create a "super NAS" server (or some other server type) by clustering N smaller NAS servers. This concept is shown in Figure 3B.19 where a CFS unifies N servers into one. Any client seeking a server may be directed (by a special IP switch or load balancing DNS or other method) to any one server in the cluster based on loading, security, and reliability criteria. Generally, clients do not know the whereabouts or identity of the individual NAS server that is providing the storage. The servers may be heterogeneous devices and located anywhere on the network consistent with the QoS requirements for the cluster. It is possible to create a server cluster without a CFS by synchronizing each of the N servers with the same file image. If one stored file is added/modified, then each of the N servers needs a file system update. Alternatively, the storage may be replicated for each server. This method is very storage inefficient, as N versions are needed compared to only one version if a CFS is used.

Aside from the NAS application, server clusters are useful for general AV computations. Animation rendering, 3D effects, cinema effects, and more are being done on Linux clusters. Each node in the cluster takes some of the computational burden. The nodes may or may not use a CFS.

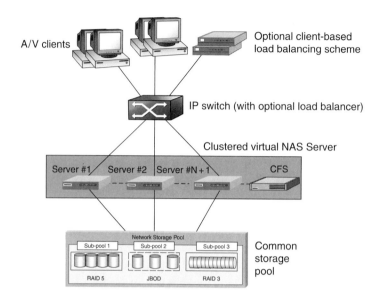

Clustered server and NAS connectivity.

Server clusters are mature and used everyday for a variety of IT operations. They are commonly applied to nonreal time operations but real time clusters do exist. See Appendix C for more information on these leading technologies.

A NAS server cluster (or general server cluster) has several very compelling advantages, among which are

◆ **$N + 1$ reliability using external load balancer**. If one server fails in a cluster of $N + 1$ servers (the 1 is the spare server), a router can direct new client requests to other working servers in the cluster. Seamlessly moving an *active client* from a failed server to a working server is not easy, as the state of any R/W storage transaction must be moved to the new server as well. Most commercial-clustered NAS servers do not automatically migrate active clients to a new server without the current R/W transaction failing. Incidentally, large Web server farms are typically load balanced using an external router or other scheme and a CFS is not normally used.

◆ **$N + 1$ reliability using client logic load balancer**. In a system where each client keeps tabs of their R/W transactions, the client may decide when storage access is below par and request another server in the cluster. This is accomplished by the client closing the existing connection to the cluster and opening one to another server. In this case, the client needs to know the identity of the servers so it can avoid the failed one. The load balancing is performed by assigning each client a list of preferred servers in the cluster, including which one to failover to. This scheme works well when the clients are part of a closed system where custom load balancing software may be installed per client.

Several strategies may be used to guarantee that servers in the cluster are never overloaded. The most popular method is the so called round-robin approach where clients are progressively assigned the next server in a circular fashion. This assures approximately equal loading of all servers. Another method is the client-based one described earlier for $N + 1$ failover.

Adding or removing servers to the cluster may be done "hot" without affecting the overall performance of the cluster. There is almost no limit on how many servers may be included in a cluster. Aggregate cluster bandwidth has been measured up to 12 GB/s in the IBM general parallel file system (GPFS) product. This system is an excellent example of a clustered NAS server. See [IBM] for a reference to a GPFS white paper. There are several installations of the GPFS system with 25+ attached professional AV editors sharing common storage. SGI also offers a Linux cluster using their CXFS AV-friendly CFS. Linux Beowulf clusters are also in general use as Web server farms and NAS file servers.

Snapshot

SAN and NAS

In its most basic form, a SAN provides **blocks** of storage to clients/servers, whereas a NAS provides **file** storage. If a clustered file system spans NAS servers, they appear as one large file server. If a CFS spans SAN clients, they have a view of all stored files.

3B.3.5   NAS, SAN, and the Future

Okay, it is time to connect all the dots. What overall picture is formed? No doubt SAN and NAS systems are finding applications in all types of AV solutions. As the forgoing sections discussed, SAN and NAS are complementary in many respects and will coexist for the foreseeable future. Figure 3B.20 outlines the chief characteristics for each technology with and without a clustered file system. Each of these four solution spaces has been discussed separately earlier in this chapter or in Chapter 3A. Remember, inclusion of a CFS allows for every attached client/server to access all permitted storage *and* files.

Looking forward, when creating medium- to medium/large-scale collaborative AV systems (>16 SD/HD edit, compositing stations, or I/O ports, for example), implementers will likely gravitate toward configurations with file sharing and with iSCSI RAID storage access (quadrant D in Figure 3B.20). This configuration enables scalable storage, bulletproof-reliable systems with an excellent price/performance ratio. The migration toward this configuration will not occur overnight, but there are compelling reasons for this direction. There are no servers or Fibre Channel HW to add complexity, and connectivity is based on an IP/Ethernet infrastructure.

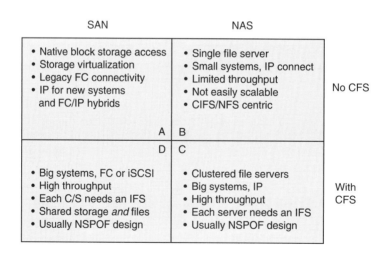

FIGURE   Sweet spots for SAN and NAS storage systems.

3B.20

The one roadblock to the wide-scale adoption of shared storage is lack of an AV industry accepted CFS. As discussed in other sections, implementing a CFS is nontrivial and typically each AV vendor offers one of their own design. As more vendors adopt the open systems approach using Linux, it is possible that a CFS may emerge that is AV friendly and embraced by the AV industry or that a particular CFS may rise to the occasion and become a darling of the AV industry. At present, this seems a distant dream but things can change quickly in the IT world so there is always hope. iSCSI SAN storage connectivity and vendor-specific CFS solutions will likely be the next step in medium/large-scale AV (shared storage) systems design.

Another configuration that shares the spotlight is based on quadrant B (small NAS version) in Figure 3B.20. Several of these systems may coexist as islands and share AV materials via file transfer. The quadrant B system may draw files from an NRT near line storage too. Building large systems out of many smaller ones adds comfort regarding security, reliability, and scalability. Due to the migration to iSCSI, the NAS-based system may take a backseat to IP SANs for large systems but not for small ones. Systems that require the services offered (data backup, for example) by a NAS server will require either a quad B or a quad C system. Of course, time is the great arbitrator in the ongoing contest of SAN versus NAS.

A Sample SAN Plus NAS AV System

A hybrid SAN + NAS AV system is shown in Figure 3B.21. The traditional AV routing infrastructure is not shown. It has the following characteristics:

◆ Quad D IP SAN system offering shared storage and file access to all clients: May scale to many AV clients and may offer excellent reliability.

◆ Quad B small NAS offering a simple island of AV clients using a single file server: Normally limited number of clients. Moderate reliability without additional NAS servers as alternates. May have more than one island if needed.

◆ IP/Ethernet connectivity at all levels.

◆ NRT second-tier storage and archive: The second-tier storage is a repository for all AV materials needed by workflows. This reduces the amount of online storage needed.

◆ Industry-accepted systems' management schemas and protocols.

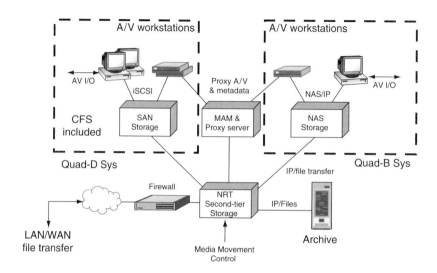

Hybrid large/medium IP SAN and NAS systems.

♦ Media asset management functions available to any client along with low bit rate proxy files.

♦ File Import/Export filtered by a firewall and possible digital rights management process.

Figure 3B.21 focuses on a representational view of what is possible in 2005 using the most appropriate technologies for IT-based AV systems. Of course, there are other configurations based on the four quadrants of Figure 3B.20, but quadrants B and D designs will become commonplace in systems architectures.

Type C will not find widespread acceptance but will be used in some large systems (IBM's GPFS NAS). The quad C server layer adds little functionality compared to the quad D (IP based) configuration for most AV applications. This statement may start a fight in some bars. Why? Well, there is a need to install a small IFS file redirector software component on every type D client/server node, whereas no IFS is needed for type C clients. Yes, the type C "hides" the CFS from the clients because it is embedded in the NAS cluster. Plus, some type C NAS servers offer loads of backup/restore services. These are big advantages. Nonetheless, a quad

D is a compelling solution and achieves excellent storage performance and file access to clients and servers. Finally, quad A will find only niche AV applications (no file sharing support), although it is very popular in general IT business environments.

Of course there are countless reductions and reconfigurations of Figure 3B.21 to meet specific workflows. Also, this discussion is focused on SAN/NAS storage access. There are other classes of systems based on streaming (over IT infrastructure) and file transfer. See Chapter 2 for a more complete discussion of methods for the accessing/transferring/streaming of AV materials. When using DAS, SAN, or NAS data flow may be improved significantly if caching is engaged. The following section outlines the advantages of caching.

3B.4   CACHING METHODS

A cache is defined as a block of memory (RAM or disc less frequently) reserved for temporary storage. Caches usually store data to/from slower disc arrays to make client access faster. When an application references a data address in a storage array, the cache is checked to see whether it holds that address. If it does, data are returned to the application; if it does not, a regular memory access occurs. Caching is not the same as buffering. A buffer is a small (seconds usually) memory for smoothing out irregularities due to network I/O jitter. An AV data cache can do the job of a buffer but its main advantages aim for higher goals. A few definitions are in order before the advantages are outlined.

◆ Cache hit—The request for an external storage R/W operation is fulfilled by the local cache. If an I/O request is met 50% of the time by the local cache, then the network infrastructure is used 50% less and the external storage is accessed 50% less.

◆ Cache coherency—This is the property that accessing a cache gives the same values as the underlying main storage values. Cached data can become stale when other processes change main storage array data.

◆ Cache location—Caches may be in clients, in NAS servers, or in the storage subsystem. Each location has a particular advantage.

Figure 3B.22 shows a typical shared storage client-attached video system with all the caches clearly identified. This system exaggerates the use of caches but for our purposes this is okay. Analyzing cache efficiency can quickly become a very complex problem due to the variables of hit rates, cache sizes/locations, I/O rates, and workflows. Instead of a quantitative view, let us have a qualitative discussion. In general, AV data caching will have advantages in the following areas.

1. Increase reliability of networked clients
   ◆ Networked clients with an internal cache have increased reliability. The local cache allows for a client to lose contact with the external storage (due to temporary connectivity or storage failure) and still function as the cache is temporarily substituted for the external storage. Consider the case where a playout client is prequeued with a playout file. The cache holds queued data. On command to play the file, the client reads from the local cache so even if the external storage connection is disrupted, the local client outputs the A/V without a glitch.

2. Increase networked bandwidth utilization
   ◆ Local cache hits effectively make an I/O appear faster. RAM-based cache R/W data rates are greater than that obtainable from

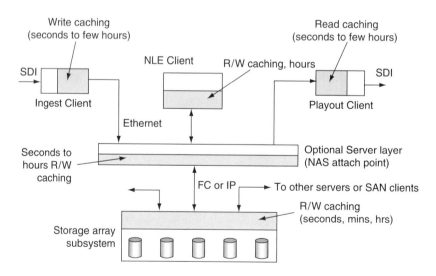

FIGURE

3B.22

Caching methods in a shared storage system.

external storage. As a result, a cached R/W operation reduces network traffic on average and appears to increase the application's read/write I/O rates.

3. Increase storage array data rate utilization
   ◆ When a storage array has a cache in the main controller, hard disc R/W operations may be block optimized to increase the array's total available data rate.
   ◆ When the HDD has cache, the R/W operation is noticeably faster.

4. Decrease system storage access latency
   ◆ Whenever a cache hit bypasses external storage hard disc access, then the apparent R/W latency will decrease.

Cache efficiency is a strong function of data workflows. Ingest clients are write intensive with almost no cache hits for any cache in the system. Playout clients are read intensive with some cache hits likely for repeated plays. Editing clients are read intensive with some write activity. Many NLE editors never modify actual master AV data but only generate compositional metadata lists to record the edit decisions. NLE clients show the most potential for cache hit advantages as users jog and shuttle around the timeline. In the worst case, because a cache adds little or no performance gain if data streams have no read cache hits, the smart system designer must not count on cache gains for worst-case operational scenarios.

The use of caches is a vendor design decision. Some vendors may not include them and another may design for their advantages. Good caching implementations will yield all or some of the advantages listed already, but only when the workflows and data access modes are favorable, which will rarely be 100% of the time. See [Exavio] for a good example of a cached storage system designed with AV applications in mind.

3B.5   IT'S A WRAP: SOME FINAL WORDS

This chapter has put some flesh on the bones of DAS, SAN, and NAS. Figure 3B.23 is a symbolic look at the overall landscape and expands the simplified view of Figure 3B.1. These three technologies are being used in AV system design every day. Expect to see the iSCSI SAN become the

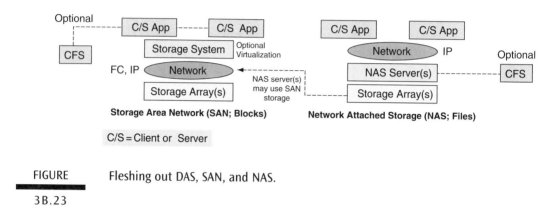

Direct Attached Storage (DAS; Blocks)

Storage Area Network (SAN; Blocks)   **Network Attached Storage (NAS; Files)**

C/S = Client or Server

FIGURE   Fleshing out DAS, SAN, and NAS.
──────────
3B.23

next wave of networked storage. It offers compelling performance, IP networking, and excellent management. Of course, a CFS is needed to extend a SAN to a shared file paradigm. Also, NAS clusters can take advantage of iSCSI as their storage access method. Storage is moving in the right direction for AV systems and its advancement will provide AV configurations with new and compelling workflows at excellent price points.

REFERENCES

[**Cameron**] Don Cameron, Greg Regnier, *Virtual Interface Architecture*, Intel Press, April 2002.

[**Chudnow**] Christine Taylor Chudnow, *Fibre channel dukes it out with IP*, Computer Technology Review, July 2002.

[**Exavio**] See www.exavio.com/examax9000.html for examples of cached storage system components.

[**FCIA**] Fibre Channel Industry Association; see www.fcia.org for more information on FC and associated technology.

[**Glass**] GlassHouse Technologies, White Paper, *Uncovering Best Practices for Storage Management*, www.glasshousetech.com, 2002.

[**Gruener**] Jamie Gruener, Giganet (now owned by Emulex), *Building High-Performance Data Centers*, 2000.

[**IBM**] *An introduction to GPFS for Linux*, www.ibm.com and search for the paper's title.

[**SNIA**] Storage Networking Industry Association; see www.snia.org and www.snia-europe.org for a wealth of information on SAN and NAS.

[**SNIA 2**] *SNIA IP Storage Forum White Paper Internet Fibre Channel Protocol (iFCP): A Technical Overview*, www.sni.

4 Software Technology for AV Systems

4.0 INTRODUCTION

Only a few years ago AV devices were hardware centric with little software value. Video product engineers were experts in real time, frame accurate, circuit, and system design. Today the roles have reversed, with software being the center of functional value for most devices. Software, coupled with sufficient CPU power, can perform almost any AV operation in real time. Thanks to Moore's law, AV-specific hardware is being relegated to I/O and some real time 2D/3D effects and signal processing. Standard definition MPEG encoding and SD/HD decoding are done easily with a common CPU. HD MPEG 2 encoding, especially MPEG 4 Part 10 (H.264), still requires hardware support. Looking down the road, hardware AV processing will become a rare commodity and software will rule. One interesting trend is to use the Graphics Processing Unit (GPU, common in all PCs) to do real time 2D/3D effects.

Figure 4.1 illustrates the software centric nature of AV systems. Of course not every element has AV I/O, but this only increases the saturation of software in the overall system. This chapter provides a working knowledge of the salient aspects of software as a system element. This includes:

- User application requirements
- Software architectural models—four main types
- Software implementation frameworks—.NET, J2EE, CORBA
- Open source systems

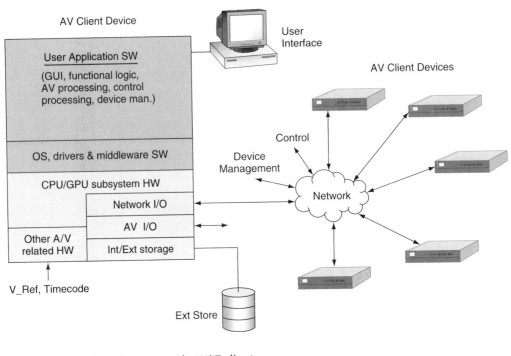

AV Client Device

User Interface

AV Client Devices

User Application SW

(GUI, functional logic,
AV processing, control
processing, device man.)

OS, drivers & middleware SW

CPU/GPU subsystem HW

Network I/O

AV I/O

Int/Ext storage

Other A/V
related HW

V_Ref, Timecode

Ext Store

Control

Device
Management

Network

FIGURE   The software centric AV/IT client.

4.1

◆ Real time systems
◆ SW maintenance and system evolution

There is no specific coverage of programming languages or practices, although they are touched on along the way. Let us get started.

4.1   USER APPLICATION REQUIREMENTS

Software user applications come in a variety of shapes and sizes. The two main user application types are server based and client based. Software "services" are used by applications but are not usually a complete application. Service concepts are covered later in the chapter. Figure 4.2

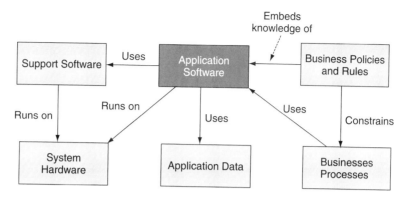

FIGURE

4.2
Context diagram for application software.
Source: Software Engineering 7 [Sommerville].

illustrates a "context diagram" for **user application software.** This high-level example shows the action verbs associated with an application. Context diagrams illuminate how a software component integrates into the bigger picture. When completing an application design, a context diagram is useful to locate missing or duplicate relationships.

The core application features and issues are as follow.

♦ Functionality—Does it meet your operational and business needs?
♦ GUI look and feel—How does the interface behave?
♦ Ease of use—Are operations intuitive? Training needed?
♦ Performance—Are benchmarks available to compare vendors' products?
♦ Quality of result—Does the AV output quality meet business needs?
♦ Standards—Does it conform where applicable?
♦ Reliability—Is it stable when pushed to limits?
♦ Network friendly—How well does it perform during network anomalies?
♦ Is there a readily available pool of trained users?

When evaluating a product, consider these minimal aspects of design. Some of the features are best evaluated by the technical staff and others by end users. Since the GUI is ever present, let us focus on the six principles for good design as outlined in Table 4.1.

Principle	Description
User familiarity	The interface should use terms and concepts familiar to most users. The interface should not break the good habits that most computer users have formed.
Consistency	Comparable actions should operate the same way. All commands and menus should follow the same format.
Minimal surprise	Users should never be surprised by behavior.
Recoverability	Users should be able to easily recover from errors—undo, for example.
User guidance	When errors are encountered, provide meaningful advice to recover. A dialog box displaying "Error, OK?" is not acceptable.
User diversity	The interface should provide different levels of operation—novice to advanced users if appropriate.

TABLE   User Interface Design Principles

4.1

Some well-meaning interface designers try to be too clever and break the first rule believing that new user paradigms are a good idea. True, there is room for innovation but designers should leverage users' good habits when possible. Some applications are self-contained and do not depend on any networked resources, e.g., using a word processor on a PC. More and more, however, applications rely on available services across a network. The end goal is a great application that users find compelling from all angles. What software architectures are available to reach this goal? The next section reviews the four main types in common usage.

4.2   SOFTWARE ARCHITECTURES[1]—THE FOUR TYPES

At some point when discussing software, religion usually enters the picture. For sure, there are priests and disciples of programming methods and languages, operating systems, and architectures. In a nondenominational

---

[1] Although our focus is on software, the concepts discussed in this section relate equally to computer systems in general so the terms *software system* and *computer system* are used interchangeably.

sense, this section reviews the central methods for solution construction using software.

What is a software architecture? Whether it is the humble microwave oven's embedded processor or Google's 15,000+ searching computers, their software is constructed using a *topology* to best match the functional objectives. If done poorly it is a pile of spaghetti code; if done well it is more like an award-winning building or well-thought out city plan.

The city plan is a useful analogy. For example, central Paris is constructed as a star centered on the Arc de Triomphe whereas Manhattan is grid based. These are high-level plans and do not constrain how individual buildings look and feel. From this perspective, let us examine four different "city plan" architectures without concern for the individual buildings. Figure 4.3 shows the taxonomy of the four plans under discussion. For sure, there are other ways to divide the pie. This illustration is not meant to be a rigid definition but merely one way to segment the architectures under discussion. The first to be considered is the centralized architecture.

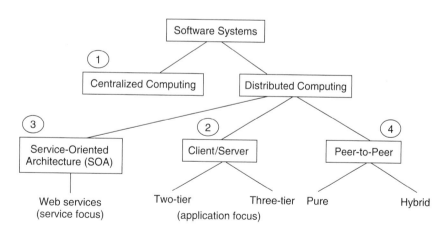

FIGURE   Software system's taxonomy.

4.3

4.2.1   Centralized Computing

This is a monolithic system ranging from a basic computer with user interface (the ubiquitous stand-alone PC) to a mainframe computer system with hundreds of simultaneous users running multiple applications. This is the most basic plan and has been in use since the days of ENIAC, the world's first electronic, programmable computer. It filled an entire room, weighed 30 tons, and consumed 200 kW of power when commissioned in 1945 [ENIAC]. Oh, the joy of Moore's law.

Many AV devices are monolithic in nature. The stand-alone video clip server, character generator, PC-based edit station, and audio workstation are all examples. Most of these are single user applications. Older mainframe systems never found a niche in AV applications and are less popular with the advent of client/server methods. Large, centralized systems suffer from scalability and reliability problems. See Figure 4.4 for a view of these two types of design.

Moving on, another class of system is distributed computing. This main class is divided into three smaller classes. The following sections review these methods.

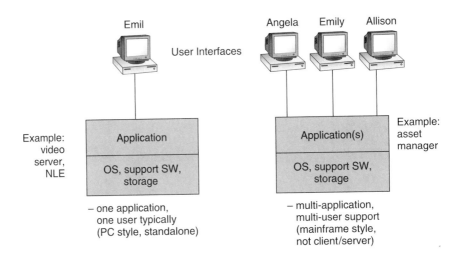

FIGURE   Single and multiuser centralized systems.

4.4

4.2.2   Distributed Computing

In this category, there are three main classes (marked 2, 3, and 4 in Figure 4.3). All share the common attribute of using networking and distributed elements: that when combined, create a solution. The three classes are as follow.

1. **Client/Server[2] (application focused)**
   a. Two tier C/S (flat)
   b. Three tier C/S (hierarchical)
2. **Service-Oriented Architecture (SOA)**
   a. Web services
3. **Peer-to-Peer**
   a. Pure
   b. Hybrid

   Let us review each of them.

4.2.2.1   The Client/Server Class

The Web as we know it rests on the bedrock of the client/server architecture. The client in this case is a Web browser and the server is a Web server accessed via an address such as http://www.smpte.org. The C/S model is found in all aspects of modern software design, not just Web-related systems. There are three layers to a client/server dialog: presentation, application, and data. These layers are glued together using various middleware connectivity protocols. Figure 4.5 (top) shows middleware as a connector that links the various layers as needed. Middleware is discussed in more detail in Section 4.3.

Figure 4.5 (bottom) shows three different but common C/S configurations.

---

[2] In this chapter, the term "C/S" is used to represent client/server and the relationship between these two elements.

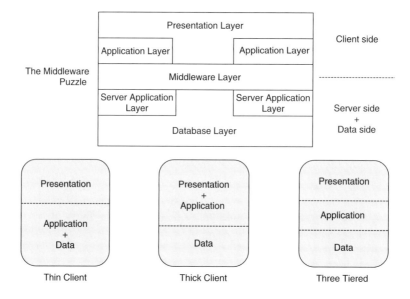

FIGURE   Middleware and layering options.

4.5

◆ **Thin client**: The presentation layer is on the client, and the application logic and data are on the server. An example of this is a terminal with a simple Web browser connecting to a Web server. The client is called "thin" because it only hosts the browser and not the application or data functions. This is a two-tier model.

◆ **Thick client**: Both the presentation and application logic are on the client; hence its thickness. An example of this is a sales report (spreadsheet) where data cells are filled in from a remote database. This is a two-tier model.

◆ **Three tiered**: In this case, the client supports the presentation, the server supports the application logic, and the data base is the third layer. Examples of this abound, and many Web servers are based on this model. The client is thin in this model.

Figure 4.6 illustrates examples of two- and three-tier models in a networked configuration.

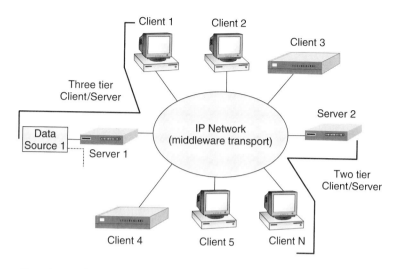

Client/server in a two- and three-tier architecture.

As the naming implies, clients and servers are separate entities that work together over a network to perform a task(s). An exact definition of client/server is cumbersome so let us define it by its characteristics. The following definitions were loosely paraphrased from [Orfali].

◆ **Server**: The server process is a provider of services, and the client process is a consumer of services. The C/S method is a clean separation of function based on the idea of a service. The service may be a complete application (Web server, file server, email server, etc.). A service may also perform a simple function, such as a file converter or a currency value converter.

◆ **Asymmetrical**: There is a many-to-one relationship between clients and servers. *Clients* initiate a dialog by requesting a service. *Servers* respond to requests and provide a service. For example, one Web server can provide Web pages to thousands of simultaneous clients.

◆ **Transparency of location**: The server may be anywhere on the network or even within the client platform. The client has no knowledge of the server's location. Client interfacing hides the connectivity to the server.

In reality, servers that are distant from the client will offer a large response time if the network QoS is poor.

◆ **Mix and match**: The client and server platforms may be heterogeneous and allow for any combination of OS and programming languages on either side. This is why a PC or Mac Web browser can access the same Linux-based Web server without interoperability problems (ideally). This is a key feature and allows programmers to choose the client/server OS and programming language that best suits their needs.

◆ **Scalability**: C/S systems can be scaled horizontally or vertically. Horizontal scaling is adding/removing clients with little or no performance impact. Vertical scaling adds servers to meet loading and performance requirements.

These client/server characteristics permit systems to be built with distributed intelligence across a network. Clients may have human interfaces. As a result, there is no reason to be dogmatic in our definition of the C/S configurations, but rather embrace the openness and flexibility of the concepts.

Take another peek at Figure 4.6. The two- and three-tier nature of C/S is illustrated. The notion of three tiers adds a database layer. Instead of integrating the database into the server, it becomes a separate element that may be shared by many servers. By separating the data storage aspects from the service aspects, it is easier to scale and manage large systems. Hierarchical systems provide for scalability and data separation at the cost of complexity. Specialized versions of C/S are grid and cluster computing, which are discussed in Appendix C.

In the framework of AV systems, the C/S configuration is quite popular. Figure 4.7 illustrates two examples. The two-tier NAS server example is discussed in Chapter 3A. With the three-tier model, media asset management (MAM) servers share a common database, which permits application server scaling independent of data. The three-tier model is a great way to scale a system. Of course the networking QoS should support the C/S sustained data rates. Failover is not shown but could be included in the design. Next, let us look at a specialized version of C/S called the service-oriented architecture.

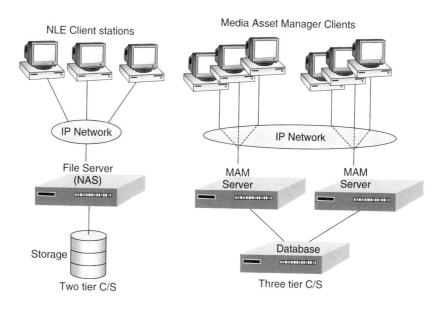

Example AV applications using client/server.

4.2.2.2   The Service-Oriented Architecture

The sage Bob Dylan once penned (1963):

> *Don't stand in the doorway*
> *Don't block the hall*
> *For he that gets hurt will be the one who has stalled*
> *— For the times they are a-changin*

Dylan's words are great advice to any who want to constrain software to the comfort of application-focused client/server or stand-alone systems. These methods are quietly giving up space to various forms of the service-oriented architecture (Figure 4.3, item 3). In the general sense, the SOA is a collection of loosely coupled services that are interoperable and technology agnostic. SOAs are not new, they have been around since computers began providing services for other computers to use.

Closely aligned with the general concepts of the SOA are **Web services**.[3] This is a specific implementation of the SOA where standardized services are made available over a network connection. The following section outlines the main aspects of a Web service.

4.2.2.3   Web Services Model

A service is a software component that provides well-defined functions using a standardized data interface. An example is a service that converts currency from dollars to Euros. The input to the module is a dollar amount, the method is to convert to Euros using the current exchange rate data, and the returned value is in Euros. If the service is well defined, then any client can call on it for the conversion service. Importantly, the service may be called by a variety of unrelated user applications. It is not difficult to imagine a collection of individual services whose aggregated functional power is equivalent to say a stand-alone application server.

Figure 4.8 shows a single service for converting dollars to Euros in a server environment. The component is invoked by some external caller and it returns the value in Euros based on the input value in dollars. Another example is a file metadata service; provide a file name and its structural metadata is returned—compression format, aspect ratio, bit rate, length, and so on. One of the more important aspects of service definition is its interface specification so that any heterogeneous client may use the service.

A Web service is hosted by a server computer. Servers may host simple services such as the currency converter or comprehensive applications such as a NAS filer. These are completely different models. An application server usually runs a single software application supporting N simultaneous clients. A Web services hosting server may run K unrelated services each supporting M clients. Basic service scaling is easy as they are divided among as many machines as needed. The next section illustrates an example of services scaling.

---

[3] Don't confuse Web services with a Web server, they use completely different software models. The differences are outlined in the course of this chapter.

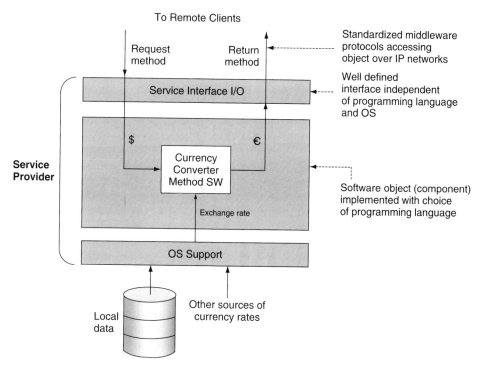

Example of a software service.

Divide and Conquer

Figure 4.9 illustrates a component-based but monolithic software application supporting one user. Component C1 is the main element and directly or indirectly calls on the other internal components (C2–C9) to perform functions. The user application example is a stand-alone MAM system with limited scalability, fault tolerance, upgradeability, and overall flexibility. It does not rely on Web services to perform any of its functions.

Now, what if we want to scale the stand-alone MAM application to allow hundreds of simultaneous users? One approach is to apply the divide-and-conquer rule: build a large system out of smaller parts. Let us break out select components and recreate them as Web services. Using services increases computing power and reusability.

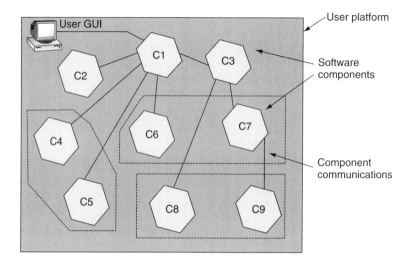

FIGURE

4.9

Stand-alone MAM application composed of software components.

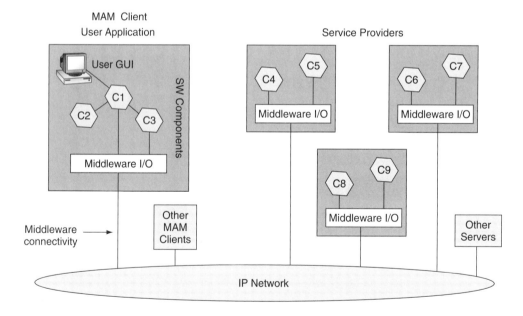

FIGURE

4.10

Distributed service computing environment.

Figure 4.10 illustrates a distributed service computing environment. Each MAM client calls the component services as needed to effectively create the functional equivalent of Figure 4.9. Each service performs a small task but not a total MAM application. In the end, it is all about one networked process calling on the services of others to create higher functional value as the result of their integration.

To no surprise, middleware is key in distributed computing. Standards guarantee that heterogeneous clients and servers can interoperate. Middleware concepts hide remote access details such as client/server language and OS differences, marshalling of data, and network interfacing. Ideally, clients should not be aware that services (C4–C9 in Figure 4.10) are remote. Of course, if the remote servers or networking have a poor QoS, then the user client application performance will suffer. The next section details a standardized method to implement the Web services model.

4.2.2.4   The W3C Web Services Model

The World Wide Web Consortium has defined a version of Web services that is in wide usage. See [Erl], [Barry], [Graham], and www.w3.org/2002/ws. The W3C specification defines the interfaces and middleware but is silent about OS, programming language, and CPU choices. W3C methods fill out many of the details left open in the generic view of Figure 4.10. Designers have great latitude in how they implement services using tools defined by the W3C.

Web services [IBM] have the following characteristics.

♦ Self-describing: Web services have a well-defined interface.

♦ Published, found, and invoked over the Web: A network is the communication media that Web services participants—requestors, brokers, and providers—use to send messages.

♦ Platform and language independent: Web services can be implemented on different platforms with a variety of programming languages.

Both Internet client/server and Web services use IP networking as a transport mechanism, but their purpose and implementation are different. Traditional Web servers return HTML text/graphics that are displayed in a browser. Web services, however, return XML messages/ data to a client process that subsequently uses the information. For the most part, Internet client/server applications are process-to-human centric whereas Web services are process-to-process centric.

Figure 4.11 shows two methods by which a client queries for the length of a news story. In the first case, the client uses the PC browser and accesses a Web server (with media asset management functionality) that provides the query/response operation. The client/server transaction is HTML/HTTP based. This is an example of a "thin client" as shown in Figure 4.5. In the second scenario, the client runs a local MAM application installed on the PC. This application calls upon the Web services query/response operator when needed. The MAM client application formats the response for display. This is an example of the "thick client" shown in Figure 4.5. The Web service query/response interface is defined using a SOAP/XML methodology. Each of these two methods has trade-offs in terms of performance and user look and feel.

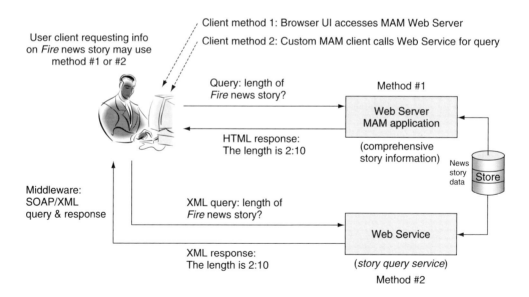

SOAP and XML—The clean way to communicate

Snapshot Pass the SOAP and XML, please. SOAP has floated to the top as a preferred way to transport XML messaging. XML is widely used for packaging messaging and data elements. SOAP/XML forms the foundation layer of the Web services stack, providing a basic process-to-process messaging framework that other layers can build on.

Under the Hood of Web Services

Web services may be advertised so that others can use them. For example, the "story query service" in Figure 4.11 can publish its service methods to a registry. Applications can then find the story query service and use it. Figure 4.12 shows the three players in the Web services dance: the service provider, the service consumer, and the service broker (a directory or registry). The dance goes like this:

1. The service provider registers its methods with the service broker. The broker knows the location and methods of every registered service.
2. Service consumers (clients) inquire of the broker to locate a service.
3. The broker returns the service address and methods.
4. Clients may then use the service as needed (transactions 4 and 5 in Figure 4.12).

The key tools in Figure 4.12 are SOAP, XML, WSDL, and UDDI. SOAP and XML are explored in Section 4.3 and the TipSheet sidebar. The Web Services Description Language (WSDL), expressed in XML, defines the methods and data structures employed by a service. It offers the first standard way for clients to know exactly what methods a service can perform. Consumers parse a WSDL document to determine the operations a Web service provides and how to execute them. UDDI is the Universal Description, Discovery and Integration protocol. A service provider registers their service functionality, expressed in WSDL, with the directory using UDDI. The discovery broker in Figure 4.12 supports both UDDI as a registering mechanism and WSDL as a service descriptor. Web services can exist without UDDI, but the services must be advertised by other means. A study of Figure 4.12 shows the common use of XML/WSDL for message exchange.

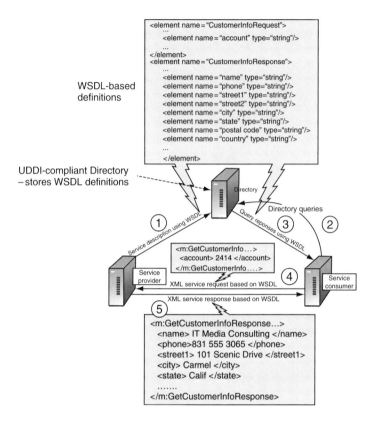

FIGURE

4.12

W3C's Web services communication model.

Concept: [Barry].

The Web services concept holds great promise for AV environments. There are many workflows used daily in TV stations, post-houses, and other AV facilities worldwide that can benefit. Imagine a collection of Web services for logging, cataloging, querying, archiving, controlling, scheduling, notifying, transferring, converting, testing, analyzing, and so on. Vendors can develop a cache of these services and use them to create turnkey solutions based on customer need or a competent AV facility staff programmer can assemble these services to perform useful applications. This may not be practical for small facilities but may be for larger ones. The possibilities are endless. Of course, the real time capabilities of Web services depend on the QoS of the service definition.

Interestingly, Google provides a free Internet query method (see www.google.com/apis) using Web services. A client process accesses the Google search engine using XML/WDSL and gets query results returned. This is similar to transactions 4 and 5 in Figure 4.12. This is especially useful for process centric Web searches.

Next, the fourth architecture under consideration, peer to peer (Figure 4.3 item 4), is reviewed.

4.2.2.5   Peer-to-Peer Computing

The term P2P refers to a class of systems and applications that use distributed resources to perform functions in a decentralized way. P2P systems may be classed as outlined in Figure 4.13 [Milojicic]. Layer two of the diagram shows the three main application domains. These are further segmented into eight specific application areas. No doubt, P2P has become a household name with the advent of Napster, Kazza, BitTorrent, Gnutella, and other file-sharing programs. However, we should not paint P2P as evil—it has plenty of legitimate applications. Let us look at the three main domains for P2P.

The first one is ***parallel systems***. They split a large task into smaller pieces that execute in parallel over a number of independent peer nodes. The SETI@Home project has aggregated tens of thousands of "client" computers to harness 2.2 million years of equivalent computer time and counting. True, this is also an example of grid computing but it uses P2P concepts. The second domain is that of ***content and file***

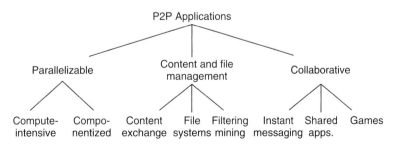

FIGURE   P2P application classifications.

4.13   Source: HP Labs [Milojicic].

management and is mainly associated with file sharing, be it legal or illegal. Streaming too is supported by some applications. See Appendix I for a novel P2P streaming model. The third domain is P2P *collaboration*. Examples of this type are AOL and Yahoo's instant messenger (IM) and multiuser gaming (MUGs). Groove's Virtual Office (www.groove.net) is a P2P application suite for sharing files, workspace, and other information. There has been little professional AV use of P2P to date, although some facilities have used it on internal, protected networks for file exchange.

P2P Architectural Examples

It is not difficult to imagine the topology of a pure P2P network (see Figure 4.14 for an example). Each node is a computer with one or more network connections to other nodes. Nodes interconnect using 1:1 communication for the purpose of data exchange. However, because any given node can support more than one P2P conversation, the diagram shows a general 1:N connection space. In reality, the connections are networked and not hard wired as the diagram may imply. There is no notion of a server or other hierarchy. This is true anarchy and one reason why it is virtually impossible to control and manage traffic

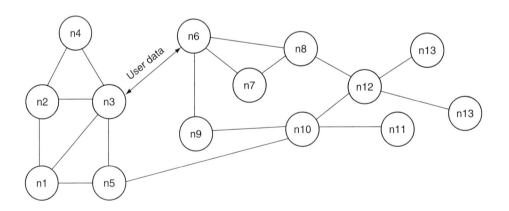

FIGURE   Pure P2P architecture.

4.14

between peers on the open Web. The Gnutella method relies on pure P2P, for example.

Aside from the pure P2P model, there is the hybrid form as seen in Figure 4.15. Anarchy gives way to hierarchy with the introduction of a directory server. The original Napster system, among others, used the idea of a main server to provide a list of files (or other information) and locations to clients. Once the client locates a file, the server connection is broken and a true P2P relationship takes over. The server makes file location a snap but is a bottleneck in what is otherwise an infinitely scalable architecture. Of course, the directory server can be replicated, but this leads to other issues. This model is good for private networks and the server adds management features. The Kazaa model uses the idea of a super-node to act as a server. Some nodes are dedicated to act as servers and to communicate to other super-nodes to create a single virtual server.

Performance of P2P networks is problematic. Because of its decentralized nature, performance is influenced by three types of resources: processing power and its availability, storage, and networking. In particular, low delivery rates can be a significant limiting factor. Data sourcing client disconnect is a major issue when transferring large files. On the plus side, P2P can scale to millions of users with a combined computing power of trillions of operations per second.

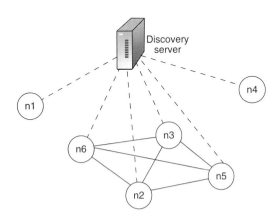

FIGURE   Hybrid P2P architecture.

4.15

4.2.3   Architectural Comparisons

So, how does all this stack up? Which of the four architectural classes in Figure 4.3 has the edge? Well, it all depends on who the "user" is and what advantages and functionality are required. All four types find practical application use. The following summarizes some key aspects of the four systems.

1. Centralized. Older, multiuser mainframe use is diminished greatly and defers to client/server methods. The single user, ubiquitous stand-alone PC rules the client world. Most legacy AV gear is stand-alone by design, such as VTRs, character generators, and NLEs. If connected to a network, the client becomes part of a C/S scenario in many cases. Dedicated devices such as A/V and IP routers are special cases of stand-alone systems.

2. Client/Server. It is the most powerful networked architecture in modern use. It is mature and offers advantages to users (inexpensive, accessible), application developers (tools galore, standards), and IT maintenance staff (management tools).

3. Service-Oriented Architectures. This space has been divided among several different Web service implementation frameworks (discussed later). Its strengths are scalability, aggregate reliability, manageability, and widely available development platforms and tools.

4. Peer to Peer. P2P is generally "out of control" in terms of IT's management, QoS, and security needs. There are some exceptions to this, but for the most part, P2P is not popular in professional applications.

The distributed architectures (2, 3, and 4) rely on various forms of middleware to tie the pieces together. The following section reviews the essentials of middleware.

4.3   MIDDLEWARE CONNECTIVITY

Middleware is the layer of functionality that connects systems over networks for exchanging information between them or, put another way, is the "glue" that ties various distributed software layers together. Most

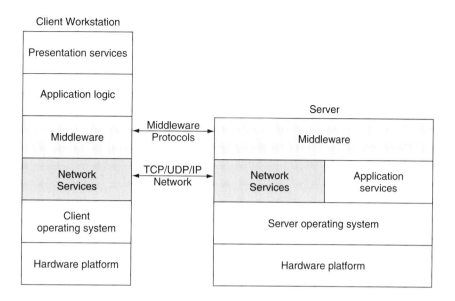

Client Workstation

Server

FIGURE

4.16

The role of middleware in a client/server transaction.

middleware technologies are platform independent but some are vendor specific. Figure 4.16 demonstrates how middleware operates as a communication layer between client and server. In general, middleware is used in a variety of distributed computing architectures.

Figure 4.17 outlines a common scenario where middleware ties the client(s) and server(s) together. For client/server interaction using middleware, the sequence of communication events is outlined in Figure 4.17 and later. The example illustrates a client calling a remote currency converter service. The sequence of events is as follows.

1. Client application formats user data structures and calls the currency converter service on the remote server.
2. Client middleware *marshals* the data into the select middleware format (RPC, RMI, HTTP/SOAP, etc.) and sends it over the network to the remote server. Importantly, the middleware data structures are independent of programming language (and OS) choices, which allows for true heterogeneous client/server communications.

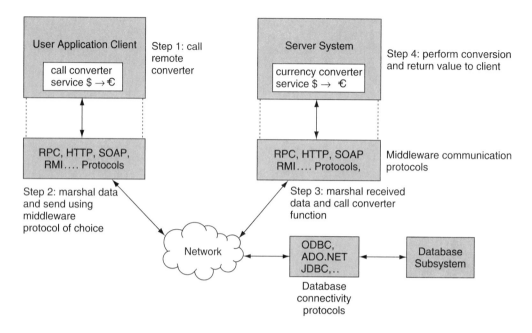

3. The remote server receives the data structures and formats them for the target function (currency converter) in the local programming language.

4. Server application formats a response, marshals the data structures, and returns them to the client over the network. At this point a complete middleware transaction has occurred. In effect, steps 3, 2, 1 are repeated in reverse order to return the response to the client.

Ideally, a remote function across the network behaves as a locally called function. However, due to network delay and other network anomalies, this may not be so. There is generally no QoS defined for these protocols, so moving real time AV with them is problematic. They are best used for nonreal time operations: query, simple control, user interface, database access, application services, and so on. With sufficient care, some may be used to stream AV if needed. These are not mutually exclusive protocols. Some systems will use one or more depending on the needs of the overall solution.

The following middleware protocol standards are in widespread use.

♦ **Remote Procedure Call (RPC)**. RPCs provide the means for one program to call the services (a procedure or other program) provided by a remote machine. The response is usually some data elements or status report. The RPC is the oldest protocol in this class. Millions of systems use the RPC library. See RFC 1831/1833 for more information.

♦ **Hypertext Transport Protocol (HTTP)**. This is the primary communication protocol for connecting browser-based clients to servers over the Web. In a secondary sense, it is also used as a generic connector between a client, not necessarily browser based, and a server.

♦ **Simple Object Access Protocol (SOAP)**. This is a basic means to move XML messaging between programs connected over a network. SOAP embeds XML data structures and the package is transported using HTTP. Typically, a SOAP message (the request) is sent to a remote receiver and it counters with another SOAP message (the response). XML is a good means for exchanging business-related information. See www.w3.org for more information on SOAP. The combination of SOAP/XML is the backbone of Web services. See Chapter 7 for a discussion of XML.

♦ **Remote Method Invocation (RMI)**. RMI is the basis of distributed object computing in a Java environment. It provides the tools necessary for one Java-based component to communicate with another Java component across a network. Think of this as an RPC for Java.

♦ **.NET Remoting**. This is a Microsoft concept for communicating between software objects in the .NET environment. .NET Remoting supports HTTP and SOAP (and other protocols) to transfer XML data structures between clients and servers, for example. This is roughly analogous to the RMI as used in a Java environment.

4.3.1   Database Connectivity Protocols

Another aspect of middleware is database connectivity (see Figure 4. 17). What does this mean? For our discussion, this relates to heterogeneous clients or servers connecting to heterogeneous databases. In the context of media, a database may store metadata that describe AV assets. Typical descriptors are title, length, owner/rights, trim points, format, descriptive key words, and so on. Edit stations, ingest control stations, browsers, traffic/programming, and device automation are among the types of clients that require database access.

The granddaddy of the database query is SQL. This is a language for accessing databases and doing adds/deletes and queries of the contents. By itself, SQL does not define how to connect to a database. Over the years several mature protocols have evolved to connect clients to databases. Highlighting the most significant, the following are in daily use.

♦ ODBC (Open Database Connectivity). This is an open standard defining how clients can connect to vendor neutral databases. Microsoft defined it but now it is an international standard and is used universally. Under the hood, ODBC uses SQL for operations on the database. Also, clients do not need to know where the database is located on a network or what brand of database is accessed. Of course, ODBC allows users to access vendor-specific features if needed.

♦ ADO.NET (ActiveX Data Objects). This is the cornerstone of Microsoft's .NET framework for database access. This is an ODBC-compliant API that exposes the features of modern databases to client applications. It was designed for the .NET programming environment.

♦ JDBC (Java Database Connectivity). This provides database access to programs written in Java and JavaScript. It uses ODBC as the core of connectivity.

These database access methods are in wide use. For more information, see java.sun.com/products/jdbc for JDBC and www.microsoft.com for ADO.NET particulars. In the bigger picture, middleware is an adhesive to create a variety of architectures made of heterogeneous, programming language-neutral components.

4.4   IMPLEMENTATION FRAMEWORKS

This section reviews the programming frameworks and major languages used for implementing the architectures discussed in the previous sections. In particular, the focus is on client/server, SOA, and

Web services models. The frameworks and platforms in common use are as follow.

- Microsoft's .NET framework
- Sun Microsystems' Java 2 Enterprise Edition—J2EE framework
- CORBA—Common Object Request Broker Architecture (middleware platform)

.NET is Microsoft's premiere development platform and Web services software architecture. Sun Microsystems developed the J2EE for a similar purpose. Both of these are competing methods for developing client/server and SOA systems. The Object Management Group (www.omg.org) defined CORBA as a platform for distributed computing.

4.4.1   The .NET Framework

The .NET Framework is an integral Windows component for building and running software applications. Figure 4.18 shows the main components in the .NET tool box. The top level relates to Web server technology. Web servers are built with .NET's Active Server Pages (ASP) and ActiveX Data Objects (ADO). The middle layer is the Visual Studio program development environment. This enables programmers to design, write, and debug software applications. The bottom layers support the W3C model for Web services. These three main divisions are mutually independent aspects of .NET.

Key aspects of the .NET Framework are:

- Supports over 20 different programming languages, mainly on X86 Intel/AMD CPUs. Visual C++, Visual Basic, and Visual C# are the most common.
- Works hand in hand with Microsoft's operating systems.
- Manages much of the plumbing involved in developing software, enabling developers to focus on the core business logic code.

.NET has found a home with stand-alone as well as distributed systems. In fact, all of the architectural classes in Figure 4.3 can be implemented

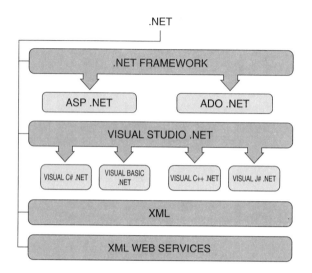

FIGURE
4.18

The .NET working environment.
Concept: Microsoft.

using .NET's tools, components, and connectivity. Many stand-alone AV software applications use the .NET framework and development tools for program creation. Its tight integration with the Windows OS makes it the preferred framework for many software projects.

4.4.2   The J2EE Framework

The Java 2 Enterprise Edition is a programming framework for developing and running distributed multitier applications. Defined by Sun Microsystems, it is a Java-based, modular service-oriented architecture methodology. J2EE is defined by method specifications and corresponding interface definitions for creating individual modules for an enterprise-level computing architecture. It supports Web server functionality and true W3C-based Web services connectivity.

In many ways, J2EE is similar to .NET: it supports distributed services, uses professional development platforms, and uses various middleware protocols for client/server communications. In fact, the .NET functionality stack in Figure 4.18 has equivalent layers in the J2EE world. One big difference is this: J2EE only supports the Java programming language. However, while .NET supporters brag about its multiple language support, Java supporters brag about its multiple OS support, including the popular open source Linux. In principle, .NET is *write many* (language choices) run *once* (only on CPUs with a Microsoft OS), whereas Java is *write once* (Java only) *run many* (choice of CPU and OS). The two camps have taken up arms over the virtues of each platform.

Figure 4.19 shows a simplified view of a hybrid J2EE environment: one browser based and the other Web services based. Browser-based clients (top left) interact directly with Java-based Web servers with Java Server Pages. This is a traditional client/server relationship in a Web environment. Non browser-based clients (lower left) interact with the Web services using W3C-defined middleware. The client executes local application code, which in turn calls the J2EE platform for services.

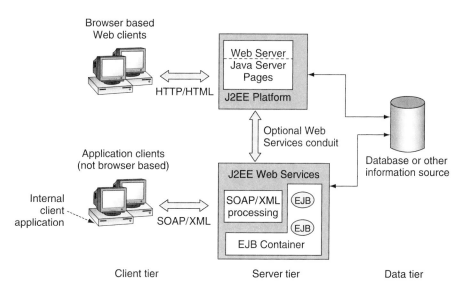

FIGURE

4.19

J2EE environment examples.

Why implement a non browser-based application client? Client-based application programs (written in the C++ or Java language, for example) provide a richer user interface than what is available using HTML with a browser. Browsers offer limited UI functionality due to security issues, e.g., no drag and drop. There are trade-offs galore between these two methods and each has found application spaces.

Figure 4.19 contains references to Enterprise Java Beans (EJB) and the EJB Container; these are J2EE lingo. Sun Microsystems calls Java software components "beans," thus continuing the coffee analogy. Enterprise Java Beans is a component architecture for the development and deployment of component-based business applications. Business logic defines the purpose and methods of a bean. The EJB Container is the run-time environment for executing beans and interfacing to the low-level platform and networking resources. By adding SOAP/XML processing, the EJB components are converted easily to Web services.

There are many vendors offering J2EE-compliant programming environments: BEA's WebLogic, IBM's WebSphere, JBoss (open source), and Sun's Application Server Platform to name a few.

Here is an example of J2EE in action. ESPN selected BBC Technology's (now part of Siemens Media) Colledia "media lifecycle management" for their digital sports broadcast center. The system is able to manage the whole broadcast and production process on a single, digital platform. Colledia uses format standards (MOS, AAF, MPEG, SMEF) and platforms (J2EE, CORBA) to integrate with components from across vendors. Colledia is used to manage and automate the contemporary sport production process and combines tools for ingest, storage, and access with specific tools that automate media workflows.

Over the years, studies have been done comparing and benchmarking .NET to J2EE given the same target application requirements. Which one produces a more responsive user experience and codes with less effort? The most famous and hotly contested benchmark is the **Pet Shop Benchmark**. Instead of taking sides in this long-running debate, read the comments for yourself on the Web. Enter **pet shop j2ee.net** into your favorite browser and jump into the fray.

Snapshot

.NET and J2EE Interoperability; Dream or Reality?

Integrating .NET and J2EE's Web services is feasible. However, there are pitfalls to cross platform integration.

- ◆ Standards are sometimes interpreted differently by the two platforms, although the conflicts are usually minor.
- ◆ Web service functionality is a common subset of both platforms. However, other middleware and messaging aspects do not have defined levels of interoperability. In this case, vendors supply bridges to cross the domains.
- ◆ Few developers are comfortable working in both environments.

4.4.3   The CORBA Middleware Platform

CORBA is an open, vendor-neutral way to enable distributed object architectures in a heterogeneous environment. It is OS, language, and CPU neutral and relies on support vendors and developers to supply the software components. Both .NET and J2EE are vendor controlled whereas CORBA is not. Think of CORBA as the detailed plan for a distributed architecture with all the critical interfaces and middleware defined. It is an open methodology for heterogeneous computing and levels the playing field by allowing anyone to create CORBA-compliant components. BEA Systems, for example, offers CORBA-compliant solutions, as does Sun Microsystems. Some vendors have created tools for CORBA, J2EE, and .NET to interoperate. Although the effort is nontrivial, it is sometimes required in multiplatform installations.

Figure 4.20 shows a simplified CORBA-distributed objects environment. Components (objects) are defined by an Interface Definition Language (IDL). This is a programming language-neutral way to describe the API of a component. Behind the IDL, the chosen programming language implements the method of the object. The ORB (Object Request Broker) is a set of run-time services that can locate remote objects for use. The ORB receives requests from clients and routes them to servers. Clients and servers register with the ORB to make their presence known. As with all distributed architectures, clients have no notion of the location of the servers. CORBA was a forerunner to the Web services model and the two methods share many principles. It is not nearly as popular as .NET or J2EE for new developments.

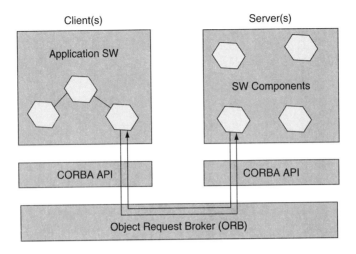

A CORBA-distributed objects environment.

4.4.4   The Connected Services Framework

Microsoft has created a predefined set of modular functions using .NET Web services referred to as the connected services framework (CSF). It includes functions that may be applied to AV system design. Some of the canned services are session management, services catalog, resource management, profile management, and standard business events. Sony Pictures Entertainment has adopted the CSF and improved workflow, enabled new services, increased interoperability, and reduced operational costs [TVTech]. For more information, see the Microsoft Web site and search for "connected services framework."

4.4.5   The Burden to Choose

With so many frameworks and platforms, it begs the question, "Which is the preferred one?" Well, it depends on many factors, some of which are application QoS performance, target HW, programmer experience/productivity, legacy IT infrastructure, choice of OS, cost of HW/SW, interoperability requirements, complexity, and available development tools. Any choice should factor in these and more. The ideal platform should map onto your overall requirements list. One other choice is open source versus vendor-controlled software. The next section outlines this.

4.5   OPEN SOURCE SOFTWARE

The basic idea behind open source programs is simple. When a mass of motivated, freelance programmers are enabled to improve and modify code and then redistribute their changes, the software evolves. If the number of programmers is large, then the speed of software evolution is astonishing [Raymond]. Open source provides free access to program source code. There is licensing required for most open source code, but the restrictions are not onerous. Changes are well controlled, tested, and folded into the next revision. The biggest open source project space may be found at SourceForge (sourceforge.net) with ~103 K registered projects. Many of these are developed by professional programmers and the quality is excellent. Scan the SourceForge for AV tools and applications to see the variety of available software.

Among open source code, LAMP is a set of programs commonly used together to run Web sites. LAMP is an acronym for Linux, the operating system, Apache, the Web server, MySQL, the database system, and the PHP server-side scripting language. Apache is used by ~65% of Web sites worldwide by some estimates. MySQL (www.mysql.com) is the most used open source database.

On the development front, Eclipse (www.eclipse.org) is a popular Java/J2EE integrated development environment. JXTA (www.jxta.org) is a set of protocols for building P2P applications. Interesting, JXTA is short for juxtapose, as in side by side. It is a recognition that peer to peer is juxtaposed to the client/server model. Of general interest is the OpenOffice Suite (www.openoffice.org), which provides desktop productivity tools.

Expect to see more open source programming included with AV vendor solutions. At present there are no "killer app" open source programs for the professional AV space. If a critical mass develops, one day we may see something like MyTraffic, MyAutomation, or even MyVideoServer as an open source program.

4.6   HIGH PERFORMANCE REAL TIME SYSTEMS

For many AV applications, real time performance is the paramount feature. There are several ways to achieve this, and this section outlines the main aspects of RT systems for AV. While it is true that not all C/S implementations are suitable for RT AV applications, some are a perfect match. Some of the important themes are the RT OS, multimedia programming extensions, GPU acceleration, and 64-bit CPUs. Let us consider each of these next.

4.6.1   Achieving Real Time OS Performance

The most common RT system implementation uses the stand-alone architecture with a dedicated OS. General-purpose, Windows-based (NT, XP, Server 2003) products can achieve excellent RT performance, despite the bad rap they sometimes get for long-term reliability in normal desktop use. This does not anoint the Win/OS as an RTOS. Instead, for some selected applications, the OS meets the performance needs for AV. For years vendors have built mission-critical, RT AV applications with the Win/OS. What is the trick?

For one, run only the target AV application—all others are persona non grata. Running unessential background applications (spyware, calendars, instant messaging, etc.) is a recipe for poor AV client performance. In general, the more insular the application, the better its performance. Another trick is to set the OS priority of the target application for maximum utilization. Fine-tuning caching and networking also improve performance. With these precautions, the Win/OS (Linux and the Mac OS too) supports AV applications with excellent performance, long-term reliability, and delivery quality.

An alternative is to base the application platform on a true RTOS, such as Wind River's VxWorks, LynxOS RTOS, Linux RTOS, and Real

Time Specification for Java (RTSJ). An RTOS guarantees excellent OS response times for AV applications. The RTOS environment runs as an embedded system and does not offer general-purpose computer resources. Embedded RTOS systems are single minded and perform exceptionally well under the stress of RT work loads.

Consequently, some AV product vendors have chosen the RTOS approach. For example, the MediaStream video server from Pinnacle Systems uses the LynxOS to control all server operations. As another example, Chyron's Duet Graphics platform uses VxWorks. The choice of RTOS versus non-RTOS depends on many factors and there are trade-offs for each camp.

4.6.2   Multimedia Extensions and Graphics Processors

Digital Signal Processors (DSP) have long been a mainstay for compute-intensive operations. Just a few years ago, real time AV processing used DSP chips or dedicated hardware. Thanks to Moore's law, the momentum has shifted from the dedicated DSP to the general CPU for standard definition video and some HD processing. Although DSP processors are still in demand for some applications, Intel/AMD processors, with DSP-like multimedia extensions (MMX), can perform RT AV operations without resorting to special hardware. The PowerPC has also been optimized for multimedia operations with its Velocity Engine.

Some vendors are only using software for real time SD MPEG encoding/decoding and HD decoding. For HD encoding (especially H.264), hardware acceleration is still needed. Looking at the crystal ball, by ~2008 it will be possible to build a four-channel video server with every AV operation performed in software, including all SD/HD decoding and encoding using only one general-purpose CPU.

Some vendors are using high-performance video/graphics cards (designed for PCs) for video processing, 2D/3D imaging, and font shading. The key ingredient here is the embedded graphics processing unit (GPU). GPUs are being used as graphics accelerators for CPU-sited algorithms. The combination of CPU software algorithms plus GPU graphics acceleration provides amazing RT video processing power.

4.6.3   64-Bit Architectures and Beyond

The jump from 32- to 64-bit processing represents an exponential advance in computing power, not just a factor of two. With 32-bit registers, a processor has a dynamic range of 2^{32}, or 4.3 billion. With 64-bit registers, the dynamic range leaps to 2^{64}, or 18 billion billion. Compute speed and memory addressing range are improved. Many popular CPUs offer 64-bit modes. Microsoft has a 64-bit version of XP and Windows Server. These are joining the mature Unix/64 and Linux/64 choices. Few AV applications have been written to take advantage of 64-bit computing, but this will change with XP/64's and Vista's availability. Porting a native 32-bit application to take advantage of 64 bits is a painful experience so most vendors will not do it. However, new applications may well be written for the 64-bit mode.

Another way to improve compute performance is to use multiple processors. If N CPUs are ganged together, the overall compute power increases. Appendix C outlines grid and cluster computing concepts.

4.7   SOFTWARE MAINTENANCE AND SYSTEM EVOLUTION

It is inevitable that software-based applications and systems will need bug fixes and upgrades. The larger the application, the more likely it will take on a life of its own. Indeed, software needs maintenance just as hardware does. Figure 4.21 outlines several questions you should ask when purchasing vendor software. Do not underestimate the effort to keep the software running smoothly. Also always ask about hot upgrades. Large, mission-critical systems have many elements; make sure that any one element can be upgraded—while the system is running—without affecting the operation of the other pieces.

Lehman's Laws

In 1972 Lehman and Belady [Lehman] published their laws of software evolution. These are reprinted in Table 4.2. They studied the history of

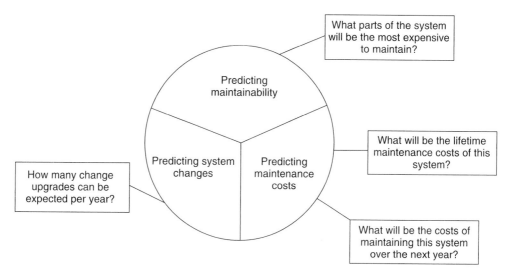

FIGURE

4.21

Software maintenance factors.

Source: Software Engineering 7 [Sommerville].

Law	Description
1. Continual change	Programs become progressively less useful over time—they age
2. Increasing complexity	Programs become more complex over time
3. Large program evolution	Program size, time between releases, and number of reported errors are approximately invariant for each system
4. Organizational stability	Over a program's lifetime, its rate of development is approximately constant and independent of the resources devoted to it
5. Conservation of familiarity	Over the lifetime of a system, the incremental change in each release is approximately constant
6. Continuing growth	The functionality has to increase continually to maintain user satisfaction
7. Declining quality	The quality of a system will appear to be declining, unless it is adapted to the changes in its operational environment

TABLE

4.2

Lehman's Laws of Software Evolution

successive releases of large programs. They found that the total number of modules increases linearly with release number but that the number of affected modules increases exponentially with release number. What does this mean? Repairs and enhancements tend to destroy the structure of a program and to increase the entropy and disorder of the system. More time is spent repairing introduced flaws and less time on developing truly useful new features.

These laws are especially useful for program developers but also for end users. For example, law #6 adds a sense of realism to a product's functionality. Users will be disappointed if the vendor does not regularly add features to the product. Law #7 indicates that as a facility changes, the unmodified products will appear less capable unless they are updated to fit into the new environment. So when selecting a product, it is wise to check with the vendor for their planned upgrade schedule. The larger the software effort behind a product, the more likely that Lehman's laws will apply. Note that these laws apply to large programs and do not necessarily apply in exactly the same way for small or medium size programs. Nonetheless, the principles have some applicability to most programming projects.

4.8   IT'S A WRAP—A FEW FINAL WORDS

AV performance is tied to software performance—and increasingly so. While it is true that many contemporary AV products use the stand-alone architectural model, expect to see distributed systems, especially Web services, applied to AV systems. Non-RT designs have relaxed QoS levels and are easier to build than RT designs. However, RT distributed systems will become part of the AV landscape as developers become more confident and experienced with service-oriented architectures.

Software evaluation, selection, configuration, and maintenance are key to a smoothly run media organization. An educated AV staff will be an agile staff. The future of AV systems' performance, scalability, reliability, manageability, and flexibility lies in software and networked systems. Keep your saw sharp in these areas.

REFERENCES

[**Barry**] Douglas Barry, *Web Services and Service-Oriented Architectures: The Savvy Manager's Guide*, Morgan Kaufmann, 2003.

[**Cummins**] Fred Cummins, *Enterprise Integration*, Chapter 10, Wiley, 2002.

[**ENIAC**] McCarthy, Scott, *ENIAC: The Triumphs and Tragedies of the World's First Computer*, Walker & Company, 1999.

[**Erl**] Thomas Erl, *Service-Oriented Architecture: A Field Guide to Integrating XML and Web Services*, Prentice Hall, 2004.

[**Graham**] Steve Graham et al., *Building Web Services with Java: Making Sense of XML, SOAP, WSDL, and UDDI*, 2nd edition, Sams, 2004.

[**IBM**] Web services definitions were derived from a course presented by IBM.

[**Lehman**] M. M. Lehman and L. A. Belady, *An Introduction to Program Growth Dynamics in Statistical Computer Performance Evaluation*, W. Freiburger (ed.), Academic Press, New York, 1972, pp. 503–511.

[**Milojicic**] Dejan Milojicic et al., *Peer-to-Peer Computing*, HP Labs Research Report, www.hpl.hp.com/techreports/2002/HPL-2002-57.pdf, March 8, 2002.

[**Orfali**] Robert Orfali et al., *Essential Client/Server Survival Guide*, Wiley Press, 1994.

[**Raymond**] Eric Raymond, *The Cathedral and the Bazaar*, O'Reilly, 2001.

[**TVTech**] TV Technology Magazine, May 4, 2005, page 1.

5 Reliability and Scalability Methods

5.0   INTRODUCTION TO HIGH-AVAILABILITY SYSTEMS

Things do not always go from bad to worse, but you cannot count on it. When money is on the line, system uptime is vital. A media services company charges clients $1K/day for editing and compositing services. A broadcaster is contracted to air the Super Bowl along with $100M worth of commercials. A home shopping channel sells $10K worth of products per hour from on-air promotions. It is very easy to equate lost revenue to reliable equipment operations. How much time and money can you afford to lose in the event of downtime? Reliability is a business decision and must be funded on this basis. Therefore, it is straightforward to calculate the degree of reliability (and money to realize it) needed to secure continuous operations. For this reason, AV facility operators often demand nearly 100% uptime for their equipment.

Of course, getting exactly 100% guaranteed uptime is impossible no matter how meticulous the operations and regardless of what backup equipment is available. Getting close to 100% is another matter. The classic "six sigma" measure is equivalent to 3.4 parts per million or an uptime of 99.9997%. In 1 year (8760 h), this equates to about 1.5 min of downtime. Adding another 9 results in 9.5 s of total downtime per year. In fact, some vendors estimate that adding a 9 may cost as much as a factor of 10 in equipment costs at the 99.999% level for some systems. Adding nines is costly for sure. This chapter investigates the techniques commonly used to achieve the nines required to support high-availability AV systems. Also, it examines methods to scale systems in data rate, storage, and nodes.

Reliability Metrics

The well-known mean or average time between failures (MTBF) and mean time to repair (MTTR) are the most commonly used metrics for predicting up- and downtime of equipment. MTBF is not the same as equipment lifetime. A video server may have a useful life of 7 years, yet its MTBF may be much less, just as with a car, boat, or other product. An even more important metric is system *availability* (Av). How do MTBF and MTTR relate to availability?

Let us consider an example. If the MTBF (uptime) for a video sever is 10,000 h and the MTTR (downtime) is 1 h, then the server is not usable for 1 h every 1.15 y *on average*. Because Av = uptime/(uptime + downtime)*100%, then Av = 99.99% availability for this example. As MTTR increases, the availability is reduced. However, if the MTBF is small (1000 h) and if the MTTR is also small (3.6 s, auto failover methods), then Av may be excellent—99.9999% for this case. MTTR is an important metric when computing Av and for achieving highly available systems.

Figure 5.1 illustrates how availability is related to MTBF and MTTR. There are two significant trends. One is as MTBF is raised, the cost of equipment/systems usually raises too. Makes sense: more reliable gear requires better components, design, and testing. However, excellent Av can be maintained even with inexpensive gear if the MTTR is reduced correspondingly. A design can trade off equipment cost against quick repair/reroute techniques and still achieve the desired Av. It is wise to keep this in mind when selecting equipment and system design styles. Even inexpensive gear has the potential of offering excellent Av if it can be replaced or bypassed quickly. Incidentally, for most TV channels, an MTTR of less than ~10 s for the main broadcast signal is crucial to prevent viewers from switching away.

Sometimes the term *fault-tolerant system* is used to describe high availability. Well, nothing is completely fault-tolerant with an Av = 100%. In most so-called fault-tolerant systems, one (or more) component failure

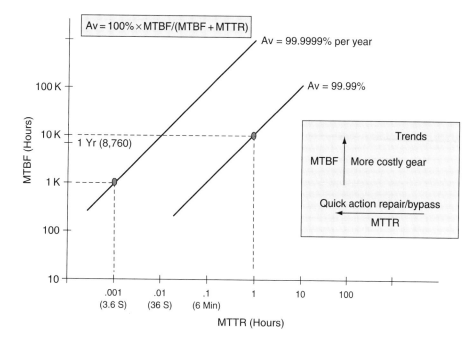

FIGURE

5.1

System device availability versus MTBF and MTTR.

can occur without affecting normal operations. However, whenever a device fails, the system is vulnerable to complete failure if additional components fail during the MTTR time.

One example of this is the braking system in a car. Many cars have a dual-braking, fault-tolerant system such that either hydraulic circuit can suffer a complete breakdown and the passengers are in no danger. Now, if the faulty circuit is not repaired in a timely manner (MTTR) and the second braking system fails, then the occupants are immediately in jeopardy.

This analogy may be applied to an AV system that offers "fault tolerance." In practice, sometimes a single system component fails but no one replaces the bad unit. Due to poor failure reporting alarms or inadequate staff training, some single failures go unnoticed until a *second* component fails months or even years later—"Hey, why are we off the air?" Next, someone is called into the front office to explain why the fault-tolerant system failed.

Detection and Repair of Faults

Figure 5.2 shows a typical fault diagnosis and repair flow for a system with many components. There are two independent flows in the diagram: automated and manually based. Of course, all systems support manual repair but some also support automatic self-healing. Let us focus on the automated path first on the left side of Figure 5.2. Automatic detection of a faulty component/path triggers the repair process. Detection may include HDDs, servers, switch ports, AV links, and so on. Once the detection is made, then either self-healing occurs or a manual repair is required. Ideally, the system is self-healing and the faulty component is bypassed (implying alternate paths) or repaired in some automatic yet temporary way. The detection and repair should be transparent to the user community. In a traditional nonmission critical IT environment, self-healing may take seconds to a minute(s) with few user complaints.

For many AV applications, self-healing needs to be instantaneous or at least appear that way. Ideally, under a single component failure,

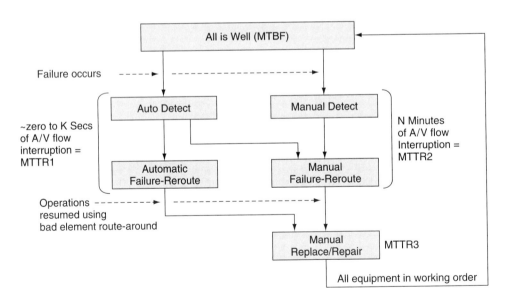

FIGURE 5.2   Failure detection and repair process flow in an AV system.

no AV flow glitching occurs. Quick failover is an art and not easy to design or test for. If done well, automated detection and healing occur in "zero" seconds (MTTR1 in Figure 5.2). In reality, most self-healing AV systems can recover in a matter of a second or so. With proper AV buffering along the way, the failure has no visual or user interface impact.

A no single point of failure (NSPOF) design allows for *any one* component to fail without operations interruption. Very few systems allow for multiple simultaneous failures without at least some performance hit. The economic cost to support two, three, or four crucial components failing without user impact goes up exponentially.

With an SPOF design, a crucial component will cause AV interruption for a time MTTR2. Even with the automatic detection of an anomaly, the manual repair path must be taken as in Figure 5.2. Usually, MTTR2 is much greater than MTTR1. This can take seconds if someone is monitoring the AV flow actively and is able to route around the failed component quickly. For example, Master Control operators in TV stations or playout control rooms are tasked to make quick decisions to bypass failed components. In other cases without a quick human response, MTTR2 may be minutes or even days. It should be apparent that availability (Av) is a strong function of MTTR. SPOF designs are used when the economic cost of some downtime is acceptable. Many broadcasters, network originators, and live event producers rely on NSPOF designs in the crucial paths at least.

The worst-case scenario is the right side flow of Figure 5.2. Without automatic detection, it often takes someone to notice the problem. There are stories of TV channel viewers calling the station to complain of image quality problems unnoticed by station personnel. Once failure is detected, the active signal path must be routed to bypass the faulty component. Next, the faulty part should be replaced/repaired (MTTR3). All this takes time and MTTR2 + MTTR3 can easily stretch into days.

In either case, manual or automatic detection, the faulty component eventually needs to be repaired or replaced. During this time, an NSPOF system is reduced to an SPOF one and is vulnerable to additional component failure. As a result, MTTR3 should be kept to a minimum with a diligent maintenance program. Examples of these system types are presented later in the chapter. The more you know about a system's health, the quicker a repair can be made. Chapter 9 covers monitoring and diagnostics—crucial steps in keeping the system availability high.

Failure Mechanisms

In general, AV systems range from small SPOF types to full mirror systems with offsite recovery. Figure 5.3 plots the available system performance versus the degree of availability for storage components. Similar plots can be made for other system level elements. Levels of reliability come in many flavors, from simple bit error correction to the wholesale remote mirroring of all online data. The increasing performance metric is qualitative but indicates a greater QoS in accessibility, reduced access latency, and speed.

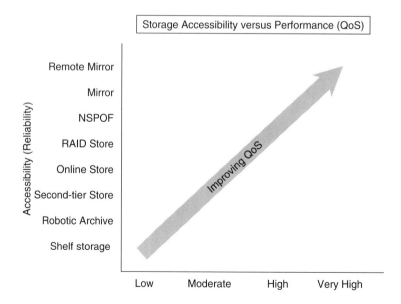

FIGURE 5.3　Storage accessibility versus performance (QoS).

Individual devices such as archives, servers, switches, near-line storage, or AV components each have an MTBF metric. Common system elements and influences (not strictly prioritized in the following list) that can contribute to faults are

◆ Individual device HW/SW and mechanical integrity
◆ Infrastructure wiring faults
◆ I/O, control, and management ports
◆ Middleware glue—communication between elements
◆ System level software—spans several elements
◆ Error reporting and configuration settings
◆ Failover control
◆ Viruses, worms, and other security risks
◆ External control of system elements
◆ Network reliability
◆ Untested operational patterns
◆ Tape and optical media integrity
◆ Poorly conditioned or intermittent power, electrical noise
◆ Environmental effects—out of limits temperature, humidity, vibration, dust
◆ Required or preventative maintenance omitted
◆ Human operational errors
◆ Sabotage

In general, the three most common failure sources are human operational error and software- and hardware-related faults. Depending on the system configuration, either of these may dominate as failure modes.

Elements and influences are often interrelated, and complex relationships (protocol states) may exist between them. Device hardware MTBF may theoretically be computed based on the underlying design. Although in practice, it is difficult to calculate and is known more accurately after measuring the number of actual faulty units from a population over a period of time. A device's software MTBF is almost impossible to compute at product release time, and users/buyers should have some knowledge of the track record of a product or the company's reputation on quality before purchase. Often a recommendation from a trusted colleague who has experience with a product or its vendor is the best measure of quality and reliability.

In the list given earlier, the upper half items are roughly the responsibility of the supplying vendor(s) and system's integrator, whereas the lower half items are the responsibility of the user/owner. Much finger pointing can occur when the bottom half factors are at fault but the upper half factors are blamed for a failure. When defining a system, make sure that the all modes of operation are well tested by the providing vendor(s).

Naturally, one of the most common causes of failure is the individual system element. Figure 5.4 shows a typical internal configuration for a device with multiple internal points of failure. It is very difficult to design a stand-alone "box" to be fault tolerant. For most designs, this would require twice of most internals to allow for a redundant spare. This is cost prohibitive for many cases and adds complexity. In general, it is better to design for single unit failure with hot spares and other methods to be described. That being said, it is good practice to include at least some internal-redundant elements as budget permits.

The most likely internal components to fail are mechanically related: fans, connectors, HDD, and structure. The power supply is also vulnerable. Cooling is often designed to withstand at least one fan failure and it is common to include a second power supply to share the load or as

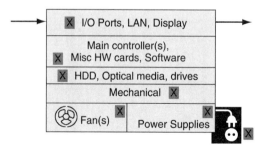

FIGURE   Stand-alone device with potential internal failure points.

5.4

a hot spare. The most difficult aspect to duplicate is the main controller if there is one. With its internal memory and states of operations, seamlessly failing over to a second controller is tricky business.

Ah, then there is software reliability. This is without a doubt the most difficult aspect of any large system. Software will fail and users must live with this fact and design systems with this in mind. The software life cycle is shown in Figure 5.5. From concept to retirement/migration, each of the eight steps should include software design/test methodologies that result in reliable code. Note that some steps are the responsibility of the original equipment vendor, whereas others belong to the operator or installer/SI.

In the classic work *The Mythical Man-Month*, a surprising conclusion was learned from designing software for the IBM 360 mainframe: in complex systems the total number of bugs will not decrease over time, despite the best efforts of programmers. As they fix one problem or add new features, they create another problem in some unexpected way.

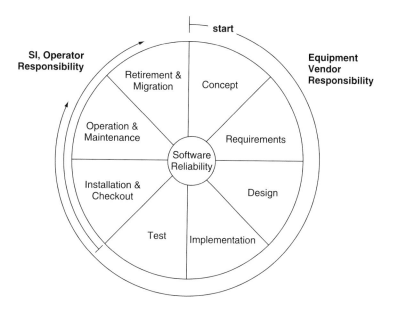

FIGURE   Software reliability and its life cycle.

5.5

There are ways to reduce this condition, but bugs will never go to zero. The good news is that software does not make mistakes and it does not wear out. See more on Lehman's laws later.

One hot topic is software security in the age of viruses, worms, denial of service attacks, and so on. Although a security breach is not a failure mechanism in the traditional sense, the results can be even more devastating. Traditional AV systems never contended with network security issues, but IT-based systems must. Of course AV systems must run in real time, and virus checkers and other preventative measures can swamp a client or server CPU at the worst possible moment with resulting AV glitches or worse. It takes careful design to assure system integrity against attacks and to keep all real time processes running smoothly. One key idea is to reduce the surface of attack. By closing all holes and limiting the exposure to foreign attacks, systems are less vulnerable. This and other security-related concepts are covered in more detail in Chapter 8.

A potential cause of performance degradation—a failure by some accounting—is improper use of networked-attached AV workstations. For example, a user may be told not to initiate file transfers from a certain station. If the advice is ignored, the network may become swamped with data and other user's data are denied their rightful throughput. This is a case of a fault caused by user error.

Before the starting the general discussion of configurations for high availability, let us investigate how reliability is measured for one of the most valuable elements in an AV design: the hard disk drive.

5.1   HDD RELIABILITY METRICS

Because disk drives are core technology in networked media systems, it is of value to understand how drive manufacturers spec reliability. Disk drive manufacturers often state some amazing failure rates for their drives. For example, one popular SCSI HDD sports an MTBF of 1.2 million h, which is equivalent to 137 years. The annual failure rate (AFR) is .73%. How should these values be interpreted? Does this mean that a typical HDD will last 137 years? It sounds ridiculous; would you believe it? What do MTBF and AFR really mean? This section investigates these questions. First, let us classify failure rate measurements into three different domains.

5.1.1 Failure Rate Analysis Domains

Measuring HDD failure rate is a little like the proverbial blind man describing an elephant—depending on his viewing perspective, the elephant looks quite a bit different. The three domains of HDD failure rate relevance are (1) *lab test domain*, (2) *field failure domain*, and (3) *financial domain.*

Lab Test Domain

The *lab test domain* is a well-controlled environment where product engineers simultaneously test 500–1000 same-vintage drives under known conditions: temperature, altitude, spindle on/off duty cycle, and drive stress R/W conditions. In this domain there are a variety of accepted methods to measure HDD failure rates. The International Disk Drive Equipment and Materials Association (IDEMA, www.idema.org) sets specs that most HDD manufacturers adhere to. The R2–98 spec describes a method that blocks reliability measurements into four periods. The intervals are 1–3 months, 4–6 months, 7–12 months, and 13 to end-of-design-life. In each period the failure rate expressed as $X\%/1000$ h is measured. In reality, the period from 1 to 3 months is the most interesting. The results of these tests are not normally available on a drive spec sheet, as evaluating a multivariable reliability metric is a knotty problem and may complicate a buyer's purchase decision.

Many electrical/mechanical components have a failure rate that is described by the bathtub curve as shown in Figure 5.6. A big percentage of "infant mortality" failures normally occur within the first 6 weeks of a HDD usage. If a vendor exercises their product (burn-in) during these early weeks before shipment, the overall field failure rate decreases considerably. However, most cannot afford to run a burn-in cycle for more than a day or two, so failure rates in the field are dominated by those from the early part of the curve. In fact, most HDD vendors test SCSI drives 24×7 for 3 months during the design phase

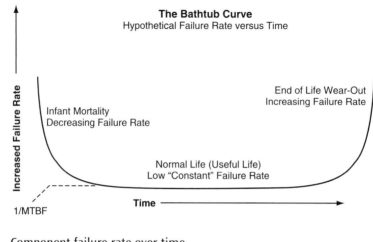

FIGURE   Component failure rate over time.

5.6

only. Correspondingly, ATA drives are often tested using stop/start and thermal cycling. This is yet another reason why SCSI is more costly than ATA drives.

However, about 10 times more ATA disk drives are manufactured today than SCSI and Fibre Channel drives combined. At these levels, ATA drive manufacturers are forced to meet very high process reliability requirements or else face extensive penalties for returned drives. As a result, one could argue that ATA drives are not inherently less reliable than SCSI drives.

The IDEMA also publishes spec R3–98, which documents a *single* $X\%/1000$ h failure rate metric. For this test, a manufacturer measures a collection of same-vintage drives for *only* 3 months of usage. For example, if an aggregate failure rate was measured to be .2%/1000 h, we may extrapolate this value and expect a HDD failure before 500,000 h (100/.2 *1000) with almost 100% certainty. However, the R3–98 spec discourages using MTBF in favor of failure rate expressed as $X\%/1000$ h over a short measurement period. Nonetheless, back to the main question, how should MTBF be interpreted?

Used, correctly, MTBF is better understood in relation to the useful *service life* of a drive. The service life is the point where failures increase noticeably. Drive MTBF applies to the aggregate measurement of a large number of drives, not to a single drive. If a drive has a specified MTBF of 500,000 h (57 years), then a collection of identical drives will run for 500,000 *device hours* before a failure of *one* drive occurs. A test of this nature can be done using 500 drives running for 1000 h. Another way of looking at drive MTBF is this: run a single drive for 5 years (service life, see later) and replace it every 5 years with an identical drive and so on. In theory, a drive will not fail before 57 years on average.

Field Failure Domain

Next let us consider failure rate as derived from units returned from the field—the *field failure domain*. In this case, manufacturers measure the number of failed and returned units (normally under warranty) versus the number shipped for 1 year. The annual return rate or annual failure rate may be calculated from these real world failures. Of course the "test" conditions are almost completely unknown, with some units being in harsh environments and others rarely turned on. The return rate of bad drives is usually lower than the actual respective failure rate. Why? Some users do not return bad drives and some drives stay dormant on distributors' shelves. So this metric is interesting but not sufficient to predict a drives failure rate.

Financial Domain

The final domain of interest is what will be called the *financial domain*. The most useful statistic with regard to HDD reliability is the manufacturer's warranty period. The warranty period is the only metric that has a financial impact on the manufacturer. Most vendors only spec a 5-year warranty—nowhere close to the 100+ years that the MTBF data sheet value may imply. For practical purposes, let us call this the *service life* of the drive. Of course the HDD manufacturer does not expect the drive to fail at 5 years and 1 day. Also, typical warranty costs for an HDD manufacturer are about 1% of yearly revenue. Because this value directly affects bottom line profits, it is in their best interest to keep returns as a very small percentage of revenue.

In reality, the actual drive lifetime is beyond the 5-year warranty period but considerably short of the so-called MTBF value. Conservatively built systems should be biased heavily toward the warranty period side of the two extremes. Of course HDD reliability is only one small aspect of total system reliability. However, understanding these issues provides valuable insights for estimating overall system reliability and maintenance costs.

5.2   METHODS FOR HIGH-AVAILABILITY DESIGN

The remainder of this chapter is devoted to various methods for creating reliable systems out of inherently unreliable devices. As Figure 5.3 shows, it is possible to approach 100% availability by relying on various techniques. So what are they? The high-availability (HA) systems' methods under discussion are RAID for storage, storage clusters, NSPOF, N + 1 sparing, dual operations, replication, mirroring, and disaster recovery.

5.2.1   RAID Arrays

The RAID [redundant arrays of inexpensive (independent, nowadays) disks] concept was invented at UC Berkeley in 1987. Patterson, Gibson, and Katz published a paper entitled *A Case for Redundant Arrays of Inexpensive Disks (RAID)*. This paper described various types of disk array configurations for offering better performance and reliability. Until then, the single disk was the rule and arrays were just starting to gain acceptance. The authors developed seven levels of RAID. Before each technique is formally defined, let us illustrate how RAID works in general terms.

The basic idea behind most RAID configurations is simple. Use a parity bit to correct for one missing (bad) bit out of K bits. Figure 5.7 shows a 6-bit data field and one parity bit. Parity measures the evenness or oddness of the 6-bit string. For example, the sequence 001100 has even parity ($P = 0$), as there are an even number of ones, whereas the sequence 101010 has odd parity ($P = 1$). If any single bit is unknown, then by using the stored parity bit, the missing bit may be reconstructed. Parity is generated using the simple XOR function. It is important to note that data bit reconstruction requires knowledge of which bit is bad. If the 0011X0 sequence in Figure 5.7 is given and $P = 0$ (even number of

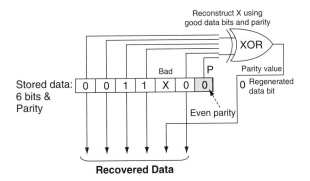

FIGURE
5.7

RAID reconstruction example using parity.

ones), then it is obvious that $X = 0$ else P could not equal zero. Of course the parity idea can be extended to represent the parity of a byte, word, sector, entire HDD, or even an array. Hence, a faulty or intermittent HDD may be reconstructed. With an array of N data drives and one parity drive, one HDD can be completely dead and the missing data may be recovered completely. Most RAID configurations are designed to reconstruct at least one faulty HDD in real time.

Figure 5.8 is typical of an HDD array with RAID protection. In this case, the disks are protected by two RAID controllers. Either can R/W to a disc or do the needed RAID calculations. In the event of one controller going haywire, the second becomes responsible for all I/O. If designed correctly, with a passive backplane and dual-power supplies, this unit offers NSPOF reliability. Note too that each HDD has a direct link to each controller. A less reliable array may connect each HDD to one or two internal buses. In this case, one faulty HDD can hang a bus and all connected drives will become inaccessible. With care, an array can offer superior reliability. Several manufacturers offer NSPOF, dual-controller, arrays ranging from a small 8 drive enclosure to an enormous array with 1,100 drives.

Incidentally, all clients or servers that access the storage array must manage the failover in the event of a controller failing or hanging. For example, if a client is doing a read request via controller #1 but with no response, it is the client's responsibility to abort the read transaction and

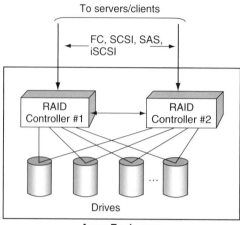

To servers/clients

FC, SCSI, SAS,
iSCSI

RAID
Controller #1

RAID
Controller #2

Drives

Array Enclosure

FIGURE   HDD array with dual RAID controllers.

5.8

retry via controller #2. As may be imagined, the level of testing to guarantee glitch-free failover is nontrivial. This level of failover is offered by a few high-end AV systems' vendors.

Two-Dimensional Parity Methods

Extending the RAID idea, it is possible to design a 2D array with two levels of parity. Figure 5.9 shows a 2D approach. One dimension implements horizontal RAID with parity for correcting data from a single faulty HDD. The second dimension implements vertical RAID and can correct for an *entire array* in the event of failure. The vertical parity method spans arrays, whereas the horizontal method is confined to a single array. The overhead in vertical parity can be excessive if the number of protected arrays is low. A four (three data + VP) array system has 25% overhead in vertical parity plus the horizontal parity overhead. Note that the parity value P3 is of no use when the entire array faults. Two-dimensional parity schemes can be complex, and they offer excellent reliability but are short of a complete mirror of all data.

Two-dimensional parity methods require some sort of master RAID controller to manage parity. For standard 1D parity, each array has its

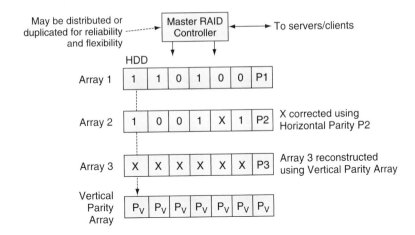

FIGURE

5.9
Two-dimensional horizontal and vertical parity methods.

own internal (normally, as shown in Figure 5.8) controller(s) for managing the parity values and reconstructing data. However, for a 2D parity method as illustrated in Figure 5.9, no single internal array controller can easily and reliably manage both H and V parity across all arrays. However, there are several different controller configurations for managing and reconstructing missing data using 2D parity. Three of these are as follows:

1. A *master RAID controller* manages all parity (H and V) on all arrays. This may be a single physical external controller (or two) or distributed in some way to span one or more physical arrays.

2. Each array has an internal horizontal RAID controller *and* some external controller or distributed controllers to manage the vertical parity. The SeaChange Broadcast Media Cluster/Library[1] supports this form of 2D parity, although the vertical parity is distributed among arrays and is not concentrated in one array.

---

[1] The SeaChange product does not reference "vertical" or "horizontal" parity in its documentation. However, in principle, it uses two levels of distributed parity to support any single HDD failure per array and any one complete array failure.

3. The vertical and horizontal parity schemes are both confined to the same array with an internal controller(s). This case allows for *any two drives* to fail per array without affecting operations. This variation is known as RAID-6 and is discussed later. Interestingly, this case is not as powerful as the other two, as it cannot recover a complete array failure. Judicious placement of the H/V controller(s) intelligence can provide for improved reliability with the same parity overhead.

Factors for Evaluating RAID Systems

Despite the relative conceptual simplicity of RAID using parity, here are some factors to be aware of:

♦ There is normally a RAID controller (or two) per array. They manage the R/W processes and RAID calculations in real time.

♦ The overhead for parity protection (1D) is normally one drive out of N drives per array. For some RAID configurations the parity is distributed across the N drives.

♦ Some arrays use two parity drives. In this case, the layout is $N + P$, with $N + P$ meaning that $2N$ data drives are protected by two parity drives. Each $N + P$ group is called a RAID set. One drive may fail per RAID set so the reliability is better than one parity drive for $2N$ data drives. For example, $5 + 1$ and $7 + 1$ are common RAID set descriptors. This is not a 2D parity scheme.

♦ HDD rebuild effort. In the event of an HDD failure, a replacement unit should be installed immediately. The missing data are rebuilt on the new HDD (or a standby spare). Array RAID controllers do the rebuild automatically. It may take many hours to rebuild a drive and the process steals valuable BW from user operations. Even at 80-Mb/s rebuild rates, the reconstruction time takes 8.3 h for a 300-GB drive. All other array drives need to be read at this same rate to compute the lost data. Also, and this is key, if a second array HDD faults or becomes intermittent before the first bad HDD is replaced and rebuilt, then no data can be read (or written) from the entire array. Because RAID methods hide a failed drive from the user, the failure may go unnoticed for a time. Good operational processes are required to detect bad drives immediately after failure. If the HDD is not replaced immediately, the MTTR interval may become large.

5.2.2   RAID Level Definitions

The next portion outlines the seven main RAID types. Following this, the RAID levels are compared in relation to the needs of AV systems.

RAID-0

Because RAID level 0 is not a redundancy method, it does not truly fit the "RAID" acronym. At level 0, data blocks are striped (distributed) across N drives, resulting in higher data throughput. See Figure 3A.13 for an illustration of file striping. When a client requests a large block of data from a RAID 0 array, the array controller (or host software RAID controller) returns it by reading from all N drives. No redundant information is stored and performance is very good, but the failure of any disk in the array results in data loss, possibly irrecoverably.

RAID-1

RAID level 1 provides redundancy by writing all data to two or more drives. The performance of a level 1 array tends to be faster on reads (read from one good disk) and slower on writes (write to two or more disks). This level is commonly referred to as mirroring. Of course a mirror requires $2N$ disks compared to a JBOD (N disks), but the logic to manage a mirror is simple compared to other RAID redundancy schemes.

RAID-2

RAID level 2, which uses Hamming error correction codes, is intended for use with drives that do not have built-in error detection. Because all modern drives support built-in error detection and correction, this level is almost never used.

RAID-3

RAID level 3 stripes *byte* level data across N drives, with N-drive parity stored on one dedicated drive. Bytes are striped in a circular manner among the N drives. Byte striping requires hardware support for efficient

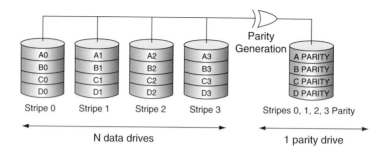

FIGURE
5.10
RAID level 3 with dedicated parity drive.
Concept: AC & NC.

use. The parity information allows recovery from the failure of any single drive. Any R/W operation involves all N drives. Parity must be updated for every write (see Figure 5.10). When many users are writing to the array, there is a parity drive write bottleneck, which hurts performance. The error correction overhead is 100% * [1/N] compared to 100% for the mirror case. A RAID-3 set is sometimes referred to as an "$N + 1$ set," where N is the data drive count and 1 is the parity drive.

Although not an official RAID level, RAID-30 is a combination of RAID-3 and RAID-0. RAID-30 provides high data transfer rates and excellent reliability. This can be done by defining two (or more) RAID sets within a single array (or different arrays) and stripe data *blocks* across the two sets. An array with K total drives may be segmented into two RAID-3 sets each as $N + 1$ drives. For example, with $K = 10$ drives, $4 + 1$ and $4 + 1$ RAID-3 sets may be defined within a single array. User data may be block striped across the two sets using a RAID-0 layout. Note that any two drives may fail, without data loss, if they are each in a different set.

RAID-4

RAID level 4 stripes data at a *block* level, not byte level, across several drives, with parity stored on one drive. This is very similar to RAID-3 except the striping is block based, not byte based. The parity information allows recovery from the failure of any single drive. The performance approaches RAID-3 when the R/W blocks span all N disks. For small R/W blocks, level 4 has advantages over level 3 because only

FIGURE

5.11

RAID level 5 with distributed parity.

Concept: AC & NC.

one data drive needs to be accessed. In practice, this level does not find much commercial use.

RAID-5

RAID level 5 is similar to level 4, but distributes parity among the drives (see Figure 5.11). This level avoids the single parity drive bottleneck that may occur with levels 3 and 4 when the activity is biased toward writes. The error correction overhead is the same as for RAID-3 and -4. RAID-50, similar in concept to RAID-30, defines a method that stripes data blocks across two or more RAID-5 sets.

RAID-6

RAID-6 is essentially an extension of RAID level 5, which allows for additional fault tolerance by using a second independent distributed parity scheme (two-dimensional, row/column computed parity) as illustrated in Figure 5.12. A horizontal parity is calculated across all drives in an array and the value is distributed across all disks, as is vertical parity. This scheme supports two simultaneous drive failures without affecting performance (ideally). This mode is not as popular as other configurations, but several vendors offer storage with this protection level. Compare this to Figure 5.9 where the 2D parity is distributed across several arrays, not only across one array.

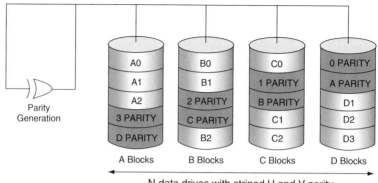

N data drives with striped H and V parity

FIGURE 5.12   RAID level 6 with 2D parity.
Concept: AC & NC.

The salient RAID aspects are as follows:

♦ RAID-0 striping offers the highest throughput with large blocks but with no fault tolerance.

♦ RAID-1 mirroring is ideal for performance-critical, fault-tolerant environments. It is often combined with RAID-0 to create a RAID-10 configuration. This is not an official RAID designation but is nonetheless a common naming. It is very popular in AV systems, despite the fact that RAID-3 and -5 are more efficient methods to protect data.

♦ RAID-2 is seldom used today because ECC is embedded in almost all modern disk drives.

♦ RAID-3 can be used in data intensive or single-user environments that access long sequential records to speed up data transfer. AV access patterns often favor this form, especially the RAID-30 configuration.

♦ RAID-4 offers no advantages over RAID-5 for most operations.

♦ RAID-5 is the best choice for small block, multiuser environments that are write performance sensitive. With large block AV applications, this class performs similarly to RAID-3. RAID-50 is also popular in AV applications.

♦ RAID-6 offers two drive failure reliability.

RAID calculations may be done in the array's I/O controller or in the attached client. In the first case, dedicated hardware is used to do the RAID calculations or the RAID logic is performed by software in the CPU on the I/O controller. However, client-based RAID is normally limited to one client, as there is the possibility of conflicts when multiple client devices attempt to manage the RAID arrays. Microsoft supports so-called software RAID in some of their products.

At least one AV vendor (Leitch) has designed a system where all RAID calculations are done by the client devices in software. This solution is called RAIDSoft and their Nexio server implements it. This system uses backchannel control locking to assign one AV client as the master RAID manager. The master client controls the disk rebuild process. If the master faults or goes off line, another client takes over. Each client reconstructs RAID read data as needed. Client-based RAID uses off-the-shelf JBOD storage in most cases.

RAID techniques are de rigueur for almost all commercial storage products. Some arrays sport dual RAID controllers for failover. RAIDed storage ranges from small products, such as the Apple Xserve RAID (1 TB minimum), to the DataDirect Networks S2A3000 storage array. The latter has four Fibre Channel I/O ports (optional 8), slots for 200 SATA or FC HDD drives, and a maximum capacity of 80 TB.

RAID and the Special Needs of AV Workflows

From the perspective of AV read operations, RAID-3 and -5 offer about the same performance for large blocks. Write operations favor level 3 because there is only one parity-write operation, not N as with level 5. Most AV-based storage systems use levels 3 or 5 (or levels 30 or 50).

For AV operations the following may be important.

◆ RAID data reconstruction operations should have no impact on the overall AV workflow. Even if the data recovery operation results in throughput reduction, this must be factored into the system design. Design for the rainy day, not the sunny one.

◆ It is likely that the reconstruction phase will rob the system of up to 25% of the best-case throughput performance. Slow rebuilds (less priority assigned than for user I/O requests) of a new disk have less impact on the overall user I/O throughput. However, slow rebuilds expose the array to vulnerability, as there is no protection in the event of yet another drive failure.

5.2.3   RAID Clusters

Another form of RAID-0 is to stripe across individual arrays (clustering). Say there are three arrays, each with RAID-3 support ($N + 1$ drives per array). For maximum performance in an AV environment, it is possible to stripe a single file across all the arrays. This increases the overall throughput to three times the throughput of an individual array on average. Typical striping could be such that data block 1 is on array 1, 2 on 2, 3 on 3, block 4 on array 1, and so on in a continuous cycle of striping. However, the entire storage is now three times as vulnerable compared to the same file stored on only one array. If any one of the three arrays faults, all stored files are lost, possibly forever. Hence, the need to guarantee that each array is NSPOF compliant and has a large MTBF metric (see Figure 5.13).

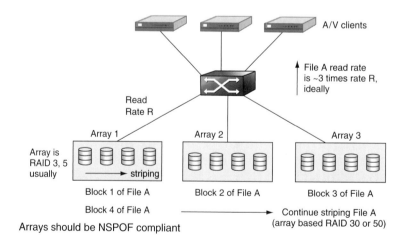

FIGURE

5.13

Array level data striping increases throughput.

Is array striping really needed? For general-purpose enterprise data, probably not. However, if all clients need access to the same file (news footage of a hot story), then the need for simultaneous access is paramount. Take the case where one array supports 400 Mb/s of I/O and the files are stored as 50-Mb/s MPEG. If 15 clients need simultaneous dual-stream access, then the required throughput would be $15 \times 2 \times 50$ Mb/s = 1500 Mb/s. To get this data throughput, the hot file should ideally be striped across at least four different arrays, providing 1600 Mb/s of read bandwidth. Many AV systems vendors support array clustering to meet this requirement.

As it turns out, it is often easier to guarantee full availability to all files than to manage a few hot files. However, some storage vendors allow users to define the stripe width on a per-file basis. Of course, there are practical issues, such as upgrading for more storage and managing the wide stripes, but these can be resolved.

Striping across arrays is a multi-RAID schema. As discussed previously, RAID levels 30 and 50 are methods primarily for intra-array data and parity layout. These RAID level names can be extended to include interarray striping as well (Figure 5.13). There is no official sanction for these names, but striping across RAID sets whether intra- or inter-based is commonly done for AV applications.

In practice, as files are striped across M arrays (a cluster), the aggregate access rates do not increase perfectly linearly. This was the case for files striped across individual HDD devices as shown in Chapter 3A. It was reasoned that striping files across N individual disks increases the access rates but not exactly proportional to N. Also, if files are striped across M arrays, the aggregate access rate is not exactly M times the access rate of one array. Access strategies vary and it is possible to approach a linear rate increase using clever queuing tactics (at the cost of increased R/W latency), but a deeper discussion is beyond our scope.

Scaling Storage Clusters

A cluster of arrays with striped files is difficult to scale. Imagine that the storage capacity of Figure 5.13 is increased by one array, from three to four. If all files are again striped across all arrays, then each file must be restriped across four arrays. Next, the old three-stripe file is deleted. This process must be automated and can take many hours to do depending on the array size and available bandwidth to do the restriping.

If the arrays are in constant use, then the restriping process can be very involved. Files in use (R/W) cannot be moved easily until they are closed. Files in read-only usage may be moved, but with strict care of when to reassign the file to the new four-stripe location. If the cluster is put offline for a time, then the upgrade process will be much faster and simpler. There are other strategies to scale and restripe, but this example is typical. Note that the wider the stripe (more arrays), the more risk there is of losing file data in the event of any array failure.

A few AV vendors offer live scaling and restriping on array clusters for selected products. It is always good to inquire about scalability issues when contemplating such a system. A few of the questions to ask a providing vendor are:

♦ Live or offline restriping? Any user restrictions during restriping?
♦ Time delay to do the restriping?
♦ Scalability range—max number of arrays? Array (or node) increment size?
♦ For wide striping, what is my exposure to an array fault? Do I lose all the files if one array faults?
♦ Are the arrays NSPOF in design?

There are other methods of adding storage and bandwidth, but they tend to be less efficient. One method is to add mirrored storage. For read-only files (Web servers, some video servers), this works well, but for file data that are often modified, synchronizing across several mirrored copies is very difficult and can easily lead to out-of-sync data. More on mirrored storage later on.

5.3   ARCHITECTURAL CONCEPTS FOR HA

"Oh, it looks like a nail-biting finish for our game. During the timeout, let's break for a commercial." Is this the time for the ad playback server or automation controller to fail? What are the strategies to guarantee program continuity? Of course, there are many aspects to reliable operations, but equipment operational integrity ranks near the top of the list. Author Max Beerbohm said, "There is much to be said for failure. It is more interesting than success." What is interesting about failure? How to avoid it!

Figure 5.14 illustrates several HA methods in one system. The design exemplifies SPOF, NSPOF, $N + 1$ sparing, network self-healing, mirroring, and client caching. A practical design may use one or some mix of these methods. Let us examine each of them. Keep this in mind: reliability and budget go hand in hand. The more reliable the overall system, the more costly it is under normal circumstances. Paths of traditional AV flows are not shown to simplify the diagram but redundancy is the stock in trade to guarantee reliable operations.

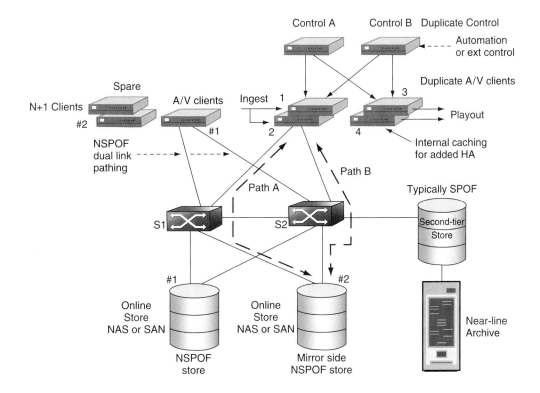

FIGURE   High availability using NSPOF, N+1, mirroring, and caching.

5.14

5.3.1   Single Point of Failure

Why use SPOF when NSPOF is available? Cost and simplicity. The cost of an NSPOF robotic archive is prohibitive for most operations. The need for reliable storage decreases as the device becomes more distant from online activities. In the case of archived AV content, most often the need for materials is predicted days in advance. Near-line storage and servers may be SPOF for similar reasons. If business conditions allow for some downtime on occasion (consistent with the availability, MTBF, and MTTR numbers), then by all means use SPOF equipment.

5.3.2   No Single Point of Failure

NSPOF designs come in two flavors: stand-alone devices and systems. A stand-alone device needs duplicated internal elements (controllers, drives, power supplies, and so on). These can be very expensive and are rare. One notable example is the NonStop brand of mainframe from HP (invented by Tandem Computers in 1975). Also, some IP switchers/routers make the claim of NSPOF compliancy. However, a system centric NSPOF design relies on judicious SPOF element duplication to guarantee continuous operations.

It is not practical to design every system element to provide NSPOF operation. However, dual SPOF elements may be configured to act like a single NSPOF element. Critical path elements may be NSPOF in design. In Figure 5.14 there are several functionally equivalent NSPOF elements: the central switches are duplicated, some paths occur in pairs, control A and B elements are duplicated, and the ingest and playout AV clients are duplicated. Here are a few of the ways that dual elements may be used to implement NSPOF.

♦ A duplicate element lies dormant until needed—a link, for example.

♦ Dual elements share the load until one faults and then the other carries the burden—the switches S1 and S2, for example. Depending on the design, a single switch may be able carry all the load or provide for at least some reduced performance.

♦ In the case of control elements, each performs identical operations. Devices Control A or Control B can each command the ingest and playout nodes. For example, if A is the active controller, then B runs identically with the exception that its control ports are deactivated until Control A faults. Alternatively, A may control ingest #1 and B may control ingest #2. If either ingest port or controller faults, there is still a means to record an input signal using the other controller or ingest port.

In some designs, AV clients are responsible for implementing NSPOF failover functionality. Take the case of recording ingest port #1. Path A is taken to record to online storage #2. If switch S1 faults, a connecting link faults or the online controller faults and then the client must abort the transaction and reinitiate using alternate path B. If path switching is done quickly (within buffering limits), then none of the input signal will be lost during the record process.

For bulletproof recording, an ingest client may record both to online stores #1 and #2 using a dual write scheme. This keeps the two stores in complete sync and guarantees that even if one fails the other has the goods. Additionally, an input signal may be ingested into ports #1 *and* #2 for a dual record. Either port may fail but at least one will record the incoming signal.

Because NSPOF designs are costly, is there a midstep between SPOF and NSPOF? Yes, and it is called $N + 1$ sparing.

5.3.3 $N + 1$ Sparing

While NSPOF designs normally require at least some 2X duplication of components at various stages, $N + 1$ sparing only requires one extra, hot spare, out of N elements. It is obvious that this cuts down on capital cost, space, and overall complexity. So how does it work?

Let us take an example. Say that N Web servers are actively serving a population of clients. An extra server (the $+1$) is in hot standby, off line. If server #K fails, the hot spare may be switched into action to replace the bad unit. The faulty unit is taken off line to be repaired. Of course the detection of failure and subsequent switching to a new standby unit require some engineering. Another application relates to a cluster of

NAS servers. In this case, if a server fails out of a population, it must be removed from service and all R/W requests are directed to a hot standby. For example, if the clients accessing the NAS are AV edit stations (NLEs), then they must have the necessary logic to monitor NAS response times and switch to the spare. Each client has access to a list of alternate servers to use in failover. Failover is rarely as smooth as with NSPOF designs, as there will be some down time between fault detection and rerouting/switching to the spare. Also, any current transaction will likely be aborted and restarted on the spare. Most NLEs do not support client-based storage failover, but the principle may be applied to any AV client.

Of course $N + 2$ sparing (or $N + K$ in general) is better yet. The number of spares is dependent on the likelihood of an element failure and business needs. Some designs select "cheap" elements knowing that $N + K$ sparing is available in the event of failure. This idea is not as daffy as it first sounds. In fact, some designs shun NSPOF in favor of $N + K$ to cut equipment costs, as NSPOF designs can become costly. This is a good trade-off based on the trends shown in Figure 5.1.

Let us take one more example. In Figure 5.15 there are N active video server I/O devices under control of automation for recording and playback. If device #2 devices fails, then by some means (automatic or manual) the recording and playout may be shifted to the spare unit.

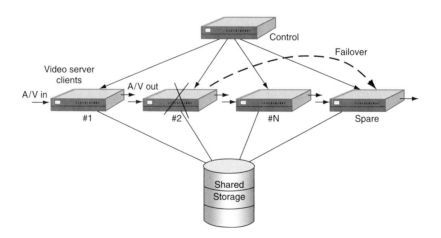

FIGURE $N+1$ sparing for a bank of video server nodes.

5.15

Of course, this also requires coordination of input and output signal routing. Also, this works best when all stored files are available to all clients. In some practical applications, $N + 1$ failover occurs with a tolerable delay in detection and rerouting. It must be mentioned that not all automation vendors support $N + 1$ failover. However, all automation vendors do support the brute force method or running a complete mirror system in parallel, but this requires $2N$ clients, not $N + 1$. Another vital aspect of AV/IT systems is network reliability. A failure of the network can take down all processes. HA networking is discussed next.

5.3.4   Networking with High Availability

Let us dig a little deeper into the methods for creating a high-availability networking infrastructure. Figure 5.16 illustrates a data routing network with alternate pathing and alternate switching. The concepts of layer 2

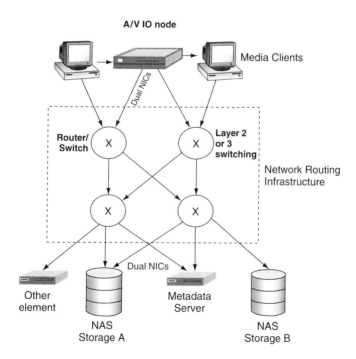

FIGURE   Data routing with alternate pathing and switching.

5.16

and layer 3 switching, routing protocols, and their failover characteristics are discussed in Chapter 6.

Figure 5.16 has some similarities to Figure 5.14. In addition to client-side route/path control, it is possible to create a network that has self-healing properties. It is always preferred for the network to transparently hide its failures than to invoke the client to deal with a network problem. For example, if one switch fails, packets may be routed over a different path/switch as needed. There are a variety of routing and switching protocols and each has its own specific automatic failover characteristics. Frankly, layer 2 switching is very practical for AV workflow applications using small networks. Layer 3 is more advanced in general but can be used to route real time AV for more complex (including geographically separated) workflows.

Finally, there is a method (not shown) for creating a fault-tolerant "virtual router" using a pair of routers. One router is in standby while the other is active. The Virtual Router Redundancy Protocol (VRRP, RFC 2338) performs an automatic failover between the two routers in the event that the active one fails. All connecting links attach to both routers so there is always routed connectivity via one switch or the other. In effect, VRRP creates an NSPOF configured router.

5.3.5   Mirroring Methods

In 1997 Alan Coleman and his geneticists amazed the world when his team cloned a sheep. Dolly became a household name. Cloning sheep holds little promise for AV applications, but cloning data, now that is a different story. Cloned data are also called a data mirror. So how can mirroring juice up storage reliability?

If used in conjunction with $N + 1$ and NSPOF methods, mirrors provide the belt and suspenders approach to systems design. Mirrors may include the following.

1. Exact duplicate store pools. Every file is duplicated on a second storage device. The mirror files are usually not accessed until there is a fault in the primary storage system. Ideally, both sides of the mirror

are always 100% consistent. Figure 5.14 illustrates a storage mirror. Keeping mirrors perfectly in sync is nontrivial engineering. Also, after one side fails, they need to be resynced.

2. Mirrored playout: N active playout channels are mirrored by another N playout channels in lock step. The second set of channels may (one or all) be anointed as active whenever its mate(s) faults.

3. Mirrored record: N active ingest channels are mirrored by another N record channels in lock step. Assume a recording of one AV signal via two inputs. Once the ingest is complete, there are two identical files in storage (using different names or different directories). One may then be deleted knowing that the other is safe or the second file may be recorded onto a storage mirror, in which case both files are saved and likely with the same name.

4. Mirrored automation methods. As shown in Figure 5.14, some facilities run two automation systems in lock step. One system may control half the channels, thereby avoiding the case of a complete system failure or each may control duplicate systems, one active and one in "active standby."

5. Offsite mirror. A storage mirror (or even complete duplicate system) gives a measure of so-called disaster recovery. If the main system fails due to power failure, water damage, or some other ugly scenario, the offsite system can offer some degree of business continuity. In broadcast TV, a facility may transmit many channels out of one facility. Keeping the channel brands alive even with reduced quality levels (using low bit rate materials) or fewer choices of programming is worthwhile for many large broadcasters. Offsite systems (broadcast applications) fall into the following categories.

   a. Complete mirror system of primary system. This can get costly but is used when business conditions warrant. One example is the BBC Center in London. The main playout occurs from a location in London with a 48-h mirror of all playout channels at another location 30 miles away. A WAN link provides the conduit for file transfer to sync the remote site.

   b. Partial mirror of primary system. The partial system may be able to sustain a few of the most important channels for a time.

   c. "Keep alive" system. In this case the offsite provides canned programming on select channels for a time. The canned programming is selected to keep viewers from turning away even if it is not the advertised scheduled programming.

One of the main worries when using a storage mirror is keeping them 100% identical. If one side of mirrored storage fails, then the other unit will likely contain new files by the time the storage is repaired. If this happens, some resync operation needs to occur to guarantee true mirrored files. This should be automatic. Using mirrors is usually based on business needs. If they can be avoided the overall system is simplified.

5.3.6   Replication of Storage

Storage replication is a poor man's mirror. Replicated storage is a snapshot in time of the primary source. As the primary storage is modified, the secondary one is updated as fast as business needs allow for. If the secondary storage is connected via a low bandwidth WAN, then the syncing may lag considerably. For read centric applications where the primary storage changes infrequently, replication is a better bet than a sophisticated mirror approach. The secondary storage may be of lesser performance and, hence, less costly. If the primary storage fails, then some logic needs to kick in to use the secondary files. Many AV system vendors and integrators can provide storage replication functionality.

Storage backup (tape, optical) finds a place in AV systems too. Inexpensive backup will have slow recovery times so design accordingly. Backup is the not the same as archive. Archive content lifetime may be 50+ years, whereas most backups last days or weeks. Some AV systems keep a spare copy only as long as the near-line or online store has the working copy. As a result, the save time can vary depending on schedules and use patterns.

5.3.7   Client Caching Buys Time

Client local caching (~buffering) also provides a measure of HA. Figure 5.14 shows several clients with AV outputs. The main programming source files for playout come from either online or near-line storage. Usually, each playout client also has a measure of local storage. If the programming is known in advance (e.g., broadcast TV), then the local client cache may be prefilled (pre-queued) with target files. When playout starts, files are read from local memory and not directly from any external stores. With sufficient buffering, it is possible to cut the umbilical cord between the playout (or ingesting) client and external storage with no ill effects for some set time. In fact, a client may play out (or record) hours or days of AV even though the main storage and connecting infrastructure are down. If the playout or record schedule is also cached in the client, then all client operations are independent of external control or storage. For sure, local caching increases the overall system reliability. Refer to Figure 3B.22 and associated text for more insights into the advantages of caching.

Many control schemas do not support local caching, preferring to run directly from online storage. One issue is last-minute changes. Given a list of prequeued files, they may need to be flushed if the schedule changes at the last minute. This may happen in a live news or sports program. The control logic is more complex with caching but worth the effort to gain the added reliability. Also, running off local client-based storage relaxes the QoS of the external storage and connecting infrastructure, as the queuing step may be done in NRT under most circumstances. Also, the internal storage will need to support the required bandwidth (say for HD rates), not just the needed storage capacity. As AV vendors make their products more IT friendly, expect to see more use of client caching.

One more use of local client caching is for remote operations. If the AV client is remote from the main storage, providing a reliable WAN based QoS can be costly. With proper client caching, remote clients may offer a high level of reliability, despite a low-grade link to main storage. This technique works best when the record/playout schedules are stable and known in advance. Remote clients are sometimes called *edge clients* because they are at the edge of a network or system boundary.

Figure 5.17 summarizes the main themes discussed so far. It is a good reminder of the choices that systems designers have at their disposal when configuring HA systems. There are other methods to build HA systems and the next section focuses on some novel approaches.

5.3.8   Other Topologies for HA

Currently, there is industry buzz about the virtual data center, virtual computing, and utility computing. Each of these describes a variant of a configuration where requests for services are routed to an available

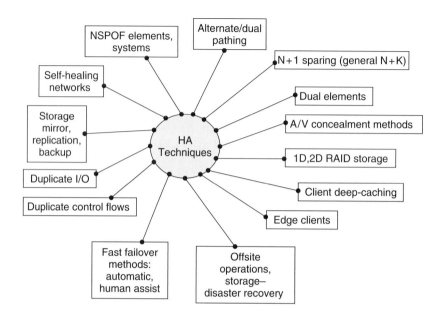

　　Summary of high-availability techniques.

resource. Imagine a cluster of servers, clients, processors, and networks all offered as undedicated resources. A managing entity can assign "jobs" to server/client/network resources; when the job is complete, the resource is released and returned to the pool, ready for the next assignment. If one resource faults, another can take its place, although not always glitch-free in the AV sense.

In enterprise IT, these new paradigms are capturing some mind share. The sense of a dedicated device statically assigned a fixed task is replaced by a pool of resources dynamically scheduled to perform as needed. Reliability, scalability, and flexibility are paramount in this concept. This idea has not yet been embraced by AV systems designers, but the time will come when virtual computing will find some acceptance for select AV (encoding, decoding, format conversing, conforming, etc.), control (scheduling, routing), and storage (NAS servers) processes. HP, IBM, Sun, Dell, and others see this as the future and offer a variety of virtual data center solutions to their customers. See [Steinke].

Although not yet applicable to AV applications (other than searching methods), one particularly interesting no-fault design is that used by Google [Barroso]. They have configured ~15,000 "unreliable" SPOF servers linked to form huge searching farms located worldwide. Query terms (video + IT + networking) are split into "shards" and each shard is sent to an available search engine from a pool of thousands. The results of each shard query are intersected and the target sites are returned to the client. The system scales beautifully and can withstand countless server failures with little impact on overall performance. There has been speculation that a Google-like architecture may be offered as a utility computing resource, ready for hire. This is an exciting area, ripe for innovation. One hot area is Web Services using the Web Services Description Language, WSDL (www.w3.org/TR/wsdl). This is discussed in Chapter 4.

5.3.9   Concealment Methods

When all else fails, hide your mistakes. Sound familiar? Not only does this happen with human endeavors, AV equipment does it as well. It is not a new idea; when a professional VTR has tape dropout problems, the output circuitry freezes the last good frame and mutes the audio until the signal returns. Concealing problems is preferred to viewing black or jerky video frames or hearing screeching audio. Similar techniques may be used when a device receives corrupted data over a link or data are late in arriving from storage. A good strategy is to hold the last good video frame and to output the audio if it has integrity or else mute it. When recording an AV signal that becomes momentarily corrupt, it is good practice to record the last valid frame along with any good audio until signal integrity returns. It is preferable to conceal problems than to fault, display, or record garbage.

A Few Caveats

When specifying an HA design, always investigate what the performance is *after* a failure. Is it less than under normal operations, is the failover transparent, and who controls the failover—man or machine? Also, what is the repair strategy when an element fails? Can the offending element be pulled without any reconfiguring steps? When a faulty element is replaced, will it automatically be recognized as a healthy member of the system? What type of element reporting is there? HA is complex, so ask plenty of questions when evaluating such a design.

5.4 SCALING AND UPGRADING SYSTEM COMPONENTS

So, the system is working okay and everyone is happy. Then upper management decides to double the amount of channels or production throughput or storage or whatever. The first question is, "Can our existing system be scaled to do the job?" The wise systems designer plans for days like this. What are some of the factors that are important in scaling AV/IT systems? Here is a list of the most common scale variables.

1. Scale networking infrastructure
   a. Network reach—local and long distance
   b. Routing bandwidth (data rate), number of supported links
   c. QoS (packet loss, latency, reliability)
2. Scale storage infrastructure (online, near-line, archive)
   a. Delivery R/W bandwidth
   b. Capacity (hours of storage)
   c. QoS (response time, reliability)
3. Scale number of clients/servers, performance, formats (ready for HD?), location of nodes
4. Scale control means—automation systems, manual operations, remote ops
5. Scale system management—alarms, configuration, diagnostics, notifications
6. Other—AC power, HVAC, floor space, etc.

Figure 5.18 illustrates each of the scale dimensions as legs of a cube.[2] The smaller volume cubes represent the current or status quo feature

---

[2] In reality, the shape may not be a cube but it is a six-sided, 3D volume.

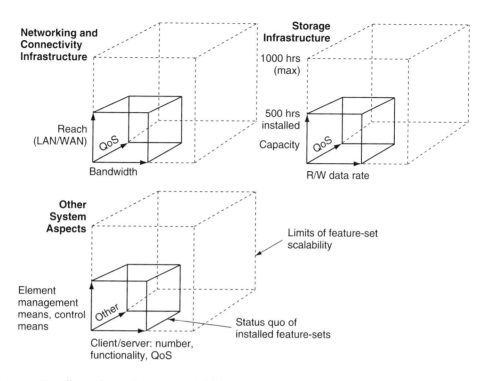

Networking and Connectivity Infrastructure

Reach (LAN/WAN)

QoS

Bandwidth

Storage Infrastructure

1000 hrs (max)

500 hrs installed

Capacity

QoS

R/W data rate

Other System Aspects

Limits of feature-set scalability

Element management means, control means

Other

Status quo of installed feature-sets

Client/server: number, functionality, QoS

FIGURE 5.18   Key dimensions of system scalability.

sets. The larger volume cubes represent the top limits of the same feature sets. Assume, for example, that the current storage capacity is 500 h of AV files but that the maximum practical, vendor-supported size is 1000 h. These values are indicated on the storage cubes in Figure 5.18. Generally, exceeding the maximum rate requires an expensive forklift upgrade of some kind. Knowing the maximum dimensions of each large cube sets limits on the realistic, ultimate system scalability. Incidentally, not every possible scale parameter is specifically sited in Figure 5.18. Hence, make sure you identify the key factors that are of value to you when planning overall system scalability.

When selecting a system, always seek to understand how each of the dimensions should be scaled. Of course, guaranteeing a future option to scale in one area or another will often cost more up front. If 5 TB of storage capacity is sufficient at system inauguration, how much more will it cost for the *option* to expand to 20 TB in the future? This cost does not count the actual expansion of 15 TB, only the rights to do it later. Paying for potential now may pay off down the road *if* the option is exercised. Sometimes it is worth it, sometimes it is not.

It is likely though, at some future time, some change will be asked for and the best way to guarantee success is to plan for it to a reasonable degree. When the boss says "Boy, are we lucky that our system is scalable," you can think "It is not really luck, it is good design." Yes, luck is a residue of good design.

Upgrading Components

Independent of scaling issues, all systems will need to be upgraded at some point. At the very least, some software security patch will be required or else live in fear of a catastrophe down the road. Then there are performance upgrades, HW improvements, bug fixes, mandatory upgrades, OS service patches, and so on. If system downtime can be tolerated during part of a day or week, then upgrades are not a big deal. However, what if the system needs to run 24×7? Well, then the upgrade process depends on how the clients, infrastructure, and storage are configured and their level of reliability.

If the principles of NSPOF, $N + 1$, replication, and mirroring are characteristics of the system design, then "hot" upgrades (no system downtime, performance not degraded) are possible. It is easy to imagine taking the mirror side out of service temporarily to do an upgrade, removing a client from operation knowing that the spare ($N + 1$) can do the job, or disabling an element while its dual (NSPOF) keeps the business running. In some cases, an element may be upgraded without any downtime. Increasing storage capacity may be done hot for some system designs, whereas others require some downtime to perform the surgery.

Always ask about hot upgrade ability before deciding on a particular system design. In a way, the ability to upgrade is more important than the option to scale. That is because upgrades will happen with 100% certainty except to the most trivial elements. However, future system scaling may never happen.

5.5   IT'S A WRAP—SOME FINAL WORDS

Yes, sometimes things do not always go from bad to worse, but you cannot count on it. Anyone who has been hit hard by Murphy's law will know the only way to outwit Mr. Murphy is to hire him as a consultant. Andy Grove of Intel famously said, "Only the paranoid survive." When it comes to reliable operations, it is okay to be paranoid. Planning for the worst-case scenario is healthy thinking, especially if it leads to worry-free sleep and a system that just keeps humming along.

REFERENCES

[**Steinke**] Steve Steinke, *Utility Computing*, Network Magazine, August 2003 issue, www.networkmagazine.com.

[**Barroso**] L.A. Barroso et al., *Web Searching for a Planet: The Google Cluster Architecture*, IEEE Micro Magazine, March 2003.

6 | Networking Basics for AV

6.0   INTRODUCTION

The kingpin of all of IT communication technologies is the network. Fortunately, we live at a time when there is one predominant network and it is based on the Internet Protocol (IP). Gone are the days when IP and AppleTalk and IBM's SNA and Novell's IPX all competed for the same air. Gone are the days when clumsy protocol translators were required to move a file between two sites. Yes, gone are the days of network chaos and incompatibility. Welcome IP and its associated protocols as the world standard of communications networks. Without IP there would be no Internet as we know it.

This chapter just touches on the basics of networking principles. The field is huge and there are countless books and Web references (see www.ietf.org and www.isoc.org) dedicated to every nook and cranny of IP networking. See too [Stallings] and [Stevens] for information on IP and associated Internet protocols. The focus combines an overview of standard networking practices with special attention to AV-specific needs, such as real time data, live streaming over LAN and WAN, high bandwidth, and mission-critical QoS metrics. It is the intersection of AV and networking that is most interesting to us. Let us begin with the classic seven-layer stack.

6.1   THE SEVEN-LAYER STACK

No discussion of networking is complete without the seven-layer stack. Figure 6.1 shows the different layers needed to create a complete end-to-end networking environment. The original Open Systems Interconnection (OSI) model is used as a reference by which to compare the Internet and other protocol stacks. The OSI stack itself may be split into three coarse levels: *link access layer, transport layer*, and *applications layer*.

The lowest level of the three coarse layers is the physical and access (addressing, access methods) layer. The transport layer relates to moving data from one point in the network to another. The application layer is self-evident. The Internet stack does not have an exact 1:1 correspondence to every OSI layer, but there is no requirement for an alignment. Each layer is isolated from the others in a given stack. This is good and allows for implementations to be created on a per-layer basis without concern for the other strata.

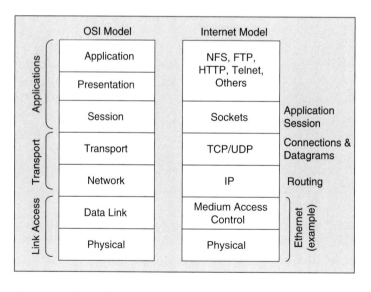

FIGURE   The OSI model and Internet stack.

6.1

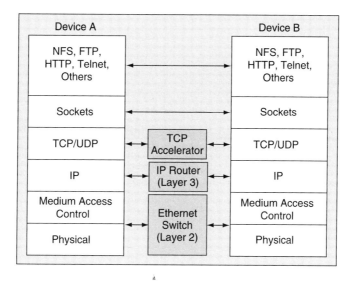

FIGURE

6.2

Layer processing using peer-to-peer relationships.

Figure 6.2 shows the value of isolated layers. There is a peer-to-peer relationship between each layer on the corresponding stacks. A layer 2 switch (e.g., Ethernet I/O) operates with knowledge of the physical and data link levels only. It has no knowledge of any IP or transport layer activity. Another example is the IP router (or IP switch). It follows the rules of the Internet Protocol for switching packets but is unaware of the levels above or below. At the Transport level, a TCP accelerator (HW-based TCP processor) can function without knowledge of the other layers as well.

Of course, some devices may need to comprehend several layers at once, such as a security firewall (or intrusion prevention device) that peeks into and filters data packets at all levels. However, each layer–process may still operate in isolation. The genius of peer-to-peer relationships has enabled stack processors to be designed and implemented independently with a resulting benefit to testing, integration, and overall simplicity.

One quick way to remember the order and names of the layers is the acronym PLANTS. From the bottom up it is P (physical), L (link), A (okay, just say and), N (network), T (transport), and S (session). Of course the application layer is always at the top.

Let us examine the layers in more detail. At the top of the stack are applications such as FTP, NFS, Web access via HTTP, time-of-day, and so on. The most common applications are available on desktops and servers as standard installs. For a list of all registered applications using well-known ports, see www.iana.org/assignments/port-numbers.

Immediately below the application layer is the session layer. A session is established between a local program and a remote program using sockets. Each end point program uses a socket transaction to connect to the network. Program data are transferred between end point programs using TCP/IP or UDP/IP. Sockets have their own protocol for setting up and managing the session. From here on, let us study the stack from the bottom up, starting with the physical and link layers.

6.1.1   Physical and Link Layers

Ethernet is the most common representation of the bottom two layers for Local Area Network (LAN) environments and has won the war of connectivity in the enterprise IT space. Just a few years ago it battled against Token Ring and other LAN contenders but these were knocked out. In addition to LANs, WANs, MANs, satellite links, DSL, and cable modem service provide link layer functionality. WANs and MANs are considered later in this chapter.

One that has become a favorite in the Telco arena is called Packet Over SONET (POS). With POS, IP packets are carried over a SONET link. Another useful IP carrier is an MPEG Transport Stream as deployed in satellite and cable TV networks. Terrestrial transmission using ATSC, DVB, and other standards also carry IP within the MPEG structure. The common DSL modem packages TCP/IP for carriage over phone lines. Ethernet too has been extended beyond the enterprise walls under the new name Transparent LAN (TLAN). This is a MAN (Metro Area Network) that is Ethernet based. TLANs and SONET are discussed in the WAN/MAN section later in this chapter. For now, let us concentrate on Ethernet as used in the enterprise LAN.

Ethernet was invented in 1973 by Robert Metcalfe of Xerox. It was designed as a serial, bidirectional, shared media system where many nodes (PCs, servers, other) connect to one cable. Sharing a snaked cable among several devices has merit for sure. Unfortunately, because any one node can hog all the bandwidth, shared media have given way to central switching (star topology). This has become de rigueur for LANs, and each node has a direct line to a switch or hub. Figure 6.3 shows a typical

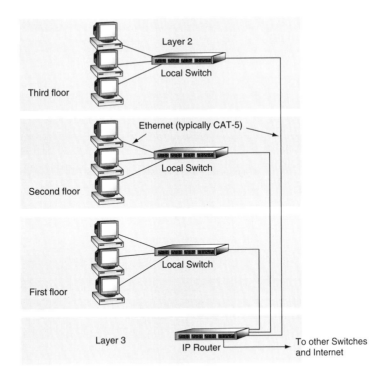

FIGURE

6.3

Hierarchical switching example.

star configuration of Ethernet-connected nodes. The star is ideal for AV networking, as it offers the best possible QoS, assuming that congestion (packet loss) in the switches is low or nonexistent.

Ethernet specs are controlled by the IEEE, and 802.3X is a series of standards for defining the range of links from 10 Mb/s to the top of the line 10 Gb/s. There are 12+ defined wire/fiber specifications. The most common spec is CAT-5 wiring and it supports 100Base-TX (100 Mb/s line rate) and 1000Base-T Ethernet. CAT-5 cable is four twisted and unshielded copper pairs. 100Base-TX uses two pairs and 1000Base-T uses four pairs.

Ten-Gb/s rates demand fiber connections for the most part, although there is an implementation using twin-axial cable instead of the more common Category 5 cabling. 10G line coding borrows from Fibre Channel's 8 B/10 B scheme (see Appendix E, *8B/10B line coding*) as do the first three links in the following list. Common IEEE-defined gigabit Ethernet links are

♦ 1000Base-LX from 500 M (multimode fiber) to 5 km (single mode fiber)
♦ 1000Base-SX from 220 M to 550 M (multimode fiber)
♦ 1000Base-CX at 25 M copper (82 feet)
♦ 1000Base-T, copper Cat 5, 100 M (327 feet) (five level modulation)

10 G links will not connect to PCs but rather as backbone transport between IP switchers and routers and some servers. There is no reason to stop at 10-G rates, and 40-G Ethernet is expected in the future. Figure 6.4 gives a history of Ethernet progress. Note that the current development run rate is beating Moore's law.

Ethernet Frames

The on-the-wire format to carry bits is the Ethernet frame as shown in Figure 6.5. As with most packet protocols, there is a preamble and address field followed by the data payload (1500 bytes max, nominal) field concluded by an error detection field. So-called "jumbo frames" carry payloads of size >1500 up to 9000 bytes. Jumbo frames are processed more efficiently with less frame-handling overhead. Each

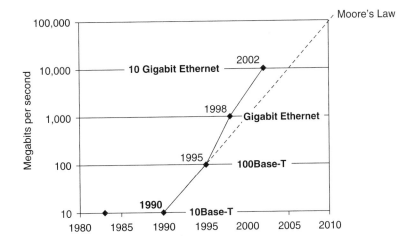

FIGURE   The evolution of Ethernet.

6.4

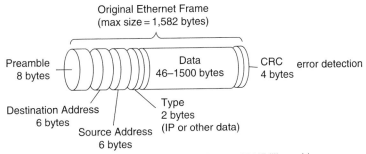

Destination/Source address are called MAC address – 256 Trillion address range
Ethernet frames ride the wire and carry all upper level data

FIGURE   The Ethernet frame.

6.5

Ethernet port has a worldwide 48-bit MAC (Medium Access Control) address that is unique per port. MAC addressing supports 256 trillion distinct ports. MAC addressing is used for many link types—not just Ethernet. Do not confuse this address with an IP address, which is discussed in the next section. Some network switches use the MAC address to forward frames. This mode of frame routing is often called layer 2 switching. Layer 2 switching is very limited in its reach compared to IP routing, as we will see.

Ethernet frames are sent asynchronously over the wire/link. There is no clock for synchronous switching as there is with an SDI signal. So any real time streaming of AV data must account for this. Several commercial attempts have filed to turn Ethernet into a time-synchronous TDMA medium, but they have not succeeded, despite the obvious advantages for AV transport. See Chapter 2 for more information on using asynchronous links to stream synchronous AV.

Let us move one layer higher in the stack to the network layer. This layer's entire data field is carried by the Ethernet frame.

6.1.2   The IP Network Layer

This is the IP routing layer. There are many ways to route signals (data) from source to destination. One way is called circuit switching, which is typified by the legacy telephone system. In this case, a telephone call is routed via switches to form a literal circuit from source to destination. The circuit stays intact for the duration of the call and the QoS of the connection is excellent. The traditional SDI router is circuit switched (crossbar normally) and connects input ports to output ports with outstanding QoS. Circuits must be set up by some external control.

On the other hand is packet switching. As an example of packet routing, let us use the analogy of sending a picture postcard of the Chelsea Bridge from London to 385 Corbett Avenue, San Francisco, USA. The postcard (a packet) enters the post office system and is routed via various offices until it reaches its destination. A clerk, or machine, at a London post office examines the destination address and forwards the packet to Los Angeles, USA. Next, the LA post office forwards the packet to the main post office in San Francisco with subsequent forwarding to the local post office nearest Corbett Ave. At each step the destination address is examined and the packet is forwarded closer to the final address.

In the end, a letter carrier hand delivers the postcard packet to street address 385. If the destination address cannot be located, then a return message is sent ("return to sender"). It is not uncommon to simultane-ously mail two postcards to the same address and have them arrive on dif-ferent days. One card may traverse via New York City while another via LA so although the routes are different, the final destination is the same. Welcome to the world of packet routing. This type of routing is often called layer 3 routing. Figure 6.6 shows examples of circuit and packet switched methods. Layer 2, MAC switching, is similar to layer 3, but there are differences, as will be shown.

As with the Ethernet frame, each packet has an address field (the IP address) and payload field. Some of the features of a packet routing are:

◆ Because each packet has a destination (and source) address field inspected at each routing point, packets are self-addressing—not true with circuit switching.

◆ Policies (routing protocols) decide how to route each packet—via LA or NYC?

◆ Congestion may cause some packets to be delayed or even dropped—the Christmas card syndrome.

◆ Packets are not error corrected (at higher stack levels they are, however).

◆ Packets associated with the same stream may take different routes (hops), resulting in out-of-order packet reception at the receiver (path A or B in Figure 6.6).

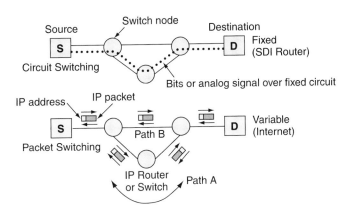

FIGURE   Example of circuit and packet routing.

6.6

◆ Packets may exhibit jitter (variation in delay) during the life of the stream.

◆ The QoS is difficult to guarantee in large networks.

◆ Packets are carried by the lower two layers in the stack (e.g., Ethernet frames).

As a result, packet switching lacks some of the more AV-friendly features of circuit switching. Despite this, packet switching offers self-addressing, resiliency to router failure, wide area routing, and IT-managed and relatively inexpensive switches. The best success story for packet switching is the Internet. Imagine building the Internet from circuit-switched elements. Some entity would need to open/close every switch point and this alone signals disaster for such a topology.

The biggest issue of using packets (compared to circuit switching) to move AV data is a potentially low or unspecified QoS. As discussed in Chapter 2, there are clever ways to smooth out any packet jitter; using TCP (next layer in stack) any packet errors may be 100% corrected. So the only real issue is overall latency, which may be hidden or managed in most real world systems.

Over small department networks, the latency through several switch hops may be well controlled. It is possible to achieve a <30-µs end-to-end latency for such a network. This is less than one raster line of video in length. As a result, real time streaming and device control using routed packets is practical. Of course a 30-µs end-to-end delay is not common for most networks, but the principle of low-latency networks is well established.

Comparing Layer 2 and Layer 3 Switching

This section sorts out some of the pros and cons of layer 2 and layer 3 switching. In many enterprise networks, switches route Ethernet frames using the MAC address (layer 2 switching) or packets using the IP address (layer 3 switching). Many commercial switches support both methods. See Figure 6.3 for a simple network using both layer 2 and 3 switching. Medium to large network domains use a mix of layers 2 and 3, whereas smaller networks or LAN subgroups use only layer 2 methods. There are trade-offs galore between these two methods, but the main aspects are as follows:

1. Layer 2 switching domain
   ◆ Switching based on MAC address in Ethernet frame
   ◆ Supports small/medium LAN groups or VLANs that confine broadcast messages. Limited scalability.
   ◆ Excellent per-port bandwidth control
   ◆ Path load balancing not supported
   ◆ Spanning Tree Protocol (STP) supports path redundancy while preventing undesirable loops in a network that are created by multiple active paths between nodes. Alternate paths are sought *only after* the active one fails.
   ◆ Easy to configure, uses lower cost switches than layer 3
2. Layer 3 switching (routing) domain
   ◆ Switching based on the IP address
   ◆ Scales to large networks—departments, campus networks, the Internet
   ◆ Routes IP packets between layer 2 domains
   ◆ Redundant pathing and load balancing supported
   ◆ Able to choose "least-cost" path to next switch hop using Open Shortest Path First (OSPF) or older Routing Information Protocol (RIP) routing protocols. OSPF has faster failover (<1 s possible) than STP.

Layer 2 and 3 switching can live together in complete harmony. It is quite common for portions of a network design to be based on layer 2 switching while other portions are based on layer 3. For AV designs, layer 2 can offer excellent QoS at the cost of slow failover if a link or node fails. STP can take 30–45 s to find a new path after a failure is detected. For this reason, RSTP is sometimes used. Rapid STP, based on IEEE standard 802.1W for ultrafast convergence, is ideal for AV networks. See [Spohn] for a good summary of layer 2 and 3 concepts and trade-offs. See also [DiMarzio] for a quick summary of routing protocols of concepts or scour the Web for information.

Another aspect of layer 2 is deterministic frame forwarding. In most cases, Ethernet frames will traverse links according to the forwarding tables (built using STP) stored in each switch. The packet forwarding paths are static,[1] until a link or switch fails. Then, if possible, a new path will be discovered by STP and packet forwarding continues. In a static network, for example, media clients accessing NAS storage should see a fixed end-to-end delay plus any switch-induced jitter for each Ethernet frame.

However, layer 3 can route over different paths to reach the same end point. Because routing occurs on a per-packet basis, this will likely introduce added jitter above what layer 2 switching introduces. See Figure 6.6 for an example of alternate pathing (path A or path B may be used as determined by routing protocols) using layer 3 routing. See Chapter 5 on how to build fault-tolerant IP routing networks. In the end, judicious network design is needed to guarantee a desired QoS and associated reliability.

Snapshot   The primary difference between a **layer 3 switch** and a **router** depends more on usage than features. Layer 3 switching is used effectively to segment a LAN rather than connect to a WAN. When segmenting a campus network, for instance, use a router rather than a switch. When implementing layer 3 switching and routing, remember: *Route once, switch many*.

IP Addressing

Just as a house has a street address, networked devices have IP addresses. The IP (IPV4) address is a 4-byte value. The address range is split into three main classes: A, B, and C. Each class has a subdivision of *network ID* and *host ID*. What does this mean? A network ID is assigned to a company or organization depending on the number of host IDs (nodes on their network) (see Figure 6.7). Classes A, B, and C are for point-to-point addressing. A special class D address is reserved for point-to-multipoint data transfer.

---

[1] It is possible that switch forwarding tables may change after a power failure or some network update so there is no guarantee that a given L2 forwarding path between selected end points will be permanent.

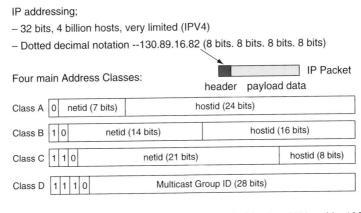

IP addressing;

– 32 bits, 4 billion hosts, very limited (IPV4)

– Dotted decimal notation --130.89.16.82 (8 bits. 8 bits. 8 bits. 8 bits)

Four main Address Classes:

Class A: Govt, HP, IBM – ½ of all IP addresses in this class (128 netids, 16 M hosts each)
Class B: campus, medium size companies (16 K netids, 64 K hosts per netid)
Class C: (2 million netids each with 254 host addresses)
Class D: Multicast Groups (268 million groups)

FIGURE   IP addressing concepts.

6.7

For example, MIT has a class A network id of 18 so the campus can directly support 16 million hosts (2^24). A smaller organization may be assigned a class C address that only supports 256 hosts. Many addresses have an equivalent network name as well. For example, MIT's IP Web address is http://18.7.22.83 (in so-called dotted decimal notation) and its equivalent name is http://www.mit.edu. A network service called a Domain Name Server (DNS) is available to look up an address based on a name. Numeric addresses, not names, are needed to route IP packets.

To better understand IP addressing, DNS address lookup, ping (addressed device response test), trace route (a list of hops), and other network-related concepts, visit www.dnsstuff.com for a variety of easy-to-run tests. Ten minutes experimenting with these tests is worth the effort. Note that it takes time (<100 Ms usually) to look up an IP address based on a name. In time-critical AV applications, it is often wise to use numeric addresses and avoid the DNS lookup delay. As a result, http://www.mit.edu takes slightly longer to reach than http://18.7.22.83 if the named address is not already cached for immediate use.

Subnets

A class A address space supports 16 M hosts. All the hosts on the same physical network share the *same broadcast traffic*; they are in the same broadcast domain. It is not practical to have 16 million nodes in the same broadcast domain. Imagine 16 M hosts broadcasting data packets! Now that is a data storm. The result is that most of the 16 million host addresses are not usable and are wasted. Even a pure class B network with 64 K hosts is impractical.

As a result, the goal is to create smaller broadcast domains—to wall off the broadcast traffic—and to better utilize the bits in the host ID by subdividing the IP address into smaller host networks. The basic idea is to break up the available IP addresses into smaller subnets. So a class B host space may be divided into say 2048 (11 bits of host ID) subnets each with ~32 hosts (5 bits of host ID)—a very practical host size. In reality, the host ID cannot be perfectly subdivided to utilize every possible host address. Still, subnetting is a practical way to build efficient networks. Each subnet shares a common broadcast domain and each is reachable via IP, layer 3, switches/routers that bridge domains.

Layer 2 versus Layer 3 Switching

Layer 2 switching uses the MAC address in the Ethernet frame to forward frames to the next node. Layer 3 switching uses the IP address in the IP packet to forward packets.

IPV6 and Private IP Addresses

No doubt about it, the Internet is running out of IP addresses. The day is near when every PC, mobile phone, microwave oven, and light switch (or even light bulb) will require an IP address. There are two solutions to this problem. One is to migrate to the new and improved version of IP, IPV6 (RFC 2460). Among other valuable enhancements, each IP packet has a 128-bit address range, which is $\sim10^{38}$ addresses. This is equivalent to 100 undecillion[2] addresses. There are an estimated 10^{28} atoms in the human

---

[2] An undecillion is 10^{36}.

body so IPV6 should suffice for awhile. IPV6 is slowly being adopted and will replace IPV4 over time. There are transition issues galore as may be imagined. One transition scenario is to support dual stacks—IPV4 and IPV6—in all network equipment. This is not commonly done but may become so as IPV6 kicks into gear.

A more common solution for living with the limited IPV4 address space is to use the Network Address Translation (NAT) method. Several addresses have been set aside for private networks as listed in Table 6.1. These addresses are never routed on the open Internet but only in closed, private networks.

The NAT[3] function is similar to what a telephone receptionist does. The main office number is published (a public IP address) but the internal phone network has its own extension numbering plan (private IP addresses) not directly accessible from the outside. The operator routes incoming calls to the correct extension by doing address and name translation. Because the private IP addresses are never routed on the open Internet, they may be reused as often as needed in private networks just as phone extension numbers are reused by other private phone systems.

NAT has effectively added billions of new virtual IP addresses, which has stalled the uptake of IPV6. Many companies use NAT services and rely on pools of internal, private IP addresses for network nodes. Many modern AV systems (playout servers, news production systems, edit clusters) also use private IP addresses. NAT uses several methods to map internal private to external public IP addresses. To learn more, see computer.howstuffworks.com/nat1.htm.

Class	Private start address	Private finish address
A	10.0.0.0	10.255.255.255
B	172.16.0.0	172.31.255.255
C	192.168.0.0	192.168.255.255

TABLE   Dedicated Private IP Address Ranges

6.1

---

[3] NAT is often referred to as IP masquerading.

The IP layer is replete with protocols to assist in routing packets over the open terrain of the Internet. For the most part, they do not influence AV networking performance so they are not covered. There is one exception—QoS. Network QoS is governed by several net protocols, which are reviewed later in this chapter. IP multicast is useful when streaming an IP broadcast to many end stations. The next section outlines the basics.

IP Multicasting

Multicasting is a one-to-many transmission, whereas the Internet is founded on unicast, one-to-one communications. Plus, multicasting is normally unidirectional, not bidirectional, as with say Web access. Multicast file transfers are not common, but there are ways to do it as discussed in Chapter 2. See also www.tibco.com for a variety of file distribution solutions to many simultaneous receivers.

The IP class D address is reserved for multicast use only. In this case, each host ID is a multicast domain, like the channel number on a TV. Any nodes associated with the domain may receive the IP broadcast. IP multicast is a suite of protocols defined by the IETF to set up, route, and manage multicast UDP packets. Most multicast is *best effort* packet delivery, although it is possible to achieve 100% transfer reliability. This is not common and becomes complex with a large number of receivers.

The key to multicasting is a multicast-enabled routing system. Each router in the network must understand IP multicast protocols and class D addressing. IP packets are routed to other multicast-enabled routers and to end point receivers. Any node that tunes into an active class D host address will be able to receive the stream.

The Internet in general does not support IP multicasting for a variety of reasons. The protocols are complex, and there is no easy way to charge for multicast packet routing and bandwidth utilization. Imagine a sender who establishes a multicast stream to one million receivers that span 100 different Internet service providers. The business and technical challenges with this type of broadcast are intricate so ISPs avoid offering the capability. However, campus-wide multicast networks are practical and in use for low bit rate streaming video applications. There is very little IP multicast used for professional AV production. Next, let us focus next on the granddaddy of all protocols, TCP and its cousin UDP.

6.1.3   The Transport Layer—TCP and UDP

TCP (Transmission Control Protocol) is a subset of the Internet Protocol suite often abbreviated as TCP/IP. TCP sits at layer 4 in the seven-layer stack and is responsible for reliable data communications between two devices. Figure 6.8 provides a simple view of TCP's relation to application-related protocols, UDP, and lower levels. Consistent with stack operations, TCP packets are completely carried as payload by IP packets. TCP supports full duplex, point-to-point communications.

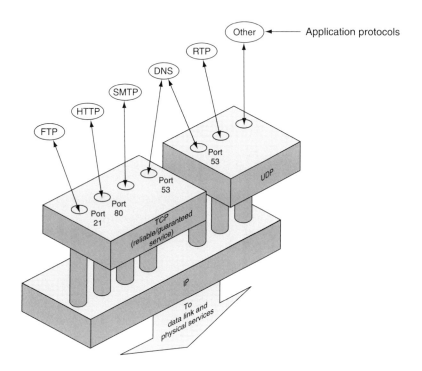

FIGURE   TCP and UDP in relation to application protocols.

6.8   Concept: Encyclopedia of Networking and Telecommunications.

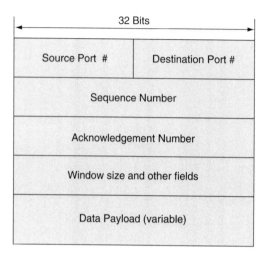

General layout of a TCP packet.

The TCP packet format is described in Figure 6.9. Some notable characteristics are:

♦ No address field
♦ Port numbers are used to distinguish application-layer services
♦ Sequence number
♦ Acknowledgment ID
♦ Window size
♦ Data payload—actual user data such as files

As Figure 6.8 shows, port numbers identify services. Many different TCP connections may exist simultaneously, each associated with a different application. For example, well-known port 21 is dedicated to FTP and 80 to HTTP for Web page access. There are 64K ports available, some assigned to specific services. Registered applications use what are called well-known ports for access.

TCP is a connection-oriented protocol. This means that a handshake protocol is used to establish a formal communication between two devices *before* any payload data are exchanged. End point connections are called

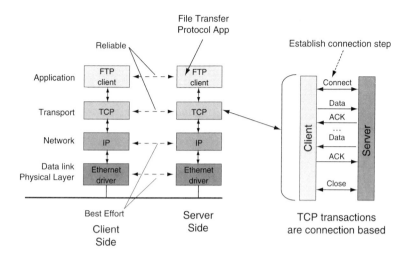

FIGURE
6.10

TCP is connection based and 100% reliable.

sockets. For example, when connecting to a Web server, a TCP connection is first established before any Web pages are downloaded. Figure 6.10 illustrates steps needed to move a file between a server and a client using FTP and TCP.

TCP connection establishment is a simple three-step sequence and is only done at the beginning of the call. Then, file data are moved between the sides. Importantly, TCP requires that *every* packet be positively acknowledged so that the sender knows with certainty that a sent packet was received without error. Because the setup phase does consume a small amount of time, AV centric applications may decide to leave the connection established ready for future use. For short transactions, the setup/close can take >50% of the total connection time.

If a packet's acknowledgment ID is not received within a certain time period then the suspect packet is resent. TCP will reduce its sending rate if too many packets are lost. This behavior helps reduce network congestion. TCP is a good network citizen. Positive acknowledgments and rate control are major features of TCP and have been both a curse and benefit to AV data transfer performance. Figure 6.11 illustrates an example of sustained TCP performance in the presence of packet loss. Note the aggressive back off and slow start up. The throughput would be constant only if packet loss was effectively zero. Although an IP packet can carry up to 64 KB of payload

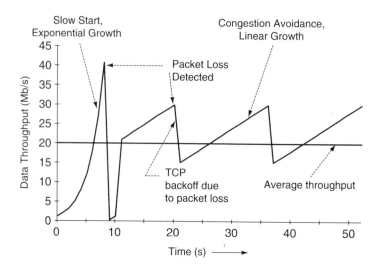

FIGURE

6.11

Behavior of TCP in the presence of packet loss.
Concept: Cisco.

data, when Ethernet is the underlying link layer, it is wise to limit IP data length to 1500 B—the Ethernet frame payload size. If a data bit error occurs at the frame or packet level, 1500 B of payload is lost for the general case.

The Sliding Window

TCP uses what is called a sliding window approach to manage transmission reliability and avoid congestion, as illustrated in Figure 6.12. There are three kinds of payload data in the vocabulary of TCP:

1. Sent and acknowledged (ACK) data packets; the receiver has the data
2. Sent and awaiting an ACK from the receiver; the receiver may not yet have the data
3. Data packets not yet sent

Data that fall into case #2 are governed by the sliding window. In most cases, the TCP window is 64 KB, although RFC 1323 allows for a much larger window with a corresponding increase in transfer rates over long-distance links. When the sender transmits a data packet, it waits for the receiver to acknowledge it. All unacknowledged sent data are considered

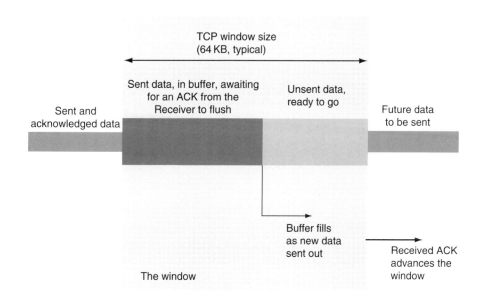

TCP window size
(64 KB, typical)

Sent data, in buffer, awaiting
for an ACK from the
Receiver to flush

Unsent data,
ready to go

Sent and
acknowledged data

Future data
to be sent

Buffer fills
as new data
sent out

Received ACK
advances the
window

The window

FIGURE

6.12

TCP's sliding data window.

"in the window." If the window becomes full, 64 KB of outstanding data, then the sender stops transmitting until the next ACK is received.

For short-distance hops, the window does not impair performance because ACKs are received quickly. For long-distance transfers (across WANs, satellites), small windows contribute to slow FTP rates because the transmission pipe fills quickly with unacknowledged data. More on this later in the chapter.

Despite some performance problems with TCP, it is the king of the transport layer. How does it compare to UDP (User Datagram Protocol), its simpler cousin? Let us see.

UDP Transport

In basic terms, UDP is a send-and-hope method of transmitting data. There are no connection dialogs, acknowledgments, sequence numbers, or rate control; UDP just carries payload data to a receiver port number. A UDP packet is launched over IP and, if all goes well, arrives at the receiver without corruption. UDP is a connectionless protocol compared to TCP being connection based.

Who would want to use UDP when TCP is available? Well, here are a few of UDP's advantages:

◆ UDP is very easy to implement compared to TCP
◆ Almost no software overhead, very CPU efficient
◆ Efficient AV streaming (VOIP uses UDP and RTP to carry voice data for a call)
◆ No automatic rate control as with TCP, transmission metering can be set as needed
◆ Minimal delay from end to end
◆ Supports point-to-multipoint packet forwarding (IP multicast)

If the network is not congested and application data are somewhat tolerant of an occasional packet loss, then UDP is an ideal transport mechanism. In fact, UDP is the basis for many real time A/V streaming protocols. When you listen to streaming music at home over the Internet, UDP is often the payload carrier.

When UDP is coupled with custom rate control it can outperform TCP. Some UDP-based file transfer protocols use TCP only to request a packet resend and set rates. Although TCP is part of the transaction, its use is infrequent and highly efficient. Some AV streaming applications use error concealment to hide an infrequent missing packet. See Chapter 2 for examples of both UDP- and TCP-based file transfer applications.

Stacking It All Up

The stack is a good way to organize the concepts and interactions of IP-related standards. The peer-to-peer relationship of the layers is an excellent way to divide and conquer a complex set of associations. Figure 6.13 summarizes how packets are encapsulated by the layer above. In the simplest form, each packet type is a header followed by a Protocol Data Unit (PDU). The IETF has set standards for each of these layers and their corresponding packet format. As trillions of packets

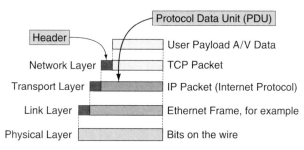

Packet encapsulation.

transit the Internet and private networks each day, the IP stack has proven itself worthy of respect.

LANs are built out of the fabric of the stack, but not all LANs are created equal. Next, the VLAN is considered.

6.2   VIRTUAL LANS

One huge, flat network easily interconnects all attached nodes. At first blush, this may seem like the ideal topology. However, dividing it into smaller subnet domains offers better QoS, reliability, security, and management. Using a VLAN is a practical method to implement the segmentation. With a VLAN, the AV domain may be on one LAN, sales on a second LAN, human resources on a third, and so on. Segmenting LANs is the ideal way to manage the network resources of each department or domain. Figure 6.14 illustrates the division of LANs. Especially important for AV applications is the isolation between LANs afforded by VLANs.

During normal LAN operation, various layer 2 broadcast messages are sent to every member of a LAN. With VLANs, these broadcast messages are only forwarded to members of the VLAN. VLAN node isolation

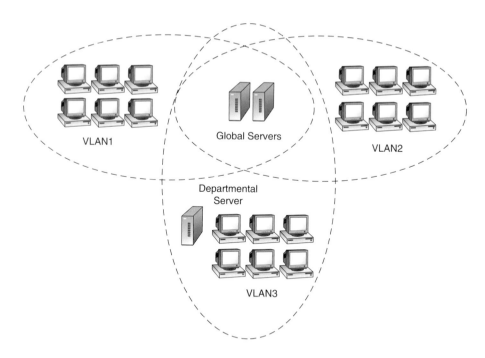

A network of isolated VLANs.

is a key to its performance gain. The IEEE has standardized 802.1Q for VLAN segmentation. This section covers the layout and advantages of VLANs over traditional LANs.

VLAN Basics

In a traditional Ethernet LAN, nodes (PCs, servers, etc.) connected to the same layer 2 switch share a domain; every node sees all broadcast frames transmitted by every other node. The more nodes, the more contention and traffic overhead are present. LAN QoS falls as the number of nodes increases. To avoid poor performance, the LAN must be decomposed into smaller pieces.

Nodal segmentation can be done by throwing hardware at the problem. Connect one set of stations to switch A, another to switch B, and so on and performance increases. This has the problem that associated nodes need to be in the same proximity. Is there a smarter way to segment a LAN? Yes.

VLANs provide logical isolation in place of physical segmentation. A VLAN is a set of nodes that are treated as one domain regardless of their physical location. A VLAN can span a campus or the world. Stations in VLAN #1 hear other stations' traffic in VLAN #1, but do not hear stations in other VLANs, including those connected to the same switch. This isolation is accomplished using VLAN tagging (see Figure 6.15). A VLAN tag is a 4-byte Ethernet frame extension (layer 2) used to separate and identify VLANs. Importantly, a VLAN's data traffic remains within that VLAN and can only cross outside with the aid of a layer 3 switch/router. Segmentation is especially valuable for critical AV workflows where traffic isolation is needed for reliable networking and achieving a desired QoS.

For example, a layer 2 switch may be configured to know that ports 2, 4, and 6 belong to VLAN #1, whereas ports 3, 5, and 7 belong to VLAN #2, and so on. The switch sends out arriving broadcasts to all ports in the same VLAN, but never to members of other VLANs.

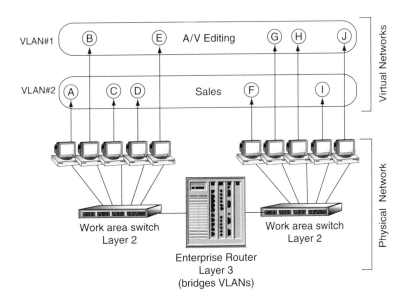

FIGURE   VLAN segmentation example.
━━━━━━   Concept: Encyclopedia of Networking and Telecommunications.
6.15

The following are VLAN advantages for a domain of A/V application clients:

♦ QoS improvement for AV VLAN segments
♦ An AV client may have two Ethernet ports, one per VLAN. With two VLAN attachments per device, it is possible to access VLAN #2 if VLAN #1 has failed. This is key to some HA dual pathing methods discussed in Chapter 5.
♦ Network problems on one VLAN do not necessarily affect a different VLAN. This is needed when the AV network needs separation from say a business LAN.
♦ More geographical flexibility than with IP subnetting

VLANs are not the only way to improve performance, security, and manageability. The next section outlines some protocols designed for setting and maintaining QoS levels.

6.3   TCP/IP PERFORMANCE

TCP has built-in congestion control and guaranteed reliability. These features limit the maximum achievable transfer rate between two sites as a function of the advertised link data rate, round trip latency, and packet loss. As discussed earlier, TCP's sliding window puts a boundary on transfer rates. Performancewise, a single TCP stream will achieve a maximum throughput of only 1.3 Mbps on a typical London to Hollywood transfer (170-ms delay, 0.5% loss) and only 174 Kbps on a typical Tokyo to Hollywood transfer (400-ms delay, 5% loss), even if the advertised link rates are much higher. TCPs average data throughput is given by the following three principles; the one with the lowest value sets the data rate ceiling.

TCP limitation 1. You cannot go faster than your slowest link.
   ♦ If the slowest link in the chain between two communicating hosts is limited to R Kb/s, then this is the maximum throughput.
TCP limitation 2. You cannot get more throughput than your window size divided by the link's round trip time (RTT).

◆ RFC 1323 does a good job of discussing this limitation and TCP implementations that support RFC 1323 can achieve good throughput even on satellite links if there is very little packet loss. A RTT of .1 s and a window size of 100 KB yield a maximum throughput of 1 MB/s.

TCP limitation 3. Packet loss combined with long round trip time limits throughput.

◆ RFC 3155 *"End-to-End Performance Implications of Links with Errors"* provides a good summary of TCP throughput when RTT and packet loss are present. In this case the following approximate equation provides the limiting transfer rate in bytes per second.

Throughput limit = 1.2 × (Packet_Size)/(RTT × SQRT (packet loss probability))

Note that TCP's throughput depends on link bandwidth only for rule #1. Rule #2 limits data throughput due to window size and round trip delay, and rule #3 limits data rate due to RTT and packet loss. Adding more link bandwidth or end-point CPU power will not increase file transfer rates if either of the other two principles limits the throughput. A file transfer from London to Hollywood using FTP takes just as long over an OC-3/155-Mbps link as over a T1/1.54-Mbps link. Throwing bandwidth at a slow transfer problem may well be a waste of money. Knowing *why* the transfer is slow gives the hints needed to improve the transfer performance.

Of course, the CPU stack processing of TCP/IP packets may also bottleneck performance, despite the efforts to optimize the three factors given earlier. There are countless ways to improve the stack's software performance, and many TCP processors use clever methods to avoid data copies and so on. Another way to improve TCP's performance is hardware acceleration with a TCP Offload Engine (TOE) card discussed later. A TOE card moves stack processing away from the main CPU to a secondary processor dedicated to TCP/IP processing. Figure 6.16 illustrates chief twiddle factors for improving TCP's performance.

So why do we use TCP at all if it has such limitations? All transfer protocols have less than ideal characteristics for some portion of their operational range. Some researchers have postulated that the relative stability of the Internet is at least partially attributed to TCP's aggressive back-off

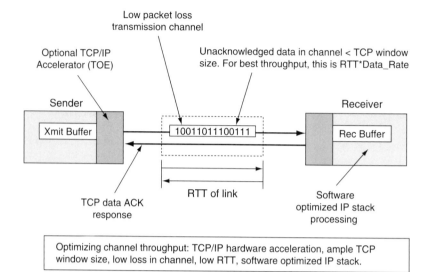

FIGURE   Optimizing TCP/IP throughput.

6.16

gentle slow startup under congestion [Aditya]. So TCP is a good network citizen. There are other TCP-like protocols that offer better throughput but they are somewhat exotic and used less commonly today. See, for example, FAST TCP as described by [Ref: Cheng Jin]. See Chapter 2 for a list of methods to accomplish fast file transfer without using TCP.

Screaming Fast TCP/IP Methods

Researchers at the University of Amsterdam [Antony] did an end-to-end file transfer experiment with the test conditions shown in Figure 6.17. They used high-end servers with 10G Intel Host Bus Adaptor (HBA) cards. These are not TOE cards. The servers ran Linux with specialized TCP stack software called TCP Vegas, provided by the NET100 group (www.net100.org). Incidentally, Linux version 2.6.6 has TCP Vegas (optimized for big windows and fast congestion recovery) as standard. One end point was in Amsterdam and the other was in Geneva. Each 10-G Ethernet LAN connected to a STM-64 10-Gb/s WAN (SONET) using a Force 10 router. The round trip delay between sites was only 17 ms. Using

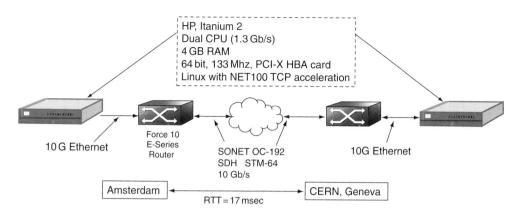

HP, Itanium 2
Dual CPU (1.3 Gb/s)
4 GB RAM
64 bit, 133 Mhz, PCI-X HBA card
Linux with NET100 TCP acceleration

10G Ethernet

Force 10
E-Series
Router

SONET OC-192
SDH   STM-64
10 Gb/s

10G Ethernet

Amsterdam ← RTT = 17 msec → CERN, Geneva

FIGURE   High-speed TCP transmission test configuration.

6.17

only CPU TCP processing, the throughput reached 5.22 Gb/s (about half of the 10G user payload) after proper tweaking of the TCP window size (socket buffer size was the adjustable parameter).

This is a very good result considering all TCP stack processing was done in software. Figure 6.18 shows measured throughput results versus TCP window size. Note that the best performance is reached when the socket buffer size is about 21 MB. Interesting, the bandwidth delay product of 5.22 Gb/s times 17 ms is about 11 MB, which should be the amount of buffer needed for optimum speed. So the test case TCP implementation has room for memory utilization improvement.

What limited the throughput performance? The researchers believe it was the internal PCI-X bus bandwidth. Also, if the WAN link had any congestion, the rate would have dropped precipitously. User data were R/W to RAM not to HDD devices so memory speeds were not an issue. The end device servers are high end and expensive. If garden-variety servers were used with untweaked TCP stacks, the performance could have been 1/10 or less. Nonetheless, the measured speed is remarkable and bodes well for lightning-fast file transfers, NAS storage access, and iSCSI SANs. With a TOE card to accelerate the stack, the performance should increase. However, there are no commercial 10-G Ethernet TOE cards yet on the market. The next sections discuss TOEs and their required operating system support.

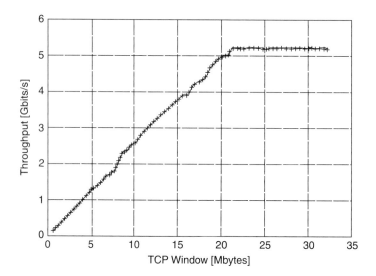

FIGURE

6.18
High-speed TCP transmission test results.

Source: [Antony].

TCP Offload Engines

A TOE card is a server or workstation plug-in card (PCI-X or similar, or on motherboard) that offloads the CPU intensive TCP/IP stack processing. To obtain the fastest iSCSI, NAS, or file transfers, a TOE card may be needed. The card has an Ethernet port and all TCP/IP traffic passes through it. At 10/100 Ethernet speeds, most CPUs can handle the processing overhead of TCP. A generally accepted rule of thumb is that a CPU clock of 1 Hz can process the TCP overhead associated with transferring data at 1 bit/s. With the advent of Gigabit Ethernet, server and host CPUs are suffocating while processing the TCP/IP data packets.

The research firm Enterprise Storage Group (Milford, MA) has concluded that "Implementing TCP off-load in hardware is absolutely a requirement for iSCSI to become mainstream. TCP is required to guarantee sequence and deal with faults, two things block-oriented storage absolutely requires. Running TCP on the server CPU will cripple the server eventually, so bringing the function into hardware is a must." Unfortunately, most TOE cards today do not work well with a Microsoft-based operating system. Integrating in a TOE alongside the OS's internal

TCP stack is a nightmare and performance and security cannot be guaranteed so Microsoft has announced an architecture for adding TOEs to a system. Their software architecture is called Chimney.

Microsoft Chimney Overview[4]

Microsoft announced its Chimney Offload Architecture for Windows at the May 2003 WinHEC Conference. The goal behind Chimney is to provide a standard interface for the integration of TOE products with the Windows OS stack for simplified development and deployment of Windows-based TOE products.

The Chimney architecture represents a significant departure from the prevalent all-inclusive approach of TCP offload. Specifically, Chimney includes offload of the TCP/IP connection data-centric path to the offload hardware (or target), such as an iSCSI HBA, while setup and teardown of accelerated TCP/IP connections and support of ancillary protocols such as DHCP will be implemented within the Windows OS TCP/IP stack. Microsoft's publicly announced plans are for Chimney to be part of the next major release of the Windows server code-named Longhorn (beta release 2006). AV workflows will depend on TOEs for superfast file transfers and high-speed iSCSI support.

6.4   THE WIDE AREA NETWORK (WAN)

A WAN is a physical or logical network that provides communication services between individual devices over a geographic area larger than that served by local area networks. Connectivity options range from plain-old telephone service (POTS) to optical networking at 160 Gb/s rates (proposed). Terms such as T1, E3, DS0, and OC-192 are often referred to in WAN literature, and frankly this alphabet soup of acronyms is confusing even to experts. There is no need to sweat like a stevedore when parsing these terms. See Appendix F, *The Digital Hierarchies*, for simple definitions and relationships of these widespread terms. Some of the links discussed

---

[4] The material in the first two paragraphs is paraphrased from the article by [Jang].

in the Appendix are used commonly to connect from a user's site to a Telco's office. Other links are dedicated to a Telco's internal switching and routing infrastructures. Usually, a WAN is controlled by commercial vendors (Telcos and the like), whereas a LAN is controlled by owners/operators of a facility or campus network. The QoS of the network depends not only on the type, but who controls it.

The four main criteria for segmenting wide area connectivity are

◆ Topologies: Switched and nonswitched (point-to-point, mesh, ring)
◆ Networks: Private and public

Figure 6.19 segments these methods into four quadrants. An overview of topologies follows.

WAN Connectivity Topologies

Each of the four types in Figure 6.20 may be used for general data communications, file transfer, storage access, and live AV streaming. Figure 6.20 expands on Figure 6.19. Each has trade-offs in the areas of QoS, cost,

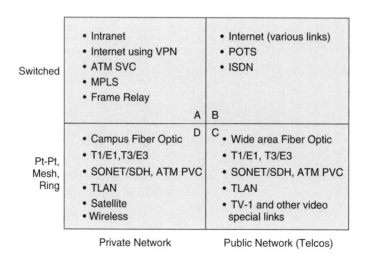

FIGURE   Wide area transport type classifications.

6.19

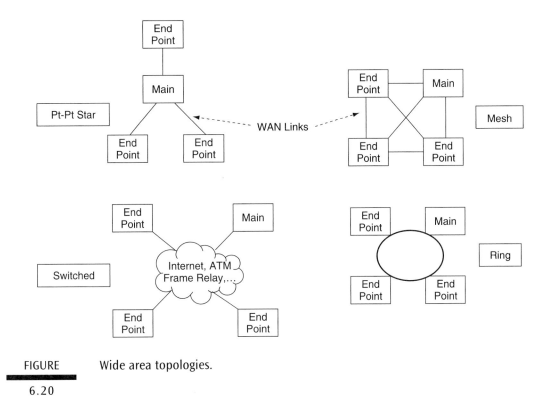

FIGURE   Wide area topologies.

6.20

reliability, security, and so on. The trade-offs are not covered in detail, but some consideration will be given to AV-specific issues.

The point-to-point form is the most common type of connectivity. One example of this may be remote AV sources (say from three sports venues) all feeding live programming to a main receiver over terrestrial or satellite links. Many businesses have remote offices configured via a point-to-point means.

The mesh allows for peer-to-peer communications without going through a central office for routing. Depending on the geographic locations of the end points, a mesh may not make economic sense. In general, the mesh has been replaced by switched networks. The complexity of a mesh rises as the square of the number of nodes.

The ring is a common configuration implemented by Telcos in a city or region. Using SONET, for example, a ring may pass by big offices or venues. Using short pt-pt links, the ring may be connected to nearby end points. Rings are often built with two counter rotating paths to provide for fault tolerance in the event that one ring dies. Many Telcos offer MAN services often based on ring technology (see later).

Finally, there are switched topologies. The most common are

◆ Internet based
◆ Asynchronous Transfer Mode (ATM) services over SONET/SDH
◆ Frame Relay
◆ POTS, ISDN

Switched methods do not always offer as good a QoS as the other three methods. Why? Switching introduces delay, loss, and jitter often not present in the other three. Of course WAN switching can exhibit excellent QoS, but only for selected methods such as ATM (or IP) over SONET/SDH and IP networks using MPLS to regulate the QoS per path. MPLS is explained later in this chapter.

Network Choices

Figure 6.19 divides WAN network choices into public and private. Public WANs are available through Telcos and other providers. They are usually available to anyone who wants to buy a service connection. Normally, anyone on the system can communicate to any other member. Quadrant B shows the most common switched networks all with low QoS. Quadrant C, however, may potentially offer excellent QoS for all types of AV communications. Telcos offer nonswitched AV products as a regular service offering. BellSouth, SBC, Sprint, Verizon, and Vyvx, for example, all offer streaming services with a QoS to meet any AV professional need.

Private networks can provide the best combination of security and QoS to meet individual needs. In the realm of switched services (quadrant A), ATM over SONET/SDH is a common Telco product. ATM was a hot topic in 1995 before the Internet took off like a rocket. It uses 53-byte cells at layer 2 as data carriers (similar to an Ethernet frame but smaller). Each cell may be switched over an ATM network using Switched Virtual

Circuits (SVC) methods or statically provisioned in a point-to-point configuration using Permanent Virtual Circuits (PVCs).

With the rise of the Internet, Ethernet, and IP as kings, ATM has lost some luster recently. The Frame Relay service is considered old technology and is being replaced with Virtual Private Network (VPN) connectivity. A VPN is a method used to tunnel private data over the public Internet. A VPN connection uses data encryption to hide all user data and forces strict access rules with multiple passwords and user names. More on this in Chapter 8. Some enterprise companies have also built a private Intranet to meet business needs of control, QoS, and access.

Most high QoS services fall into quadrant D. This area gives the user the most control over the data communications. Using point-to-point linking is a good way to guarantee QoS at the cost of managing separate links.

Whether a network is considered public or private, Telcos and other service providers can offer the equipment and links to build the system. The distinction between public and private is one of control, security, QoS, and access more than anything else. Given the right amount of packet reliability and accounting for delay through a network, any of the quadrants will find usage with AV applications. In general, the order of AV streaming quality spans from D (highest QoS) to C to A to B (lowest). Also, the main distinctions between quadrants C and D are reach and security.

The Video Services Forum (VSF, www.videoservicesforum.org) is a user group dedicated to video transport technologies, interoperability, QoS metrics, and education. They publish guidelines in the following areas:

◆ Multicarrier interfacing for 270 Mb/s SDI over ATM (OC-12)
◆ Video over IP networks
◆ Video quality metrics for WANs
◆ Service requirements

The VSF sponsors VidTrans, an annual conference where users, Telcos, and equipment vendors gather to share ideas and demonstrate new AV-networked products.

Another topic of interest to AV network designers is the MAN. It is a specialized, local reach WAN. The next section outlines this method.

6.5   THE METRO AREA NETWORK (MAN)

A MAN is a specialized WAN configuration that spans from a few miles to 50 miles or so. The common carriers, such as SBC, Sprint, Verizon, and so on, offer MAN services to businesses in a region, usually a city. Because a MAN has limited reach, both ends are controlled by the same service provider, resulting in a simplified contact and one-stop servicing for problems. Traditional MANs are not Ethernet based but use SONET/SDH rings or T3/E3 connectivity and routing. These links are expensive, difficult to provision, and at odds with the end customer's in-house networks that they interface to.

Enter the TLAN or Transparent LAN. This is an Ethernet-based MAN (at the end points especially). The beauty of TLANs is their seamless connection to the end-user IT network (see Figure 6.21). There are countless startups along with the incumbents entering this field and

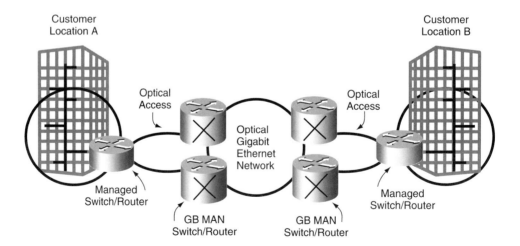

FIGURE   Example of a MAN (TLAN) that is all Ethernet based.
6.21   Concept: Yipes Communications.

there will be a shakeout for sure when TLANs come into maturity. There is a theme here and it is simply this—local, national, and global networks are migrating toward layer 2 Ethernet and layer 3 IP routing. This is great for interoperability and lowering end-user costs. Some vendors suggest that TLANs are one-tenth the cost of traditional WAN connectivity at the gigabit per second range.

The research firm Heavy Reading (www.heavyreading.com) reported that 75 carriers in North America offer several hundred Ethernet connectivity and access services. Carriers of all stripes are rolling out solutions at a steady clip. This reinforces the direction of Ethernet in the MAN (and WAN too); it is exploding. To learn more, visit www.metroethernetforum.org. See too www.yipes.com for an example of the new breed of TLAN service provider.

6.6 UNDERSTANDING QUALITY OF SERVICE FOR NETWORKS

The heart and soul of high-quality, digital AV networking is the QoS[5] metric; low delay, low jitter, controlled bandwidth, low packet loss, and high reliability. Hand-wringing is common over maintaining QoS levels; who sets them, how can they be guaranteed, and when are they out of limits? These are common concerns. Link QoS may be specified in a contract called a Service Level Agreement (SLA). Service suppliers provide SLAs whenever contracted for LAN or WAN provisioning. The elements of an SLA are useful criteria for any network design. QoS-related items are:

◆ Delay. Also called latency, this is the time it takes a packet to cross the network through all switches, routers, and links. Link delays are always evil and the absolute value of an acceptable delay depends on use. Control signaling, storage access, file transfer, streaming (especially live interviews), and so on, each has different acceptable values. Delay may be masked by using AV prequeuing and other techniques. Control has the strictest requirement for low delay and may be less than one

---

[5] QoS can be applied to services of all types—networking, application serving, storage related, and so on. Each of these domains has a set of QoS metrics. For this section, networking QoS is the focus.

line of video for some applications. However, for most applications, a control signal delay less than ~10 ms (less than half a frame of video) is sufficient. For LANs a 10-ms max delay is well within range of most systems.

◆ Jitter. This is the time variation of delay. Jitter is difficult to quantify but knowing the maximum expected value is important.

◆ Controlled bandwidth. Four common ways (some or all) to guarantee data rate are:

   1. Overprovision the links with sufficient bandwidth headroom. Meter the ingress data rate to known values (e.g., 5 Mb/s max).

   2. Do loading calculations for each link and switch to guarantee no switch congestion or link overflow at worst case loading.

   3. Use reservation protocols to guarantee link and network QoS.

   4. Eliminate all IP traffic that does not have predictable data rates so that uncontrolled FTP downloads of huge files are not allowed over specified LAN segments. A rate shaping gateway may be used to tame unpredictable IP streams.

◆ Packet loss. The most common cause comes from congested switches and routers. A properly configured switch will not drop any packets, even with all ports at 100% capacity. Of course traffic engineering must guarantee that ports are never overloaded. AV clients that are good network citizens will always control their network I/O and thus help prevent packet congestion.

◆ Reliability. This is considered at length in Chapter 5 but is typically one of the most important elements of an SLA.

It is a good plan to work with AV equipment providers that understand the subtleties of mission critical networking and guaranteed QoS. See Chapter 2, Section 2.4.1.2 for an illustration of network-related QoS metrics in action.

6.6.1   QoS Management Techniques

The Internet is a connectionless packet switched network and all services are best effort. In contrast, leased lines and SONET/ATM are connection oriented and data are delivered in predictable ways. Guaranteeing the

QoS for a general Internet connection is impossible in 2005. The Internet carriers do not all agree on how to set and manage QoS criteria, someone has to pay for the extra level of service, and there is little motivation to change the status quo. ATM, however, has well-defined QoS levels/services and carriers are eager to offer it. TLAN providers also offer predictable QoS metrics. Then too there are specialized IP networks where the provider guarantees QoS using Multiprotocol Label Switching (MPLS). This discussion does not make a distinction between class of service (CoS) and QoS, although they are different in principle. A CoS is a routing over a network path with a defined QoS. Incidentally, MPLS is designed to be network layer independent (hence the name, multiprotocol) because its techniques are applicable to *any* network layer protocol but IP is the most common case.

What are the chief categories for QoS control? Here is a list of commonly accepted techniques.

◆ **Congestion management**. Methods to reduce or prevent congestion from occurring.

◆ **QoS classification techniques**. IP packets are each marked (tagged) and directed to queues for forwarding. The queues are prioritized for service levels.

◆ **QoS reservation techniques**. Paths are reserved to guarantee bandwidth, delay, jitter, and loss from end to end.

Let us consider each one of these in brief.

Congestion Management

TCP has built-in congestion management by detecting packet loss and backing off by sending fewer packets and then slowly increasing the sending rate again (Figure 6.11). TCP is a major reason for the inherent stability and low congestion loss of the Internet. Within the network, routers sense congestion and may send messages to other IP routers to take alternate paths. Also, some routers may smooth out bursty traffic and reduce buffer overflows along the path. A router may use the Random Early Detection (RED) method to monitor internal buffer fullness and drop select packets before buffers overflow. Any congestion for critical AV applications is bad news. High-quality streaming links cannot afford congestion reduction—they need congestion avoidance. File transfer can live with some congestion, as TCP will correct for lost packets.

QoS Classification Techniques

These methods are based on inspecting some parameter in the packet stream to differentiate and segment it to provide the desired level of service. For example, if the stream is going to a well-known UDP port address (say a video stream), then the router may decide to give this packet a high priority. Sorting on port numbers is not the preferred way to classify traffic, however—it breaks the law of independence of stack layers. The generally accepted classification methods in use today are based on tags. The three most popular means are as follows:

♦ **Ethernet frame tagging**. This is based on an IEEE standard (IEEE 802.1D-1998) for prioritizing frames and therefore traffic flows. It has limited use because it is a layer 2 protocol and cannot easily span beyond a local LAN. For AV use in small LANs, this type of segmentation is practical and many routers and switches support it. In a similar way, ATM is a layer 2 routing protocol with explicit QoS but for wider areas than Ethernet normally spans.

♦ **Network level ToS tagging**. The type of service (ToS) is an 8 bit field in every IP packet used to specify a flow priority. This layer 3 field has a long history of misuse but was finally put to good use in 1998 with the introduction of IETF's Differentiated Services (Diffserv) model as specified by RFC 2475. Diffserv describes a method of setting the ToS bits (64 prioritized flow levels) at the edge of the network as a function of a desired flow priority, forwarding each prioritized IP packet within the network (at each router) based on the ToS value, and traffic shaping the streams so that all flows meet the aggregate QoS goals. Diffserv is a class of service method to manage data flows. It is a stateless methodology (connectionless) and does not enforce virtual paths as ATM and MPLS do.

♦ **MPLS tagging**. This technique builds virtual circuits (VCs) across select portions of an IP network. Virtual circuits appear as circuit switched paths, but they are still packet/cell switched. VCs are called label switched paths (LSPs) and are similar to ATM and Frame Relay virtual circuits. MPLS is an IETF-defined, connection-oriented protocol (see RFC 3031 and others). It defines a new protocol layer, let us call it "layer 2.5," and it carries the IP packets with a new 20-bit header, including a label field. The labels are like tracking slips on a pread-dressed envelope. Each router inspects the label tags and forwards the MPLS packet to the next router based on a forwarding table. Interestingly, the core MPLS routers do not examine the IP address, only the label. The label carries all the information needed to forward IP packets along a path across an MPLS-enabled network. Paths may be engineered to provide for varying QoS levels. For example, a path may be engineered for low delay and a guaranteed amount of bandwidth. MPLS operation is outlined in a later section.

These tagging methods are used in varying proportions in business environments and by Internet providers in the core of their networks. Several Telco carriers offer MPLS VPN services. AV applications, including streaming, critical file transfers, storage access, and real time control, can benefit from tag-enabled networks. Diffserv and MPLS are sophisticated protocols and require experts to maintain the configurations. Routers also need to be Diffserv and/or MPLS enabled. MPLS and Diffserv may indeed work together, as there is considerable synergy between the two methods. There is more discussion on these two methods in following sections.

There is one more CoS method that does not rely on tags of any sort: Weighted Fair Queuing (WFQ). Router (layer 3)-based WFQ schedules low-volume traffic first, while letting high-volume traffic share the remaining bandwidth. Each network router assigns a weight per IP flow, where lower weights are the first to be serviced. This implies that low rate flows would experience less congestion loss. In AV applications, WFQ is not always dependable for mission critical services so it is best not to bank on it.

QoS Reservation Techniques

ATM and MPLS virtual circuits can guarantee a QoS level while travers-ing across a broad network landscape. Each can carry IP packets as pay-load. Before routers pass any cells or packets, the QoS resources should be reserved. There are several ways to set up a virtual path with guaran-tees. One is to use the Resource Reservation Protocol (aptly named RSVP, RFC 2208, and others). RSVP is an out of band signaling protocol that communicates across a network to reserve bandwidth. Every router in the network needs to comprehend RSVP. As it turns out, it does not scale well and finds application in enterprise Intranets and in conjunction with MPLS to reserve path QoS.

Diffserv is a simpler, practical way to forward packets via what are called per-hop-behaviors (PHB). Hops are defined (by the IETF) with different QoS metrics, such as minimum delay, low loss, or both. When a packet enters a router, its tag is inspected and processed according to the PHB it is assigned to. Admittedly, it is more concerned with class of service than QoS, a subtle distinction.

The QoS Pyramid

Figure 6.22 illustrates the QoS pyramid. At the top of the pyramid is the trusty point-to-point link. There is no packet switching or sharing

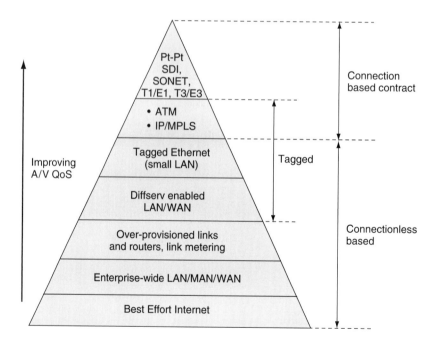

FIGURE   The QoS pyramid.

6.22

of bandwidth—it offers premium service at the sacrifice of self-addressed routing flexibility. The SDI link falls here. Dropping down one notch, ATM offers four general classes of service. A Telco-provided ATM path with >600 Mb/s, <10 ms delay, <<1 ms jitter, and 10e-8 cell loss is achievable over a 500-mile distance. IP/MPLS is almost as robust but with a packet loss of 10e-3 (typical) as offered by most Telcos.

At the bottom is the wild west of the Internet—the father of best effort service with routing (addressability) as its number one asset. All the other choices in the pyramid are specialized means to guarantee QoS to various degrees. Note that some of the methods are connection based so a contract exists between end points, whereas others are connectionless with no state between end points. This is independent of the fact that layer 4 (TCP) may establish a connection over IP as needed. ATM is branded as a "tagged" service, but this is slightly poetic because it is really a layer 2 routing protocol. Some of the divisions may be arguable, but in general going up the pyramid provides improved QoS metrics.

6.6.2   MPLS in Action

Before we leave QoS, let us overview a simple MPLS-enabled network. As mentioned, MPLS is a connection-oriented protocol so a contract exists between both ends of an MPLS network path. Figure 6.23 shows the chief elements of such a network. It is link layer independent. Standard IP packets enter the label edge routers (LER) for grooming, CoS classification (usually <8 classes defined, although more are available), and label attachment. MPLS packets traverse the network, routed by label switched routers (LSR). The label is used to route the MPLS packets at each LSR and not the IP address. Packets follow a label switch path (LSP) to the designation LER where the label is striped off as it enters a pure IP routed network. LSPs may be engineered for a range of QoS metrics. MPLS networks are becoming more common and are used in Internet carrier core networks, as offered by Telcos for private networks and for enterprise Intranets. Expect to see MPLS applied to AV applications, as it has a great combination of defined QoS levels and support for IP.

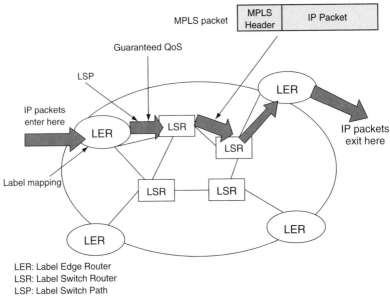

MPLS packet | MPLS Header | IP Packet

Guaranteed QoS

LSP

IP packets enter here

LER

LSR

LER

LSR

IP packets exit here

Label mapping

LSR   LSR

LER

LER

LER: Label Edge Router
LSR: Label Switch Router
LSP: Label Switch Path

FIGURE   An MPLS routing environment.

6.23

6.7   IT'S A WRAP—SOME FINAL WORDS

Networking is the heart and soul of IT-based media workflows. Just a few years ago, network performance was not sufficient to support professional AV applications. Today, with proper care, LAN, WAN, and TLAN are being used to transport AV media and control messaging with ample fidelity. MPLS and Diffserv enabled connectivity offers a good choice for high-quality networking with performance guarantees. With IP networking performance and availability ever increasing, AV transport is a common occurrence. True, dedicated video links will be with us for many years to come, but AV-friendly networking is taking more and more of the business once the province of specialized AV suppliers.

REFERENCES

[**Aditya**] Aditya Akella et al., *Selfish Behavior and Stability of the Internet: A Game-Theoretic Analysis of TCP*, Proceedings of the 2002 ACM conference on Applications, technologies, architectures, and protocols for computer communications, pages 117–130, 2002.

[**Antony**] Antony Antony et al., *A new look at Ethernet: Experiences from 10 Gigabit Ethernet End-to-End networks between Amsterdam and Geneva*, University of Amsterdam, The Netherlands, October 23, 2003.

[**Cheng Jin**] Cheng Jin, David X. Wei, and Steven H. Low, *TCP FAST: Motivation, architecture, algorithms, performance.* Proceedings of IEEE Infocom, March 2004. http://netlab.caltech.edu

[**DiMarzio**] Jerome DiMarzio, *Teach Yourself Routing in 24 Hours*, Sams, April 2002.

[**Jang**] Saqib Jang, *Microsoft Chimney: The Answer to TOE Explosion?* Margalla Communications, www.businessquest.com/margalla/, 8–19–03.

[**Spohn**] Darren Spohn, *Data Network Design*, McGraw-Hill Osborne Media, third edition, September, 2002.

[**Stallings**] William Stallings, *Computer Networking with Internet Protocols*, 2003, Addison-Wesley.

[**Stevens**] Richard Stevens, *TCP/IP illustrated, Volume 1*, 1994, Addison-Wesley.

7 | Media Systems Integration

7.0   INTRODUCTION

The previous six chapters outlined the core elements of any IT-based AV system design, including file transfer, streaming, storage, servers, HA methods, software platforms, and networking. This chapter ties these elements together to create world class media workflow systems. Additionally, the foundations of media types, metadata, control methods, nodal management, and asset management are introduced to more fully describe networked media systems.

As a house is made of bricks, so a media system is composed of its constituents. But a pile of bricks does not make a house anymore than a collection of servers and a network create a media system. It is the organization of the bricks that makes the house livable. So what are the organizational principles of AV systems? Let us start by describing the three planes.

7.1   THE THREE PLANES

Is there a unified way to simply categorize all the disparate elements of an AV system? Figure 7.1 is a pictorial of the three disciplines commonly used in most AV/IT systems: **data/user, control, and management planes**. Each plane has an associated protocol stack—LAN (TCP/IP), SDI,

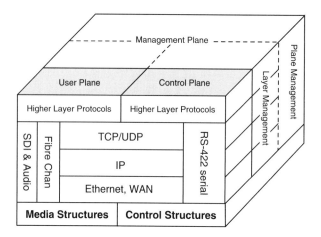

FIGURE   The three planes: Data/user, control, and management.

7.1

audio, or other as depicted. Figure 7.1 shows alternate stacks per plane depending on whether the system is based on traditional AV or networked media. As a result, AV (data plane) may be passed over an SDI link in one case or TCP/IP networking used in another. Due to the legacy of older control and management protocols, the RS232/422 links will be in use for years to come. The stacks in Figure 7.1 are representational and not meant to document every possible stack for each plane. Although the planes are independent, they are often used together to accomplish a specific operation. For example, commanding a video server to play a file will involve both user and control planes. Here are brief descriptions of the three planes.

◆ Data or user layer: Moving AV data across links in RT or NRT is a data plane operation. The data types may be all manner of audio, video, metadata, and general user data. This plane is alternatively called data or user. One term describes the *data format* aspects of the plane whereas the *user* handle denotes applications-related aspects, not shown, at the top of the stack. Editing a video that is stored on a remote networked device is a user plane operation.

◆ Control layer: This is the control aspect of a video system and may include automated and manual protocols for device operations (master control switcher, video server, video compositor, router, VTR, archive, etc.), live status, configuration settings, and other control aspects. This plane includes control applications, not shown, at the top of the stack.

♦ Management layer: Device management for alarms, warnings, status, diagnostics, self-test, parameter measurements, remote access, and other functions. This plane includes management applications, not shown, at the top of the stack.

Another way to view the three planes is illustrated in Figure 7.2. In this case, a general AV device is divided up into three functional domains. For sake of viewing, the LAN ports are repeated for data, control, and management, but in reality there may be only one LAN port and all three functional areas share the LAN. However, in some cases the management LAN port would be a second port to completely isolate management from applications-related operations. Why do this? Device management operations should be nonintrusive and not affect the AV operations in any way. The separate LAN port makes it easier to

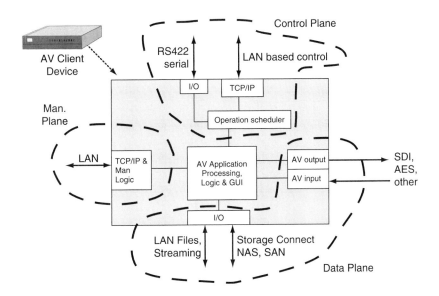

FIGURE   The three planes: Physical view of client side.

7.2

build and operate nonintrusive management operations. For example, blade servers typically have a dedicated Ethernet port for management use (see Appendix J).

In some cases, LAN isolation may apply to the control layer too. The choice of one, two, or three LAN ports is left up to the equipment manufacturer. Of course, choosing more than one LAN port can complicate the external network infrastructure if different QoS requirements are placed on each LAN connection.

Examples of the Three Planes

Complete industries exist to serve these layers. For example, automaton companies such as Florical Systems, Harris Broadcast Communications, Hitachi Systems, Masstech Group, Omnibus Systems, Pebble Beach Systems, SGT, Sundance, and others sell products for the control layer. Traditional video equipment companies sell data/user (A/V equipment of all sorts) plane products. Device management solutions have traditionally been vendor specific, but Miranda (iControl) and Snell & Wilcox (RollCall) for example offer general device management solutions, despite a lack of industry-wide standards. Let us consider a few examples in each plane.

7.1.1   The Control Plane

Traditionally, the control layer has been forged from custom solutions and lacks the open systems thinking that is prevalent in the general IT world. For example, many AV devices still rely on RS-422-related control protocols and not LAN-based ones. For controlling video servers, the Video Disk Control Protocol (VDCP) has been used for many years over the RS-422 serial link and many manufacturers are reluctant to move away from it, despite several vendor attempts to introduce LAN-based control protocols. The common Sony BVW-75 VTR control protocol is also in wide use and is RS-422 based. At present there is no LAN-based A/V device control protocol sanctioned by SMPTE, although several automation and server companies have developed private LAN-based protocols. For example, some of the current *vendor-specific* LAN control protocols (and APIs) for networked AV devices (especially servers) are:

♦ Avid's TransferManager Automation SDK/API for device operation and VDCP over LAN for server control

♦ Harris Automation's NDCP (Networked Device Control Protocol)

♦ Media Object Server (MOS) from Associated Press (AP) and the MOS user group

♦ Omneon's Server Control protocols; Player Control API and Media API

♦ Omnibus' G2 Control Protocol with G3 to follow soon

♦ ClipNet protocol from Quantel

♦ SGI's Multiunit Video Computer Protocol (MVCP)

♦ Thomson/GVG Profile Server native control

♦ Sony, SeaChange, Leitch, and others offer proprietary LAN-based control protocols

Vendors have developed device frame accurate, custom LAN-based protocols for controlling servers, file transfer, logo inserters, real time compositors, A/V routers, character generators, format converters, and more.

For now, these incompatible protocols will coexist in AV/IT systems. Of course this is not ideal and creates interoperability issues, but until SMPTE or some industry group standardizes a method(s) or a de facto one is selected by the market there will be confusion and competition among protocols.

The MOS Example

One exception to the rule is the MOS (Media Object Server) protocol designed by the MOS Group for *story list management* in AV devices. It has achieved excellent market acceptance as an IP-based protocol. The MOS Group is an industry body composed of representatives from many industry companies. The protocol is applied to news production for creating, organizing, deleting, and modifying the news "run-down list" of stories for a newscast. Video playback servers, character generators (CG), video compositors, teleprompters, and even robotic cameras need to know what activity to do per-story entry. MOS manages and synchronizes the activity lists across devices.

The following is a sample list of device activities needed to run story #3 for the newscast.

◆ Story 3 needs a lower third text crawl so the CG has a run-down story entry "Story 3, text crawl "Snake River overflows banks . . .""
◆ Story 3 requires an over-the-shoulder video clip of the swollen river so the video server has a story entry "Story 3, play clip Snake-Flood.dv"
◆ The teleprompter has a run-down entry "Story 3, file Snake-Flood.txt"

The MOS protocol works in the background in nonreal time creating run-down activity lists in all equipment. It is not considered a real time control protocol. At story time, a separate scheduling engine (or manual operation) triggers the individual devices to execute the list entry for story #3, thus creating a well-orchestrated harmony across all equipment. List management is an ideal activity for an IP-based protocol because no frame accurate video control is required. See www.mosprotocol.com for more information.

With the success of MOS, industry leaders are looking at ways to use the framework of the protocol (XML message passing) for general, real time, frame accurate, and device control over IP networks. Of course, new commands are needed, including the prequeuing methodology discussed here. What methods are needed to use a LAN and still achieve real time control? Let us see.

Techniques for Control over IP

Why have LAN-based device control protocols been adopted so slowly? Most traditional RS-422 serial device control protocols are video frame accurate by the nature of the point-to-point wiring. There is never congestion or meaningful latency using a serial link. It is proven.

In a broad sense, there are three "cause (command to do some action) and effect (action)" timing relationships in AV systems.

1. Hard real time, frame accurate control. The response latency is fixed at one frame or less measured from the command transmit event. Another version is where latency is longer than one frame, but fixed. For example, "in exactly N frames from transmit of the command, action X will occur."

2. Quasi RT control. The latency is bounded but there is jitter. For example, with a maximum of three frames of latency from command transmit (one to three frames range), action X occurs or there is a delay range for device execution; N frames $+-2$ frames.

3. Nonreal time control. Unbounded latency and jitter. An action X may occur any time after transmit of the command. In practice there is an upper bound that is acceptable to users.

For most AV operations, the first timing case is preferred, although case 2 is acceptable for some actions; case 3 is rarely acceptable unless bounded. LAN-based control has the potential of latency, jitter, and packet loss, which is an anathema when controlling device frames accurately. The proprietary LAN-based protocols cited earlier use two ways to circumvent the problem cases and to achieve hard real time control. Let us call the first method type S (action **S**cheduled) and second type N (action **N**ow). Both are illustrated in Figure 7.3.

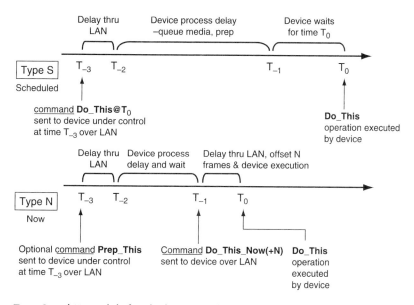

FIGURE

7.3

Type S and N models for device control over LAN.

Not to scale.

Type S—LAN-Based Scheduled Real Time Control

This model is based on *prequeuing* a list of actions in the target device. Queued items range from a simple command to play a clip to a complex multielement video composite. Each queued item has an exact, frame-accurate, future execute time, T_0. As long as the device reliably receives the command instructions adequately before T_0, then any IP jitter or packet loss is of no consequence. By allowing the device under control to, in effect, schedule the future operation, any small LAN delays will be absorbed. Of course the controlling intelligence must cooperate by sending commands before they are to be executed at T_0.

Reviewing Figure 7.3., the type S timeline shows three critical periods from the initial command reception to command execution. A **Do_This@T_0** command (with *This* implying some device operation) is sent to target device at T_{-3}. Delay through a small LAN network is normally <1 ms (much less than one frame of video) if there is no router congestion. The target and sender device TCP/IP processing delay are both in series with the LAN delay, which can be significant if not managed. The next period (T_{-2} to T_{-1}) is allocated for the device to queue any AV media and prep for the desired action at T_0. This may take from one to N video frames based on traditional serial control methods. In the world of VTRs, this is called the *preroll time*. Next, there is a wait period until T_0 occurs referenced to a time code clock (usually synced to the facility time-of-day clock). At T_0, the desired operation is executed, frame accurately. The T_{-1} until T_0 delay can range from one frame to hours.

Figure 7.4 illustrates a video server with a deep queue using type S control. The external storage does not require a low latency response, as the server has ample time to queue the clips. Of course the *average* storage access bandwidth must meet the needs of the server. Type S does not require a deep queue (one level may be sufficient), but the deeper the queue, the more forgiving the overall system is to temporary LAN and storage access anomalies. In fact, a type S control schema considerably enhances overall system reliability if queuing is used judiciously.

A type S control has ideal frame accurate characteristics as long as prequeuing timing is observed. The minimum practical time from command reception to execution is less than one frame of video. The maximum time

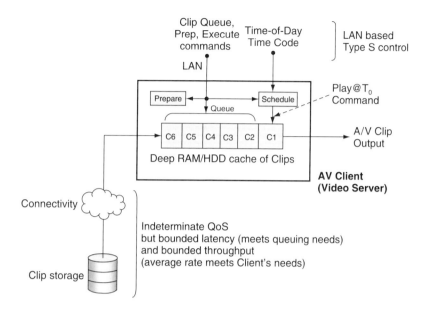

FIGURE

7.4

Deep queuing with quasi-RT storage and type S control.

depends on several factors, such as queuing time and the QoS of any external storage, and may require 7 s or more for reliable, repeated execution. Many typical operations (video server plays Clip_C1, for example) need 3 sec or less from T_{-3} to T_0. If the target device does not support scheduled operators or the application is not suited for this model, then type N may be used.

Type N—LAN-Based Immediate Real Time Control

For this scenario, the concept is based on a **Do_This_Now** command plan. In some cases, such as selecting signal routing, immediate execution is required with no prequeuing or prescheduling possible as with a type S. A low LAN delay is crucial (less than one frame of video) for immediate execution of some commands. For other scenarios, prequeuing is required so a **Prep_This** command is issued *before* the **Do_This_Now** is executed. Figure 7.3 shows the prep command in the type N timeline. Command execution is not prescheduled as with a type S, but follows the **Do_This_Now** command being received by the target device. In general, the execute command needs to have an offset of N (0,1,2,3,4, . . .) frames in the future to allow for the frame accurate alignment of other coordinated AV devices—each with a potentially different execute latency. As a result, **Do_This_Now(+N)** is a more general case where N is device specific. This is not a new problem and exists with RS-422 command control today.

There may be several prep commands issued before the corresponding **Do_This** command. For example, the sequence **of Prep_This_1, Prep_This_2** may precede a **Do_This_2_Now** followed by a **Do_This_1_Now** execution sequence. The order of execution is not fore-ordained. The most crucial time period is from T_{-1} to T_0 and should be less than one video frame (~33 ms with 525 line video). Modern LANs can meet this requirement.

For most type S and N control cases, the relaxing of storage access latency implies that the storage and connecting infrastructure is easier to build, test, and maintain. Plus quasi real time (latency may on occasion exceed some average value) storage is less expensive and more forgiving than pure RT storage. Of course, if the workflow and reliability demand immediate access and playout without the advantage of deep queuing, then the storage QoS will be rigid. There is no free lunch, as prequeuing clips in local client memory (RAM usually but disk also possible for some cases) adds a small expense. A client cache that can hold 50 Mb/s encoded clips for 1 min needs to be at least 375 MB deep. This is not a huge penalty but it is a burden. Also, the logic for deep queuing may be nontrivial and some automation controllers may not be designed with deep queuing in mind. Also, if the playout sequence changes in the last seconds (news stories), then the queue needs to be flushed or reordered, which adds complex logic to the workflow. See the section on user data caching in Chapter 3B for more insight into the art of caching.

It is inevitable that LAN methods will replace legacy serial links. With certainty the generic **Do_This@T$_0$** and **Do_This_Now** with associated deep queuing/prep commands will be implemented. Many industry players predicted (hoped!) that LAN control would overtake the serial link by 2005 but this did not happen. However, because there has been some recent industry activity in LAN-based control protocols, we may see the transition over the next year or so. Next, let us consider the management plane.

7.1.2   The Management Plane

The management plane (see Figure 7.1) is the least mature of the three because there are too few AV product management standards to gain the momentum needed to create a true business segment. The general IT device management solution space is very mature with hundreds of vendors selling to this domain. However, because AV equipment manufactures have been slow to develop standardized management plane functionality, many AV-specific devices are managed in an ad hoc manner. SMPTE is encouraging all vendors to assist in contributing to common sets (general and per device class) of device status metrics but the uptake has been slow. See Chapter 9 for a complete coverage of the management plane.

7.1.3   The Data/User Plane

The data/user plane is the most mature of the three, with many vendors offering IT-based NLE client stations, AV servers, browsers, video processors, compositors, storage systems, and other devices. For example, Sony offers the XDCam camera family (field news gathering) using the Professional Optical Disc, Panasonic offers the P2 camera family using removable flash memory, and Ikegami offers the EditCam3 with a removable 40-GB HDD. These are a far cry from the video-tape centric cameras of just a few years ago. The P2 and XDCam have LAN ports for offloading AV essence,[1] usually wrapped by MXF with included metadata. Generally, most recently developed AV devices show a true hybrid personality with traditional AV connectors, a LAN (or FC) port, and other digital I/O ports such as IEEE-1394 or USB2. Incidentally, the P2 camera offers 16 GB of removable flash and a gigabit Ethernet port supporting download rates of 640 Mb/s. This storage is equivalent to 1.42 hr of DV/25 recording that may be downloaded to permanent storage in only 3.3 min. There are interesting and compelling tradeoffs among these three camera styles.

The types of data plane AV essence in use are varied from uncompressed digital cinema production quality ($\sim$7 Gb/s) to low bit rate compressed proxy video at 100 Kb/s. Audio too can range from multichannel, 24-bit uncompressed, 2.3 Mb/s per channel to MP3 (or a host of others)

---

[1] The term "essence" denotes underlying A/V data structures such as video (RGB, MPEG2, etc.), audio (AES/EBU, WAV, MP3, etc.), graphics (BMP, JPEG, etc.), and text in their base formats.

at 64 Kb/s. Due to the wide variety of AV compression formats, video line rates, and H/V resolutions, achieving interoperability among different vendors' equipment can be a challenge. Although the data plane is standardized and mature in many aspects, creating workflows using different vendors' equipment can be a challenge.

The protocol aspects of this plane include network protocols such as TCP/IP, storage access protocols such as SCSI and iSCSI, and file server access protocols such as NFS and CIFS. The main goal of access protocols is to get to data—the AV and metadata gold that resides on disk arrays and archive systems. These protocols are discussed in detail in Chapter 3B.

The data structures layer is rich in variety and detail. SMPTE and other standard bodies have devoted hundreds of standards to describing these structures. Chapter 11 specializes in the AV data/user plane with coverage of the fundamentals of AV signal formats, resolutions, interfaces, compression, transmission formats, and many more. You may want to read Chapter 11 first before continuing here if you are unfamiliar with the basics. If not, let us move on to wrapper formats, including MXF, AAF, and XML. See [SMPTE] for a good tutorial series on MXF and AAF.

7.2 WRAPPER FORMATS AND MXF

The AV industry is not lacking for file formats. A laundry list of formats confronts designers and users daily: MPEG1, 2, 4, WM9/VC-1, H.264, DV (25, 50, 100 Mb/s), HDCAM, Y'CrCb, RGB, audio formats, and the list continues. As shown previously, files are indispensable when acquiring, logging, browsing, storing, editing, converting, transferring, archiving, and distributing AV materials. Is there a way to tame the format beast? Can we select one format that all users would support? If so, then interoperability would be a snap and file exchange between users would rarely hit a snag. Additionally, AV equipment interoperability, vendor neutral solutions, and one archive format all follow when a universal file format is chosen. Despite the desire for interoperability, very few users would accept a *one format* policy. Why not? Each format has its strengths and weaknesses. Depending on business needs (acquisition format, cost, quality, bandwidth, simplicity, legacy use, etc.) format A may be a better choice than format B. In the end, the one format policy can not be legislated, despite all its benefits.

Fortunately there is an acceptable tradeoff: a standardized, universal, professional *wrapper format*. A wrapper does exactly what the name implies—it wraps something. In the broadest sense, that something may be AV essence, graphic essence, metadata, or generic data. Like peas inside a pea pod, a wrapper is a carrier of lower level items. A universal wrapper fosters interoperability between users and equipment at several levels. Figure 7.5 illustrates the concept of a wrapper. Note the various essence mappings into the wrapper file.

A wrapper format is not the same as a compression format (e.g., MPEG2 Elementary Stream). In fact, many wrappers are compression agnostic even though they carry compressed essence. The QuickTime.mov format from Apple is a wrapper. The ubiquitous .avi file format is a wrapper. A File.mov or File.avi that carries MPEG essence or DV does not disclose which by its file extension, unlike File.dv, which is always a DV format. Many AV essence formats have documented mappings into file wrappers. The term "essence agnostic" is often cited regarding MOV, AVI, or MXF but is only partially true. The wrapper must provide for the underlying essence mapping with supporting official documentation. An undocumented mapping is useless. For an excellent reference to MXF and other file formats, see [Gilmer] and also the SMPTE Engineering Guidelines EG–41 and EG–42.

Despite the existence of AV wrappers, all legacy formats fall short of the needs of professional AV. The ideal wrapper requirements for our needs are

◆ Open and standardized (QuickTime is not open or standardized)
◆ Supports multiplexed time-based media

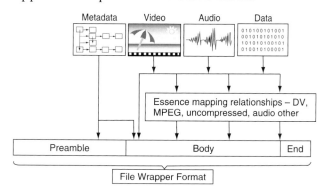

FIGURE

7.5

Example of a file wrapper format.
Concept: File Interchange Handbook, Chapter 1.

♦ Supports multiplexed metadata

♦ Targeted for file interchange

♦ Essence agnostic in principle

♦ OS and storage system independent

♦ Streamable

♦ Extensible

Wrapper requirements were identified by the SMPTE/EBU Task Force report of April, 1997 (see www.smpte.org for a copy of this online report). Following that, the ProMPEG Forum (www.pro-mpeg.org) was formed to define and develop a wrapper format that met the requirement list given earlier. The initial work started in July of 1999 and was called the Material eXchange Format or MXF. After nearly 4 years of effort, the forum submitted their documents to SMPTE for standardization in 2003. In 2005, there are 24 MXF-related standards, proposed standards, and engineering guidelines. SMPTE 377M is the fundamental MXF format standard. MXF has been favorably embraced by the AV industry worldwide. Of course it will not replace existing wrappers or dedicated formats overnight. It will take time for MXF to gain enough steam to become the king of the professional AV format hill. MXF is expected to have minimal impact on consumer product formats.

7.2.1   Inside the MXF Wrapper

There are two chief ways to view an MXF file: the physical layout and the logical layout. The physical view is considered first. Figure 7.6 shows the physical layout of a typical MXF file. The A/V essence, metadata, and optional index file (associates time code to a byte offset into the file) are all multiplexed together using basic key/length/value (KLV) blocking. KLV coding is a common way to separate continuous data elements and allow for quick identification of any element. The key is a SMPTE registered 16B Universal Label (SMPTE 336M) that uniquely identifies the data value to follow (audio, video, metadata, etc.). Length indicates the number of bytes in the value field. The value field carries the data payload, including audio samples, video essence, metadata, index tables, pointers, and more.

The KLV sequences are divided into three general groups: the header, body, and footer. The *header* contains information about the file,

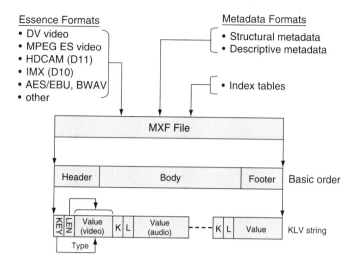

Physical views of an MXF file.

such as operational pattern (explained below), clip name, length, creator, aspect ratio, encoding rate, frame rate, and so on. This information is referred to as *structural* (in contrast to descriptive) metadata. The header also contains descriptive metadata that may be time synchronous with the A/V essence. The *body* contains A/V multiplexed essence. The A/V essence is mapped according to the rules per each data type. For example, MPEG (including MPEG 1, 2, MPEG 4 and H.264/AVC) has a mapping (SMPTE 381M), DV has a mapping (SMPTE 383M), AES/EBU audio has a mapping (382M), and so on. There is a mapping expected for JPEG 2000 in full motion mode as well. Most mappings locate each video frame on a KLV boundary for convenient, fast frame access, but there is no absolute requirement for this. Finally the *footer* closes the file with optional metadata. Additionally, index tables (frame tables) are optionally included in the header, interleaved in the body, or stored in the footer.

MXF: The Logical View

The second way to view an MXF file is logically. In this case, the focus is on the organization of the information, not how it is sequenced in the file. Figure 7.7 (top) illustrates a very simple MXF file with only sound

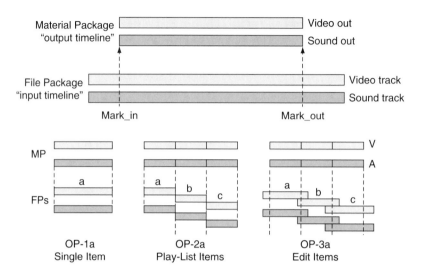

Logical views of an MXF file.

and video essence tracks. Of course data are stored as KLV sequences, but the organization shows a File Package (FP) and Material Package (MP). By analogy, the File Package is the "input timeline," a collection of files in effect, whereas the Material Package is the "output time-line"—how the MXF internal files are to be read out. The example shows the output to be a portion of the stored essence. A small amount of internal metadata sets the mark_in and mark_out points and is changed easily.

This is only the tip of the organizational iceberg of MXF and much of its documentation is devoted to describing its logical layout. It is not hard to imagine all sorts of ways to describe the output timeline based on simple rules between the File Package and the Material Package. These rules are called Operational Patterns. Consider the following in reference to Figure 7.7:

◆ Single FP, single MP. This is the most common case and the FP is the same as the MP. This is called OP-1a in MXF speak and is referenced as SMPTE 378M. An example of this is DV essence, with interleaved audio and video, wrapped in a single MXF file.

- Multiple File Packages, Single Material Package. This is case OP-2a (SMPTE 392M) and defines a collection of internal files (a, b, and c) sequenced into one concatenated output.
- OP-3a (SMPTE 407M) is a variation of OP-2a with internal tracks a, b, and c each having mark_in and mark_out points.

There are seven other operational patterns (2a, 2b, 2c, 3a, 3b, 3c, and OP-ATOM), each with its own particular FP to MP mapping. The simplest, OP-ATOM (SMPTE 390M), is a reduced form of OP-1a where only one essence type (A or V not both) is carried. Many vendors will use this format for native on-disc storage but support one or more of the other OPs for file import/export. Frankly, the abundance of OPs makes interoperability a challenge, as will be shown.

Descriptive Metadata

A distinguishing feature of MXF is its ability to optionally carry time synchronous *descriptive metadata*. Other wrappers are not as full featured in this regard. An example of this type of metadata is the classic opening line of the novel *Paul Clifford*:

> *It was a dark and stormy night; the rain fell in torrents—except at occasional intervals, when it was checked by a violent gust of wind which swept up the streets, rattling along the housetops, and fiercely agitating the scanty flame of the lamps that struggled against the darkness.*
>
> —*Edward George Bulwer-Lytton* (1830)

It is not hard to imagine this text associated with a video of a rainy, night-time London street scene. As the video progresses, the descriptive metadata text is interleaved scene by scene in the MXF wrapper. Once available for query, the metadata may be searched for terms such as "dark and stormy" and the corresponding video timecode and frames retrieved. The promise of descriptive data is enticing to producers, authors, editors, and others. The entire value chain for descriptive metadata is nontrivial: authoring the text, carrying text, storing searchable text separate from corresponding video, querying the text and retrieving corresponding video, editing the text, archiving it, and so on.

Our industry is struggling to develop applications that use metadata to its fullest potential. Because metadata spans a wide range of user applications, no one vendor offers a comprehensive, end-to-end solution set. SMPTE has standardized some of the more common descriptors and documented them as DMS-1 (Descriptive Metadata Schema, SMPTE 380M). MXF uses DMS-1. In addition, SMPTE has also defined a metadata dictionary (RP 210) with room for custom fields as needed. Interestingly, when Turner Entertainment documented their cartoon library they invented 1500 new terms to describe cartoon activities that rarely occur in daily life, such as stepping off a cliff, slowly realizing that the ground is far below, and then falling.

Several vendors support the budding metadata management world. A few tools in this space are MOG's Scribe and MXF Explorer (www.mog-solutions.com), Metaglue's Diffuser (www.metaglue.com), and OpenCube's MXF Toolkit (www.opencube.fr). Do not confuse metadata management with digital asset management (DAM). DAM is considered later in this chapter. Incidentally, Snell and Wilcox provides an open, free MXF SDK found at www.freemxf.org. Information on SMPTE's MXF interoperability efforts is located at www.smpte-mxf.org.

The Group of Linked Files (GOLF) Concept

The overarching goal of MXF is to package data formats of various flavors under one wrapper using operational patterns to define the packaging. An archived program may include some or all of the following data types:

◆ Video tracks—one or more, SD versions, HD versions
◆ Audio tracks—one or more
◆ Descriptive metadata
◆ Closed caption files (per language)
◆ Descriptive narration files (per language)
◆ Proxy files—VC-1 or similar low bit rate (A + V)
◆ AAF compositional metadata file
◆ Other (rights use, etc.)

MXF defines the wrapping rules for many of these data types, but not all of them. For example, the proxy and closed caption files may remain separate, never to be wrapped by MXF. The audio and video could be wrapped into a single MXF file; however, there are reasons to keep them discrete.

While it is true that some of the file types in the list may be wrapped into a single MXF file, at times it is wise to keep *all* these files separate. Using the concept of a file directory, all included files become linked or associated together. Let us call this a group of linked files. A GOLF uses a directory to wrap files and thus mimic some, but not all, of the wrapping features of MXF. For access purposes, a user may retrieve all or parts of the program, including partial access within an individual file/track. By referring to the named directory, it is easy to move all its parts in total to another location without fragmentation.

Figure 7.8 shows an example of a GOLF for the program title "Basketball_Finals." Notice that only the video tracks are wrapped in MXF using Op-ATOM, the simplest operational pattern. The index file is a key element and defines the contents of all the files in the GOLF. The indexer could be an MXF file (OP-2b, or OP-2C for example) that only describes or points to other individual files in the same directory or an XML index file could be used but no standards exist yet for this purpose. The index file creates a "smart directory" of sorts. It should be noted that currently not every GOLF file type has a SMPTE-supported unique identifier but this is remedied easily.

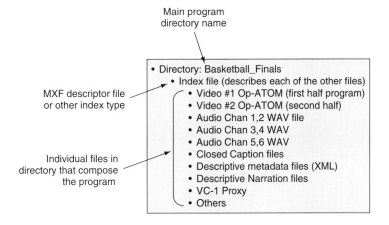

FIGURE 7.8   Group of linked files (GOLF) example.

The GOLF files are accessed as a function of the needs of a workflow. For example, for AV editing the separate audio and video files are accessed as needed. For broadcast playout, the audio, video, and closed caption files are retrieved and sequenced together in time. For low-resolution browsing, only the proxy file is needed. As a result, a GOLF enables easy random access to target files. Using an all-encompassing MXF wrapper, all included tracks must be retrieved to access even one track.

The upper level applications need to assure proper A + V + data timing when combining files for synchronous playing. Incidentally, this is something that MXF does inherently well. The GOLF method has other advantages compared to a fully wrapped MXF file—less data wrapping and unwrapping to access and insert tracks.

Let us consider an example. Assume a 1-h MXF program file with interleaved A + V (with 50 Mb/s MPEG essence). Accessing, modifying, and restoring an audio track require these operations: the audio track is demuxed/removed, modified by some audio edit operation, and remuxed back into the MXF file. As might be imagined, these are data-intensive operations and may involve 45 gigabytes of R/W storage access even though the target audio track is about 650 MB in size. Using the GOLF, only the target audio track is retrieved, modified, and restored with a huge savings in storage access time. Also, the index file may be updated to indicate a new version of the audio file.

For some applications and workflows, working with a GOLF is simpler and more efficient than using fully wrapped MXF. In general, access and restore are easier using the GOLF, especially partial file/track access. There is room for MXF centric and GOLF centric designs and each will find its application space.

7.2.2   Working with MXF and Interoperability

It's interesting to note that one of the goals for MXF is to foster file interchange and interoperability between users/equipment and not to define an on-disc AV format. What is the consequence of this decision?

Equipment vendors are not required to store MXF, as their *native file format* enables others access over a network. Consider a networked editing system that stores all AV essence in the AVI format. If an external user expects to connect to this system via a NAS and directly access stored MXF files, he or she will be disappointed. However, if the system supports MXF file import/export using FTP, then the same user will be able to exchange MXF files, even though the storage format is natively AVI. Of course, this requires an AVI/MXF file conversion step as part of the import/export process. As a result, MXF does not guarantee interoperability for all system access modes but it is a step in the right direction. Some vendors have chosen to work with natively stored MXF but this is not a requirement of the standard.

One example of a system with mixed formats is illustrated in Figure 7.9. The networked editing system is "closed." The attached NLEs have direct access to stored AV essence, which may be in AVI, QT, or even MXF formats. Outsiders have access to the stored essence via the gateway. If the internal format is AVI and the system advertises MXF compliancy, then the gateway is responsible for all format conversions. External users do not need to know that the internal format is AVI for the most part. As long as the gateway provides for the import/export function then all is well. Or is it?

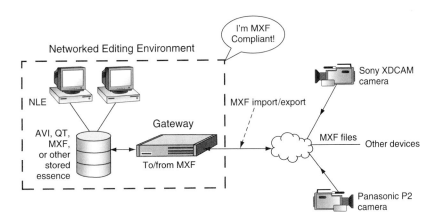

FIGURE   A sample MXF interchange environment.

7.9

There is a world of difference between MXF *compliancy* and MXF *compatibility*. The system of Figure 7.9 is MXF import/export compliant but it may not be MXF compatible. If it meets all the legal MXF specs—*how* it is formed—then it is compliant. However, in a two-sided transaction, both parties need to agree on exactly *what* will be transferred for compatibility. Assume that an external source has an MXF file that is OP-3a formatted, MPEG-4 IBP essence with no index tables. If an internal location only supports OP-1a, MPEG-2 with an index table then there is a conflict. From the standpoint of the internal site, the external MXF file is not *compatible* even if it is *compliant*.

Figure 7.10 shows a stack of possible external formats, and MXF as the preferred internal format. The pyramid relates to the relative number of files in production today with MXF at the top because it is rare. A gateway (GW) sits between the external source/sink of files and the internal source/sink. The purpose of the GW is to massage the files and make them MXF *compliant* and *compatible* for import/export. Legacy files will always be with us so the gateway is legacy's friend.

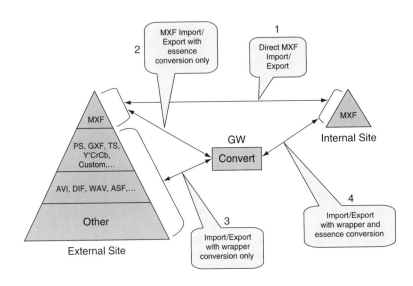

FIGURE   File conversion gateway operations.

7.10

The File Conversion Gateway

The more choices MXF allows for (and there are plenty) the less likely that any two-party transaction will succeed without some format manipulation. The gateway performs at least four different kinds of operations per Figure 7.10:

◆ Case 1. MXF import/export compatible and compliant to both sides. In this case the GW does no format changes. This is the trivial case.

◆ Case 2. MXF compliancy on both sides but the MXF essence layers are not compatible. For example, the GW may need to transcode from MPEG to DV. Another possible change is from OP-3a to OP-1a. This step may cause quality degradation and delay the transfer due to slow transcoding.

◆ Case 3. The external wrapper is not MXF compliant (may be AVI) but the essence, say DV, is compatible. The GW unwraps the DV and rewraps it under MXF. This is a fast transaction, with no quality loss, but metadata may be lost when going from MXF to a non-MXF format.

◆ Case 4. The external wrapper layer is not MXF complaint and the essence layer is not compatible. This is the worst case and costs in quality and time. Avoid if possible.

There are several vendors providing all-purpose file gateways, among which are Front Porch Digital (www.fpdigital.com), Masstech Group (www.masstechgroup.com), and Telestream (www.telestream.net). Each of these vendors either offers MXF conversion or has plans to so.

In general, gateway operations are governed by the following principles:

◆ Speed of conversion. Transparent RT is ideal but few gateways operate in RT for all operations.

◆ Loss of quality during conversion. Transcoding a DV/25 file to MPEG2 at 10 Mb/sec will cause a generation loss of quality

◆ Assuring that all the information in the input file (A/V, metadata, etc.) is not lost but somehow accounted for in the output file. Often some input information is deliberately left on the floor during the conversion.

◆ Testing all the conversion combinations is often not practical. For example, cross conversion support among only 10 file format types leads to 90 conversion pairs that need to be tested and supported.

Gateways are a fact of life but careful planning can reduce their heavy usage. With the advent of MXF, our industry will standardize on one wrapper format. Another use of a gateway is to create a proxy file from a higher resolution file. For example, a gateway (really a conversion engine for this example) can watch a file folder for signs of any new files. When a new file arrives, the engine can encode to say a WM9 file for use by browsers facility-wide. Gateways will become more sophisticated in dealing with metadata too. The field of metadata mapping between AV formats is unplowed ground for the most part. Also, Moore's law is on the side of the transcoding gateway as it becomes faster each year.

You Only Get What You Define

Okay, so you have decided all your time-based media will be MXF. To reach this goal, it is best to publish an import/export specification to set the format ground rules. With adherence to these guidelines, format compatibility is all but guaranteed. Unfortunately, some suppliers will still provide MXF files that differ somewhat from desired. In many cases the imported file will be compatible. In other cases a gateway is needed to force compatibility. Some of the MXF specs that should be nailed down are:

- SD and HD resolutions, 4×3 or 16×9, 4:2:2, 4:2:0, duration
- Video essence layer—MPEG format and type (IBP or I-only), DV, other
- Video essence compression rate (e.g., <=50 Mb/sec)
- Audio essence layer—AES/EBU, Bwave, other, number of channels
- Operational patterns. OP-1a and OP-ATOM will be the most common for many years to come
- Use of metadata—DMS-1, other, or none
- Streamable or not—MXF streams are not in common use
- Frame-based edit units or other segmentation
- Advanced topics: length of partitions, alignment of internal fields, index table location(s), VBI carriage, other

Early success with MXF depends on sticking to a formula for MXF file parameters. Without an interoperability document, MXF interchange quickly becomes a bad dream.

7.3 ADVANCED AUTHORING FORMAT—(AAF)[2]

AAF is a specialized metadata file format designed for use in the postproduction of AV content. Imagine a project where three different people collaborate on the same material. One person does the video edits, another does the audio edits and mix, and a third does the graphics. They all need to see the work of the others at different stages of the development. Figure 7.11 shows a typical workflow for such a production. The following is a list of common operations used in post workflows:

◆ Editing materials
◆ Visual effects
◆ Compositing
◆ Animations
◆ Mixing audio
◆ Audio effects
◆ Captions

It is obvious that a common language for material interchange is needed. At the essence level, MXF meets the need, but what is the best

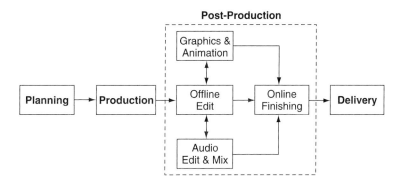

FIGURE

7.11

Workflow to create typical AV program material.

Source: File Interchange Handbook, Chapter 6.

---

[2] This section is loosely modeled after and paraphrased from parts of Chapter 6 (AAF) by Phil Tudor, File Interchange Handbook [Gilmer].

way to describe the assembly of the material? How are all the edits, mixes, compositions, effects, captions, and so on assembled to create the final program? This is where AAF comes in. At the most basic level, AAF is categorized as an edit decision list (EDL) format. Because it is a record of every edit operation, an EDL plus the essence completely defines the media project at any stage of development. Many proprietary EDLs exist with little interoperability and limited feature sets. There is a need for an open, extensible, full-featured "super EDL" and AAF meets these needs.

AAF was developed as a response to the SMPTE/EBU Task Force's recommendations for such a format. In time the AAF Association (www.aafassociation.org) took up the mantle to manage AAF's development as an open format although technically not a standard. The Association also promotes AAF through a series of awareness events.

Methods of AAF File Interchange

AAF supports two methods to interchange edit information between assembly tools. These are the import/export and the edit-in-place models. Figure 7.12 shows the two methods. With the import/export method (top of Figure 7.12), tool A creates a new AAF file that is read by tool B. Tool B creates a new AAF file that is read by tool C. The two interchanges are

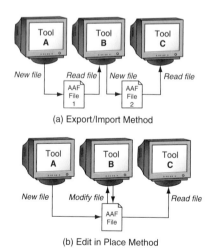

(a) Export/Import Method

(b) Edit in Place Method

FIGURE   AAF export/import and in-place-edit interchange methods.
7.12   Source: File Interchange Handbook, Chapter 6.

independent. This model is appropriate for simple exchanges between two tools but has limitations for moving data among multiple tools. However, the edit-in-place method allows for any tool to read/modify a common AAF file as needed. Any data created by tool A can be read by tool C with no dependence on tool B. When AAF files are created or modified, a record of each application's operations is made to leave an audit trail.

AAF supports internal or external A/V essence. Internal essence is practical for small projects. For larger ones, keeping the essence external (e.g., MXF) is desired. This is especially true if there are many essence files. Loading all essence into a single AAF file could easily create an impenetrable 50 GB file for just a few hours of raw video essence.

AAF Reference Implementation

The AAF Association provides an open-source software reference implementation of the AAF specification (the AAF SDK). It is distributed as C++ open-source code with ports to several computer platforms. The reference implementation is recommended for use in products to reduce compatibility problems when crossing between different vendor implementations.

MXF and AAF share some common technology. MXF reuses a subset of the AAF object specification but maps it differently using KLV (SMPTE 336M) encoding. Parts of the object specification dealing with clips and source material are reused in MXF; parts dealing with compositions and effects are removed. By using a common data model, metadata in an MXF file are directly compatible with AAF. This allows AAF and MXF to work in harmony across a broad range of applications.

There are virtually no limits to the types of effects that a composition may contain. Vendor A may offer a super 3D whiz bang effect that vendor B does not support. In this case, how does AAF help because the effect cannot be interchanged? While it is true that not every possible effect is transportable between tools, AAF supports a subset of effects that meets the needs of most creative workflows. The AAF edit protocol defines this practical subset.

The edit protocol is designed to codify best practices for the storage and exchange of AAF files [McDermid]. It constrains the more general

Dissolve effects	Layered 2D DVE effects
Wipe effects	Key effects
Motion effects	Alpha channel matte key definition
Frame repeat effects	Alpha key over video
Flip and flop effects	Luminance key
Spatial positioning and zooms	Chroma key effect
(2D DVE) including:	Audio gain effects
Moving the image	Audio clip gain and track gain
Cropping the image	Audio track pan effect
Scaling the image	Audio fade effect
Rotating the image	
Corner pinning	

TABLE

7.1

Constrained Effects: Defined for Interoperability Using AAF

AAF to a subset of all possible operations to guarantee a predictable level of interoperability between tools. One area that requires constraint is effects. Interchanging effects is one of the most challenging aspects of AAF. Table 7.1 shows the classes of defined effects supported by the edit protocol. Other effects will need to be rendered into a video format before interchange. In the end, AAF is a life saver for program production across a collaborative group. AAF levels the playing field and gives users an opportunity to choose their tools and not be locked into one vendor's products.

7.4   XML AND METADATA

XML (eXtensible Markup Language) has become the lingua franca of the metadata world. When XML became a standard in 1998, it ushered in a new paradigm for distributed computing. Despite its hype, XML is simply a meta language—a language for describing other languages. For the first time, XML enabled a standard way to format a description language. Its use is evident in business systems worldwide, including AV/IT systems. XML makes it possible for users to interchange information (metadata, labels, values, etc.) using a standard method to encode the contents. It is not a language in the sense of say C+ or Java but rather one to describe and enumerate information. Let us take an example to get things started.

Your vacation to London is over. You took plenty of video footage and now it is time to describe the various scenes using textural descriptions (descriptive metadata: who, what, when, and where). Using XML it may look like the following:

```
<vacation_video>
<location> London, August, 2005 </location>
<scenes>
    <time_code> 1:05:00:00 </time_code>
        <action> "arriving at our South Kensington hotel" </action>
        <action> "strolling down Pond St in Chelsea" </action>
        <action> "walking along the King's Road with Squeak and Dave" </action>
</scenes>
<scenes>
    <time_code> 1:10:12:20 </time_code>
        <action> "visiting the Tate Museum" </action>
        <action> . . . and so on . . .
</scenes>
</vacation_video>
```

The syntax is obvious. All the information is easily contained in a small file, e.g., London-text.xml. Importantly, XML is human readable. The labels may take on many forms and these are preferably standardized. Several groups have standardized the label fields (<scenes>), as described later. For example, one of the early standards (not A/V specific) is called the Dublin Core. The Dublin Core Metadata Initiative (DCMI) is an organization dedicated to promoting the widespread adoption of interoperable metadata standards and developing specialized metadata vocabularies for describing resources that enable more intelligent information discovery systems (www.dublincore.org).

Due to the popularity of XML, there are tools galore to author, edit, view, validate, and do other operations. See www.xmlspy.com for a variety of examples and tools. See too [XML] for a collection of XML resources and standards. Because editors and producers do not want to be burdened with the details of XML, the AV industry is slowly creating high-level applications (authoring, querying, browsing) that use XML under the hood.

Querying metadata is a very common operation. Let us assume a collection of 10,000 XML files each describing associated AV essence files. What is the best way to query metadata to find a particular scene of video among all the essence? One customary method is to extract all metadata and load into an SQL database. A database query is supported by a variety of tools and is mature. Is it possible to query the 10K files directly without needing an SQL database? Yes and one tool to assist is XQuery.

XQuery is a query language specification developed by the World Wide Web Consortium (W3C) that is designed to query collections of XML data or even files that have only some XML data. XQuery makes possible the exciting prospect of a single query that searches across an incoming AV metadata file in native XML format, an archive of catalog data also in native XML format, and archived metadata held in a relational database. It will take some time for the AV industry to appreciate the value of this important new query language.

Many professional video products offer some fashion of XML import/export. Descriptive metadata is the lifeblood of AV production for documenting and finding materials. Expect XML and its associated metadata to touch every aspect of A/V workflow. From acquisition to ingest/logging, editing, browsing, archiving, and publishing, metadata is a key to managing media. Several industry players are defining how to use XML schemas to package metadata. The next section outlines some current efforts.

7.4.1   Metadata Standards and Schemas for AV

We are at the cusp of standardized metadata that crosses tool and system boundaries. MXF supports SMPTE 380M for metadata descriptions. Also SMPTE supports the Metadata Dictionary, RP210. This is an extensible dictionary that may be augmented by public registry. SMPTE is also crafting an XML version of MXF descriptive metadata. This is a work in progress but is expected to be available by late 2005. In addition, the AV industry has developed several metadata frameworks, each with its own strength.

The BBC has defined a Standard Media Exchange Framework (SMEF) to support and enable media asset management as an end-to-end process across its business areas, from production to delivery to the home. The SMEF Data Model (SMEF-DM) provides a set of definitions for the information required in production, distribution, and management of media assets, currently expressed as a data dictionary and set of entity relationship diagrams.

The EBU (www.ebu.ch) project group, P/META, defines and represents the information requirements for the exchange of program content between the high-level business functions of EBU members: production, delivery, broadcast, and archive. The P/META scheme provides defined metadata to support the identification, description, discovery, and use of essence in business-to-business (B2B) transactions. Their work effort is based on an extension of SMEF.

MPEG-7 is an established metadata standard for classifying various types of multimedia information. Despite its name, MPEG-7 is not an A/V encoding standard such as MPEG-4. MPEG-7 is formally called a "Multimedia Content Description Interface." For an overview of MPEG-7 technologies, see [Hasegawa]. The standard supports a wide range of metadata features from video characteristics such as shape, size, color, and audio attributes such as tempo, mood, and key to descriptive elements such as who, what, when, and where. MPEG-7 has found little use in professional AV production so far. However, it has found application by the TV-Anytime Forum (personal video recorder products). Their defined metadata specification and XML schema are based on MPEG-7's description definition language and its description schemas.

Finally, the IRT (Institut für Rundfunktechnik) in Munich and MOG (www.mog-solutions.com) have codeveloped an XML mapping of the MXF metadata structures (DMS-1). The IRT has also developed an AV metadata framework specific to AV production applications. These are not yet standardized solutions but will likely find applications in some quarters.

7.4.2   The UMID

Without a way to identify metadata types and essence files explicitly, they quickly become lost in a sea of data. The Unique Material Identifier (UMID, SMPTE 330M and RP 205) is a global way to identify AV materials. It is the kingpin in the quest for a universal way to unambiguously tag every piece of essence and metadata. UMIDs identify every component part of a program and provide a linkage between the essence and its associated metadata. The UMID is a 32-bit (64 in extended form) field with the potential to identify every AV file with a granularity of frames if desired. For example, the UMID hex value of #A214F07C could represent the unique AV essence of NASA's original video of Neil Armstrong's first step on the moon. MXF relies on UMIDs for content ID. Some of its characteristics are:

- It is a globally unique identifier
- It identifies any level of material granularity, from a single frame to a completed final package
- It can be automatically and locally issued, which means that access to a central database or a registration authority is not needed
- It may be used in different applications, i.e., not only as a global material identifier, but also as a local identifier with some specific local applications

Figure 7.13 puts all the concepts together in a metadata registry example. It is server based, stores XML metadata, and provides for common client metadata operations. The different layers describe functions and aspects needed to implement a searchable metadata repository. There are no standardized and commercially available metadata application servers on the market. Each vendor offers something unique and fine-tuned for its products and supported workflows.

Metadata management solutions range from hand-searched lists to federated networked systems with millions of metadata entries. No one architecture, schema, or vendor solution has won the hearts of all AV users. Time will tell how metadata management solutions will pan out and what schema(s) becomes the king of the hill. Admittedly, several may rise to the top, as there is room for specialized schemas across the range of AV businesses.

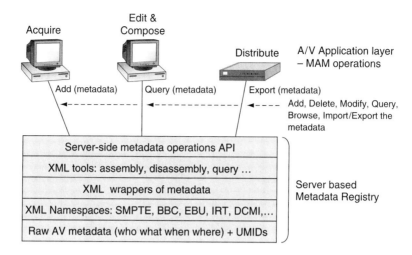

XML-centric metadata registry: Server based.

7.4.3   ISAN and V-ISAN Content ID Tags

The ISO has standardized ISAN (International Standard Audiovisual Number) as a 64-bit value to identify a piece of programming. The ISAN goes beyond the UMID by providing fields for owner ID, content ID, and episode number. It should be embedded into the material (watermark is one way) so that the ISAN value and content it points to are inseparable. Think of the ISAN value as representing a collection of AV objects that are in total a program. V-ISAN is a 96-bit version that includes the version number, indicating language, edited for TV rating, and subtitles.

Metadata and its associated tools are only small cogs in the big wheel of media asset management (MAM). In what way is MAM part of the AV/IT revolution? Let us see.

7.5   MEDIA ASSET MANAGEMENT

There is an old saying in the AV business that goes something like this: *"If you have it but can't find it then you don't have it."* With a MAM solution, enabled users can—ideally—quickly and easily locate content they possess.

With the proliferation of media assets and Web pages with embedded AV, MAM solutions are becoming commonplace in business. More generally, digital asset management (DAM) solutions (not media centric) are used to manage text documents with graphics. Think of MAM as DAM with the ability to manage time-based media. In the big picture, both MAM and DAM are content management (CM) concepts. According to a Frost & Sullivan report, the worldwide MAM market will grow from $327 million in 2003 to $1.37 billion in 2010 at a compound annual growth rate estimated to be 20.2%. The overall market includes all types of media production and delivery, including Web based.

One definition of MAM is the process of digitizing, cataloging, querying, moving, managing, repurposing, and securely delivering time-based media and still graphics. It supports the workflow of information between users for the creation of new and modified media products.

But what is a media asset? On the surface, any media that sit in company storage may be considered an asset, but this is far from the truth in practice. Figure 7.14 shows the asset equation: an asset is the content *plus* the rights to use it. Many broadcasters have shelves full of videos that they cannot legally play to air because the use contract has expired. Also, the content is the essence *plus* the metadata that describes it. In the end, both metadata and rights are needed to fully qualify and manage a media asset. In fact, we need to modify the opening quote to reflect the true reality: "*If you have it and can find it but with no rights to it then you don't have it.*"

Rights management is a complex topic. It involves aspects of copyright law, contracts, payments, and windows of use and reuse. A single program

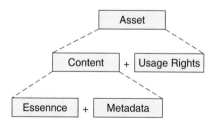

FIGURE   The asset equation.
7.14   Source: SMPTE.

may have sequences each with its own rights clauses. Rights age so what is legal today may not be tomorrow. All aspects of production require knowledge of media rights. See Section 7.52 for a primer on DRM.

The MAM Landscape

This section examines the major components in a MAM solution. Figure 7.15 outlines the MAM onion. The outer layer represents the applications and solutions needed by business processes. AV-related ones are

- ◆ A/V production
- ◆ Broadcast automation
- ◆ News production

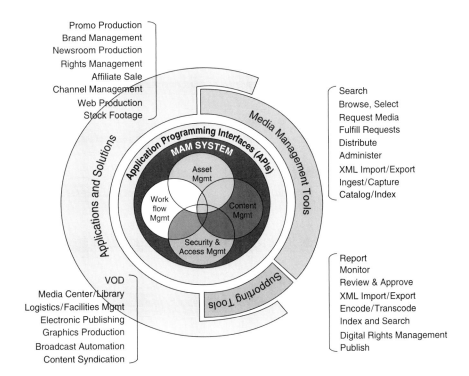

FIGURE   The MAM onion.
7.15   Source: Perspective Media Group.

◆ Web production

◆ Rights management

◆ Video on demand

◆ Graphics production

◆ Content syndication

Each of these application areas may require a full-featured MAM system. The next layer comprises tools for ingesting, browsing, querying, and so on. Applications make use of these features as needed. Augmenting user functions are the support tools for reporting, review/approve, publishing, and so on. Applications and tools are connected to the center of the diagram using defined APIs. Finally, in the center are the core processes as listed. One area not yet discussed so far is workflow management. This is a relatively new frontier for AV production and provides methods to manage an entire project from concept to delivery. Workflow methods are examined later in the chapter.

No doubt, full-featured MAM solutions are complex. It is very unlikely that a shrink-wrap MAM solution will meet the needs of any large real world business.[3] Open market MAM solutions rely on customization to meet existing business process needs. Also, there are many vendor-specific aspects of these systems from AV proxy formats (MPEG1, WM9/VC1, MPEG4, MXF, etc.) to metadata formats (DCMI, SMEF, IRT, SMPTE, custom, etc.) to the APIs and middleware that connect all the pieces together. See [Cordeiro] for insights into a unified API for MAM. Ideally, the MAM system should fit like a glove with the existing AV systems architecture with its formats, workflows, control, and applications use. Unfortunately, the rather liberal use of "standard" formats prevents MAM systems from interoperating at even the most basic levels. Upgrading a MAM system from vendor A to B is a painful and often impossible task so choose your MAM system wisely, as you will live with it for a long, long time.

Choosing a commercial MAM system for a legacy business requires a large dose of compromise and realignment of internal processes to the abilities and functions of the MAM system. Many media operations have

---

[3] Shrink-wrap MAM solutions often meet the needs for simple workflows (Web page asset management) with a small number of users.

developed totally custom solutions because open market ones were not sufficient. Of course when developing a new complex workflow from scratch, it is wise to base it on available MAM functionalities to enable the use of open market solutions.

7.5.1 MAM Functions and Examples

To fulfill the needs of a full-featured MAM system, the following functions [Abunu] are required:

- One-time media capture and indexing of metadata (including rights, program information, usage, etc.) made accessible to all workflow participants.
- Standards for media assets for interoperability across the workflows.
- Implementation of a metadata set to support all workflow operations.
- Search functions to identify and locate AV essence. This may range from a simple file name search to a query based on people, places, things, and activities.
- Shared views and access to media across an organization mediated by access control.
- Media life cycle management—from ingest to composing to converting to archiving.
- Workflow process support—assignments, approvals, releases, ownerships, usage history.
- Functionalities to package and distribute media according to business needs.

Exploring the intricacies of these items is beyond our scope. However, to learn more about the details of MAM functionality (with support for time-based media and focus on broadcast and AV production), study the representational offerings from companies such as Artesia Technologies (www.artesia.com), Avid (www.avid.com), Blue Order (www.blue-order.com), Harris Broadcast (www.broadcast.harris.com), IBM (www.ibm.com + content manager), and Omnibus (www.omnibus.tv). The Perspective Media Group (www.perspectivemediagroup.com) specializes in workflow consulting to media companies. Virage (www.virage.com) pioneered A/V indexing and turnkey MAM solutions. Also, check out G-SAM (Global Society for Asset Management, www.gsam.org) for links to most vendors and reference materials.

A classic case of integrating a MAM with AV editing gear occurs in broadcast TV news production systems. Today many media companies from a large CNN to a small local TV station rely on IT-based news production systems for day-to-day operations. For example, Avid, GVG, Leitch, Quantel, and Sony, all offer a range of IT-based news production systems incorporating a restricted MAM. These systems support end-to-end unified workflows from ingest to play-to-air of news stories. Metadata management plays a big role in these systems. Most of the traditional automation vendors also offer MAM as part of their overall product portfolio.

Example of an Index/MAM Query Operation

This section examines the indexing and querying operations. These are two common operators in any MAM system. Indexed and cataloged metadata are the lifeblood of any asset tracking system. Figure 7.16 illustrates the relative volume of metadata versus positions in the media workflow. As a project develops the metadata volume increases to a peak during the editing and compositing stage. Little metadata is produced or consumed at either end of the production cycle. However, this trend may change as metadata methods become more mature. In the future it is likely that more descriptive information will be produced at image capture time.

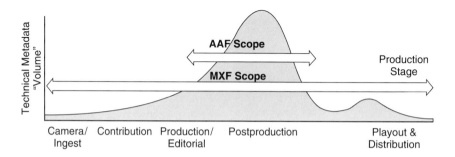

FIGURE

7.16

Volume of technical metadata associated with a clip during production.
Source: File Interchange Handbook, Chapter 5.

Human entry is often the most accurate and certainly the most detailed. It is also expensive and time-consuming. Ideally, an automatic indexer will identify some of the more common elements of a scene as outlined in Figure 7.17. It will be a long time before a machine can describe the subtle interaction among four people playing poker. Still, indexing technology is steadily improving and already generates a good deal of searchable metadata.

Figure 7.17 provides a divide-and-conquer approach to indexing an A/V clip. Some of the operations are straightforward and mature, such as shot detection, whereas others are state of the art like speech to text in the presence of music. In the realm of science fiction is face recognition in a dense crowd. For less demanding scenes, such as TV news anchor ID, it is practical today. For each element there is a defined metadata type. The more powerful the indexer, the more valuable the searchable metadata. A/V indexing is a hot area of university research.

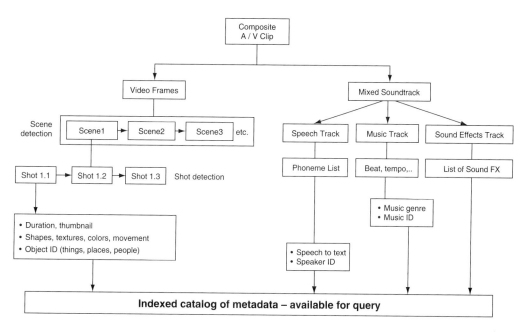

FIGURE   A/V media indexing hierarchy.

7.17

Content Owner: WNET

Story 3   8/9/05 Business News Hour
Scene 3.1 – Introduction by Anchor; NYSE Stock story

Duration: 5:02:00:00 to 5:02:12:00 (12 seconds)
Script: "The NYSE market hit a record high for the year today....."

Shot 3.1.1 Anchor   Shot 3.1.2 NYSE floor traders

FIGURE

7.18

Typical query response to "**Find:** *NYSE stock news, market high.*"

An example of a query response is illustrated in Figure 7.18. In this case the query was "Find: *NYSE stock news, market high.*" Assuming the required metadata exists in a catalog, then the response is formatted as shown. Because there are no standards for query method or response format, these will remain custom methods for years to come, although an XML-formatted response would make sense. Once the material is located and the access rights determined, then it may be incorporated into a project.

7.5.2   Using DRM as Part of a MAM Solution

Digital rights management is all the buzz for end consumer use of AV media. Microsoft has its DRM 10 and Apple's iPod uses FairPlay, for example. DRM provides features to keep files secure and to determine how the content may be used. Although not currently used in bulk for professional applications, DRM has a place in the broadcast/AV workflow. Today, for the most part, contracts or custom solutions are used to define rights usage at the production level. However, traditional contracts tend not to be machine friendly, whereas DRM technology is machine friendly.

The following are common features of a DRM protected file:

♦ Encrypted file content—only users with an owner-provided key can open the media file.

♦ Rights use—time windows, platforms (Desktop, mobile, etc.), number of viewings, copy rights, sharing rights, and so on.

♦ License granting—provided with file, on-demand, or silent background methods to obtain the license/key to use a file(s).

Think of DRM as a workflow, not just a file use enforcer. A total DRM environment includes contract authoring, file encrypting, license and key distribution, and runtime contract enforcing. So why use it in the professional domain? If you cannot afford to lose control of your distributed media, then consider DRM as one way to manage it. A compromise to a full-featured DRM is to use only file encryption and manual key transfer. This achieves a level of protection without all of DRM's features.

One promising technology is from the Open Digital Rights Language initiative (odrl.net). This group has developed a rights expression language for general use and it may find application in professional production MAM systems.

7.5.3   Tastes Like Chicken

The single most important factor in leveraging all things digital is smooth, efficient workflow. Nearly every component in a well designed project workflow has the MAM stamp on it. MAM functionality is the glue that ties all the pieces together. Figure 7.19 outlines the various classes of MAM products, tools and solution providers. There is no such thing as a one size fits all product or solution.

When specifying MAM functionality for a project, think holistically. MAM should not be some add-on, plug-in, or attachment but rather its presence is felt systemically at all levels of the design. Imagine MAM as a personality feature of a well-designed workflow. For new designs, MAM functionality should be spelled out as part of the overall workflow not only on a per component basis. Be specific as to what formats, operations,

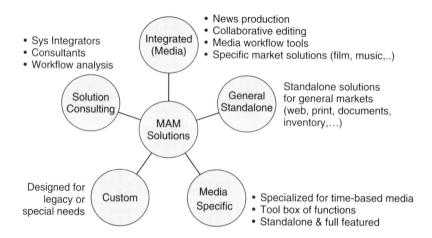

FIGURE   The MAM product and solution landscape.

7.19

scale, and UI functionally are needed. Especially give care to the total interoperability among the various components. Also, be a realist. Your idea of the ideal workflow will not necessarily map into what is available commercially. It is often smarter to evaluate what is available and then pattern your workflow accordingly. Workflows also deserve mention at this point so let us consider some of these aspects.

7.6   AV WORKFLOW METHODS

What is a workflow? It is the process by which a series of tasks is executed in a specific sequence. It allows the flow of work among individuals, processes, and/or departments. For many AV production projects, there are five layers of operational aspects needed to fully create and distribute a program. For a typical TV news story these are:

1. Acquisition layer—Acquire original AV sources
2. Asset management layer—MAM functions
3. Creative layer—Graphics, video, audio editing, creation, and processing

4. Control layer—Sequence finished program for distribution, playout

5. Presentation layer—Composite additional graphics for the desired on-air look

Roughly, these operations occur in series. Of course there are many other steps, such as story identification, reporter assignment, and so on, required for the total workflow. For now, let us concentrate on the AV flows: ingest clips (stories from the field), edit them, and play the final story to air. Figure 7.20 shows the process steps required from ingest of field-captured AV clips to the final story playout during the newscast. Also shown are the

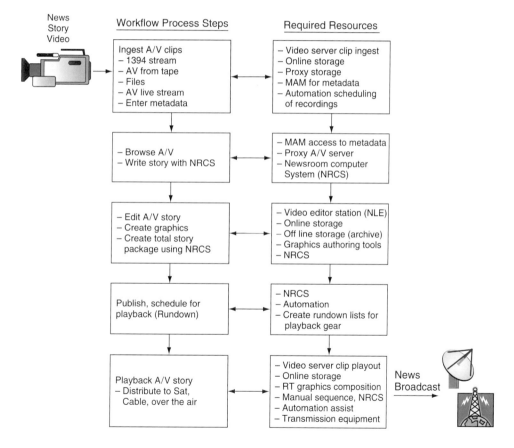

FIGURE
7.20

Production processes and resource usage for news story creation.

major hardware and software application resources required at each step in the story creation.

Much of this diagram is the food of discussion throughout this book—servers, storage, networking, and so on. The question is this: what are the methods to accomplish the flow as outlined? Figure 7.21 is a version of Figure 7.20 but showing the flow of AV and other data types across the chain.

Although not obvious from Figure 7.21, there are at least two data flow models that may be implemented. Let us call the first one *complete file flow*. A process example is as follows:

◆ A field camera is connected to the ingest station (or a live feed from the field is the source).

◆ An operator ingests all the relevant AV as one file (assume this for now), which is stored on a central system. It takes 20 min to ingest all unedited clips. Cameras that support faster than RT file transfer (say 2 or 10×) have a distinct advantage.

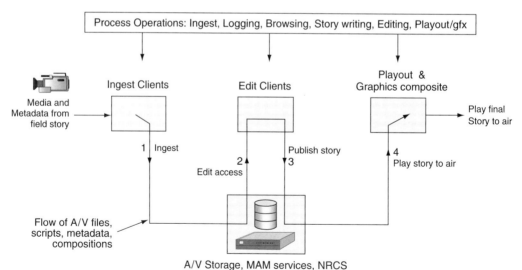

FIGURE   Simplified AV workflow example for news story production.

7.21

◆ An editor is informed of the available AV and begins to edit and create the final story complete with subtitles, voice-over, and supporting graphics. Say it takes 60 min. for editing. The editor finishes the story and informs the news producer. In most cases, the story is now one complete file (in the central store) ready for playback.

◆ The news director plays the edited AV story at the appropriate time: 3 min. playback time.

In this case each step must complete its function entirely before the next step can begin. The editor must wait for the ingest process to finish before the edit can start. This workflow is similar to moving a box of video tapes from step to step. There is an inherent inefficiency in this flow; for time critical operations such as news and sports it can stand improvement.

Let us call the second method *continuous file flow*. In this case, the processes overlap. As the A/V ingest is occurring, the edit may start and even the playout may occur before the entire edit is complete. This is a form of pseudo streaming of files. Some call this process "edit while ingest" or "record to timeline." As simple as it sounds, file management, avoiding file corruption with multiple users, updating the live end point, and managing metadata are nontrivial. Modern AV/IT news and sports editing systems (think ESPN half-time show highlights reel) aim for this type of workflow to cut down on the total latency from ingest to on-air playback. This method must be done using files not tape.

Three Classes of AV Flow

In fact, there are at least three different classes of serial AV flows for many real world processes. Figure 7.22 outlines these three types of flows for a sample multiprocess serial operation. The previous examples illustrated class 2 (continuous file flow) and class 3 (complete file flow) flows. Let us add to these the class 1 *streaming flow* method. It is the most common in legacy systems and is not file based. Rather, it relies on standard SDI, AES/EBU streaming, or similar serial connectivity of individual processes. Streaming always has the lowest delay from input to output compared to the other classes. Some processes, such as editing or browsing, cannot be implemented using streaming, whereas a video filter, for example, can have continuous stream I/O. For purpose of explanation, the processes in Figure 7.22 may deal with

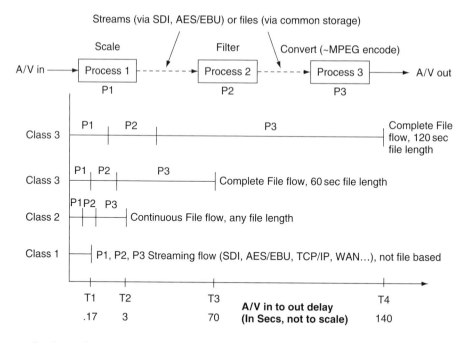

FIGURE

7.22

The three classes of serial A/V flows.

streams or files. Each may have different inherent delays. Let us examine each of the classes.

The class 1, streaming flow, total in–out delay (T1) is 0.17 s. This is reasonable and represents five frames of 30 FPS video, one frame of delay each for P1, 2, and 3 frames for the MPEG encoding process P3.

The class 2, continuous file flow, total in–out delay (T2) is 3 sec. For this example, a file of any length (>3 sec. in this case) is segmented into 1 s pieces. Each file piece is sequentially accessed from a common store, processed, and returned to the store wherein the next stage processes the same segment. In this way the three processes introduce a 3-s total delay from in to out, assuming each process also takes 1 s. Naturally, the in–out delay is independent of the total file length. This is a pseudo streaming flow and the processes must be designed knowing that they cannot consume faster than they receive. In practice, as the example in the previous section illustrated, the file would be segmented into chunks much larger than 1 s so the in–out delay is typically much larger.

Class 2 is a true serial process; processes 1–3 are simultaneously working on different portions of the same stored file. In practice, each process needs simultaneous access to shared storage. The advantage of this method is speed compared to class 3; the first part of the output file is available before the entire file is completely processed. True, class 1 has a smaller delay but it is not file based.

For class 3, each procedure must completely process the entire file before the next stage may begin—it is a bucket brigade. The process delay is a strong function of process complexity; the MPEG encoder's (P3) delay is larger than the simple scale function of step 1. The class 3 total in–out delay scales linearly with file length. Consider the example in Figure 7.22 of the 60-s file length scenario. The total in–out delay is 70 sec. This assumes a 5-s delay for P1, 5 s for P2, and 60 s for P3. The second example shows a 120-s file length and has 140 s of in–out delay or twice the 60-s file case.

Of course, if more than one serial workflow exists, then it may be possible to run them in parallel. Executing N tasks in parallel may reduce the overall execution time by a factor of N if all tasks are equally weighted. Let us call the parallel workflow case class 4 (not shown in Figure 7.22). This is just a special case of classes 1–3. Managing tightly coupled parallel workflows is nontrivial, but the time saved using parallel flows is often worth the effort. Some parallel flows may require time synchronous configurations. If possible, plan for nontime synchronous flows to reduce operational and testing complexity.

So, which class of media flow is preferred? Actually, there is no right answer. Each class has its own sweet spot. All three may coexist in a facility. In general, class 1 is for RT operations that do not require intermediate storage or human intervention. Class 2 is ideal for time critical workflows as illustrated earlier (news and sports programming). Class 3 is the simplest to implement and is commonly used for collaborative editing projects of all types and any operation where complete files move from step to step. Use Class 4 whenever low overall execution delay is crucial and the individual tasks are paralelable.

In a growing number of broadcast facilities it is common to work with both SD and HD parallel workflows for some or all of the delivery chain. Ideally, the same personnel can manage both chains simultaneously but this is not always the case. Some vendors have developed the idea of "one workflow, two outputs." This enables portions of both SD and HD signal paths to be manipulated by operators in various ways as though they are only working with a single signal type. There are trade-offs for sure and this would not fly for all cases but it will for some.

Workflow Tools

The actual AV data flow as described in the previous section is only part of the entire workflow process. In the bigger picture, job assignments, quality review, rights clearance, standards and practices review, and job process status are all part of many human centric workflows. Some integrated solutions for the production of programming have process monitoring built in. One example of this product type is the Workflow Process Manager (WPM) from Harris Broadcast; another is the Workflow Manager from Omnibus.

The WPM tool provides the ability to define a specific series of tasks to be executed in a certain order to produce an expected result. It integrates the tasks that are performed by people and automated systems to ensure that the human touch is minimized. At the highest level, WPM interfaces with content management and scheduling systems that provide inputs to broadcast playout and media/asset management applications. Tasks such as ingesting media from digital delivery services can be assigned as an automated workflow, thereby reducing manual operations.

Automated workflows and process management are not mature or widely accepted in broadcast operations. As file flows become the standard, automated processes will become the norm and process management will see more light of day.

Auxiliary Data Workflows

In addition to the AV flows described earlier, nonreal-time informational flows are used to coordinate and control many operations in a broadcast station or AV facility. One of the more common informational flows is between a traffic system (a manager of programming playout schedules) and the device automation system. Traffic generates playlists that the automation system implements. Traffic also informs automation when to purge select programming from stores. Automation provides an as-run list to traffic proving that the schedule was implemented as desired.

As may be imagined, numerous data types are passing between domains. These data structures have been proprietary and create vendor lock in. In 2004 SMPTE formed the S22-10 TV Systems Data Exchange Working Group. The group is busy defining a standard data dictionary and XML schema for describing the transactions cited previously. Plus, protocols are being defined for the data exchange process. Once complete, the standards will enable information flows between traffic, automation, programming management, and content delivery systems. This is a very exciting work effort and it will have profound positive results once implemented by industry vendors.

7.7   TYING IT ALL TOGETHER

During this chapter and the previous seven, the elements of media systems were developed. Capable system designers can use these tools to create world class workflows of almost any imaginable type. Figure 7.23 illustrates the chief components in a high-level system. Of course each block may be subdivided into more well-established components. There is no defined workflow here, just available components on which to build specific business operations. In fact it supports a mix of streamed, file flow, stored, nonstored, automated, and manual operations. Because there is information flow between processes, sticking to standards is key to getting efficient flows. Having to do data and link conversions between steps should be avoided.

Of course there is no magic formula for designing an IT-based media workflow, but there are best practices, some of which were discussed in previous chapters. At the highest levels of integration the following should be observed:

◆ Define the required and potential workflows and processes needed to run the business. Maximize automated operations. Plan for expansion and change.

◆ Define a tentative system's architecture but allow for change due to available equipment and vendors' ideas.

◆ Leverage networking, control, and management IT-based standards; use open systems where possible for all three planes.

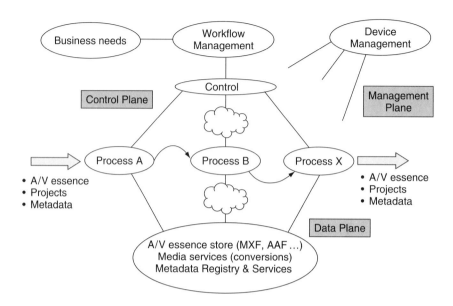

FIGURE   Tying it all together: The integrated IT media system.

7.23

◆ Define media types (SD, HD, uncompressed, MPEG, DV, Proxy, etc.) and AV data rates for all operations, including import/export. When possible, insist on MXF/AAF for intra- and interdomain compatibility. Plan for essence conversion gateways. Aim for interoperability at all levels.

◆ Refine desired workflows based on available MAM functionality. Think holistically. Do not piecemeal the MAM functions, but be realistic and do not try to boil the ocean.

◆ Define the schema and dictionary for metadata types that the MAM system will use. If possible, use existing formats and solutions provided by vendors.

◆ Identify the required storage hierarchy, reliability, and QoS needs. Choose open IT storage if possible. There are always trade-offs between AV vendor-supplied storage and generic storage. AV storage providers stand behind their QoS metrics, whereas generic storage providers often do not fully appreciate the QoS needs of AV workflows.

◆ Determine the needs for archiving and disaster recovery.

◆ Decide on control and automation requirements.

- Determine overall I/O, storage, and bandwidth requirements.
- Determine who will manage (faults, alarms, status, configuration, diagnostics, etc.) the system's elements. This will affect your choice of management system—IT centric or specialized A/V (more on this in Chapter 9).
- Develop a security plan for virus checking, worm prevention, firewalls, and so on. Securing RT equipment is more challenging than traditional NRT gear (more on this in Chapter 8).
- Plan for a great deal of social engineering, as the move to IT from traditional A/V can be gut-wrenching for some people. Change management training may be needed.
- Plan for equipment upgrades, expansions, and maintenance. What is your obsolesce plan? How long will a vendor support quickly changing IT-based products?

 Architect Louis Sullivan preached, "Form follows function." In video systems, technology should follow workflow needs. Do not let the technology dictate the workflow.

Any large system should comprehend all these factors. Even the simplest of systems with only one or two components will benefit. When evaluating a vendor's system proposal, make sure to look for discussions of these items. When developing an RFP for vendor response, include these factors in your write up. Of course each point in the list given earlier is only a headline, so make sure you understand the details behind each item. Many of these points are discussed in detail elsewhere in this book. See Chapter 10 to learn more about AV/IT transition issues from the change management and human side of the equation. It also provides an FAQ on system design pointers.

REFERENCES

[**Abunu**] D. Abunu et al., *The BBC in the Digital Age: Defining a Corporation Wide MAM Approach*, page 417, Conference Publication of the IBC, 2004.
[**Bhaskaran**] Vasudev Bhaskaran et al., *Image and Video Compression Standards*, 2nd edition, 1997, Kluwer Press.

[**Bosi**] Marina Bosi, Richard E. Goldberg, and Leonardo Chiariglione, *Introduction to Digital Audio Coding and Standards*, Kluwer Press, 2002.

[**Cordeiro**] M. Cordeiro et al., *The ASSET Architecture: Integrating media applications and products through a unified API*, SMPTE Motion Imaging Journal, September 2004.

[**Gilmer**] Brad Gilmer, *File Interchange Handbook: For professional images, audio and metadata*, Focal Press, 2004.

[**Hasegawa**] Fumio Hasegawa, Haruo Hiki, *Content Production Technologies*, Wiley, 2004.

[**Marpe**] Detlev Marpe et al., *Performance evaluation of Motion-JPEG2000 in comparison with H.264/AVC operated in pure intra coding mode*, Proceedings of SPIE—Volume 5266, February 2004, pp. 129–137.

[**McDermid**] Ed McDermid, *AAF Edit Protocol: Introduction and Overview*, SMPTE Motion Imaging Journal, page 225, August 2004.

[**Poynton**] Charles Poynton, *Digital Video and HDTV—Algorithms and Interfaces*, Morgan Kaufmann, 2003.

[**SMPTE**] *AAF and MXF Tutorials*, SMPTE Motion Imaging Journal, July/August 2004.

[**Symes**] Peter Symes, *Digital Video Compression*, McGraw Hill/TAB, October 2003.

[**Wiegand**] Thomas Wiegand, Gary J. Sullivan, Gisle Bjontegaard, and Ajay Luthra, *Overview of the H.264/AVC Video Coding Standard*, IEEE Transactions on Circuits and Systems for Video Technology, July 2003.

[**XML**] For more information on some key XML definitions, learn about the XML Schema and Namespaces as defined by the W3C at www.w3c.org/xml.

8 | Security for Networked AV Systems

CHAPTER

8.0   INTRODUCTION AND SCOPE

Information systems security has never been more critical.[1] At the same time, protection of information systems is increasingly complex. As AV facilities reinvent their service infrastructure to meet business demands, traditional boundaries are disappearing. The cyber security threats lurking outside those traditional boundaries are real and well documented. Security by exclusion is both more necessary and more difficult, but at the same time not sufficient. The enterprise must also practice security by inclusion to allow access to the services that field offices, customers, suppliers, and business partners are demanding.

Information security is not only a technical issue, but also a business and governance challenge that involves risk management, reporting, and accountability. Effective security requires the active engagement of executive management to assess emerging threats and to provide strong cyber security leadership. Figure 8.1 provides a good look at the three main building blocks for a secure enterprise.

This chapter provides a summary of the basics of security in light of AV systems. Our focus centers on the process of developing a sound security plan, what the threats are, and how to protect networked AV systems

---

[1] This paragraph was paraphrased from [NAC].

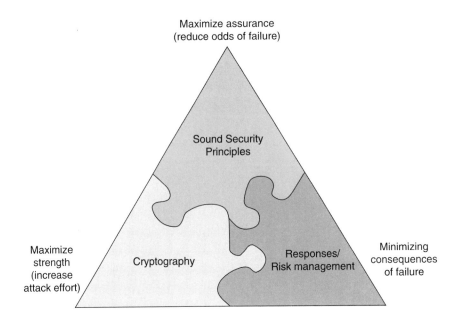

The building blocks of security.
Concept: Cryptographic Research, Inc.

against them. Detailed examinations of all security aspects can be found in a number of books and Web resources. This chapter is organized around the following ideas:

◆ The threat matrix
◆ Intrusion prevention tactics and security planning
◆ Prevention technology
◆ Cryptography concepts

At one level, security is founded on the world's most sophisticated mathematics. At another, it is about bribery, loose lips, and poor processes. A decent percentage of security breaches occur from unhappy employees who have easy access to internal networks and systems. Figure 8.2 illustrates the two extremes of system security: plotting effort versus probability of attack success. The ideal curve is solely proportional to data encryption strength. In practice, the curve is composed of a mix of human, software, and process weaknesses. Most

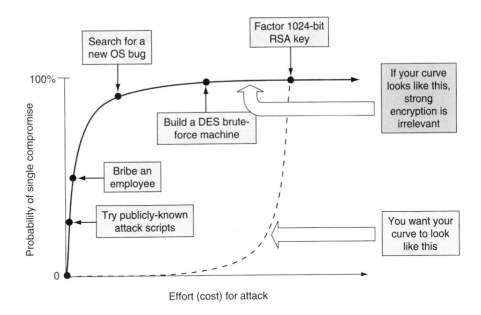

FIGURE

8.2

Security should be proportional to the effort it takes to crack it.

Concept: Cryptographic Research, Inc.

experts agree that encryption is rarely broken these days by hackers, although there are well-known examples; the breaking of the data scrambler for the DVD being a prime example. Rather, systems are compromised by other means. Let us look into what the threats are and then counter them with a summary of prevention and detection methods. An overview of cryptography is presented later in this chapter. The RSA key in Figure 8.2 is also explained later, giving you a chance to win $200,000.

8.1   THE THREAT MATRIX

Ideally, AV equipment in mission critical applications is 100% protected against all threats. Before examining how to prevent threats, let us look at the threat landscape. In general, a networked computer system threat has a life cycle. The following five-step sequence is typical of the life cycle.

1. **Probe the system.** This may take place via port probes or studying for vulnerable access points. Outsiders often probe every known portal for access.

2. **Gain access.** This step allows a malicious entity (program, person, or machine) to gain access to a system or system element using the access point identified in step 1. If the access allows foreign code to execute, a virus, worm program, or code fragment is now free to execute. If unauthorized access is made (e.g., password compromise), then foreign or malicious internal users have complete access to all element resources.

3. **Execute malicious code or operation.** The execution of foreign code may be completely benign ("Hello!" message) at the low end of trouble up to deleting every file or stealing highly confidential information at the top end.

4. **Propagate.** Once a program executes, it can then propagate itself to other machines via network services, email, or other means.

5. **Removal.** Once the culprit is identified, it can be removed from the compromised device, assuming it has not already destroyed itself in a Samson-like death. It is common for virus checkers to scan a disc and remove any harmful code for example. If the threat was weak access security, then stronger entrance passwords are warranted.

The life cycle may be cut short at any step if preventative measures are effective. For example, a port probe may be detected and the foreign data denied entry. Or, an anti-virus program identifies the offender and removes it before execution.

Another threat is a denial-of-service (DOS). The goal is not to gain unauthorized access or run foreign code but to deny legitimate users access to a service. Attackers may flood a network with large volumes of data or deliberately consume resources. Typical of such DOS attacks is to flood a TCP port (say for the FTP service) with requests for a connection. One example is the well known SYN flood associated with the initial steps in setting up a TCP connection. DOS attacks may consume a large share of main CPU clock cycles thus preventing rightful use.

8.1.1   Viruses, Worms, Trojan Horses, and Malware

Four of the biggest offenders are viruses, worms, Trojan horses, and malware. These four sometimes confusing terms are defined next.

Virus

A virus is a program designed to infect a computer and spread via innocent human assistance. It often announces its presence to the user and may do damage to the target system's files or steal secrets. The virus attempts to spread via email attachments typically. In most cases a human unknowingly runs the virus program, thinking it is a friendly program or file. Always beware of executing unknown source files with .exe extensions. Plus, use caution with Microsoft Office macros, ActiveX, and some Java scripts.

Worm

A worm enters a computer via a network connection and executes a downloaded program fragment—usually in data memory—without any human action. A worm is often described as a subclass of a virus, although the two are very different in how they infect a system. Worms can spread much faster than viruses by orders of magnitude. For example, the Code Red worm infected 359 K networked machines in 12 h. Simulations of worm spreading show potential rates of 7.5 to 30 K infected machines per second! To make matters worse, the spreading is exponential in growth. A typical entry point is via a TCP/IP service port. In 2004 Microsoft documented 45 different security vulnerabilities (MS04–045 is a reference to the last documented violation in 2004) and most can be classed as a worm.

Trojan Horse

This is a program that initially looks benign but allows for backdoor, undesired actions. One example is free downloadable programs claiming to do some desired action (a drawing program) but also performs other undesired actions, such as installing pop-up advertising software. Beware of free programs!

Malware

Malicious software is designed to hijack some or all of the user experience and turn innocent grandmothers into porn providers. It includes viruses, worms, Trojan horses, Spyware, and some pop-ups. Spyware is software that tracks usage and reports it to others, such as advertisers. Usually the tracking is concealed from the user. A pop-up is a new browser window that usually appears unrequested on the screen brandishing ads. Particularly maddening are those termed exit pop-ups: browser windows that launch when you leave a site or close a browser window. Within a scripting language these are called "onUnload" and "onClose" events. Pop-ups turn the browsing experience into a sleazy carnival midway, complete with flashing lights and loud music.

Because of the prevalence of Microsoft OS and derivatives, many hackers target these systems for *worm* access. Other operating systems are not usually targets. Although Linux and the MAC OS have vulnerabilities, these are exploited infrequently. Several organizations document virus and worm threats. The CERT Coordination Center, www.cert.org, and SANS, www.sans.org, are excellent resources for the early notification of security threats. Many IT managers subscribe to their services for early notification. If the threat is a virus, then antivirus vendors strive to find a prevention method ASAP. If the threat is a worm, then the OS provider usually offers a software patch.

It is valuable to know the types of threats but it is more important to stop them cold. The next section considers prevention tactics.

8.2   PREVENTION TACTICS

Many, if not most, computer security vulnerabilities can be eliminated if the systems are properly configured against attacks. Consistency is a key factor in security. A plan is needed for all devices that trade off usability against security. It is not difficult to wall off a computer to the extent it is practically unusable—no email access, no Web access, no internal network access, and so on. However, full and unfettered access to any and all network resources breeds trouble. Finding the balance between the two extremes is a science.

Developing a security process for an organization is the most important preventative measure. Passwords, antivirus, firewalls, and so on are of value but a cohesive prevention deployment process applied consistently across the organization is the most important aspect of a comprehensive security solution.

Let us put the regions of attack in perspective. Figure 8.3 shows typical boundaries between networks and systems for a large deployment. Four regions are identified, A–D, each with its own security needs. Region A is a typical element—server, desktop PC, and so on. B is a walled off A/V system requiring very high security. This could be the news production system of a TV station, for example. Region C is the company Intranet. Region D is the unbounded WW Internet. In most cases, region A or B is the target for access. C and D are the starting points of the attack. D is the most common starting location. However, internal attacks (C attacking A) can occur maliciously but at times out of ignorance too. For example, a virus may enter a building on a laptop or USB memory stick without the carrier even knowing it.

There are three security boundaries for this model. Figure 8.3 outlines typical methods to secure a boundary. For example, A, B, and C are

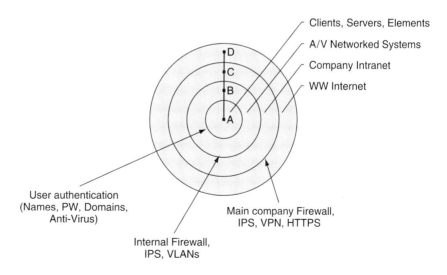

FIGURE

8.3

Security boundaries in large systems.

protected from D by the use of firewalls, intrusion prevention systems, and VPNs. Each prevention method is explored in the discussion to follow.

8.2.1 Developing a Security Plan for System Elements

This section outlines the questions to resolve as part of a security plan for system elements. The answer to each question should be incorporated into an overall security implementation plan. For each case ask what the implications are for RT A/V gear. Specific prevention technology is covered later. The following QA list was loosely paraphrased from information available on the CERT Web site.

1. Identify the purpose of each system element.
   a. What is the nature of this element? What categories of information reside on it? Is it crucial to RT A/V production?
2. What network services will be provided by this element?
   a. Email, Web access, Web services, file transfers, media converter, etc.
   b. For each service document whether the device will be configured as a client, server, or both.
   c. Disable all other services per device. The list of active services should be well documented and no new ones added without permission. It is well known that rogue and poorly designed network services are a source of easy access into a device or network. Also, for AV clients, unnecessary network activity can disrupt (cause glitches or worse) the RT nature of a client.
3. Identify the network service software to be loaded on this element.
   a. Are the services bundled with the OS and/or are third-party services to be loaded?
   b. Pay special attention to the security aspects of any third-party applications.
4. Identify the users or categories of users.
   a. Roles of the users.
   b. Actions performed, services needed.
5. Determine the file privileges for each category of user.
   a. What file actions are allowed: read, write, delete files, directory access, and machine access.

6. Determine how users will be authenticated.

   a. User names, passwords (and stale password change methods), SecureID cards, or other. Many networks rely on Microsoft's Active Directory (AD) for system-wide user/password registration. AD allows an admin. to enter a user/pw once and this registry is consulted by all user applications across a range of products. AD enables "single logon" for users. AD also supports password aging and prevents breakable passwords from being used.

7. Access to information control.

   a. Is all information available to all users? Is data encryption needed to protect sensitive information?

8. Develop intrusion detection strategies for select elements.

   a. Decide on what information is to be collected for login logs and audit methods.

9. Develop backup and recovery for devices that require it.

   a. Document method to restore a defective element from scratch.

   b. Set up a backup method for devices that require it. This is especially crucial for mission critical devices.

10. Develop a documented plan for installing the OS of a device.

    a. Include what security aspects should be turned on.

11. Determine how any system elements will be connected to the network.

    a. Always, sometimes, or never connected. Determine if a device needs to reside in a DMZ (extra secure area of company intranet) or external hosting site for maximum security.

    b. Define a clear policy when attaching foreign laptops to the internal network.

    c. If remote computers need to use the internal network, define a VPN strategy.

12. Identify an antivirus strategy.

    a. Do not install any software that may interfere with the RT nature of AV system elements.

    b. Work with your AV vendor to find a way to provide for antivirus software. This is tricky, as every vendor's products have different requirements regarding when, at what level, and for how long a virus scan may operate.

13. Establish a plan to patch the OS as security alerts are announced.

   a. This is crucial so make sure your AV vendor has a good plan in this area.

   b. Assure that your AV vendor tests for the most crucial OS patches on mission-critical devices. Because vendor patch verification will always lag the availability of a patch, the latency needs to be defined.

14. Keep the security plan current and promote awareness within the company.

   a. Monitor and evaluate policy and control effectiveness.

Of course there are other items needed to define the full constellation of a security solution. However, the 14 items just listed are the most common for any system. The deeper the device is located away from the Internet/email (Fig. 8.3), the less likely it is to be attacked. Still, internal attacks are possible although unlikely. A security policy may not allow any Internet access on some elements. Some vendors rely on Internet access to diagnose and repair their equipment under a service contract. More on this topic in Chapter 9.

The Window of Vulnerability

Worms and viruses are quick acting. An IT manager may only have seconds to secure a device(s) against a new network-disseminated worm threat. Because an organization can react immediately, a firewall or software patch is relied on to prevent worm infections. More on firewalls in the next section. Viruses are slower acting than worms due to the need for human action to spread. It is common to get an email warning message from IT announcing something like: "Do not open any attachment named *I Love You*." For viruses there is a window of vulnerability as illustrated in Figure 8.4. Figure 8.4 also applies to worms but the time period is much smaller.

The window shows four periods: one before a virus or a "worm hole" is detected and three after. The window of vulnerability is the time when devices are open to possible attack. The *avert* period is the time when IT sends messages to all users not to open named attachments for viruses or to patch their computers against worms. This period is sometimes called the zero-day attack time. The implication being that attacks can start on

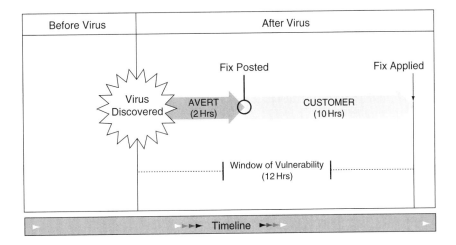

FIGURE

8.4

The window of vulnerability.

Concept: McAfee.

the heels of (or before) the public announcement of a vulnerability and before a protection method is available.

Once an antivirus vaccine is produced, then all vulnerable systems should be updated with it. In most corporate environments, antivirus updates occur automatically and invisibly using antivirus management applications. The longer this takes (the *customer* period), the longer the period of vulnerability. Within hours of detection, an antivirus vaccine is normally available. Again, installing virus scanners on RT AV equipment must be done in cooperation with the equipment provider to guarantee RT performance when scans are active or scheduled for off hours.

For RT gear it is especially important to have confidence that any software patch will not affect performance. Should IT install the patch, hurriedly test, and deploy, hoping that the patch works, or should they wait until more is known about its ramifications? These are difficult decisions and keep the window of vulnerability open. For worms, OS providers often notify the community of the vulnerability and then provide the patch. The delay before the patch is installed gives attackers time to exploit defenseless system elements.

8.3   PREVENTION TECHNOLOGY

In the end, it is the prevention technology that will keep out the pirates. In general, there are five main means to prevent/discover attacks over a network.

1. Main firewall
2. Intrusion Prevention System (IPS)
3. Intrusion Detection System (IDS)
4. Antivirus methods
5. Virtual Private Network (VPN)

Figure 8.5 shows the overall landscape to prevent outside attacks against internal, private networks. Of course there are other configurations, but let us use this one for the purposes of discussion.

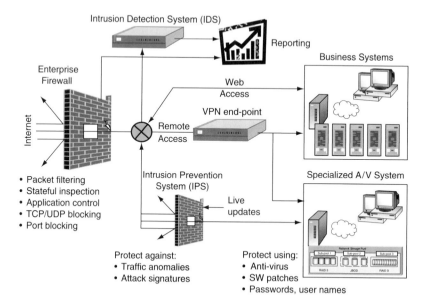

FIGURE   Strategies for protecting business and A/V systems.

8.5

8.3.1　The Main Firewall

This is the classic method used to protect against outside intrusion. Firewalls come in many flavors from a variety of companies. Some are host based and run on desktops, servers, and so on. Microsoft's XP *internet connection firewall* is a prime example. Others are network based, such as FireWall-1 from Check Point Software and Cisco's PIX Firewall family. Figure 8.6 illustrates the four main functions of a generic firewall. Some firewalls have added loads of other functions, such as NAT translation, VPN, and so on, but these are auxiliary to the main purpose behind a firewall with the possible exception of VPN.

A firewall blocks malicious packets by using one or more of the following strategies.

◆ Packet inspection, filtering ports, packet types, IP addresses, etc.
◆ Transport layer filtering, TCP/UDP blocking, select connections permitted

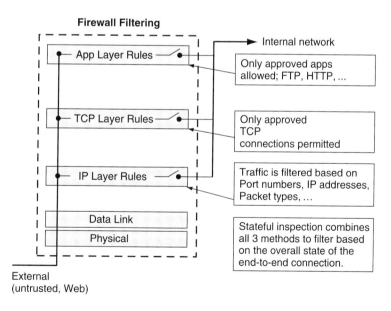

FIGURE　　　Firewall filtering methods.

8.6

◆ Application layer logic, approved apps such as FTP, HTTP, and so on

◆ Stateful inspection technology (also known as dynamic packet filtering) tracks connection "state information." It uses this intelligence to decide when to allow/disallow comminucation from remote computers.

Of course the firewall should be configured by a competent IT security expert for the most effective blocking. There are several subtle settings that only a skilled expert would be aware of.

If AV applications move data via a firewall then attention must be given to bandwidth and other QoS needs for remote access. Does the remote user expect to transfer files at high rates? Will the transfer application be FTP? If so it may be more practical to locate the FTP server in a third-party service center completely isolated from the enterprise network. Offsite FTP services allows for scalability, very high transfer rates, and complete isolation from business systems. The XDrive (www.xdrive.com) service is a practical way to share large files with vendors and customers (see www.yousendit.com for a free basic service).

Also, it is not uncommon to have remote user access AV files for proxy viewing and editing. It is problematic to allow direct access even via a firewall. In this case a secure VPN connection should be forged to guarantee secure access.

8.3.2   Intrusion Prevention Systems

The IPS is a relatively new class of device with a higher level of blocking than a firewall. There is much industry debate about the need for this in addition to a firewall. In 2005 most of the IPS vendors do not attempt to duplicate all firewall functionality. However, some functions are indeed duplicated along with many functions not found in a firewall. If one is installed, a FW must also be used, as shown in Figure 8.5. The hand-writing on the wall seems to indicate that eventually the IPS will likely assume firewall functions (or the firewall will assume IPS functions) as the product category matures. The IPS protects the AV system but not the business system in Figure 8.5 but it could also protect the entire internal network.

Higher levels of IPS security include:

- Performance—support gigabit speeds, low latency, reliably. Ideally, appear as a "bump on the wire" as installed. Some units sport through-out delays of <250 μsec. The unit should be totally nonintrusive. It should only filter actual threats with no false positives (stopped a non threat) or false negatives (did not stop a valid threat). Clustered IPS units exceed 8 Gb/sec of throughput. The device needs to precisely discriminate between benign and attack traffic. It may also filter traffic in both directions.

- Protection—protocol analysis, anomalous behavior, identify and filter signatures of known methods of attack, statistical analysis, fragmentation attacks, usage patterns, port usage, more.

- Near real time updates of the IPS filter engine. The vendor should supply updates to keep the protection engine "smart." For example, when a new worm vulnerability is identified, the vendor updates the IPS to stop the worm from passing into the network.

The idea that an IPS appears as a bump on the wire is interesting. Most IPS units do not have a MAC or IP address and are simply inserted into the desired key path (Ethernet link) without any configuration. Their ability to analyze data streams for attack signatures and to stop any suspect data is a powerful feature. For example, some external malevolent probes look for device TCP port buffer overflows (and then take command of a CPU), but an IPS can detect this kind of activity and abort its operation.

The power to filter streams enables the *virtual software patch*. What is this? In most cases, the discovery of a worm vulnerability is accompanied by the release of a software patch for a program or OS. Ideally, an enterprise IT department will immediately install the patch on every target server and desktop. In reality there may be a long delay between the availability of a patch and its installation on all vulnerable devices. It takes time to qualify a patch and then time to distribute the patch. Then too for real time AV equipment (on air video server) the patch should be qualified by the AV vendor *first* before the end user installs it. All this amounts to the window of vulnerability being stretched into days or even months in some cases.

Enter the virtual software patch. As soon as a vulnerability is announced the IPS vendor can update its attack signature database to include this new threat. The vendor then downloads this new attack filter into every IPS under contract for real time updates. In a matter of hours after a worm vulnerability is discovered an entire network of computers can be protected against the new danger. This is a powerful feature and protects devices before they have installed the latest software patch for a particular exploit. Figure 8.7 illustrates this idea. No AV vendor testing, no enterprise testing, and virtually immediate protection. That is the power of the virtual patch. Should the enterprise still install the recommended patch? Likely, but now time is not as critical and a methodical plan to perform updates is in order. No rushing, no errors.

As a point of illustration, the UnityOne IPS from TippingPoint Technologies is one such product that provides for virtual software patches (see www.tippingpoint.com for more information on these ideas). The IPS is a valuable product category and plays an important role

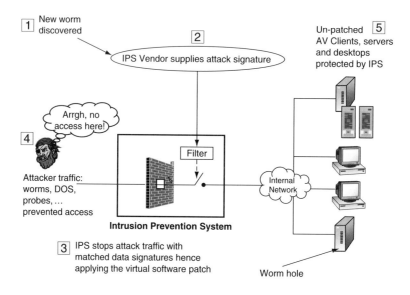

FIGURE 8.7   The IPS and the virtual software patch.

in protecting mission-critical AV gear.[2] Especially important is that device protection does not require the AV vendor to qualify the suggested software patch immediately. Other companies offering IPS products are Network Associates, ISS, NetScreen (Jupiter Networks), Top Layer Networks, and Fortinet, among others.

The IPS can become a lightning rod of blame when there are network problems. True, on occasion it can exhibit false positives if not tuned correctly. Albert Einstein once said "Not everything that is counted counts, and not everything that counts can be counted." Due to the complex nature of blocking threats, some false positives and false negatives will occur so some enterprises are slow to install an IPS because it *may* block legitimate traffic. Then too if all traffic crosses through the IPS, it is a single point of failure so a failover means is needed. Looking back 10 years, the newly introduced firewall was a punching bag when access problems occurred. Today the firewall is a necessary, noncontroversial system element. The IPS is maturing and over time it will likely reach a point of acceptance where it becomes de rigueur as a system element.

8.3.3   Intrusion Detection System

The IDS inspects data traffic and looks for problems. When irregularities occur, they are logged with optional notification to management. The IDS does not block traffic, but indicates that traffic may be harmful. It is a fire alarm, not a fire extinguisher. The IDS signals attacks explicitly addressed by other security components (such as firewalls and even IPS) and also attempts to provide notification of new attacks unforeseen by other components. Intrusion detection systems also provide forensic information that potentially allows organizations to discover the origins of an attack. However, in 2004 the respected industry source Gartner Research predicted the marginalization of the IDS over the next few years.

As the IPS matures it will replace the IDS for many applications. In theory, a full-featured IPS is able to detect, report, *and* block threats, so

---

[2] Of value for insight is the TippingPoint White Paper, *The Science of Vulnerability Filters*, by Victoria Irwin.

investing in both technologies may be a waste of resources. Some consultants see the IDS as an essential component for sniffing at select parts of the network so it may well survive for some time. For example, when a virus or other threat is carried into the enterprise via a USB memory stick, the IDS should detect the traffic and send an alarm. Keep in mind that the IPS may not catch a threat that is released inside an organization. The demise of the IDS is a controversial conclusion so time will be the arbiter.

In the open source world, Snort has become the de facto IDS standard (see www.snort.org for information and downloads). This Web site has lots of information about threats and how to identify them. See too [Beale] for the complete bible on Snort.

Intrusion detection devices are not tuned for AV gear or applications so there is nothing special to expect from them in this regard. They are not in series with mission critical data flows so their failure will not immediately affect business operations. Looking forward, it seems that the firewall and full-featured IPS are the future of enterprise filtering and intrusion detection.

NX Nails Worms

Snapshot

Worms commonly use data memory to execute their rogue program fragments. NX comes to the rescue—No eXecute—by blocking program execution from data areas. Before NX, CPU memory did not distinguish between permission to read and permission to execute instructions. NX changes that by marking memory as executable or not so a worm may indeed enter a memory area but NX stops it from running. AMD, Intel, others, and some OSs now provide NX functionality.

8.3.4   Antivirus and Client Shell Software

Despite the power of the IPS, many will not block malicious virus attachments. As a result, it is good practice to keep up-to-date virus scanners on every desktop and server. Scanners are mature and updates can occur in real time once an antivirus is produced. However, using antivirus programs on real time AV gear is problematic. Because most of these programs are not respectful of real time devices and steal a good portion of CPU power to do a scan, it is prudent to schedule the scan for off hours if possible. If the device is in service 24×7 then the AV vendor needs to supply a solution that works in harmony with your needs. It is possible to place the scan at a low priority so as to only minimally steal CPU resources with no adverse affects on AV performance.

The enterprise perimeter has become fluid as it passes through tele-workers, mobile employees, and contractors. Security policies should be enforced among a decentralized user base as effectively as they are on the corporate network. Employees and contractors, whether deliberately or inadvertently, are in a position to seriously compromise existing security practices. The fast-changing pace of technology, such as the widening adoption of VPN and the rise of the "zero-day exploit" requires new methods to stop threats from spreading. One means to add security is via a client shell. This is an example of a host-based IPS.

Cisco's Security Agent, NetIntelligence's End Point, and other prod-ucts are software shells that monitor all I/O network activity and user actions on end-point devices such as a PC. Some shells can be configured to only allow for selected user operations. By combining a firewall, antivirus, filters, application restriction, and usage monitoring of all sorts, these programs offer a high level of localized protection. However, they may even be more invasive than a vanilla virus scanner in terms of affect-ing AV real time operations so do not install one of these on critical AV gear unless the supplying AV vendor guarantees performance.

8.3.5   The Virtual Private Network

The heart and soul of secure remote access are bound up in the VPN. The basic idea is to encrypt the TCP/IP data packets from external users to hide them from prying eyes as they traverse the Internet. Also, the log-on process for these users is secure, using time-stamped passwords and other means to make unauthorized access almost impossible. The VPN is the vehicle to secure a tunnel from the external user to the internal network. For all practical purposes, remote users are an extension of a private network.

A VPN creates a secure "tunnel" through the public network, so the protocols used to establish the connection are called tunneling protocols. Figure 8.8 shows the three most common ways to use tunnels for modern VPN implementations: L2TP with IPSec, IPSec alone, and SSL/HTTPS. The acronym soup will be explained next.

L2TP is the Layer Two Tunneling Protocol (RFC 2661) and can run over ATM, IP/UDP, and others and carry various protocols in its tunnel. It also supports authentication means for user access. IPSec (IP Security) is a method used to secure IP packets. All packet data, except for the IP address header, are encrypted for passage over unsecured networks. As a result, it is obvious that the TCP and UDP payloads are also encrypted. IPSec is a suite of protocols (see RFC 2411 for a good summary). IPSec uses the Internet Key Exchange method (IKE, RFC 2409) to obtain the encryption keys per connection. The IKE uses Diffe-Hellman (DH) Public Key exchange. DH is described later.

The Secure Sockets Layer (SSL) is used most often to secure HTTP, and the combination is called HPPTS (as seen with https://). Virtually all common Internet browsers support SSL natively, which is a big convenience for "any client" (kiosks, wireless hotspots, Internet café, etc.) remote access. While SSL can add security to any protocol that uses TCP, it occurs most commonly with the HTTPS access method. HTTPS serves

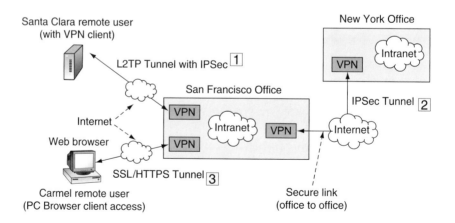

FIGURE 8.8   Using tunneling protocols to create secure VPNs.

to secure Web page access. SSL uses public key cryptography and public key certificates to verify the identity of end points.

Three Secure VPN Methods

What are the differences and trade-offs among the three VPN methods as illustrated in Figure 8.8? The L2TP/IPSec method carries user data IP/UDP/TCP payloads by L2TP, which in turn are carried by IPSec. This is a common method for remote users that need complete secure access to a corporate network with strong authentication. Most often specialized VPN software must be loaded on any remote machine to support this form of VPN.

For office-to-office connections it is possible to only use IPSec, as there is no user authentication. The connections are permanent and the tunnel provides transparent access for any IP payload.

The third method with only SSL usually supports HTTPS. This allows remote users to access HTTPS Web mail as supported by Microsoft's Exchange Server, for example. Importantly, even thought SSL is secure, it is also application based. Remote users do not have access to the entire internal network, only to the device and application (e.g., Web server) that terminates the SSL connection. As a result, SSL adds security by tying a remote user to an application and not the entire internal network.

Some SSL-based VPN solutions permit access to more than Web applications using a proxy mapping method (see www.aventail.com for SSL/VPN solution examples). However, each application must be "webified" either natively or via the proxy mapper so that it may be accessed via a remote browser. SSL/VPN falls short of offering 100% complete internal network access, but for most remote users this is preferred. There is currently a huge marketing battle between IPSec VPN vendors and SSL-based ones.

For AV applications, L2TP/IPSec is a likely choice for remote proxy browsing, AV editing, and file transfer. The remote users may have access to all the resources within the AV system but the IPS (remember, it is bidirectional in Figure 8.5) can limit access into the corporate network as needed. SSL/VPN providers claim equivalent performance to L2TP/IPSec, but each vendor will offer some slightly different model of operations, as the SSL/VPN is still browser-based. Because SSL is TCP specific, UDP streaming applications are not supported, whereas with IPSec they are. With L2TP/IPSec, applications are browser-independent.

Strictly speaking, VPN is a tunnel between end points over a network. Most references refer to VPN as secure (as our examples do), but some authors refer to VPN as a tunnel—secure or not. For example, Generic Routing Encapsulation (RFC 2784), IP-in-IP, and MPLS are tunneling protocols but are not encrypted. Often these are combined with an encryption method (such as IPSec) to create a secure VPN.

Next, a cornerstone of security is covered—cryptography. As mentioned earlier, total security is bound up in process and technology as per Figure 8.2 so hiding data behind mathematics is only a part of an overall way to secure the enterprise. This fascinating aspect of security is considered next.

Protecting the Crown Jewels

Snapshot Stored data accessed via SAN and NAS has traditionally been protected with simple username/password schemes. Enter a new class of storage security that combines secure access, authentication, and strong data encryption to provide a new level of data safekeeping. One vendor supplying these services is Decru. See www.decru.com to learn more.

8.4   BASICS OF CRYPTOGRAPHY

Quiet, I've got a secret to tell you. These words are whispered millions of times a day in a variety of networked transaction scenarios. Keeping secrets is one of the most important activities in an IT environment. No discussion of security can be complete without at least a cursory look at the basics of cryptography—the basics of keeping secrets. This section introduces four fundamental elements of secure transactions: **encryption, keys, key management**, and **digital signatures**. With the hacker's appetite to break into every nook and cranny of networked systems, cryptographic methods are applied to transactions of all kinds.

The history of secure transmissions is as old as mankind. One of the most famous persons of antiquity to employ coding of messages to foil eavesdroppers was Julius Caesar. In *The Gallic Wars*, Caesar describes using a substitution cipher to deliver a military message to Cicero, whose troops needed encouragement during a particularly difficult campaign. The author of the message substituted Greek letters for Roman letters, rendering the message inexplicable to the enemy. Caesar used three of our four themes: (1) encryption—the substitution cipher method, (2) a key—the "trick" to the cipher/decipher, swap Roman letters for Greek, and (3) key management—Cicero and only Cicero should know how to decode the message. Over the course of human development, thousands of ciphers have been developed to secure messages. So let us jump ahead two millennia and peek into the state of the art of these four themes.

8.4.1   Modern Encryption Methods

There is an ocean of methods to en/decrypt messages. This dialogue is limited to several of the most popular methods: DES, Triple DES, and IDEA. Figure 8.9 shows the simplest picture of a cryptosystem. Let us concentrate on the en/decryption methods: the keys used to uniquely code and

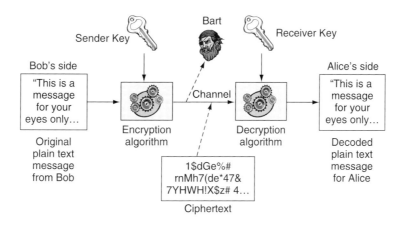

FIGURE   A basic crypto system.

8.9

decode the messages. For many systems, the two keys are identical. Our story has three players: sender Bob, receiver Alice, and eavesdropper Bart.

The Data Encryption Standard (DES) was developed in the 1970s by IBM for the U.S. government. This was the first "data mangler" to find wide acceptance, be free of licensing fees, simple to implement in hardware, well documented, and fast. It is a symmetrical design, i.e., the same algorithm is used to decrypt as is to encrypt. Considering the amount of data morphing that DES does, this is an amazing achievement. The basic idea is shown in Figure 8.10. A message (parsed into 64-bit chunks or blocks) enters at the left side, is permuted by the initial permutation (IP, a remapping of the input bits) and then is mangled 16 times by a combination of the all important cycle operator (CO) followed by an XOR function. At the final stage, the output permutation (OP) exactly undoes the IP operation. The CO function is a relatively involved combination of a bit permutation followed by an XOR (with an internal key as its second input) followed by yet another substitution/permutation of bits. Each cycle makes the input message more and more unrecognizable. After so much data morphing, it is nearly impossible to examine the output and thereby determine its input without knowing the key.

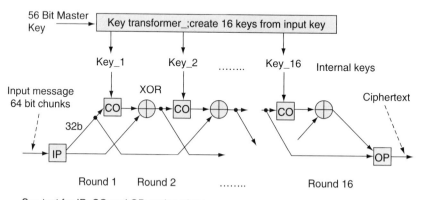

See text for IP, CO and OP explanations

FIGURE   Mangling numbers: Highly simplified DES design.

8.10

The internal keys Key_1 to Key_16 are derived from the 56-bit master key. Each internal key is a different circular bit shift and permuted version of the master key. Also, the decoder is amazingly the same device with the same 56-bit master key that the encoder used but with the 16 internal keys reversed, i.e., Key_1(decode) is Key_16 (encode) and so on. Truly DES is an object of beauty. To learn more about CO function, do an Internet search on *DES encryption* and feed to the heart's desire or visit csrc.nist.gov/publications/fips to learn more about DES in general. See also [Stallings] for a good coverage of cryptography and DES.

At first, the DES algorithm was kept a national secret, as the thought of providing a recipe to nefarious Bart was abhorrent. It was finally published, which proved a good idea, as the "hacker/cracker" community could test its muscle. In fact it did. A prize of $10,000 was offered to crack DES by finding a particular 56-bit key value. In 1997, a worldwide user community of 14,000 PCs running a cracker program for 4 months finally broke DES. Mind you, this was 4 months to discover the value of *one particular* key. However, the cat was out of the bag and the security experts needed a better algorithm than DES. Interestingly, knowing the architecture of DES was of no help. The key was discovered by brute force testing of all (or until the key was found) key possibilities.

What was DES's biggest sin? The master key length was too short at 56 bits. Let us assume that a 56-bit key could be discovered in 1 sec. by a cracker. This is very optimistic, as the world record to crack DES is 22.5 h using a massive array of PCs. For more information on how this was done, see www.distributed.net. By simple scaling, it would take 4 min. to crack a 64-bit length key; 76 bits takes 12.1 days, 112 bits takes a billion years, and 256 bits takes 10^{52} years. So the trend is obvious and comforting to Bob and Alice and troubling to Bart. Clearly Bob's message is safe for eons and then some as the key length becomes moderately large.

Beyond DES

Since a single DES seems doomed, the crypto community tried a novel idea—triple DES. Consider a DES encryption (key1), followed by a DES decryption (key2), and then again by a DES encryption (key1 again). The overall effect is a 112-bit keyed cipher that is super secure. Not content and looking for efficiencies, two cryptographers in 1992 developed the International Data Encryption Algorithm encrypt engine. This works with a 128 length key, is twice as fast as DES methods, is more software friendly, and looks like a close cousin of DES in terms of operation. It has achieved the status of triple DES and is included in many cryptosystems in everyday use, despite the fact that it is patented and needs a license to use. Other coders in common use are the Advanced Encryption Standard and the stream cipher RC4 (encodes a byte at a time, not a block at a time). Incidentally, these crypto methods can function in real time to process high rate AV data streams if needed.

8.4.2   Keys and Key Management

Let us look again at Figure 8.9. Focus on the two secret keys. They must be the same for DES or the other common symmetrical en/decryption engines to operate properly, but how do both sides agree on a common key? Here is one way.

Dear Alice,

Now that we have both purchased an EnigmaMan cryptosystem let's start using it. My secret key is 831 408 625 989. To keep things simple, I plan to use this key for the next 10 years.

Cheers, Bob

Eavesdropper Bart (who is always listening) loves this type of message, as he now knows the key's value and its lifetime. Whoopee! Imagine the living nightmare of securely administering and distributing the keys for millions of multiparty coded conversations between Bobs and Alices. Simplifying this problem eluded cryptographers until 1976 when Whitfield Diffie and Martin Hellman published their seminal paper, *New Directions in Cryptography* (DiffHel). They introduced the idea of a public key and a private key instead of using two identical secret keys as implied in Figure 8.9. The basic idea is that different keys are used for asymmetrical encryption and decryption (DES is a symmetrical algorithm). The public key is used for encryption and the private key is used for decryption. The first key is publicly known and the latter is kept strictly private.

A brief survey of the concepts behind the idea is worth our time, but a full discussion of this method is beyond our scope. With the assistance of Figure 8.11 we can see the essence of the public/private key method. The lower portion of the diagram is essentially the same as Figure 8.9. The upper portion shows a "secret key" exchange method using a public key and a private key. Some of the salient aspects of Figure 8.11 are as follows:

◆ The plaintext message is encoded and decoded using the DES method or similar symmetrical algorithm. Coding and decoding use the same "secret key."

◆ Alice's public key is available to any Bob and is used to encrypt the secret key that is utilized by Alice to decode the plaintext message. Alice has a private key designed to decrypt any "message" that Bob sends. In this case the message is the secret key. The private key belongs to Alice and never leaves her possession, whereas the secret key must be used by both Bob and Alice. This is subtle and vitally important to the overall scheme.

◆ Pub_Enc and Priv_Dec are not DES or even similar to DES. Also, because these two algorithms are *not symmetrical*, the keys that operate them are not identical either. This is an important point of the public/private method.

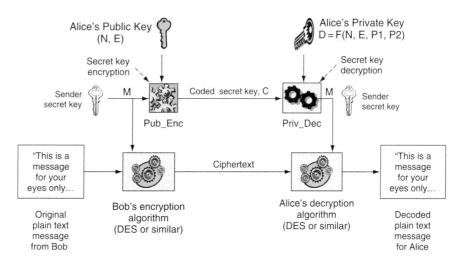

FIGURE   A hybrid method of coding using public/private keys.

8.11

Your first thought may be "this is complex with three different keys and three different crypto methods." Think of it this way: in the big picture, this is the simplest way to solve the secret key distribution problem. One of the beautiful aspects of this method is the concept of a public key. It may seem that making a key available publicly as part of a cryptosystem is outlandish and just plain stupid. After all, why provide Bart with any hints? Despite publishing the public key, this method is extremely secure and has not been broken by any cracker.

A plain text message is sent from Bob to Alice as follows:

1. Bob looks up Alice's public key in a directory.
2. Bob encrypts his secret key using Alice's public key and sends the encoded key to Alice.
3. Alice decrypts the secret key using her private key. At this point, both Bob and Alice have the secret key.
4. Bob now encodes his plain text message using the secret key and Alice decodes it using the same secret key.

Because the key exchange cryptosystem is only used for sending keys and not to encode the target plain text message, the architectures of Pub_Enc and Priv_Dec need not be especially efficient or fast (order of 1000 times slower than DES is okay), as they are used occasionally and only for short (<2048 bits) keys. The magic of the public/private concept is embedded in the way in which the keys are created and how Pub_Enc and Priv_Dec function.

The Public/Private Key Method

Diffie and Hellman invented a creative and beautiful key exchange framework. Their main thesis is the following: What function $Y = \text{Fun}(P)$ is easy to solve in one direction but fiendishly difficult to solve in the inverse?

An example of this is the deceptively simple one-way function $Y = P1 \times P2$, where P1 and P2 are prime numbers. Computing Y for values of P1 and P2 is easy even if the primes have hundreds of digits. For example, if $P1 = 13$ and $P2 = 19$, then $Y = 247$. However, if asked to find P1 and P2 given the value 247, you would need to put in some effort.

Now if the Ps are hundreds of digits long, imagine how difficult it would be to factor the resulting product if you had no hints. The current state of mathematics provides no fast methods to factor large numbers. Oh yes, there are tricks galore to speed up the factoring problem but no quick fix methods exist. Given a factoring engine capable of ~10^{12} operations per second (state of the art for supercomputers in 2005), it would take over 1000 years to factor a 250 digit number [Stall] and about a million years for a 350 digit number. A composite number of 600 digits is currently beyond the scope of any machine to factor in a lifetime of the universe.

Diffie and Hellman did not utilize the factoring method but rather discovered another one-way function called the discrete logarithm. Finding secure one-way functions is very challenging, and their method ranks among the truly great discoveries in cryptography. It turns out that by utilizing one-way functions, both public and private keys can be generated. Their paper inspired three other cryptographers to improve on the idea. In 1978, Ron Rivest, Adi Shamir, and Len Adleman of MIT proposed a method of public/private key generation now called the RSA algorithm. Their method proved so successful that RSA Security (www.rsasecurity.com) was formed to commercialize the concepts. The RSA algorithm relies on the inability of machines to factor 200+ digit decimal numbers. The RSA algorithm is particularly complex, yet beautiful too. The basic idea is (refer to Figure 8.11):

◆ Alice produces a number $N = P1 \times P2$. She also chooses a value E (small, normally 3 or 7 or 65537) that has a special relationship to P1 and P2. She publishes her public key pair = (N, E) for Bob to use. N is normally hundreds of digits long. She keeps primes P1 and P2 private.

◆ Alice also needs to compute her private key (D) and uses the function $D = F(N, P1, P2, E)$ to do so. Note that she has the advantage of knowing P1 and P2, whereas Bob and Bart do not. F() is defined by RSA and is not described here.

◆ Bob can access Alice's public key (N, E) whenever he wants to send Alice a secret key.

◆ Bob encrypts his message M (the secret key) by computing the value of $C = M^E \pmod N$. C is the cipher data that he sends to Alice. This RSA function is Pub_Enc in Figure 8.11. The encryptor function raises M to the power of E and then applies Mod N of the result. Mod N is a reminder operator. For example, if $X = A \bmod (B)$, then A is the integer reminder when X is divided by B. If B = 9 and X = 12, then A = 3, where A, B, and X are integers.

♦ Alice receives the encrypted data stream and decrypts it using Priv_Dec. RSA defines the decrypted value as $M = C^D \pmod{N}$, which is the recovered secret key in our example. Note the simple elegance of the RSA functions Pub_Enc and Priv_Dec.

Bob and Alice now have the same secret key so they can proceed to send the actual message of interest using the lower part of Figure 8.11. Many books on cryptography spend 50+ pages to describe the public key method. Obviously many details have been omitted for the sake of simplicity. For an enjoyable and enlightening coverage of this method, see [Singh].

In practice, many real world systems use either the Diffie-Hellman or the RSA Public/Private key exchange method. For example, IPSec uses Diffie-Hellman key exchange and SSL uses RSA methods. Even with the wonderful invention of the public/private key technique, there is a need for trusted agencies to accept, store, and publish public keys. As you might imagine, there are all sorts of things that can go wrong unless someone manages the keys properly. An entire industry has been created to manage keys. Certificate Authorities (CA) do the job of guaranteeing binding between the public key and the owner, thereby preventing masquerading. The Public Key Infrastructure (PKI) is a complete system for managing public keys and includes policies and procedures and digital certificates. A digital certificate is a short record that holds information about a person or organization, including any associated public key. A certificate binds a public key to its owner. For more information on CA, see, for example, www.verisign.com for practical solutions and white papers. Standard ITU-T X.509 specifies all the relevant details to implement a PKI system.

8.4.3   Kerberos

The much-used public key method is still a complex beast. As an alternative the Kerberos (Greek spelling of the mythical three-headed dog that guards the entrance to the underworld) protocol is sometimes used. This method supplies identical private keys to Bob and Alice for their use in straightforward symmetrical DES en/decryption. It tends to be used at universities and within companies where a certain amount of trust can be placed in the operators. Over the raw Internet the PKI is preferred over most private key exchange means. Still Kerberos is widely used and the open source code is available from MIT (RFC 1510).

The basic idea is that Kerberos uses two trusted third parties at the same time: the Kerberos server and the ticket granting server. Bob and Alice transact with these servers to get a common secret key that they will subsequently use for exchanging their target coded information. The full transaction explanation is beyond our scope [Wenstrom]. Before leaving cryptography, we need to cover one more topic, digital signatures.

Snapshot

Factoring Digital Monsters

Wars have been lost when a cipher was broken by the opposing side so the interest in secure ciphers has led mathematicians to study factoring these long digit count monsters. Several organizations offer challenge money of $100 to $200,000 to factor a given number. The amount of money is small compared to the effort expended. However, like climbing Mt. Everest, many will try to top it because "it is there." Search the Internet for topics such as "RSA challenge" or "factoring large numbers" to learn more. One current challenge offered by RSA Security is titled *Challenge RSA-1024*. There is a $100,000 prize to find the two factors of N (P × Q = N, find P and Q) of the following 309 digit decimal number (1024 bits). If you succeed, there is a 618 decimal digit monster waiting for you with a $200,000 prize attached. Happy computing!

135066410865995223349603216278805969938881475605667027524485143851526510604859533833940287150571909441798207282164471551373680419703964191743046496589274256239341020864383202110372958725762358509643110564073501508187510676594629205563685529475213500852879416377328533906109750544334999811150056977236890927563

8.4.4   Digital Signatures (DS)

As the name suggests, a DS is a digital fingerprint of a data file. As with a traditional signature on a document, a digitally signed document attaches a person's acknowledgment or approval to the document. A DS is a form of checksum (or DNA strand by analogy) that may be used to validate a target data file's contents. Let us call a plain text message PT and the DS of this as DS(PT). A DS is a hash function (also called a message digest) that "compresses" an entire PT no matter how long into a single value normally less than 256 bits. For example, the digitally represented signature of this book is a unique DS value. This value may be used to verify that an electronic file copy is indeed 100% identical to the digital master DS. Some of the aspects of a DS are as follows:

◆ DS(PT) is a value that uniquely identifies the PT. There is no other PT with the same signature ideally.
◆ Most signatures are relatively short, a la 160 bits.
◆ From the DS(PT) value no one can reverse the function and produce the original PT. The function is secure.
◆ DS algorithms are published for open use.

There are a variety of hash functions in use today, with the most popular being SHA-1 (Secure Hash Algorithm), MD5 (RFC 1321), and RIPEMD-160.

As with most signatures, a digital signature may be used to verify who sent a PT message. Assume that Bob sends Alice a coded PT message but Alice wants to know for sure that Bob sent it and not someone else (authentication). An example of this is the following:

◆ Bob calculates a single DS(PT) value for his plain text message.
◆ Bob encrypts the value of DS(PT) using his private key and sends the encrypted value to Alice. Bob also sends Alice the PT as per the secure methods discussed earlier.
◆ Alice receives and decrypts Bob's PT coded stream, called PT_Recovered.
◆ Alice also receives the encrypted value of DS(PT) and decrypts it using Bob's public key.
◆ Alice now computes DS(PT_Recovered) and compares it to the received value of DS(PT). If the two match, then the received message was indeed sent by Bob (he is authenticated) and the message itself was unaltered.

The last step is the significant phase in authenticating that Bob is who he says he is and that the received PT is the correct message. Digital signatures are used for a variety of applications and this example is only one such instance. Message digests are well-accepted components in the big scheme of security, public key management, authentication, and the validity of messages.

The overall basics summarized in this section should provide you with sufficient understanding to plow through the minefield of cryptographic jargon. Don't feel bad if these concepts don't smoothly roll off your tongue; after all they are the results of hundreds of cryptographers' efforts combined over 40 years. Fortunately too, most applications hide the gory details from users. But it's good to have a general knowledge of the main themes that are being employed daily in IT systems and the Internet.

Remember that cryptography is not the total solution to security. It's really about process not math. Encoding rules are only a small part of overall security methods.

8.5 IT'S A WRAP—SOME FINAL WORDS

Security methods will likely never become simpler than they are today. As threats increase, methods to protect against them will become increasingly more complex. This is a fact of life in the digital age. The networked requirements of AV force security methods to account for real time applications as never before. When deciding on security policy, factor in the real time needs of AV or pay the price of poor performance for applications.

REFERENCES

[**Beale**] Jay Beale et al., *Snort 2.1 Intrusion Detection, 2nd Edition*, Syngress Press, May 2004.

[**DiffHel**] W. Diffie and M. Hellman, *New Directions in Cryptography*, IEEE Transactions of Information Theory, IT 22/6, 1976.

[**NAC**] Networking, Analysis, Collaboration (www.netapps.org), *Enterprise Security Architecture: A Framework and Template for Policy Driven Security, 2000, Executive Summary.*

[**Singh**] Simon Singh, *The Code Book*, Anchor Books, 1999.

[**Stallings**] William Stallings, *Network and Internetwork Security*, Prentice Hall, 1995.

[**Wenstrom**] Mike Wenstrom, *Managing Cicso Network Security*, Cisco Press, 2001.

9 | Systems Management and Monitoring

9.0 INTRODUCTION

Managing the IT infrastructure is one of the thorniest problems facing business executives today. It is not easy, vacuums up resources, and is ever changing. To some, the cost of managing IT is pure overhead with no apparent positive return on investment. However, when the gains of productivity, availability, and efficiency are counted, coaxing out every ounce of performance is wise and contributes to the bottom line.

This chapter reviews the fundamentals of systems management for pure AV systems and hybrid AV/IT systems. Monitoring is a part of systems management and is covered with sufficient emphasis to be showcased in the chapter title. The following topics are discussed:

◆ Systems management 101: The FCAPS model
◆ A summary of traditional AV monitoring
◆ IT monitoring methods
◆ An AV/IT system monitoring framework
◆ Systems management IT standards
◆ Diagnosing problems

Remember, the management plane is part of the three-plane model discussed in Chapter 7 so it plays a pivotal role in IT systems. However it is the least developed of the three planes *for AV systems*. Still, it is fitting to discuss the principles of the management plane, its developmental status, and how it can grow to meet the needs of AV.

Who are the users of management systems? Broadly, they can be classed as

◆ Access to a device by ***local service personnel***. They typically need the most detailed device reporting and diagnostics with hands-on access.

◆ Systems management for a campus or enterprise IT infrastructure—managing groups of devices from a central location by ***IT staff***.

◆ Access to devices by **remote vendor service personnel**—ideally do any management operation remotely that can be done on site. This challenges some AV gear but enables remote troubleshooting.

The concepts discussed in this chapter apply to all three types of users.

Figure 9.1 illustrates the landscape of managed systems and devices. A "managed" device or system component (including software applications) is one that exposes its internal states to external observers over a network. A stand-alone device with only front panel error reporting does not fall into

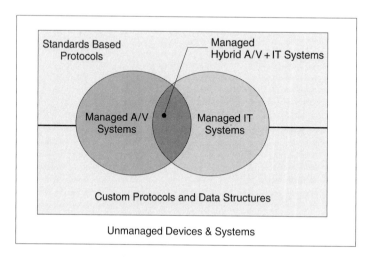

FIGURE
9.1
The landscape of managed systems.

this category. This would be an unmanaged element. There are two general techniques to manage an element: using management standards or proprietary methods. Our focus is on standard methods. Also, there are three management domains for purposes of our discussion: traditional A/V, standard IT, and hybrid AV + IT. All are considered. So let us get started.

9.1   THE FCAPS MODEL

In service of the telecoms industry, the ITU-T derived the FCAPS acronym to describe the salient aspects of systems management. It has been applied to managing IT as well. FCAPS (fault management, configuration, accounting, performance, and security) is a categorical model of the working objectives of network management. There are five levels: the fault management level (FM), the configuration level (CM), the accounting level (AM), the performance level (PM), and security level management (SM). Table 9.1 outlines the function of each level. Monitoring is an amalgam of select FM, AM, and PM functions.

The categories are self-describing, and Table 9.1 provides hints for each functional definition. This chapter focuses on fault management

Fault management	Configuration management	Accounting management	Performance management	Security management
Probe for measurements	System turn-up	Track service usage	Data collection	Control user access
Trouble detection	Device configuration	Bill for services	Report generation	Enable user functions
Alarm handling, logs access	Auto discovery		Test scripts	Access logs
Trouble correction with diagnostics tools	Back up and restore		Status reports	Secure devices
	Database handling			

TABLE   FCAPS Breakdown

9.1

and performance management—the shaded columns. But why not cover every column? Configuration management is vital of course but there are precious few standards today. Although it is fundamental, it also tends to be vendor specific so it will be skipped for now. Accounting is also vendor specific and is applicable to facilities that rent equipment per hour or project for the most part. The security column was covered in Chapter 8. The lion's share of systems management, for our purposes, is related to monitoring, reporting, diagnosing, and repairing devices and systems.

Although not originally encompassed, the FCAPS model may be extended to cover Web applications management. It is not enough just to manage the IT infrastructure but ignore the applications layers. Modern systems' management solutions can drill into applications as they run and report status, resource problems, performance, security issues, and so on.

Ideally, all device/link/application-related FCAPS functions can be managed from a centralized station(s) connected to an IP network. Then hundreds of links, devices, and processes can all be monitored from one or more stations with integrated reporting across the entire system. This sure beats having to manage a multitude of devices individually with specialized protocols and methods.

If possible, every component, device, link, and network is 100% monitored and faults (or preventative indicators) are reported with appropriate alarms. In some cases the cause of a fault is obvious such as "*Storage Array ABC, Disc 5 failed.*" There is no need to hunt down the bad element. The guilty party is replaced with a new disc drive. At the other end of the scale, the root cause of a fault may not be apparent. How should a technician respond to the reported fault "*Protocol XYZ failure: audio level parameter L3 out of bounds?*" Logs need to be scanned and interpreted and diagnostic tools run to discover the root cause(s) of the fault. These can be tricky problems to debug, and diagnostics tools are mandatory to avoid protracted troubleshooting. Of course there is no magic bullet to resolve all problems, but applying the FCAPS model is a step in the right direction.

FCAPS implementation in the IT space has become an industry with many vendors supplying standards-based solutions. However, we are also interested in management solutions for hybrid AV + IT systems, and this combination has been vendor specific with a only smidgen of IT-based

FCAPS thrown in. Still, there is huge promise for FCAPS to be adopted by the AV industry and this chapter shows its potential. Of course, adopting the model is just a start. What is really needed is adoption of the *standards* that support the model. Before exploring this potential, the status quo of AV monitoring and problem resolution is outlined.

9.2   TRADITIONAL AV MONITORING METHODS

The maturity of AV standards has enabled a variety of monitoring techniques and methods. Figure 9.2 illustrates an exaggerated monitoring landscape. There are six monitor and reporting classes shown (the device class, the

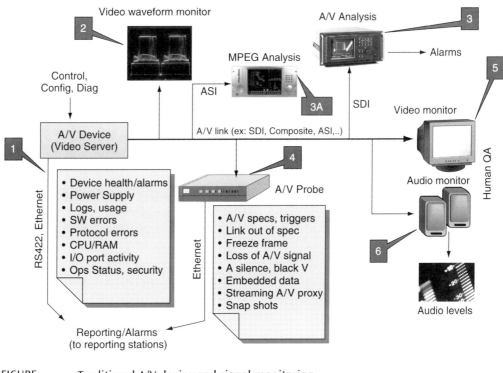

FIGURE   Traditional A/V device and signal monitoring.

9.2   see [Sources].

visual viewing class, and so on) and each is discussed in this section. The source of AV is a video server for this example but could be any AV source.

The most common monitoring method is to examine the internals of the device under test, point #1 in the diagram. This class enables the managed A/V device—the left lobe in Figure 9.1. Typical internal measured data points are listed. Monitored data are reported to remote observers over LAN or serial RS422. There are several protocol means to report on the device health over IP networks. Many are proprietary but one is based on an IT standard: the Simple Network Management Protocol (SNMP). This is an IETF standard for accessing measured device data over an IP network. SNMP is the workhorse for monitoring IT gear of all sorts. SNMP reads device internal data values arranged in a Management Information Base (MIB). MIB data reside inside the target device. A MIB is a tree-like data structure populated with measured values specific to the device under observation (alarms, power supply health, storage stats, I/O status, etc.). SNMP was designed to read this tree of data and return the values to a monitoring station. SNMP and MIBs are explained in more detail later in this chapter. Unfortunately, and this is key, there are very few *standardized* MIB definitions for AV gear. Video servers, routers, switchers, and so on that have MIBs use proprietary ones for the most part. True, MIB data structures are usually published by the vendor to enable reporting but they are still proprietary.

Device management is often based on vendor-specific technology and data structures. This frustrates plans for uniform facility monitoring as is available for IT systems. There is a nascent interest in establishing MIB A/V standards but the work has been slow. However, MIBs for IT gear are plentiful and mature.

Monitor point #2 in Figure 9.2 is the time-honored video waveform monitor class. This time-based device displays one or more horizontal video lines. Video amplitude and timing-related specs are checked most commonly. A close cousin is the vectorscope used to measure color parameters. Even some nontechnical users refer to the waveform display for a confidence check of min/max video luminance values. Some models can be configured to report over a network when illegal values are encountered. For a representative sample of signal monitors, refer to

Tektronix (www.tektronix.com), VideoTek (www.videotek.com), and Magni Systems (www.magnisystems.com).

Monitoring point #3 in Figure 9.2 shows the venerable VM-700 from Tektronix. This is the granddaddy of video measurement gear and can test every conceivable video spec. Some facilities use this as a quality and confidence monitor for master output feeds. Because these are expensive, simple-minded A/V probes are more practical for multilink monitoring. Point #3A in Figure 9.2 is a related method for monitoring MPEG TS streams over ASI links (and other links). The DVStation from Pixelmetrix (www.pixelmetrix.com) is such a device. Because DVB, ATSC, ISDB (Japan), and digital cable TV standards are all MPEG based, there is ample need to monitor/report on streaming MPEG signal integrity for these systems.

A relatively new class of monitor is the A/V probe (point #4 in Figure 9.2). These devices can be scattered throughout a facility and probe critical or suspect A/V links for signal integrity. They do not have an embedded display, such as a waveform monitor, but rather send a wide variety of real time data points to centralized reporting stations. The method supports remote monitoring from virtually any Internet access point, which is powerful for multifacility monitoring from a central location. Each probe can be configured to report only when a trigger threshold has been reached. For example, say that the audio of a link is intermittent. A monitoring probe can be programmed to send a report only when the audio is silent (the trigger) for more than say 3 s. There is no end to the number of measured parameters and thresholds that can be programmed. Judicious configuration can find odd problems that rarely occur, which is a life saver for big system debugging. They can also be programmed to report continuously on select parameters for display on a central console.

Several vendors offer A/V probes with centralized reporting stations. Figure 9.3 shows an example PC screen shot from Miranda's iControl (www.miranda.com). It illustrates a full-featured reporting display that receives its data from Miranda A/V probes. All manner of stats, data points, alarms, trigger thresholds, latched triggers, meters, and proxies are displayed. Other providers include Evertz (www.evertz.com) with their VistaLINK series signal monitoring and

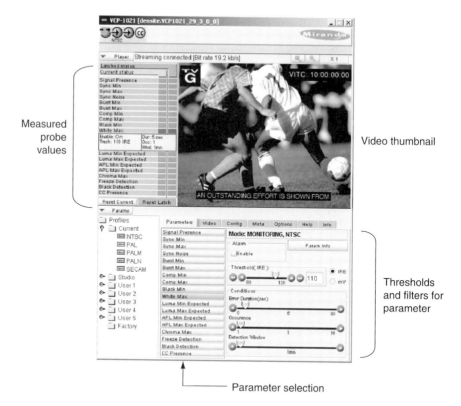

Measured probe values

Video thumbnail

Thresholds and filters for parameter

Parameter selection

FIGURE

9.3

A/V probe-reported data.

Image courtesy of Miranda Technologies.

reporting. Also, Videotek (www.videotek.com) offers the Signal Quality Manager series with probes and reporting displays. Video Frame Systems (www.videoframesystems.com) provides a variety of A/V probes (VTECS model) as well.

Monitor points #5 and 6 in Figure 9.2 are legacy visual and aural monitors. With stand-alone video, monitoring problems are detected only if someone is watching/listening at the moment of signal corruption. Modern control rooms and sports vans often use a monitor wall showing many channels simultaneously. They have embedded signal alarms and triggers based on AV analysis. Barco's iStudio, Evertz' MVP, and Miranda's Kaleido are among several products that combine video images with overlaid data monitoring and alarms on the same display. See Figure 9.4 for a representative example.

FIGURE

9.4

Integrated wall display for A/V channel monitoring and stats.

Image courtesy of Miranda Technologies.

The Challenge

Monitoring methods 2–6 are alive and well. They are based on existing
A/V standards and signal links. A/V probes (#4) use custom data structures and reporting. Ideally, this could be standardized, but market
pressure to do this is minimal at present. However, monitoring method
#1 is problematic. A medium-sized facility may have 200+ devices from
possibly 30 different vendors. Device management using 30 different
protocols, data structures, and reporting screens is a nightmare. There
are too few standards, and most solutions are ad hoc and vendor specific.
Progress is needed to standardize device-specific MIBs with agreements

on how to use Microsoft's Windows Management Instrumentation (WMI) for reporting OS, device resource, and application layer parameters. WMI is Microsoft's implementation of WEMB discussed in Section 9.4.

One exception to the status quo is a Sony effort to set a company-wide standard for professional AV device MIBs. They call this the Pro-AV MIB and it spans all their new AV equipment. The MIB was first defined in 2001 and is now included with all new Sony professional products. Figure 9.5 shows a general outline of the structure of this MIB across product lines. Actually, the Pro-AV MIB is defined by combining MIBs

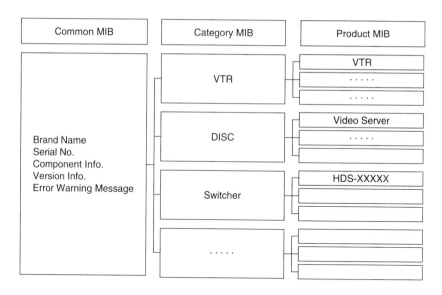

As shown, the Pro-AV MIB is defined as a three-layered structure.

- Common MIB: Common information for all professional products
- Category MIB: Product category (i.e., VTR, camera, switcher)
- Product MIB: Product-specific information

FIGURE
9.5

Sony Pro-AV MIB general overview.
Concept: Sony.

from individual products. It is not yet a SMPTE standard but they do have category MIBs for the most common AV elements.

9.3   AV/IT MONITORING ENVIRONMENT

As systems migrate to hybrid AV + IT technology, are strict AV monitoring methods sufficient to meet user's needs? No, new monitoring methods are needed. Ideally, we need to add *functionality* to Figure 9.2 to include at least the following:

1. IT systems integrity—links, routers, security, rates, QoS measurements, alarms, performance, and usage. Storage system health, stats, reports (on-line, near-line, off-line and archive) (Mon 1, 1A)
2. File transfer progress reporting (Mon 3)
3. A/V file analysis, integrity, proxy viewing (Mon 4)
4. Metadata browsing (Mon 4)
5. AV stream taps. Monitor an AV stream over a network connection (possibly UDP/IP or ATM based) with a nonintrusive monitor probe (Mon 2)
6. Workflow reporting, job progress reporting

This domain is the merged overlap area shown in Figure 9.1. *Mon 1–4* in the above mentioned list indicate reporting methods referenced in Figure 9.6.

All but the first item in the list are AV specific. Standard IT means are sufficient to meet just about any network and storage measurement or monitoring scenario (#1 in list). However, functions 2–6 are not commonly available on centralized reporting displays, although some of these are available using vendor-specific tools.

Figure 9.6 illustrates a full-featured AV/IT monitoring environment. It uses all the methods shown in Figure 9.2 and augments these to include the functions in the list given earlier. The added items are identified as Mon 1/A, 2, 3, and 4. They are shown separately but could be combined into one or more stations for convenience as needed. Each one will be outlined.

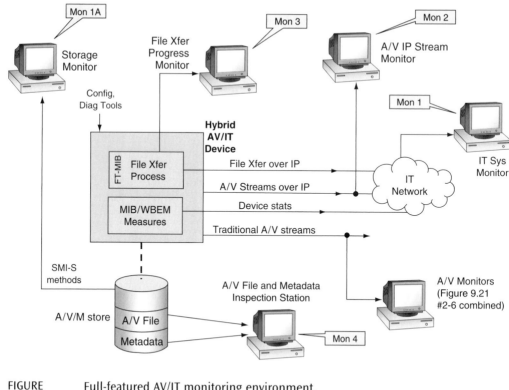

Full-featured AV/IT monitoring environment.

9.3.1   Traditional IT Device and Network Monitoring (Mon 1)

Mon 1 is the traditional IT infrastructure monitor means. This is the right lobe in Figure 9.1. Using[1] MIBs (data structures populated with monitored and static values) and SNMP (the protocol used to retrieve MIB elements), most IT elements may be monitored. **Mon 1A** in Figure 9.6 is dedicated to storage management, but is really just a subset of Mon 1. This area is well developed with hundreds of vendors supplying reporting

---

[1] MIBs, SNMP, and WBEM are described in more detail in Section 9.4. If you cannot wait, read ahead to learn more about these important IT-related specifications.

gear based on many standardized MIBs and other data structures. For example, the following grouping is of common network device-related MIBs as defined by the IETF.

RFC 1493 Bridge MIB; RFC 1213 MIB II; RFC 2096 IP Forwarding Table MIB; RFC 2737 Entity MIB; RFC 2665 Ethernet MIB; RFC2819 Four groups of RMON: 1 (statistics), 2 (history), 3 (alarm), and 9 (events); RFC 2021 RMON probe configuration; RFC 1850 IP Routing MIB

In fact, 101 official IETF RFCs in early 2005 referenced the word MIB in their title. In addition, there are thousands of proprietary MIBs. A few standards of noteworthy mention are MIB-I, MIB-II, and RMON MIBs. One of the first MIBs to be defined is called MIB-I (RFC 1156) and is used to manage the TCP/IP protocol suite. MIB-II is an updated version and is included in most devices that support TCP/IP. It is shown later in Section 9.4. The MIB is a tree structure with the upper part leading a path to the actual data elements in the lower part.

The RMON (versions 1 and 2) specification is an extension of MIB-II. RMON stands for remote monitoring and was designed to enable vendor-neutral IP stack network monitoring. An RMON-compliant probe (an IP stack parameter measurement device) can accumulate data and report when thresholds are reached. See Figure 9.7 for the breakdown of RMON 1 and 2 measurement domains. Because RMON defines a MIB standard, vendors can compete by selling probes and centralized reporting stations, knowing that the entire food chain is defined. The RMON equivalent for AV-specific gear and links does not exist, yet. However, the Pro-AV MIB described earlier comes close.

In addition to MIBs and SNMP, the Web-Based Enterprise Management Initiative (WBEM) is a separate set of technologies developed to manage enterprise computing environments (integration platforms). WBEM provides the ability to deliver an integrated set of standard management tools that leverage Web techniques. More on this in Section 9.4. One special area is storage management. The Storage Networking Industry Association (www.snia.org) has defined how to use WBEM to manage storage systems. Networked video relies heavily on storage, so let us review the development of SNIA.

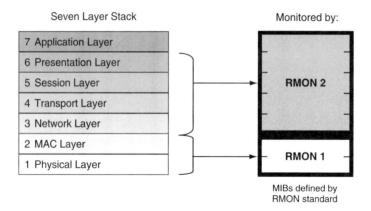

Seven Layer Stack

| 7 Application Layer |
| 6 Presentation Layer |
| 5 Session Layer |
| 4 Transport Layer |
| 3 Network Layer |
| 2 MAC Layer |
| 1 Physical Layer |

Monitored by:

RMON 2

RMON 1

MIBs defined by
RMON standard

FIGURE   RMON MIB monitoring for the IP stack.

9.7

The Storage Management Initiative (Mon 1A)

The SMI was developed by the SNIA in response to the crying need for
storage management across heterogeneous platforms. At its core the SMI
is composed of the following:

◆ Enable and streamline the integration of multivendor storage systems

◆ Leverage established management methods

◆ Encourage management consolidation (end the nightmare of five
  management consoles for five different storage systems)

◆ Provide a common management interface for vendors to develop
  compatible products

◆ Interoperability and testing suites

◆ SMI-S—the technical specification

SMI is more than a specification, it is an initiative spanning education, specs, interop testing, and marketing of the concepts. SMI-S is the
specification portion, which is our focus. The SNIA predicts that 60% of
all new Fibre Channel SAN-based storage will be SMI-S compliant in early
2005. Because virtually all storage vendors support this initiative, eventually most SAN storage systems will support it. The SNIA added NAS and
iSCSI storage support in mid-2003.

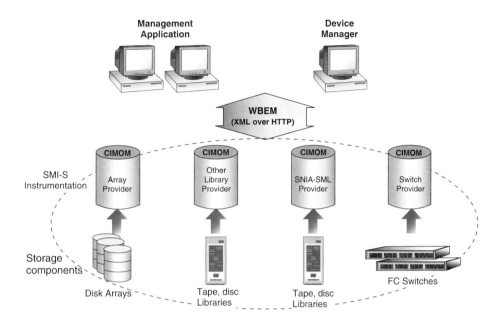

FIGURE
9.8

Overview of SMI-S management methods.
Concepts: SNIA.

Figure 9.8 is a top-level view showing arrays, libraries, HBA, and FC switches being managed using WEBM. The basic idea is to leverage WBEM along with CIM (see Section 9.4 for details) for element, application, and system management. CIM is an information model, a conceptual view of the managed environment that unifies and extends the existing management standards (SNMP, MIBs) using object-oriented constructs and design. The CIM model (CIM Object Model in Figure 9.8) is populated with reported data values that a management station may query to determine the state of a device or process.

The SMI-S 1.1 specification documents a secure and reliable interface that allows storage management systems to identify, monitor, provision, configure, and control physical and logical resources in a storage system. Importantly, SMI-S is much more than dumb element monitoring (report bad fan) and includes configuration and a hierarchy of managed objects. The bottom line is this—administrators can manage heterogeneous storage platforms using a standardized management interface and vendor neutral management stations. Storage administrators can use one application for many of the operations that traditionally take several vendor-specific management products. This brief coverage only scratches the surface of SMI-S (refer to www.snia.org/smi for a deeper look).

Centralized Enterprise Reporting Stations (Mon 1, 1A)

At a higher level, there is an entire industry providing enterprise-wide management stations that hide the complexity of MIBs, SNMP, and WBEM. After all, what users really want are reports and notifications informing them of alarms and potential troubles and assisting with problem diagnostics and resolution. No one wants to read strings of MIB variables or CIM models to find a problem. Managers want the fewest people to administer the most system components. Figure 9.9 illustrates a simple

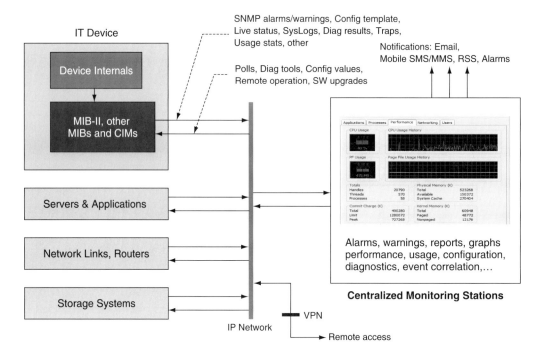

FIGURE   IT element monitoring environment.

9.9

monitoring configuration with a centralized station(s) monitoring potentially thousands of IT elements.

Some valuable performance attributes of the reporting station are as follow.

◆ General alarm reporting, including notifications to email, SMS/MMS, and so on.

◆ Support for all standard reporting means—standard MIBs, SNMP, WMI, WBEM, OMI, and so on.

◆ Resolving power—report the root cause of a problem if possible. Some problems can cause an alarm storm due to cascading errors. A good reporting tool will determine the root cause and give it priority over possibly hundreds of other cascading alarms.

◆ User-friendly screens—ability to dig as deep into a system as needed. This may include embedded configuration diagrams for easy tracing of problems.

◆ Settable thresholds—this allows for a user to set trigger points in a device for select parameters and report only when the trigger has been reached. For example, only report when the storage capacity reaches 10% free space.

◆ Copious reporting choices—charts, graphs, and textual reporting of all sorts.

◆ Optional IT element diagnostics, configuration, performance, usage, event log viewing, and status are valuable features. Depending on the element(s) being managed, configuration, diagnostics, performance, and so on may only be available from the element's vendor as a stand-alone function and not integrated into a generic reporting station.

It is not easy to monitor AV gear in real time, especially accessing internal, low-level parameters. The procedure of monitoring may interfere with the AV operation. By way of analogy, this is related to Heisenberg's uncertainty principle. The more precisely a measurement is made, the more likely it is to interfere with process operations. It is left to the AV vendor to design their devices to be monitored noninvasively in real time. Nonreal time monitoring is easy but a nuisance, as it may miss critical events.

There is a world of choice when selecting enterprise systems management software. HP's OpenView, IBM's Tivoli Management Software, and

Computer Associate's Unicenter are the big three providers. Of course there are 30+ smaller providers that often specialize to differentiate in some manner. The big three offer a complete line of management solutions, whereas others usually offer vertical solutions in select areas. None of these players specialize in AV systems. However, several AV vendors offer entry-level, vertical management platforms dedicated to their own products and some third-party ones. Some sample offerings are Avid's Administration Tool for Unity, GVG's NetCentral, Leitch's CCS Pilot, Miranda's iControl, Snell and Wilcox' Roll Call, and Sony's MMStation.

Look ahead to Figure 9.17, which demonstrates an example of a hierarchical system configuration as viewed on a management station. Users may drill deeper into any subsystem by selecting it for exposure. This example shows two levels, but more are likely for larger systems. At the lowest level, dashboards of device health are common. This example shows a video server the MIB with particular focus on the configuration details of the device. This aspect of Figure 9.17 is discussed later in the chapter.

9.3.2   A/V IP Stream Monitors (Mon 2)

This class of monitoring reports on A/V stream signal integrity over IP links. In a way, it is an extension of traditional A/V monitoring (class 3 in Figure 9.2) except for IP links. One such method uses UDP/IP and the RTP streaming protocol to carry MPEG, DV, uncompressed HD (RFC 3497), or other A/V payloads. Another model carries MPEG over IP/ATM directly. MXF has stream support but there is little usage so far. Expect to see more IP usage as SDI is replaced by IP connectivity. However, as mentioned in Chapter 2, SDI will not replace IP streaming anytime soon for live event scenarios. The DVStation from Pixelmetrix is one such monitoring device, but this class is immature at present.

9.3.3   File Transfer Progress Monitor (Mon 3)

The usage of file transfer to move AV assets has become commonplace. Many everyday operations, once based on SDI or composite links, are now performed using files. Anyone who has waited for a file transfer to complete knows the value of a monitoring display showing the stats of the transfer—time to go, percentage complete, stalled, failed, and so on. Frankly, there should be a federal law forcing vendors to always provide a meaningful progress monitor—the hourglass icon does not count!

As file transfers consume a larger part of overall AV operations, it makes sense to have a unified way to monitor their status. One could argue that separate vendor-supplied custom monitors (usually embedded in an application) will always be acceptable, but then there is no consolidated view of system-wide transfer operations. Incidentally, if the file transfer is considered a stream, then the Mon 2 method may be used in some cases. Generally, however, monitoring the actual file as it moves across a link has little value and is difficult to implement.

One way to enable a universal view is to define a file transfer MIB populated with live stats. If 10 products from different vendors are all moving files independently and each supports this proposed FT-MIB, then a central station can easily monitor all transfers on one display. The FT-MIB would reside in the box titled "File Xfer Process" in Figure 9.6. Some may reason that the individual transfers lose their meaning on a centralized report. However, a centralized knowledge of all transfer stalls/failures, completion of crucial scheduled transfers, and aggregate consumed bandwidth is valuable information for managing the overall facility. Defining the FT-MIB is a simple task and possibly ~15 parameters would suffice. A suggested parameter list is as follows.

◆ File name, file size
◆ Transfer ID tag (tracking number)
◆ Source machine name, process name, and ID
◆ Destination machine(s) name, process name, and ID(s)
◆ Time of transfer start, estimated time of completion
◆ Percentage complete (updated every 2 s or so)
◆ Average Mb/s transfer rate, peak, minimum
◆ Status: transfer in progress, stalled for N seconds, failed (failure code)

There is an old saying, "If you can't measure it then you can't improve it." The FT-MIB is a step in the right direction in improving file transfer efficiency and overall infrastructure utilization.

9.3.4   AV File and Metadata Inspector (Mon 4)

When inspecting a video tape, text labels are indispensable for identifying the contents. It is a snap to read a tape's label and/or preview it on any active VTR. When using files, it may not be as straightforward to know what is in a file or to preview it. Enter the *file inspector*. This class is not strictly monitoring but rather examination. There are no alarms, warnings, or MIBs. Rather this class enables easy viewing of stored assets and associated metadata. It is a MAM element as discussed in Chapter 7. A short list of file inspection criteria is

◆ Query for and locate one or more files.
◆ Browse file on a desktop client, view basic properties.
◆ Read the associated structural and descriptive metadata as appropriate.
◆ Move a file across the network as an option.

These steps are an analogy to the tape-based inspection case. Most MAM vendors offer file browsing with these features. Having access to inspection browsing reduces user anxiety in tapeless environments. Plus, with sufficient determination, it allows personnel to debug problems, find misplaced assets, and locate poorly indexed metadata. As it happens, several vendors provide utilities for testing file format (MPEG, MXF, XML metadata, etc.) legality; this is beyond the basic requirements outlined in the above mentioned list.

So, there it is. Figure 9.6 outlines the salient aspects of a full-featured monitoring system. Most systems will have some subset of this universal viewpoint. Those who ignore monitoring will suffer when troubles arise. Some of the pieces are in place today, some are coming on the scene, and some are long overdue. As IT moves deeper into AV systems, expect to see more growth and standards in these areas. If you are a user, query any potential vendor for their response to the issues and features that make up the management plane.

9.4   STANDARDS FOR SYSTEMS MANAGEMENT

The world of managed systems is built on a strong foundation of standards. Actually, layers of standards. There are standards for data types, data structures, access methods, and transport. Figure 9.10 shows a

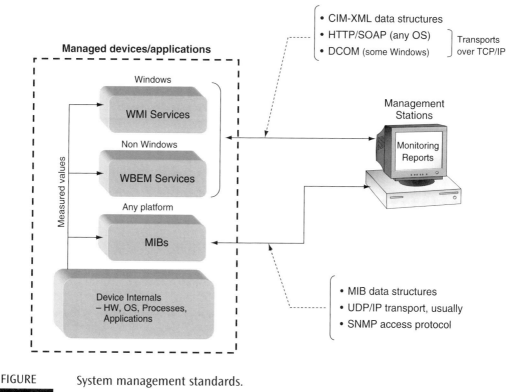

FIGURE

9.10

System management standards.

high-level view of the relevant device and application management standards that impact IT and AV systems. Of course there are countless custom ways to create management systems, but this section focuses on industry standards and their functions.

The chief standards and controlling bodies are

◆ Management Information Base—IETF body

◆ Simple Network Management Protocol—IETF

◆ XML, SOAP, HTTP, TCP/IP data wrapping and transport standards—W3C, IETF

◆ Web-Based Enterprise Management Initiative (WBEM)—DMTF body

  ◆ Common Information Model (CIM)—DMTF

◆ Windows Measurement Instrumentation (WMI)—Microsoft implementation of WBEM

◆ CIM extended for Windows environment (de facto standard)

Each of these is explored in order to shed some light on their underlying function and to place in the overall management food chain.

9.4.1   The Management Information Base

A MIB is a tree structure containing human readable data values. Its base
standard is RFC 1155. Each node in the tree contains an element value.
In fact, all the values are ASCII textual values. Any text processor can
display the contents of a MIB in much the same way that an XML file can
be examined. An example of a MIB is shown in Figure 9.11. The tree
structure is obvious. Each node is labeled with a number, the object ID
(OID). The label identifies an associated value. The OID is a kind of
address. To locate any element in the MIB tree is as simple as following
the OID pointer. Some key nodal values are:

◆ International Standards Organization (ISO); node OID = 1
◆ Organization; node OID = 3 (an ISO-recognized body)
◆ Department of Defense (DOD); node OID = 6
◆ Internet; node OID = 1
◆ Mgmt; node OID = 2 (all elements below this node are management
data)
◆ MIB-II; node OID = 1 (standardized IP stack measures)

The full OID 1.3.6.1.2.1 points to the top of the MIB-II data structure.
Just for fun, enter this number into an Internet search engine to appreciate
the ubiquity of MIB-II in managed products. MIB-II nodal objects are
defined by RCF 1213. One example of a MIB-II node element value is
"IP_Address_Error" at OID = 1.3.6.1.2.1.4.5 descending from the node
IP(4) in the MIB. This value is defined by MIB-II and is the count of received
IP address errors. Of course the full MIB-II contains several hundred nodes.

There are thousands of defined MIBs, some standardized and some
private. The private MIB "enterprise" OID always begins with 1.3.6.1.4.1.

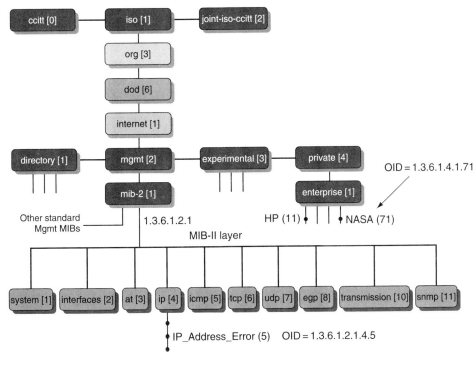

For example, 1.3.6.1.4.1.11 is reserved for all of HP's custom MIBs. Do an Internet search using this exact value to prove it. All companies with private enterprise MIBs need an assigned OID.

End users rarely have to worry about building MIBs; that is left up to the equipment vendors. So the gory details of how to compile a MIB and what variables to include should not be an issue for end uses. However, viewing the MIB may be required if the management station does not recognize it. In that case, most stations will display (using a MIB browser) the values of the MIB without knowledge of their root meaning. It is not easy to understand raw MIB values, as the viewer needs a MIB dictionary (maps OIDs to the value of a node) to make sense of the data. Make sure your equipment vendor supplies a dictionary for any MIBs that are not standardized. You never know when the dictionary will be needed when debugging odd problems.

The MIB structure is designed to be "crawled" to read out its values and SNMP is designed specifically to do this. The next section provides the basics of this universal tool.

9.4.2   The Simple Network Management Protocol

SNMP is the foundation protocol for monitoring system elements. Because simplicity breeds ubiquity, SNMP is supported by nearly 100% of IT-based devices. Its main function is to interact with element MIBs. Figure 9.12 provides a glimpse of a monitoring environment and why SNMP is indeed simple; it only has five commands. See [Mauro] for a good introduction.

Figure 9.12 shows four main components: the management station, the managed element with the SNMP agent and associated MIB, and the SNMP. Agents are software modules that reside in system elements. They

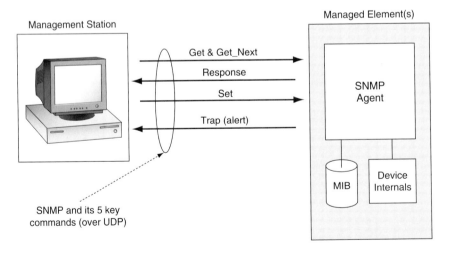

FIGURE   Basic monitoring using SNMP.

9.12

collect and store management information (errors, stats, counters, etc.) in the MIB and provide SNMP support to R/W MIB variables. The five main commands shown in an illustrative way are

◆ Get(1.3.6.1.2.1.4.5)—read a variable from a MIB at node OID
◆ Get_Next(OID)—read the *next* consecutive element in the MIB tree (OID + .1)
◆ Response (returned value)—value from Get or Get_Next request
◆ Set(OID, value)—set the MIB element at node OID to value
◆ Trap(returned value)—trap sent in response to some threshold reached

It is a snap to read a MIB using the Get or Get_Next commands. Sets can be useful for writing values into a MIB but it is suggested that this feature not be overused because it quickly leads to poor data management and access rights issues. Get_Next is useful for efficiently traversing the elements of a MIB. Traps are responses to some target MIB variable reaching a critical threshold. If too many traps are set or their trigger threshold is too low/high, trap storms can arise when some upstream problem occurs. Use traps and sets judiciously.

There are three versions of SNMP: SNMPv1 (RFC 1155), SNMPv2C, and SMNPv3, each in turn with more functionality. SNMPv1 and SNMPv2C define administrative relationships between SNMP entities called *communities*. Communities group SNMP agents that have similar access restrictions with the management entities that meet those restrictions. All entities that are in a community share the same *community name*. To prove you are part of a community, access is tested against the community name during the SNMP dialog. SNMPv3 defines the secure version of the SNMP protocol.

SNMPv3 addresses security by adding two new features: authentication via hashing and time stamps and confidentiality via encryption. A management application is authenticated via a SNMPv3 remote device before being allowed to access the MIB variables. In addition, all of the requests/responses between the management station and the remote device are encrypted to prevent snooping.

Interestingly, SNMP runs over UDP not TCP. Why? Because UDP requires low overhead, the impact on a network's performance is reduced. SNMP has been implemented over TCP, but this is more for special-case situations over long distances. It is the responsibility of the management station to guarantee data integrity, which can be done using time-outs and retries. Also, the **set** operation is problematic, as there is no guarantee that it will actually change the desired variable.

In AV applications, many devices support SNMP. The real issue is whether the MIBs that are accessed are standards or vendor proprietary. If custom, then users are practically restricted as to their choice of management stations, usually vendor supplied. Of course if all management is Web based (Web server in each managed device), then this is a moot point and SNMP is not involved. The plea for AV MIB standards cannot be proclaimed loud enough or else users will be forced into using closed, vendor-supplied, management stations.

MIBs and SNMP do not have a monopoly on management standards. The next section considers the other standards cited in Figure 9.10.

9.4.3   Web-Based Enterprise Management (WBEM)

The Distributed Management Task Force (DMTF) is the leading industry organization for the development of management standards and integration technology for enterprise and Internet environments. Its roster has reached 3000 participants, from nearly 200 organizations. Many of its participants provide IT devices enabled with WBEM technology.

The WBEM initiative was created to provide common management infrastructure components for instrumentation, control, and communication in a platform-independent and technology neutral way. DMTF technologies include information models (CIM), communication/control protocols (WBEM), and core management services/utilities.[2]

The goal of the DMTF was to create a set of standard methods to manage devices, applications, and infrastructure at a high level. The aim is more far reaching than monitoring a set of MIB variables.

---

[2] Some of the information in this section is paraphrased from the www.dmtf.org Web site.

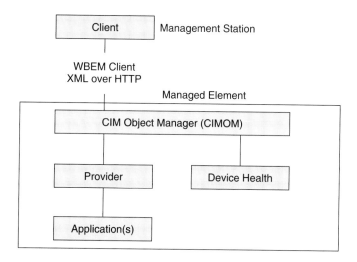

FIGURE

9.13

WBEM-based device monitoring.

A basic outline of the architecture is shown in Figure 9.13. A core piece of the puzzle is the Common Information Model (CIM). The CIM is based on a description language. This is an object-oriented model, describing an organization's computing and networking environments (its hardware, software, and services). All managed elements are positioned within this model, streamlining integration by enabling end-to-end multivendor interoperability in management systems. As a crude analogy, its counterpart is the MIB. Although a MIB has no notion of object-oriented design, both concepts describe management information schemas.

Each management area, such as networks or applications, is represented in a CIM schema. Different management areas are worked on by different DMTF specialty groups. Figure 9.14 shows how existing CIM schemas are conceptually layered. A core schema is at the center, and schemas then build on each other to represent more specific management areas. At present there are 10 (not all shown in Figure 9.14) CIM management schemas. See www.dmtf.org for full definitions of the CIM schemas.

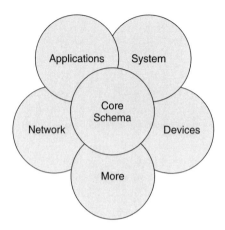

FIGURE   CIM management schemas.

9.14

The CIM data models are managed by the CIM Object Manager (CIMOM) component. It communicates with the management station using an XML mapping of the CIM data elements over HTTP. Think of the CIMOM as a way to access data that the CIM schema describes. XML/HTTP is a common method in Web environments to interchange data elements. Again, by way of simple analogy, this is similar to SNMP, but much more flexible in operation. One advantage is that it uses TCP transport compared to SNMP's unreliable UDP. This is especially valuable when management stations span the Web.

In theory, anything that can be managed using MIB/SNMP can be managed using WBEMs. However, the converse is not true due to the power of WBEM methodology. For example, monitoring of user application's performance, security, and status is rarely done using MIBs but is common using WBEM. WBEM encourages high-level monitoring of applications, devices, and networks simultaneously to get the most information of overall system performance and status. With the hegemony of Microsoft in enterprise IT, it is wise to ask if they support WBMS. Well, yes and no. They developed an implementation of WBEM and it is called WMI.

9.4.4   Windows Management Instrumentation (WMI)

Windows Management Instrumentation is a component of the Windows operating system that provides management information and control in an enterprise environment. Using CIM standards, managers can use WMI to query and set information on desktop systems, applications, networks, and other enterprise components. Developers can use WMI to create event monitoring applications that report when incidents occur. One area of incompatibility is how an application writer codes to WMI versus WBEM. WMI provides an API to access the CIMOM and this API is not the same as, for example, a Linux implementation. As a result, this incompatibility complicates application porting. The Microsoft Web site offers many tutorials and white papers on WMI and its use in systems monitoring.

Because WMI is part of the Windows OS, practically any OS operating parameter may be monitored locally or by remote means. For example, Figure 9.15 shows a screen shot from the EventTracker product available from Prism Microsystems (www.prismmicrosys.com). This tool collects and consolidates all the Microsoft event logs from remote Windows devices. It can be configured to dig as deeply as needed to report on virtually any device-related parameter. User applications that are WMI compliant may be monitored with this tool. The Windows OS supports hundreds of WMI-monitored parameters. Many hardware-related stats may also be monitored using WMI.

To see what a local Windows XP machine event log looks like, examine the tools at Start, Control Panel, Admin Tools, Computer Management for a glance at some useful reporting screens.

The bottom line is that more and more IT devices, networks, and applications will depend on WBEM/WMI for management. It is not yet common to use these methods for A/V-related applications. The usual mantra applies—as IT digs deeper into traditional A/V applications space, these methods will find use. So get ready! It is always good form for users to query A/V vendors on their product's management ability, including support for application level WBEM/WMI.

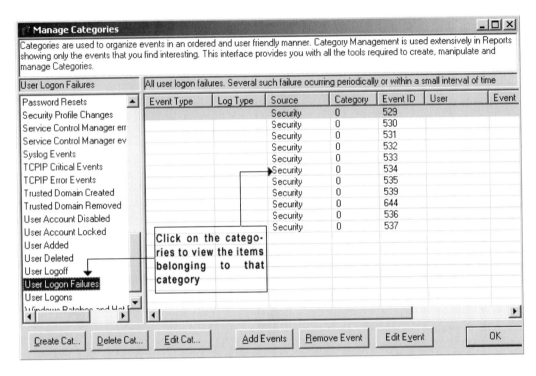

FIGURE

9.15

Console screen shot of EventTracker application (relies on WMI).

Source: Prism Microsystems, Inc.

9.5   SERVICE DIAGNOSTICS

Reporting system events is only one aspect of overall management. Another is diagnosing the root cause of a problem. Some critical application servers can easily generate thousands of events a day, although this would be uncommon in most AV systems. It is tough to comprehend this massive flow of data. Many of these events are also cryptic and make it difficult to pinpoint specific problems. As a result, some sort of event filtering is needed for big systems. Some vendors of IT management stations offer event correlation tools that make connections between hundreds of events to spot the likely cause.

Another scenario is finding the root cause for an event such as *"Video Server application: Failure: Play File ABC: Port 4, 10:24 AM."* System logs need to be scanned and interpreted for clues. At times, diagnostics tools are needed to run tests to uncover the root cause. Vendor-supplied management stations should offer some rudimentary tool set for debugging problems. Of course, there are no standards for troubleshooting, but some common techniques are available and widely used. The following is a list of general tools that *should* be made easily available on every modern A/V device to aid in troubleshooting.

♦ Easy access to the venerable Ping command. This polls a remote IP address for life. See Chapter 6 for ideas on simple network testing.

♦ Log access. When a problem occurs, the first place to turn is the device event log. Applications that log events using WMI (or WBEM) or MIBs should be queried easily. Incidentally, RFC 3164 defines a SysLog format that should be adhered to by device designers or at least modified to suit instead of a totally proprietary log format.

♦ Remote access to read internal device logs, read/change configuration settings, and perform operational tests. Vendor access using a VPN along with tools such as PCAnywhere or VNC (a multiplatform product, available for free) enables many device problems to be debugged and repaired remotely. Remote troubleshooting and device upgrades can cut downtime by orders of magnitude compared to on-site vendor visits.

♦ Configuration management (See later).

♦ Live status reporting for AV gear. Instead of poll to read events (pull method), devices should also support a pushed "live status stream" over IP. The stream (maybe 30 Kb/s) could contain select real time monitored values, including small proxy snapshots of a target AV I/O port. Think of the data stream as representing a configurable RT monitoring probe into device internals.

♦ If one were to dream, every I/O port should have the equivalent of an attached A/V probe as discussed in Section 9.2. The more nonintrusive eyes and ears watching and listening for anomalies, the easier it is to find and isolate problems. No real world devices support this today, but it is a laudable goal.

Figure 9.16 outlines the ideal features of a system element that provides for the full gamut of testing and diagnostics tools in the list just given. It is meant to be illustrative and would have one Ethernet port and not three as shown. For the most part, diagnostics tools are a vendor afterthought as a product feature. It is always good to ask any potential vendor what tools are supported. Also, brace up to the fact that remote access

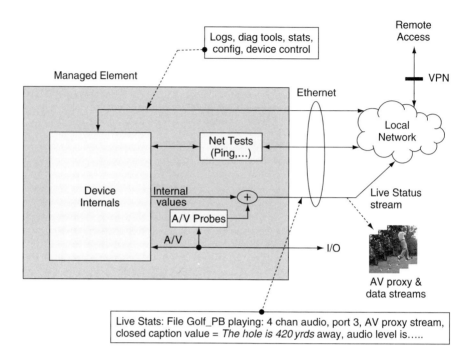

FIGURE   The well-diagnosed AV element.

9.16

(over secure VPN) for a vendor on a service contract is a good way to repair and upgrade equipment without the need for an on-site visit. It saves time and money.

Configuration Management

Device configuration parameters have been on a long leash for many years and need to be tightened up. Figure 9.17 illustrates a suggestion for MIB-based configuration data structures. While it is true that some MIBs do support configuration data (see Figure 9.5, for example), the coverage is often ad hoc and not complete. The suggested parameters fall into the following areas:

◆ Product specs—summary of product specs; this is very useful when new personnel are doing troubleshooting

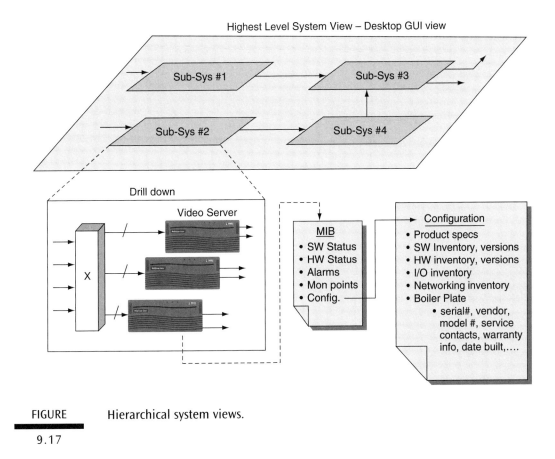

Highest Level System View – Desktop GUI view

FIGURE   Hierarchical system views.

9.17

♦ HW, SW, I/O, and networking inventory along with versioning information

♦ Boiler plate information as listed in Figure 9.17

This is offered in the spirit of a unified vendor configuration data structure. True, it is not complete, but with a little vendor cooporation, the details could be nailed down in short order. Some parameters need to be updatable to reflect changes in device SW and HW inventory and versioning. As a result, the update method needs to be obvious and easy to use. Well, that is it for the status quo of device and system management; what does the future portend? Let us see.

9.6   FUTURES—DCML

Managing more for less is the CFO's mantra. Only by using standards and leveraging the world of open systems will this happen. Managed IT sets the stage for how AV should be managed. Progressive vendors see this and others are following.

On the bleeding edge of managed systems is the work effort by Organization for the Advancement of Structured Information Standards (OASIS) (www.oasis-open.org). OASIS[3] is a not-for-profit, international consortium that drives the development, convergence, and adoption of e-business standards. The consortium produces more Web service standards than any other organization, along with standards for security, e-business, and standardization efforts in the public sector and for application-specific markets. Their standards encompass much more than device management. At the center of their efforts is the Data Center Markup Language (DCML).

DCML provides the first specification that provides a structured model and encoding to describe, construct, replicate, and recover data center environments and elements. Using DCML, companies have a standard method to enable data center automation, utility computing, and system management solutions.

DCML provides the only open XML-based specification designed to do for the data center what HTML did for content and IP did for networking: achieve interoperability and reduce the need for proprietary approaches. It does this by providing a systematic, vendor-neutral way to describe the data center environment and policies governing the management of the environment.

The methodology is the first standard model to describe both a recipe and a blueprint of the data center environment. As a culinary recipe provides both the list of ingredients and the instructions for successfully combining them, DCML provides both an inventory of data center elements and the desired functional relationship between them. In this way, all of its component relationships, dependencies, configuration,

---

[3] Some of the information in this section is paraphrased from the OASIS Web site.

operational policies, and management processes are well documented so that automated processes can take over the load of running and maintaining business processes.

The DCML Draft 1.0 Framework Specification was released in May 2004. The specification will continue to evolve in the OASIS DCML technical committees. Admittedly, DCML will not change the world of AV systems overnight. For small systems, it may never have any impact, but for larger AV systems, DCML holds the promise of a structured way to manage the infrastructure from the highest levels.

9.7   IT'S A WRAP—SOME FINAL WORDS

If you cannot measure it, then you cannot improve it. This chapter provides an overview of the big picture for monitoring and diagnostics of IT and AV/IT equipment and systems. Use this information to ask providing vendors what management solutions they offer, how they integrate with existing IT monitoring gear, and what standards are supported. You will not likely find the ideal solution, as the AV industry has only recently started providing standards-based management solutions. So, accept the immature status quo of current solutions and support industry efforts to create progress toward the nirvana of 100% managed AV/IT systems.

REFERENCE

[**Mauro**] Douglas Mauro, et al., *Essential SNMP*, O'Reilly, 2001.
[**Sources**] Element 3A reproduced with permission of Pixelmetrix, Inc. Element 3 reproduced with permission of Tektronix, Inc.

10 | The Transition to IT:
CHAPTER | Issues and Case Studies

10.0   ISSUES IN THE TRANSITION TO IT

The move to IT will have its share of pains and joys. Despite the rosy picture painted in Chapter 1 about the workflow benefits to hybrid IT + AV infrastructures, there remain practical issues that can be daunting for some. Depending on your starting point and end goals, the road to IT may be fairly simple or dreadfully complex. In the latter case, the IT pill may kill the patient. How can we avoid this sorry end? As with most new adventures, proceed with caution and with eyes wide open. The section that follows outlines the key factors that should be considered before embarking on any infrastructure change.

Following the transition issues will be coverage of three case studies: KQED's digital plant, PBS's NGIS project, and Turner Entertainment's new digital facility. Finally a short FAQ will cover some common questions.

Look before You Leap

Moving to IT/AV likely will not be a knife switch cutover for most users. Consider the following possible transition scenarios:

◆ New facility from ground up—no or little legacy equipment or formats. This is the green-field case.
◆ Upgrade select pieces of traditional AV with the IT hybrid.
◆ Wholesale upgrade of existing facility—legacy issues galore.

In all but a few cases, the move to IT should improve media workflows, but will it? This depends on what the end design goals are. Some choices to consider are:

1. Replace traditional VTR/tape workflow with IT/servers but keep tape-like workflow.
2. Replace portions of old workflows with improved workflows.
3. Wholesale upgrade to new workflows.

One error some planners make is to duplicate the old workflow but use new equipment (#1). It is tempting not to change what works. It is tempting to keep all the people and institutional experience in place even though new workflows have major advantages. One case where the old workflows were completely discarded is the PBS engineering project called NGIS. This is one of our case studies and shows what wonderful benefits can be achieved by implementing #3.

Changing from an old but culturally established workflow to a new one (despite the proven advantages) can be a gut-wrenching experience for the operations and maintenance staff. Just the thought of changing from the comfortable to the new is difficult for many of us. So what factors need to be accounted for? Figure 10.1 shows the three domains that are normally affected by any new infrastructure or major workflow change. The stakeholders from each domain need to be involved before any migration plan is in place. If not, there will unhappiness and discord in many parts of your organization as they realize that the changes did not involve them even though they are affected in major ways. Let us see how each of these domain members are stakeholders in the process of change.

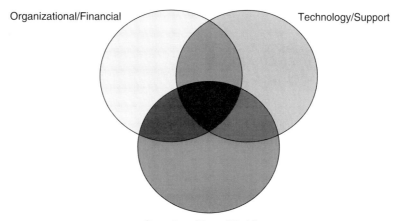

Organizational/Financial

Technology/Support

Operations/Users/Workflow

FIGURE   Transition planning: Stakeholders of interest.

10.1

10.1   ORGANIZATIONAL AND FINANCIAL

When the horizon of change becomes apparent, we often hear reasons why the move is a bad idea. Consider a few classic lines:

"It is too risky to change now"

"It will not work in our market"

"The union will never approve of this"

"We cannot afford that"

How can an organization reduce the staff's anxiety level? It is understandable that some resistance will occur. Change management is an art. Cultural change does not occur overnight. Some of the steps needed to move forward with a project are as follow.

◆ Education for all those who will be affected—why, when, and how.
◆ Have a change leader in the organization to evangelize the new work-flows and infrastructure.
◆ Sell the vision in small steps.

◆ Consider consolidating the media engineering and IT staffs or, at the very least, cross-pollinating these groups. This is a politically charged issue no matter which way it tips.

◆ Stay focused on short-term goals but always keep the long-term vision as a guiding light.

◆ Secure visible support from executive management.

◆ Do not bite off more than you can chew.

◆ The transition strategy should include "what-if" scenario planning.

No project should move forward without a proper justification for the funding. For grand visions, the CEO and CFO will demand to see the return on investment (ROI) and total cost of ownership (TCO) analysis before proceeding. ROI can be a difficult metric to calculate, especially if the new workflows are unfamiliar. For more modest transitions, some of the questions may not be fitting but they are still good reference points for consideration. Questions of interest are as follow.

◆ Will it generate new revenue potential, how much, and when?

◆ What are the most compelling reasons to make the change?

◆ Will it lower the TCO compared to current operations? Fewer operational staff, lower maintenance costs, less ongoing capital spending, less floor space, less power usage?

◆ What is the equipment lifetime?

◆ Do we have the skill sets needed to be successful? Should we merge the video engineering and IT departments? Make changes in staff skill set? Redeploy some resources? Training needed?

◆ What is the initial capital cost for the equipment and installation?

◆ What are the costs to upgrade the building for air-conditioning, power, and security to support the new installation?

◆ Timeline for the transition? Will it be done in phases? Will there be any disruption in our current operations and delivered product?

◆ What is the overall ROI expected over the lifetime of the installation?

All these factors were important to the participants involved with the case studies considered in this chapter. For the Turner Entertainment and PBS cases, planning and execution were several-year events. The scale of the execution is enormous, as we shall see. It is beyond our scope to detail each of the forementioned questions. However, if you are planning a transition, having solid answers to these questions is essential for your success.

10.2   TECHNICAL OPERATIONS AND SUPPORT

The *second* domain of stakeholders comprises engineering and ongoing technical support. In some ways, the change to IT/AV is the most challenging for this group. Why? Because traditional AV experts are not always comfortable in the IT world. Also, the IT experts may lack a working AV knowledge. *IT Media Engineer* is a new title and few of the staff are fully comfortable taking on its mantle and working in both spheres. Some of the classic complaints are:

"IT networks cannot carry video in real time."

"No one is trained to operate or repair it."

"We have tried that before and it did not work."

"The viruses and worms will kill us."

Of course the eight technical advantages discussed in Chapter 1 are not all peaches and cream. Each has some counterpoint in reality. Every engineering choice is a verdict; give me this for that in effect. Very rarely is an engineering course set without weighing the pros and cons. So what are the main technical issues to weigh when contemplating the switch to the IT/AV world? Figure 10.2 outlines the five main topics for this discussion. The list is not exhaustive and assumes that equipment performance, reliability, and scalability are already factored into the system transition plan.

Life Cycle Issues

This is a red flag for many engineering managers. Some IT components, such as PCs, servers, some software, Ethernet cards, disk drives, and more, have notoriously short life spans. In a way, Moore's law is responsible for this. We might call it Moore's law of obsolescence. This is not just a headache for end users, but for equipment manufacturers too. They must

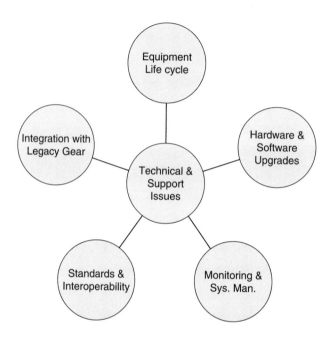

support obsolete gear and stock a lifetime supply (5 years normally) of some spare parts or continue the product in production. Also, manufacturers often have to quickly redesign products due to lack of parts. This is a royal pain. Competent vendors account for this and deflect any obsolescence anguish away from the end user as much as possible. In the end, any purchase decision should factor life cycle into the plans.

Live Hardware/Software Upgrades and Repair

In the normal IT environment, upgrading components can be done during off hours. Likely, we have all seen the message: "The email server will be down for 30 minutes tonight between 8 and 8:30 for a software upgrade. You will have no email access during that time." We learn to live with and work around the small inconvenience, but imagine a similar message, "The TV station's video server will be down tonight between 8 and 9 to install a software patch." This will not fly. $24 \times 7 \times 365$ is the mantra for many media facilities.

Knowledgeable vendors have designed much of their equipment to be upgradeable while in use. At first blush this may seem nearly impossible. However, with a degree of equipment redundancy (to support fault tolerance) this is practical. For example, a video server may be configured as $N + 1$ (see Chapter 5) and the spare unit may substitute for the component being upgraded. There are many clever methods to upgrade while "live." It is important that you query the vendor on these matters before a purchase decision. Incidentally, for many upgrades, an AV and IT expert may need to be present. Depending on either alone may result in long delays when trouble is encountered, especially during off hours.

Another aspect is the initial transition from the old workflow to the new. How will this transition be managed? What sorts of interruptions will we encounter? What is the most intelligent way to manage this with minimal disruption to our operations? Should we run the new workflow in parallel with the old for a time to test for compliance and equivalence of functionality? Should the new workflow be enabled and tested in phases? For cases where the system is composed of multiple versions of the same basic idea (e.g., station group implementation for 10 stations), should we implement one first and then follow with the others? These questions should be answered before making the leap to any new workflows.

Integration with Legacy Equipment and Systems

When building a new AV facility, the issue of legacy integration may be a moot point. However, for most transitions, the move from old to new cannot be done without accounting for legacy systems and media/metadata formats. Take the case of CNN's new digital feeds and edit system. In 2003 they initiated a phased installation to an AV/IT-based news production architecture from a tape-based one. As part of their New York City facilities, CNN installed 29 SD ingest encoders for recording news feeds from the field and elsewhere, 20 SD playout decoders, 15 professional NLEs, and 50 proxy editor/browsers. Media clients attach to ~950 h of fault-tolerant, mirrored AV storage. Most interconnectivity is based on Ethernet, mirrored IP switches, and some Fibre Channel. A similar system is also installed at CNN's Atlanta headquarters. These are not green-field installations, and on-air news production needed to continue as migration to the new system was phased in. Of course the CNN integration is not typical of most transition scenarios due to its size and scope.

Let us not forget about HD. How will SD and HD flows be supported? Any broadcaster or service facility needs to have a handle on their HD strategy. No one wants to purchase SD-only equipment with the prospect of having to do a forklift upgrade to add HD functionality. Make sure you pepper any prospective vendors with a range of questions on their SD/HD strategy. Then too are the inevitable decisions as to how to manage, produce, and distribute both SD and HD versions of the programming. There is no one way to produce simultaneous SD and HD content. One producer may start with HD and downconvert to SD, keeping in mind the safe areas for the 16×9 to 4×3 conversion. Another may choose to develop the SD and HD independently with as much overlap in content as practical. This is more costly but yields better production value per program. In the end, any new workflow should meet not only the needs of the SD world, but also those of SD + HD.

Monitoring and Systems Management

Every system, whether traditional AV or hybrid IT, needs some sort of fault, warning, and diagnostic reporting provision. The IT world offers a standardized, mature, and encompassing solution set as shown in Chapter 9. Compared to standard AV gear reporting, IT systems management is very sophisticated and holistic. Most vendors provide their own user interface for access to the most common management operations.

Standards and Interoperability and Vendor Lock-In

Most IT/AV systems are composed of different vendor's equipment in a tightly integrated configuration. Ideally, the end user has the choice to substitute one system element for another. However, regarding hybrid IT/AV systems, most providers require that no third-party "substitutes" [commercial off the shelf (COTS)] be used. For example, a data server element in a live-to-air environment may require very special operational specs to meet the needs of live failover or an element (Fibre Channel switch, IP router, etc.) is located in a critical data flow and requires guaranteed throughput. For most standard IT applications, a little slower or faster element may not impact workflow at all, whereas for IT/AV the element specs are crucial for operations. A two video frame (~65 ms) equivalent delivery delay in an email application will have zero impact on the end user. Compare that to the same delay for a critical A/V application where a lip-sync problem manifests itself. Even such content-neutral elements such as IP routers and switches can have a major impact on system performance under corner case loading and failover scenarios. As a result, while the end user may be tempted to substitute COTS equipment in a configuration, the reality of guaranteed performance under all operating modes makes this a risky decision.

Product support is another aspect of using COTS in an end-user configuration. A vendor's system design is normally tested and validated with known equipment. Each element may have specific error and status reporting methods that the system provider is depending on. The overall system status and health are strongly dependent on knowing the exact nature of each element. If a COTS element is substituted for a vendor-provided element, the vendor support contract may be breached. After all, configuration documentation is the heart of any big system, and changing components to suit the needs of the end user (normally to save money or repair time) will make support a nightmare. All similarly specified IP routers are substitutable, right? Well, for some applications this may be true, but the performance and operational characteristics are never exactly equivalent between say a Cisco router and one from Foundry. Configuration methods are often completely different, internal components are rarely the same (power supply diagnostics will be different), and so on. Any substitute of a mission critical system component will only cause long-term grief to the end user and the providing vendor.

With that preamble, it is not difficult to see that some vendor lock-in is inevitable. However, this comes with the upside of guarantees in performance and support. No end user wants to be completely locked into a vendor's products. That is why standards and interoperability are still of value. After all, most systems need to import files from external sources so the file formats should be "open." Also, metadata need to be open in terms of access and formats. When evaluating a vendor's solution, make certain that the environment is open for file import and export. Because many systems have control points (record input A/V, playback, and so on), associated APIs and protocols should be well documented and open for third-party access. Ask many questions of any provider so you know which system domains are open and closed. Only then can you make intelligent buying decisions.

10.3 OPERATIONS, USERS, AND WORKFLOW

The *third* category of interest is where the rubber meets the road—the user experience. The end user usually gets the ear of the engineering and management staff when selecting new gear. Many purchase decisions are a direct result of what the operations staff demand. Changing workflows or the operational experience is never easy and end users are often reluctant to venture into uncharted waters. Some operators (especially A/V editors) are comfortable with their favorite interface and can be intransigent when it comes to trying something new. This behavior comes from several motivations.

◆ If it is not broken, do not fix it.
◆ We do not know if the new way will work.
◆ I like vendor XYZ's user interface, do not ask me to learn a new one.
◆ Changing products now will slow us down—too much to learn. If you want it done today, then let me use what I already know.

For sure, these are valid comments, but in the context of the greater good, they are inhibitors to more efficient workflows and all that IT promises to deliver. Let us look at some of the factors that may impede the adoption to IT/AV systems.

Managing Disruptions during the Transition

This is a crucial aspect of the move to any new workflow. Planning needs to be done to minimize any potential reduction in the quality and amount of output. Using a mirror training system is one way to reduce staff anxiety and opportunity for error. In the case of Turner Entertainment, they built a new facility and ran a new channel in parallel before decommissioning the old channel. This gave the staff some time to learn the new workflows and iron out the bugs. Of course, this was a challenge since the staff needed to operate both old and new simultaneously but this proved a wise choice in the end.

Training is a key to smooth transitions. This may come from vendor-provided classes or in-house mentoring. As with most of us, once we are comfortable with a new process then we are eager to spread our wings. Without proper training we should expect the worst—problems at every turn. The poet Longfellow said, "*A single conversation across the table from wise man is better than ten years' mere study of books.*" How true. So get educated by attending industry events such as SMPTE Technical Conferences and Networld + Interop conferences—meet the people driving AV/IT forward. Attending conference-related tutorials is a great way to learn. Subscribe to several AV and IT industry trade magazines. Subscribe to free Web-based AV and IT newsletters. Attend local AV and IT industry events.

Know thy Workflow

During the course of developing this chapter, several facility engineers and end users were interviewed. When contemplating the change to a new workflow, there was the inevitable step of reviewing the documentation of the *existing* workflows. "Where is the documentation for our workflows?" was the refrain. No one answered back. As it turns out, existing workflows were part of the culture of doing the job and not some well thought out and documented procedure. This was an eye opener to some of those about to embark on improving the old workflow since they did not have a good handle on what they wanted to improve! This is a dangerous stating position for a new venture. Of course every case is different and each transition plan eventually comprehends the status quo to the extent needed. The lesson was clear to all; you cannot improve what you do not understand. If you are thinking of changing workflows, take the time to document what you have so the transition to new ones will not have as many surprises.

Chapter 7 reviews the fundamentals behind all AV workflows. This is a high-level discussion but will give you some food for thought as you plan new workflows.

10.4   CASE STUDIES

The three short case studies to follow investigate the workflows, challenges, and successes of each new design. In all cases, the existing media enterprise planned and implemented (or using a systems integrator) the transition from traditional AV to an AV/IT system. In some cases the transition is a work in progress, whereas for others the job is done. For each case study, stakeholders were interviewed for their take on the success and issues with the undertaking. These three are representative of many similar facilities worldwide. One is a typical public TV station, one is a TV network facility, and one is a large multichannel broadcaster. The coverage is brief and you may not find a direct parallel to a project you have in mind. Nonetheless, the general methods and lessons from these studies are applicable to just about any size AV/IT project. The following case studies are covered.

♦ KQED San Francisco—A flagship station of public broadcasting and a provider of PBS programming. It is one of 349 member stations serving commercial-free programming. In 2003, KQED replaced their tape-based master control chain with an IT-based one.

♦ PBS—They are executing on a long-term plan to convert their member station AV stream feeds over satellite to file transfers. Migrating from traditional video feeds to file transfer yields great economies.

♦ Turner Entertainment Networks—In September 2003 TEN rebuilt their entire broadcast operations center in Atlanta. As one of the premiere broadcasters worldwide, TEN has developed an IT-based, distributed operations center for 22+ channels.

10.4.1   Case Study: KQED, Channel 9, San Francisco

KQED[1] is a major public broadcaster and PBS affiliate. In 2003, on-air operations were based mainly on tapes and VTRs for time-delaying PBS programming. Yes, they have some live local programming, but the lion's

---

[1] This case study is based on information provided by Larry Reid, Sr., Director/Chief Broadcast Technology Officer of KQED.

share of on-air content comes from stored materials. Most delays were anywhere from a few hours to a few years. Their workflow is not identical to a commercial station but there are many similarities.

In 2003 they replaced most of their manual video tape chain with an automation system, a video server system, and a data tape archive. Figure 10.3 shows the major components in the system using IT-based control and stored program content. The legacy system had all the classic inefficiencies inherent in a tape-based system.

◆ Linear, nonnetworked material

◆ Tape-based, VTR maintenance headaches

◆ Little automation, no HD chain

◆ Upgrading to multichannel could not be supported

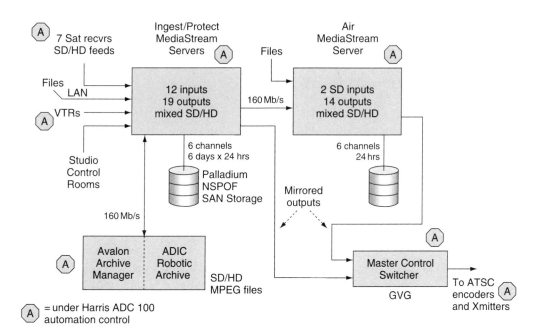

FIGURE   KQED digital on-air system.

10.3   Concept courtesy of KQED.

Planning a new infrastructure should comprehend more than eliminating the pain of the old one. In addition to moving beyond video tape, some of the goals of the new infrastructure were:

◆ Moving from 20 h per day to broadcasting 100 h (six channels) without increasing staff.

◆ Maximize the use of automation—ingest, file movement, storage management, playout, and switching.

◆ Support for HD along the entire chain.

◆ Support for eight audio channels per video channel.

◆ File transfer based. Support for ingesting files (e.g., from PBS), archiving files, and playing out files. PBS file ingest is a future need so the new system also supports recording and playing of traditional A/V streams.

The Configuration

Figure 10.3 shows the chief components of the new system. Central to all operations are two video servers using Pinnacle Systems' (now Avid) MediaStream. Each is attached to separate SAN storage. Two servers provide protection in the event of one failing. One is used primarily as an ingest server (it has 31 I/O) and the other as a playout air server (16 I/O). In the event of one malfunctioning, the other one can take over. Material comes in from satellite or tape and is recorded automatically into the ingest server. Once it is ingested, trimmed, and QA'd by personnel, it is pushed to archive and to air server if it airs within 24 h.

The ADIC Scalar 1000 archive system is a major system component. It has a capacity of 1000 tapes. AIT-3 tapes are used with a capacity of 100 GB each so each tape supports 18.5 h of MPEG2 at 12 Mb/s (SD) per tape for a total of 18,500 h for the archive. A total of 12,000 hours of mixed SD/HD is a practical limit. HD is stored at 19.3 Mb/s and some at 45 Mb/s so this also reduces total storage hours. When AIT-4 tapes are used, the capacity will double. EMC's AVALONidm storage management software automatically and transparently manages files in the ADIC tape system, optimizing the placement of data to match service levels.

Most of the stored materials are received from PBS. KQED has the rights to rebroadcast a show four times over a 3-year period for most of the programs. The automation is provided by Harris Automation, ADC100. It manages all A/V movement. Six days in advance of air time, the traffic department gives automation a list of programs for all channels. The Harris ADC100 locates the programs in the archive and moves them to the ingest server. Twenty-four hours before air time, they get copied to the air server from the ingest server's storage. Six days, notice is required for the "pull list"—that gives plenty of time to resolve any material location problems. The day before air time, interstitials are pulled from archive and loaded into the ingest/protect and air servers. At air time, both servers playout in parallel all channel programming with fault tolerance and peace of mind.

When PBS initiates program delivery via file transfer, KQED will be ready for this new form of ingest. PBS has yet to define the exact AV file format. It will likely be a constrained MXF file with MPEG2 essence; it should be resolved in late 2006. Operations are running smoothly and the engineering staff and operators are gaining confidence in the new work-flow. National TeleConsultants was the systems integrator for the project.

Of course, not every aspect of the migration went smoothly. KQED had issues with device configuration and establishing stability of some software elements. Some vendors overpromised their deliverables. The learning curve from traditional manual to full automation operations took time to negotiate.

10.4.2   Case Study: PBS, NGIS Project

PBS[2] is the main public broadcaster in the United States with 170 non-commercial, educational licensees operating 349 PBS member stations. In October 2002, 75.7 million households representing 143.6 million people watched public television. Headquartered in Alexandria, Virginia, PBS broadcasts several programming genres, each on a different channel, which in turn are consumed by the member stations. For many years, program distribution to member stations has been via satellite AV streaming. Local stations recorded the feeds and schedule playback based on their local needs, as discussed in the KQED case given earlier.

---

[2] Much of this material is based on a presentation (and private discussions) given at the NYC SMPTE Technical Conference on November 12, 2003 by Thomas Edwards, Senior Manager, Interconnection Engineering, PBS. Thanks also to André Mendes, Chief Technology Integration Officer of PBS for fruitful discussions about NGIS.

PBS is engaging the Next Generation Interconnect System (NGIS) project, which will completely revamp how they receive (from content providers) and distribute programming to member stations. This case study outlines the issues with the old workflow and the motivations and plans to upgrade to a file-based workflow nationwide. NGIS is a work in progress (2006 phase in) but the ideas are instructive for review even though it is not complete. To put the project into perspective, Figure 10.4 illustrates media flow among providers, PBS, and member stations. NGIS targets the programming flow in and out of PBS.

Motivations to Move from the Status Quo

Let us start off by reviewing the current roadblocks to smooth program exchange between entities in Figure 10.4. The next list breaks the issues

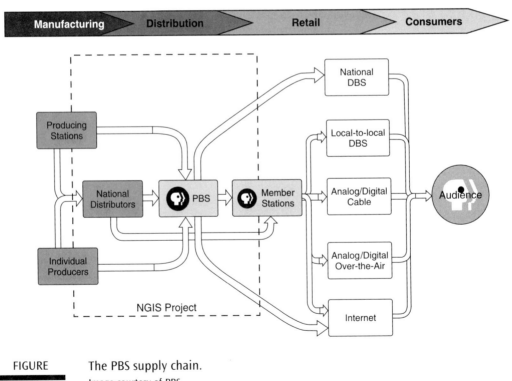

FIGURE	The PBS supply chain.
10.4	Image courtesy of PBS.

into three camps: programming inputs to PBS, PBS output streams, and member station operations.

1. **Programming produced by outside sources**
   - Much of the content is initially rejected. Quality, closed caption, SAP, issues
   - Metadata are inaccurate, gross timing errors, tape problems
   - Time-consuming tape movement and storage

2. **Real time streaming distribution to member stations**
   - Metadata continue to be inaccurate
   - Same program fed multiple times
   - Satellite rain fades, dropouts
   - Use 125,000 h to send 7000 programming hours (18X ratio)

3. **Station side**
   - 179 stations do basically the same thing:
      - Each piece of content is ingested, trimmed, QA'd, stored at each location
      - Enormous redundancy caused by: upstream content discrepancies, unreliable distribution technology, and outdated workflows

Table 10.1 outlines advantages to moving to a file-based ingest/playout workflow and away from tape ingest and AV stream feeds to member

Characteristic	Status Quo	With NGIS
Meets the needs of program distribution	▲	▲▲
Support for DTV and enhanced interactive services	▲	▲▲
Peer-to-peer connectivity		▲
Flexible workflows		▲
Optimizes the distribution resources (better satellite BW utilization, lower costs, other)		▲

TABLE 10.1   Comparative Workflow Advantages of NGIS (▲ Meets Needs, ▲▲ Improved Performance)

stations. NGIS is aimed at removing the current inefficiencies and adding new performance features along with future proofing the design.

The last entry in Table 10.1 enables a big savings in satellite use and overall distribution bandwidth. By sending files instead of streams the overall transmission efficiency is increased by about a factor of 6. Fortunately, because PBS member stations do not broadcast network programs live for the most part, transferring program files (especially HD) to stations using nonreal time delivery saves considerable satellite bandwidth and is a great way to cut costs.

The NGIS System Outline

The following list outlines the salient features and technical advantages of the NGIS.

◆ All SD and HD files are compressed MPEG (or other) wrapped in MXF
◆ Most content distributed as files using IP over satellite
◆ Send content once, accurate content distribution
◆ Automated operations as much as possible
◆ Received content temporarily cached on edge server at station side
◆ Reduces number of transponders and costs
◆ Missing packets are requested and resent using Internet connection

Sending files from point to multipoint over satellite is nontrivial. One missing bit can ruin nearly a second of MPEG video so any loss is unacceptable. NGIS uses two strategies to guarantee 100% file delivery integrity. The first is a very robust forward error correction (FEC) means to correct up to 20 min of lost data! This requires sophisticated coding but is achievable. It is a necessity during a heavy rain fade. A 20-min loss at 80 Mb/s (transponder rate) is equal to 12 GB of recoverable data. Very impressive. See Chapter 2 for more information in FECs and error correction strategies. The second strategy is to ask for a retransmission of corrupt packets if the FEC cannot recover the errors. The back channel request must be used sparingly or retransmissions will kill the file transfer advantages. For example, a FEC that can recover only .1 s of data will force many retransmissions and the satellite bandwidth usage will be worse than with legacy AV streaming.

Figure 10.5 shows a NGIS test configuration for the PBS side of the equation. At a scheduled time, automation retrieves files from the ADIC archive, prepares them for transmission, and feeds them to member stations over satellite. Note the Internet connection. It is required for retransmission requests and for member station requests for nonscheduled programming materials. On the station side (Figure 10.6), IP packets are received by the "catch PC." It applies the FEC to correct file data errors, asks for retransmission if needed, and optionally reformats the file for the member station legacy video server. Most stations already have video servers, supplied from the usual suspects, and it is not practical for PBS to send files formatted for *each* server type; that would waste bandwidth. As a result, the catch PC optionally reformats (lossless normally) the incoming PBS MXF file into a format usable by the installed legacy server. The prototype shows an Omneon Spectrum server. For the final rollout, various models will be used, depending on legacy installations on a per-station basis (see the KQED case given earlier).

NGIS also defines format requirements for vendors supplying programming to PBS. When WGBH produces a new Frontline episode for

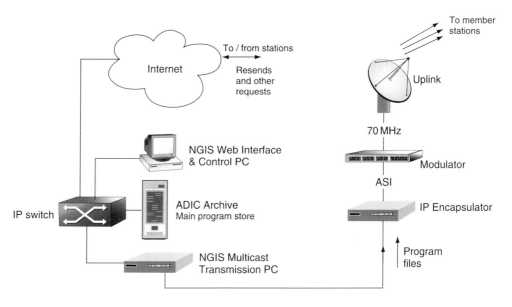

FIGURE
10.5

Prototype NGIS PBS-side hardware.
Concept from Thomas Edwards, PBS.

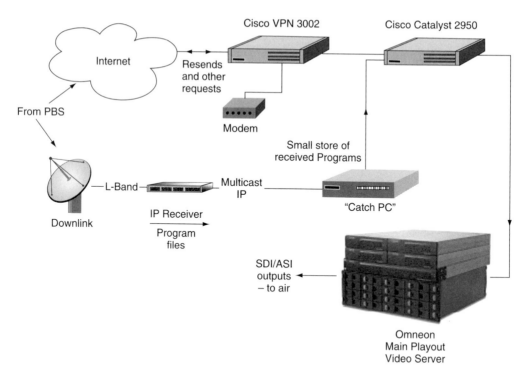

FIGURE

10.6

Prototype NGIS station-side hardware.
Concept from Thomas Edwards, PBS.

PBS, they would format it within the NGIS guidelines for metadata, closed caption, MPEG format specs, and so on. Any errors inherent during PBS ingest may get propagated to all member stations. Hence, NGIS is keen to define a standard ingest file format and improve the quality of the total distribution process.

Upon completion, NGIS promises to be a very efficient and practical way for PBS to receive and distribute programming. NGIS sets a model for how syndicated programming, news, and commercials may be distributed to commercial stations. Of course, there is activity in this area. See, for example, the services and products from BitCentral (www.bitcentral.com) and Pathfire (www.pathfire.com) that are in general use and similar to the overall themes of NGIS.

Making the transition to NGIS is filled with challenges. Some of the issues needing to be resolved are the following.

- Member stations are currently using video servers from a host of vendors. The master PBS file format will likely be MXF with MPEG2 essence. However, because this format is not compatible with all installed video servers at stations, a new edge server will be installed at each station and act as a format bridge and local cache. The device may convert the PBS file format to the local station's server format or, on command, the edge server will output an AV signal (SDI) of any stored file.

- PBS will package metadata with each program file. Local stations may decide to use this data to improve their operational workflow.

- PBS needs to coordinate with the 349 member stations so they have the proper file receive infrastructure as discussed earlier. These stations need to start thinking files not streams as the new workflow.

- Funding from the Corporation of Public Broadcasting (CPB) is needed to complete NGIS. Writing proposals and working with the budget process are time-consuming and filled with iterations.

- The current DigiCypher satellite transmission system will likely be replaced with DVB in 2005/2006. There is a need to coordinate with the member stations. DVB-S is effective for live streaming and file transfer. Over time, PBS will enhance the transmission format by switching to DVB-S2, which offers better C/N performance and consequently more efficient file throughput.

10.4.3   Case Study: Turner Entertainment Networks—New Centralized Broadcast Operations

In January 1970, Ted Turner purchased UHF channel 17 (WJRJ) in Atlanta and renamed it WTCG. From that humble beginning, TEN[3] now operates 22 network feeds (plus time zone feeds), including three of the top five cable networks in the United States—downtime is not an option. Channels are fed to satellite and cable distributors in North and South America. In September 2003, TEN moved all broadcast operation to a

---

[3] The materials for this case study were provided by Clyde Smith, Senior VP, Broadcasting Engineering R&D, QA and Metrics of the Turner Broadcasting System; Naveed Aslam, Senior Director, Broadcast Technology and Engineering; Jack Gary, Director Projects and Integration Engineering; and Rick Ackermans, Director of Engineering, Turner Broadcasting Systems Network Operations.

new 198,000 square foot building (see Figure 10.7). Migration from a videotape-based to an IT and file-based architecture was likely the biggest broadcast related project of its kind in 2003.

The following list enumerates the motivations behind the project.

◆ Provide for anticipated network growth
◆ Improve control and management of Turner physical and intellectual property assets
◆ Reduce current operational compromises and meet the growing demands of the Turner Entertainment Group
◆ Provide a platform for implementation of new media-based business initiatives

FIGURE

10.7

New broadcast operations building—part of the TEN campus in Atlanta.
Image courtesy of TBS.

◆ Consolidation of technical resources

◆ Implement a total digital infrastructure with fiber optic connectivity for file exchange

◆ Facilitate the implementation of HD digital TV

◆ Facilitate the migration from a videotape-based storage and workflow to a digital asset-based environment

◆ Enable upgrade of the traffic system and other key broadcast specific operating systems

Now, that is a tall order. Figure 10.8 illustrates a high-level view of TEN's broadcast inventory management (BIM) system. At its heart is the media operations center (MOC). This portion is responsible for ingesting AV materials from tape, utilizing six short form bays, four long form bays, and 20 cache engines. Tape ingest formats include IMX, D2, and SRW (Sony HD) tape formats. Ingest video servers are

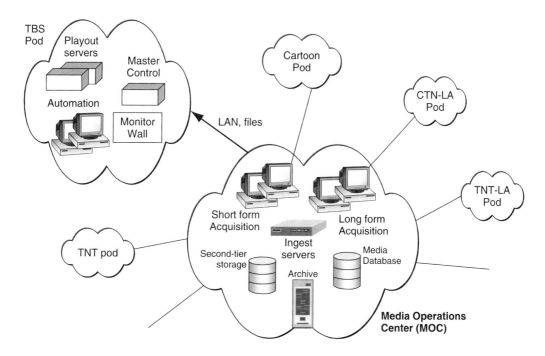

FIGURE   Broadcast inventory management system.

10.8   Concept courtesy of TBS.

used to temporarily cache newly ingested commercial and promotional content. Next, the cached materials are transferred as files into EMC near-line storage arrays and the Asaca AM 1450 DVD (Blu-ray Disc) backup libraries. Pro-Bel Automation's Sextant software moves the programming files via the AVALONidm (storage management software) from the EMC CLARiiON FC4700 arrays to the playout pods as determined by channel scheduling needs. Program content is cached directly to the air playout servers.

Each pod is designed with parallel playout chain redundancy. Each channel chain (A and B) has separate automation control. Two Pinnacle MediaStream 900 servers (mirror of content) synchronously play out the channels under Pro-Bel control. GVG MC2100 master control switchers are used. There are 49 automation/air chains in all, with a total of 200+ associated computers.

The Cartoon Network has two dedicated StorageTek Archives (Powderhorn 9310) for storing 6000 cartoons. Total capacity for the archive is 240 TB. While all other channels have near-line storage (with backup, not archive), Cartoon relies on deep archive due to the

FIGURE

10.9

Composite view of TEN's 500 racks of equipment.
Image courtesy of TBS.

frequency of playback and total storage needed. Figure 10.9 shows a composite view of the 500-rack equipment room.

Figure 10.10 outlines the benefits–payoffs for the BIM project. The five payoffs on the right side are of universal value to any commercial media operation. It is obvious that migrating to IT has big advantages for TEN. Of course there were challenges along the way. A few of the biggest obstacles were:

◆ Building one of the first SMPTE 292M (serial HD link) compliant facilities required unique installation methods to preserve the long-term integrity of the cabling.

◆ Developing the BIM system. This is not an off-the-shelf solution and required the cooperation of five major vendors in order to complete the system successfully.

◆ Painstaking analysis of current workflows in order to best understand what BIM should provide.

◆ Work with many vendors over 12–24 months to develop new products in order to meet our vision of what the file-based, HD-compliant infrastructure needed to deliver.

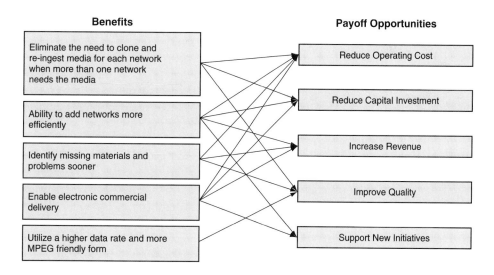

Benefits

Eliminate the need to clone and re-ingest media for each network when more than one network needs the media

Ability to add networks more efficiently

Identify missing materials and problems sooner

Enable electronic commercial delivery

Utilize a higher data rate and more MPEG friendly form

Payoff Opportunities

Reduce Operating Cost

Reduce Capital Investment

Increase Revenue

Improve Quality

Support New Initiatives

FIGURE
10.10

Benefits–payoffs of the BIM project.
Concept courtesy of TBS.

10.5   GENERIC AV/IT SYSTEM DIAGRAM

In the final analysis, the three case studies and many others not outlined here are patterned after the generic converged AV/IT video system shown in Figure 10.11. Figure 10.11 illustrates the major architectural themes discussed in this book. By rearranging, factoring, scaling, and duplicating elements, any AV/IT system can be implemented, including the three case studies. For sure it is overly simplified, but it represents the new paradigm for IT-based video systems. Note the use of the four classes of media clients as discussed in Chapter 2. Also note the use of three levels of storage including SAN/NAS as outlined in Chapter 3. Prominent too is the use of IP networking as discussed in Chapter 6. Ideally, all elements are tied into centralized systems management. Concepts such as media formats, protocols, security, software architectures, and reliability

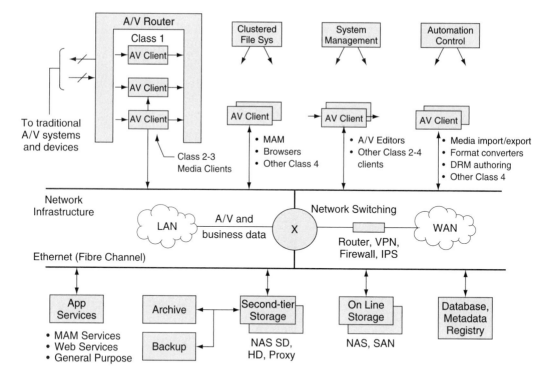

FIGURE   The generic converged AV/IT video system.

10.11

are implied but not distinctly shown. Of course there is not a single central IP router; the one in Figure 10.11 represents an aggregate of network switches, including redundancy methods.

Figure 10.11 is useful as a touchstone when developing converged AV/IT systems. It is a reminder of the chief elements required for many designs.

Well, that concludes the three case studies. If space would permit, many more from Europe, Asia, and the United States could be reported on. Just about every new broadcast and professional installation has a large component of IT spread throughout. The FAQ to follow concludes the discussion about AV/IT systems. Chapter 11 is an overview of traditional AV technology. The contents are a flash course in digital video basics.

10.6   THE IT-BASED VIDEO SYSTEM—FREQUENTLY ASKED QUESTIONS

Thinking of migrating to a converged AV/IT system? If so, the following FAQ will be of value to you. It covers select issues commonly encountered by facility planners. The FAQ is brief; likely it will not answer all of your questions. However, it should give you a springboard to start your planning process.

Q1: What is a practical plan to convert to an IT-based AV workflow?

A: Do not boil the ocean. Convert one workflow at a time. Start with ingest or playout or archive or editing or graphics. If you are starting from scratch, you may be able to do a complete IT design. For most designs, the move to IT will be incremental and must integrate with a legacy system.

Q2: Is there is downside to the migration to IT-based video?

A: Sure. Creating video systems using IT is not a panacea. There are hidden costs, operational issues, and implantation issues. Some are staff education, interop often falls short of vendor promises, too many standards to track, proprietary aspects, maintaining the desired network QoS, keeping it secure, software upgrades, IT gear obsolescence, unified element management, and consistent metadata and format use. Despite these issues, each can be overcome by applying the principles outlined in the book's chapters. Proof too is demonstrated by many successful IT/AV installations worldwide.

Q3: How should a small TV station or other AV facility approach the move to IT?

A: Work with trusted vendors and SI's who have a proven track record in offering and implementing IT-based systems. Educate yourself and the staff. Visit facilities that have made the move and interview the stakeholders. Make decisions based on the expertise of the IT **and** A/V staff; do not go it alone.

Q4: Where should I expect the most gains from the switch to IT?

A: Networked efficiencies and reach, content tracking and usage, less pure video to test and calibrate, flexible workflows, speed of content access, virtual facilities not bounded by distance, no video tape handling, ride the IT wave to lower costs, and higher performance.

Q5: What aspects of IT-based media client video flow will dominate: file transfer, IP streaming, or RT direct-to-storage access?

A: Based on current trends in facility design, file transfer is most common, followed by direct-to-storage access followed by streaming. Low-bit rate proxy video will be streamed to client stations. Your mileage may vary based on workflow needs.

Q6: What standards should we give special attention to?

A: For AV file interop, focus on MXF and MPEG/DV; for storage access, CIFS, NFS, and iSCSI; for metadata, MXF, XML, SMEF, SMPTE, and EBU recommendations; for networking, IETF and IEEE; for editing, AAF and, of course, SDI and countless SMPTE standards for traditional AV interfacing.

Q7: How should we approach asset management?

A: There is no simple answer. It depends on size of the installation, workflow needs, amount of programming, material repurposing plans, and other factors. Spend time to get this right as it is the key to many workflow efficiencies. Again, learn from others who have already made the move. Do not try to boil the ocean.

Q8: In what format should we archive our AV materials?

A: It depends on several factors so there are several answers. If you ingest materials from digital cameras, save in the camera's native compressed format. If you ingest from legacy video tape or live video feeds, select a facility-wide encoding compression format. Choices range from DV 25/50/100, one of the many MPEG bit rates and line structures (HD, SD), to 10 to 450 Mb/s or fully uncompressed video for very high-end work. Audio formats range from uncompressed 16/20 bit, Dolby-E, AC3, AAC, or a variety of other formats. Archive choice also depends on material repurposing plans. For SD/HD play-to-air only applications, lower video bit rates suffice. As MXF becomes mature, many facilities will choose to work and archive with it.

Q9: What are the key IT/AV design parameters?

A: Give attention to the **Top 10**.

1. Functionality of the total workflow (includes MAM)
2. Interop with legacy systems and intersecting workflows
3. Essence and metadata formats
4. Element and system reliability (SPOF, NSPOF, MTTR)
5. System scalability (number of clients, storage, network size, bandwidth)
6. Network topology and QoS
7. Software architectures (Web services, Middleware, J2EE, .NET, standalone)
8. Storage requirements (on-line, near-line, and archive, hours, QoS)
9. Security across all system elements
10. Element management (system management techniques)

Q10: We are thinking of developing new IT-based workflows for our AV needs. How should we start?

A: Know thy current workflow first. Spend time to document how you do things now before you design replacement workflows. Time spent up front will enable you to design better workflows later. Make sure any providing vendors agree to your system requirements.

Q11: How should we qualify a new AV/IT installation?

A: Develop acceptance test criteria. Before signing the check for a completed systems installation, make sure it all works according to plan. Develop a list of test actions. A target list may contain items such as glitch-free AV recording for 5 h, glitch-free playout for 5 h (or a lot more), file transfer speeds, storage access rates, component failure responses, device failover responses, security audit, media client responsiveness, power cycle responses, alarm reporting, MAM functionality, and many more. The bottom line is: make sure you are buying a useful system that is not filled with holes.

Q12: Any parting words?

A: AV/IT is maturing. It is still experiencing growing pains. Some workflows are mature and ready for prime time (news story production, ingest, playout, proxy browsing, cataloging, graphics playout, and production). Others are taking baby steps as with live production. Understand your workflow and map to stable technology. Do not bet on the latest unproven concepts for mission-critical applications. Traditional AV technology is not dead. The fat lady is not singing, but she is practicing her scales.

Q13: What do you see in the crystal ball for technology?

A: Oh boy. Well, looking near the surface, IT costs will continue to decline and element/link performance will continue to increase. That is an easy one. Traditional AV will find applications for years, but AV/IT will continue to move into broadcast and other professional applications. Storage will support 1000 "viewing quality" HD movies on a single 7-TB disc drive by 2013. Looking deeper, high-end HD media clients will support 10G Ethernet for NAS and SAN (iSCSI) storage access by ~2008. Open systems will take hold, and A/V vendors will offer (begrudgingly, for all but the pioneers) media clients to work with third-party online COTS storage for mission-critical applications. The forces are aligning for this to occur in the next ~4 years. There are QoS support issues with the COTS model at the present. Expect more and more software SD/HD processing with less and less video-specific hardware Video tape will find shelf space at the Smithsonian. Looking deeper—now this is amazing—wait, it is getting cloudy. We will just have to wait and see.

Q14: What do you see in the crystal ball for AV systems design?

A: Well, open systems for sure. Expect more use of Web services possibly using Microsoft's Connected Services Framework. Expect to see rich media clients of all types, workflow management tools, more MAM, lots of creative tools for graphics, video and audio editing, and authoring. File transfer will rule the day with AV streaming taking a back seat. Live event production will continue to use traditional AV methods for many years. It takes a pioneer to change the status quo of event production and there is not one on the horizon. AV devices will be managed using IT methods—at last. Oh yeah, and of course, IP- and Web-based everything.

10.7   IT'S A WRAP—SOME FINAL WORDS

Well, that is it—insights from the real world on the convergence of AV + IT. Yes, the AV/IT train is moving down the track at high speed propelled by Moore's law and the eight forces outlined in Chapter 1. The future looks bright for AV system design, and it will be a fun ride over the next few years as the remaining transition issues get settled. Keep your saw sharp and you will not be left behind as our industry moves forward. The next chapter outlines traditional AV technology without special attention to IT. If you are new to AV, then this chapter will be of interest.

11 | A Review of AV Basics

CHAPTER

11.0   INTRODUCTION TO AV BASICS

Coverage in the other chapters has been purposely skewed toward the convergence of AV + IT and the interrelationships of these for creating workflows. This chapter reviews traditional video and audio technology as stand-alone subjects without regard to IT. If you are savvy in AV ways and means, then skip this chapter. However, if chroma, luma, gamma, and sync are foreign terms, then dig in for a working knowledge. Chapter 7 presented an overview of the three planes: user/data, control, and management. This chapter focuses on the AV user/data plane and the nature of video signals in particular. Unfortunately, by necessity, explanations use acronyms that you may not be familiar with so check with the Glossary as needed.

The plan of attack in this chapter is as follows: an overview of video fundamentals including signal formats, resolutions, AV interfaces, signal processing, compression methods, and time code basics.

11.1   A DIGITAL VIEW OF AN ANALOG WORLD

Despite the trend for all things digital, we live in an analog world. In 1876, Bell invented his "electrical speech machine" as he called it—the telephone—a great example of analog design. However, analog signals are susceptible to noise, not easily processed, not networkable, suffer loss during transmission, and are difficult to store. Digital representations of analog signals generally overcome these negatives. Sure, digital has its trade-offs, but in the balance it wins out for many applications. Figure 11.1 shows the classic transform from the analog domain to the digital. Transformation is performed by an A-to-D converter that outputs a digital value every sample period at rate Fs. Better yet, some digital video and audio signals are never in analog form but are natively created with software or hardware. Often, but not always, the digital signal is converted back to analog using a D-to-A operator.

There will always be analog diehards who claim that digital sampling "misses the pieces" between samples. Examining Figure 11.1 may imply this. The famous Nyquist sampling theorem states: "The signal sampling rate must be *greater than twice* the bandwidth of the signal to prefectly reconstruct the original from the sampled version using the appropriate

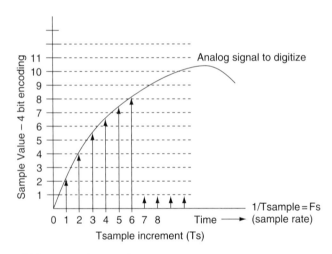

4 bit per sample example

Sample Point	Analog Value	Digital Value	Error
0	0	0	0
1	2.12	2	−.12
2	4	4	0
3	5.41	5	−.41
4	6.51	7	.49
5	7.35	7	−.35

Error term approaches zero as bit length increases. Error for 12 bit sampling is only ±.012%

FIGURE   The analog digitization process.

11.1

reconstruction filter." For example, an audio signal spanning 0 to 20 kHz and sampled at >40-kHz rates (48 or even 96 kHz is typical for professional audio) may be perfectly captured. It is one of those wonderful facts dependent on math and does not sacrifice "missing pieces" in any way.

Okay, there are two "pieces" involved here. One piece is along the horizontal time axis, as snapshot values only occur at sample points. However, according to Nyquist, zero signal fidelity is lost if samples are spaced uniformly at a sufficiently high sample rate. The second piece is along the vertical (voltage) axis. In practice, the vertical domain must be digitized to N-bit precison. For audio signals, a 24-bit (16 and 20 also used) A–D is common, which yields vertical impression that cannot be detected aurally. For video, 12-bit precision is common for some applications, which yields noise that is well below visual accuity. The ubiquitous serial digital interface (SDI) link carries video signals at 10-bit resolution. Admittedly, 10-bit, especially 8-bit, resolution does produce some visual artifacts. Here is some sage signal-flow advice: digitize early, as in the camera, and convert to analog late, as for an audio speaker or not at all as for a flat panel display. Yes, core to AV/IT systems are digital audio and video.

It should be mentioned that capturing an image with a sensor is a complex operation and that it is nearly impossible to avoid some sampling artifacts (aliasing) due to high-frequency image content. With audio, Nyquist sampling yields perfect fidelity, whereas with video there may be some image artifacts due to scanning parameter limitations with "random" image content.

11.2 PROGRESSIVE AND INTERLACE IMAGES

The display of the moving image is part art and part science. Film projects 24 distinct frames shuttered twice per frame to create a 48 image per second sequence. The eye acts as a low-pass filter and integrates the action into a continuous stream of images without flicker. Video technology is based on the raster: a "beam" that paints the screen using lines that sweep across and down the display. The common VGA display uses a *progressive* raster scan, i.e., one frame is made of a continuous sequence of lines from top to bottom. Most of us are familiar with monitor resolutions such as

800×600, 1024×768, and so on. The VGA frame rate is normally 60 or 72 frames/s. Most VGA displays are capable of HD resolutions, albeit with a display size not large enough for the comfortable 9-foot viewing distance of the living room. By analogy, a digital or film photo camera produces a progressive image, although it is not raster based.

The common analog TV display is based on an interlaced raster. Figure 11.2 illustrates the concept. A frame is made of two fields,[1] interleaved together. The NTSC frame rate is 30^2 frames per second (FPS) and it is 25 for PAL. The second field is displaced from the first in time by 1/60 (or 1/50) second and vertically offset by one-half field-line spacing. Each field has one-half the spatial resolution of the resultant frame for nonmoving images. A field is painted from top to bottom and from

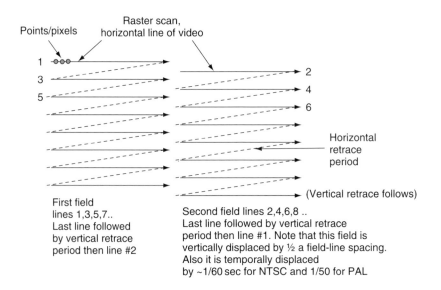

FIGURE

11.2

An interlaced picture frame: first field followed by second field in time and space.

---

[1] In practice, field lines are numbered sequentially across both fields. To simplify explanations, however, they are numbered as odd and even in Figures 11.2 and 11.3.

[2] The frame rate of an NTSC signal is ~29.97 frames per second, and the field rate is ~59.94 fields per second. These strange values are explained later in this chapter. However, for simplicity, these values are often rounded in the text to 30 and 60, respectively. The PAL field rate is exactly 50 and the frame rate is 25 FPS. SECAM uses PAL production parameters and will not be explored further.

left to right. Why go to all this trouble? Well, for a few reasons. For one, the eye integrates the 60 (50) field images into a continuous, flicker-free, moving picture without needing the faster frame scan rates of a progressive display. In the early days of TV, building a progressive 60-frames/s display was not technically feasible. Second, the two fields combine to give an approximate effective spatial resolution equal to a progressive frame resolution. As a result, interlace is a brilliant compromise among image spatial quality, flicker avoidance, and high scanning rates. It is a form of video compression that saves transmission bandwidth at the cost of introducing artifacts when there is sufficient image motion.

Why does the interlace process introduce motion artifacts? Figure 11.3 shows the outline of a football as it is captured by two successive fields. Each field has half the resolution of the composite frame. Note that the ball has moved between field captures so horizontal lines #1 and #2 display different moments in time but are adjacent in a spatial sense. A print-out of a single frame (a frozen frame) with image motion looks ugly with jagged tears at the image edges. This can be seen in Figure 11.3. Fortunately, the eye is not highly sensitive to this oddity at 60 (50) fields per second. Also, when a captured image has detail on the order of a single display line height, then some obnoxious flicker will occur at the frame rate. With the advent of HD resolutions, both progressive and

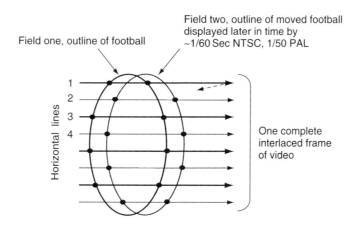

FIGURE

11.3

Interlace offsets due to image movement between field scans.

interlace formats are supported. Progressive frames appear more filmlike and do not exhibit image tearing.

 Having trouble remembering the difference between a frame and a field? A farmer took a picture of his two fields and framed it. There are two fields displayed in the frame.

11.3   VIDEO SIGNAL TIMING

In order to understand the basics of video timing, an example is posited based on a monochrome (gray scale) signal. Color video signals are considered later but the same timing principles apply. At each point along a horizontal line of video the intensity (black to white) is relative to image brightness. To paint the screen either progressively or using an interlaced raster, we need a signal that can convey image brightness along with the timing to trigger the start of a line, the end of a line, and the vertical retrace to the top of the screen. The luma[3] signal in Figure 11.4 meets our needs. The luma signal represents the monochrome or lightness component of a scene. The active video portion of a line is sourced from file data, image sensors, computable values, and so on. It is of value to note that most AV files do not carry horizontal or vertical timing information. Timing must be added by hardware circuitry as needed by the delivery chain.

The receiver uses the horizontal timing period to blank the raster during the horizontal beam retrace and start the next line. The receiver uses the vertical timing to retrace the raster to the top of the image and blank the raster from view. The vertical period is about 21 unseen lines per field. Lines ~12–21 (of both fields) are often used to carry additional information, such as closed caption text. This period is called the vertical blanking interval (VBI). The vertical synchronizing signal is complex and all its glory is not shown in Figure 11.4. Its uniqueness allows the receiver to lock onto it in a foolproof way.

---

[3] Technically, only the active picture portion of the signal is the luma value. However, for ease of description, let us call the entire signal luma. Luma (Y′) and chroma are discussed in Section 11.5.

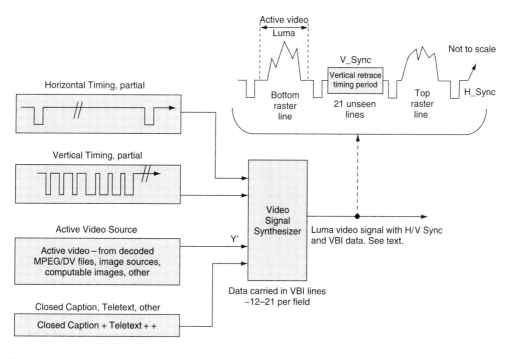

FIGURE
11.4

Synthesis of a monochrome video signal.

11.4 VIDEO RESOLUTIONS AND ASPECT RATIOS

We see a moving 2D image space on the TV or monitor screen, but it requires a 3D[4] signal space to produce it. Time is the third dimension needed to create the sensation of motion across frames. Figure 11.5 illustrates a sequence of complete frames (either progressive or interlace). There are four defining parameters for a color digital raster image.

1. Number of discrete horizontal lines—related to the vertical resolution. Not all of the lines are in the viewing window.

2. Number of discrete sample "points" along a horizontal line and bit resolution per point—both related to the horizontal resolution.

---

[4] Video has the signal dimensions of horizontal, vertical, and time (HVT) so it may be called a 3D signal. Do not confuse this with a moving stereoscopic 3D image, which is a 4D signal.

Frames (~30 per second for NTSC, 25 PAL)

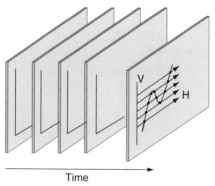

Time

FIGURE

11.5

Video is a 3D spatiotemporal image.

Not all of these points are in the viewing window. Each "point" is composed of three values from the signal set made from R, G, and B values. (see section 11.5).

3. The number of frames per second—related to the temporal resolution. This is ~29.97 for NTSC and 25 for PAL, for example.

4. The image aspect ratio. AR is defined as the ratio of the picture width to its height. 4×3 is the traditional AR for analog TVs and some computer monitors. 16×9, so-called widescreen, is another popular choice.

Next, let us look at the scanning parameters for the standard definition video image. There is a similar set of HD metrics as well and some are covered in Table 11.1. Figure 11.6 outlines the key measures for a frame of SD video. These are as follow.

◆ **HL_total**—total horizontal lines. For NTSC SD production, this is 525 lines and 625 for PAL.

◆ **HL_active**—lines in the active picture area. For NTSC production, this is 480 lines and 576 for PAL. Only these lines are viewable. Usually, the first viewable line starts at the ~22nd line of each field.

◆ **H_samples_total**—digital sample points across one entire line, including the horizontal blanking period. There are 858 points (525 line system) and 864 points (625 line system) using a 13.5-MHz sample clock and a 4×3 aspect ratio.

Common system name active lines/frames per second (fields per second)	Active picture scanning size H_samples_active × HL_active	Total picture scanning size H_samples_total × HL_total	Display aspect ratio
480i/30 (60) or 525i/30 (60) SD	720 × 480	858 × 525	4 × 3
576i/25 (50) or 625i/25 (50) SD	720 × 576	864 × 625	4 × 3 and 16 × 9
480p/60 SD+	720 × 480	858 × 525	4 × 3
720p/60 HD	1280 × 720	1650 × 750	16 × 9
720p/50 HD	1280 × 720	1980 × 750	16 × 9
1080i/30 (60) HD	1920 × 1080	2200 × 1125	16 × 9
1080i/25 (50) HD	1920 × 1080	2640 × 1125	16 × 9
1080p/30 HD	1920 × 1080	2200 × 1125	16 × 9
1080p/25 HD	1920 × 1080	2640 × 1125	16 × 9
1080p/24 HD	1920 × 1080	2750 × 1125	16 × 9

[a] The line count and sample metrics were defined earlier in this section (see Figure 11.6 for SD reference). The "i" term indicates interlace, the "p" indicates progressive scanning. It is common to refer to a 1080i system as either 1080i/30 or 1080i/60; the difference being the reference to frame versus field repeat rates. This reasoning applies to the other interlaced scanning standards as well. The 480p system falls between legacy SD and HD. It has twice the temporal resolution (60 frames per second) of SD formats, but because the horizontal resolution is still 720 points, it will be classed as SD+. Each of the frame rates 24, 30, and 60 has an associated system scaled by 1000/1001. NTSC uses the 525/30 system, and PAL uses the 625/25 system. A "point" along the horizontal line is composed of an RGB signal set.

TABLE

11.1

Common SDTV and HDTV Production Scanning Parameters[a]

♦ **H_samples_active**—digital sample points in viewing window. There are 720 active points for 525 and 625 line systems. This is a key metric for video processing and compression.

The horizontal sampling rate for SD production is 13.5 MHz. Other SD rates have been used but this is widely accepted. For HD resolution, a common sampling rate is ~74.25 MHz. What is the total picture bit rate for an SD, 525, 4×3 digital frame? Consider: **525_bit_rate** = 525 lines × 858 points/line × 3 samples/point × 29.97 frames/s × 10 bits/sample = 405 Mb/s. Another way to get to this same result is 13.5 MHz × 3 samples/point × 10 bits/sample = 405 Mb/s.

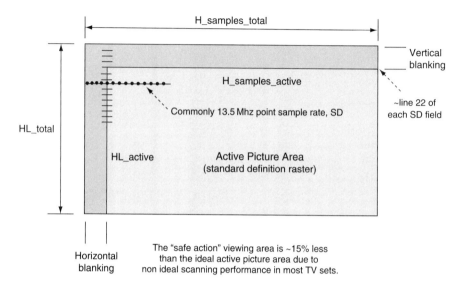

Image frame sizes and metrics.

A common data rate reduction trick in image processing is to reduce the color resolution without adversely affecting the image quality. One widely accepted method to do this, explained in Section 11.54, reduces the overall picture bit rate by one-third, which yields a 270-Mb/s (= 405 Mb/s × 2/3) data rate. This value is a fundamental data rate in professional standard definition digital video systems.

Incidentally, 10 bits per sample is a popular sampling resolution, although other values are sometimes used. Surprisingly, for a 625 (25 frames/s, same one-third bit rate reduction applied) system, the total picture bit rate is also exactly 270 Mb/s. See Appendix G for more insight into this magic number. Note that this value is not the *active picture* data rate but the total frame payload per second. The active picture data rate is always less because the vertical and horizontal blanking areas are not part of the viewable picture.

Table 11.1 outlines a few of the common SD and HD system names and associated scanning parameters. NTSC, PAL, SECAM, DVB, ATSC, and ISDB (Japan) transmission systems use a selection of these scanning rate formats (and others). Common in-home TV displays usually offer reduced resolutions. For example, an HD consumer display that supports the 1080i/30 format will usually have resolutions on the order of 1280 horizontal points/line × 768 lines. This is less than the production resolution. Most home sets resize the received image to fit the display. Of course, display resolutions will improve but for now full resolution displays are too expensive for the masses. The standards in Table 11.1 are production related and the transmitted or displayed versions may provide less resolution.

Most professional gear—cameras, NLE's video servers, switchers, codecs, graphics compositors, and so on—spec their operational resolutions using one or more of the metrics in Table 11.1. In fact, there are other metrics needed to completely define the total resolution of a video signal, and Section 11.5 digs deeper into this topic.

Aspect Ratio Conversions

One of the issues with scanning formats is display mapping. Programming produced in 16 × 9 and displayed on a 4 × 3 display, and visa versa, needs some form of morphing to make it fit. Figure 11.7 shows

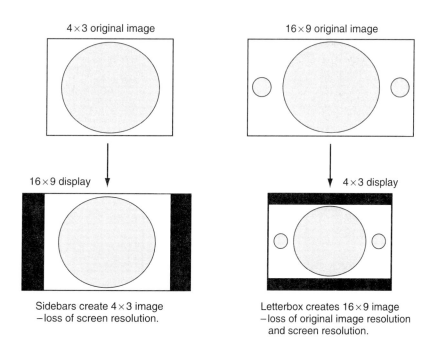

FIGURE   Common aspect ratio conversions.

11.7

the most popular methods to map one AR format into another for display. Another method includes panning and scanning the 16 × 9 original image to select the "action areas" that fit into a 4 × 3 space. This is used commonly to convert widescreen movies to 4 × 3 without using letterbox bars. Still another method uses anamorphic squeezing to transform images from one AR to another. This technique always creates some small image distortion, but it utilizes the full-screen viewing area. Whatever the method, AR needs to be managed along the signal chain. Generally, both 16 × 9 and 4 × 3 formats are carried over the same type of video links.

11.5   VIDEO SIGNAL REPRESENTATIONS

There are many ways to represent a video signal and each has some advantage in terms of quality or bandwidth in both analog and digital domains. Figure 11.8 outlines eight different signal formats. Figure 11.8 is conceptual and no distinction is made between SD/HD formats. The H/V timing is loosely applied (or not applied) for concept only. It is not a design specification, but a high schematic level view of these important signal formats. In practice, some of the signals may be derived more directly via other paths so consider Figure 11.8 as representational of the conversion processes. The "matrix Fx" term indicates mathematical operations for signal conversion and is different for HD and SD matrix operations. Keep in mind that all the operations are reversible, i.e., R′G′B′ can be recovered for display from say Y′CrCb or S_Video but there is always some loss of fidelity due to the effects of the matrix math. Let us examine each signal and conversion path in Figure 11.8.

11.5.1   The RGB and R′G′B′ signals

At the start of the image chain is a camera imager or other means to generate a raw RGB signal. Red, green, and blue represent the three primary color components of the image; 0% RGB is pure black and 100% is pure white. The signal requires three channels for transport: one per pixel component. The three time-based signals are shown by example in

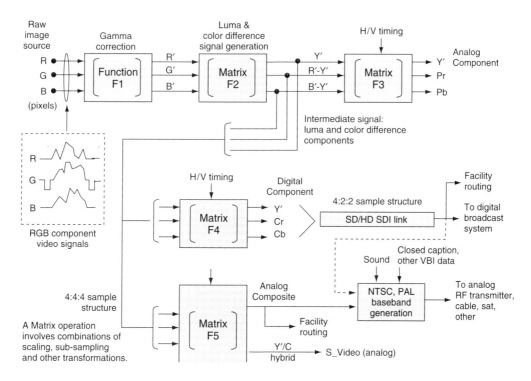

the dotted box with the green signal having horizontal syncs indicating the start and end of a line. This signal set is rarely used stand alone but needs conversion to a gamma-corrected version, R′, G′, and B′. Basically, gamma correction applies a power function to each of the three RGB components. The general function (F1) is of the approximate form, $A' = A^{.45}$ where the .45 is a typical gamma value. An apostrophe is used to represent a gamma-corrected signal. According to [Poynton], "Gamma is a mysterious and confusing subject because it involves concepts from four disciplines: physics, perception, photography, and video. In video, gamma is applied at the camera for the dual purposes of precompensating the nonlinearity of the display's CRT and coding into perceptually uniform space." Charles Poynton does a masterful job of explaining the beauty of color science, gamma, luma, and chroma so consult the reference for a world class tour of these important parameters and much more. For our discussion, gamma correction is an exponential scaling of the RGB voltage levels. In the context of Figure 11.6, each "sample point" refers to the three pixels as a data set.

11.5.2   The Component Color Difference Signals

A full bandwidth R′G′B′ signal is a bandwidth hog and is only used for the most demanding applications where quality is the main concern (graphics creation, movies, and other high-end productions). Ideally, we want a reduced bandwidth signal set that still maintains most of the RGB image quality. We find this at the next stop in the signal chain: conversion to the Y′, R′-Y′, B′-Y′ signal components. These are not RGB pixels but are derived from them. The Y′ term is the luma signal (gray scale) and the other two are color difference signals often called chroma signals. Interestingly, statistically, 60–70% of scene luminance comprises green information. Accounting for this and removing the "brightness" from the blue and red and scaling properly (matrix F2) yields two color difference signals along with the luma signal. What are the advantages of this signal form? There are several. For one, it requires less data rate to transmit and less storage capacity (compared to R′G′B′) without a meaningful hit in image quality for most applications. Yes, there is some nonreversible image color detail loss but the eye is largely insensitive to a high degree due to the nature of F2's scaling. In fact, there is a loss of 75% of the colors when going from an N-bit R′G′B′ to an N-bit color difference format. If N is 8 bits, then some banding artifacts will be seen in either format. At 12 bits, artifacts are imperceptible. Despite the loss of image quality, the transformation to color difference signals is a worthwhile trade-off, as will be shown in a moment. See [Poynton] for more information on this transformation.

To give a bit more detail, the following conversions are used by matrix F2 for SD systems.

$$Y' = .299R' + .587G' + .114B' \text{ (the luma signal)} \tag{11.1}$$
$$R'\text{-}Y' = .701R' - .587G' - .114B' \text{ (a chroma signal)} \tag{11.2}$$
$$B'\text{-}Y' = -.299R' - .857G' + .886B' \text{ (a chroma signal)} \tag{11.3}$$

The coding method is slightly different for HD formats, as HD and SD use separately defined colorimetry definitions. Other than this, the principles remain the same.

11.5.3   The Y'PrPb Component Analog Signal

The color difference signals are intermediate forms and are not transported directly but are followed by secondary conversions to create useful and transportable signals. Moving along the signal chain, the Y'PrPb signal set is created by the application of matrix operation F3. Y'PrPb is called the analog component signal and its application is mainly for legacy use. The P stands for parallel, as it requires three signals to represent a color image. Function F3 simply scales the two chroma input values (R'-Y' and B'-Y') to limit their excursions. The Y' signal (and sometimes all 3) has H/V timing and its form is shown as the middle trace of Figure 11.10.

11.5.4   The Y'CrCb Component Digital Signal

Matrix F4 produces the signal set Y'CrCb, the digital equivalent of Y'PrPb with associated scaling and offsets. The C term refers to chroma. Commonly, each component is digitized to 10-bit precision. This signal is the workhorse in the AV facility. The three components are multiplexed sequentially and carried by the SDI interface. More on this later. One of the key advantages to this format is the ability to decrease chroma spatial resolution while maintaining image quality, thereby reducing signal storage and data rate requirements. Sometimes this signal is erroneously called YUV, but there is no such format. However, the U and V components are valuable and their usage is explained in Section 11.5.5.

Chroma Decimation

The Y'CrCb format allows for clever chroma decimations, thereby saving additional storage and bandwidth resources. In general, signals may be scaled spatially (horizontal and/or vertical) or temporally (frame rates) or decimated (fewer sample points). Let us focus on the last one. A common operation is to decimate the chroma samples but not the luma samples. Significantly, chroma information is less visually important than luminance, so slight decimations have little practical effect for most applications. Notably, chroma-only decimation cannot be done with the RGB format—this is a key advantage of the color difference format.

Our industry has developed a short-form notation to describe digital chroma and luma decimation, and the format is A:B:C. The A is the luma horizontal sampling reference, B is the chroma horizontal sampling factor relative to A, and C is the same as B unless it is zero and then Cr and Cb are subsampled vertically at 2:1 as well. It is confusing at best so it is better not to look for any deep meaning in this shorthand. Rather, memorize a few of the more common values in daily use. The first digit (A) is relative to the actual luma pixel sample rate, and a value of 4 (undecimated luma) is the most common. Luma decimation, in contrast to chroma decimation, sacrifices some observable image quality for a lower overall bit rate. In most cases, it is the chroma that is decimated, not the luma. Some of the more common notations are as follow.

- 4:4:4—luma and 2 chroma components are sampled equally across H and V.
- 4:2:2—chroma (Cr and Cb) sampled at half of luma rate in the horizontal direction (1/2 chroma lost).
- 4:2:0—chroma sampled at half of luma rate in H *and* V directions (three-fourths chroma lost). The DV-(625/50) format uses this, for example.
- 4:1:1—chroma sampled at one-quarter of luma rate in H direction (three-fourths chroma lost). The DV-(525/60) format uses this, for example.
- 3:1:1—as with 4:1:1 except one-fourth of luma samples also discarded. A 1920 sample point HD line is luma subsampled to 1440 samples. Sony HDCAM format, for example.
- 4:4:4:4—the last digit indicates that an alpha channel (transparency signal) is present and sampled at the luma rate.

It turns out that 4:2:0 and 4:1:1 have an equal number of chroma samples per frame, but the samples are at different locations on the grid. Figure 11.9 shows examples of the Y', Cr, Cb sample grid for different methods. The common SDI studio link normally carries 4:2:2 SD/HD video at 10 bits per sample. Conceptually, the sequential order of carriage over SDI for 4:2:2 samples is Y' Cr Y' Cb Y' Cr Y' and so on. It is easy to see the one-half Cr and Cb chroma rate compared to the luma rate. For 4:2:0 there are one-half as many chroma samples compared to 4:2:2 and one-fourth compared to 4:4:4 (Y' Cr Cb Y' Cr Cb Y', etc.). In practice, the decimated Cr and Cb samples are derived by averaging several adjacent chroma values from the 4:4:4 signal. This gives a slightly better

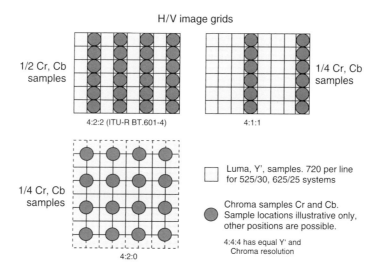

FIGURE

11.9

A comparison of chroma sampling in 4:2:2, 4:1:1, and 4:2:0 formats.

result than unceremoniously dropping chroma samples from the 4:4:4 source.

The 4:2:2, 4:2:0, and 4:1:1 decimations are used as the source format for many video compression methods, including MPEG and DV. In fact, these codecs get an extra boost of compression when they decimate the chroma before the actual compression starts. Both DVB and ATSC digital transmissions systems utilize 4:2:0 decimated chroma at 8-bit resolution luma and chroma. The 4:4:4 HD R′G′B′ format is used for high-end applications, and a dual-link HD-SDI method (2 × 1.485 Gb/s data rate) is defined for carrying the three synchronous signals.

11.5.5   The Analog Composite Video Signal

The analog composite[5] video signal is output from matrix F5 as shown in Figure 11.8. This signal is illustrated in Figure 11.10 (top trace). The middle trace is the luma (plus H/V timing) signal. The bottom trace is the

---

[5] CVBS, composite video burst and sync, is shorthand used to describe a composite signal.

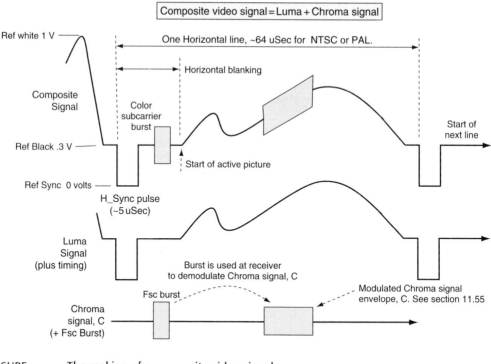

Composite video signal = Luma + Chroma signal

Ref white 1 V

One Horizontal line, ~64 uSec for NTSC or PAL.

Horizontal blanking

Composite
Signal

Color
subcarrier
burst

Start of
next line

Ref Black .3 V

Start of active picture

Ref Sync 0 volts

H_Sync pulse
(~5 uSec)

Luma
Signal
(plus timing)

Burst is used at receiver
to demodulate Chroma signal, C

Modulated Chroma signal
envelope, C. See section 11.55

Fsc burst

Chroma
signal, C
(+ Fsc Burst)

FIGURE

11.10

The making of a composite video signal.

Note: These are conceptual diagrams only and some details are simplified (not to scale).

chroma signal (plus color burst, explained shortly). The top trace is composed of the sum of the bottom two signals and contains color and brightness information in one signal. A receiver can recover the H/V timing, brightness, and color details from the signal.

The composite signal is a wonderful invention, has a long history of use, and is the basis of the NTSC and PAL transmissions systems. Over the last 50 years, most TV stations and AV facilities have used it as the backbone of their infrastructure, although the digital component SDI link is quickly replacing it. Most consumer AV gear supports composite I/O as well. Also, there is a digital composite version of this often referred to as a "$4F_{sc}$ composite" but it is used infrequently.

So what is the trick for carrying color and luma as one signal? Actually, there are several. First, let us define the U and V signals. Simply, these are scaled versions of the two color difference signals B'-Y' and R'-Y', [Eqs. (11.3) and (11.2) (Section 11.5.2)].

$$U = .492 \ (B'-Y') \ \text{and} \ V = .877 \ (R'-Y')$$

To reduce the bandwidth further, U and V are bandwidth filtered and scaled. Next, they are combined into a single color signal, C, by quadrature modulating a subcarrier at frequency F_{sc}.

$$C = U \times \sin(\omega T) + V \times \cos(\omega T), \qquad (11.4)^6$$

where $\omega = 2\pi F_{sc}$ and F_{sc} is the color subcarrier frequency. C is formed by AM modulating $\sin(\omega T)$ with U and $\cos(\omega T)$ with V both at the same frequency F_{sc}. C is shown as the bottom trace of Figure 11.10 along with the color burst reference signal, explained later.

F_{sc} is chosen at ~3.58 MHz for NTSC and ~4.43 MHz for most PAL systems. Now, the composite base band video signal is

$$\text{Composite signal} = Y' + C + \text{burst} + \text{H/V timing} \qquad (11.5)$$

By selecting the value of the color subcarrier F_{sc} judiciously, the Y' and C terms mix like oil and water; they can be carried in the same bucket but their identity remains distinct. Ideally, a receiver can separate them and, via reverse matrix operations, recreate the R'G'B' signals ready for display. See again Figure 11.10 and imagine the bottom trace (C) and the middle trace Y' summed to create the top trace—this is Equation (11.5). In reality, due to a variety of factors, R'G'B' is not perfectly recovered but close enough in practice. Also, the C component is bandwidth limited by a filter operation before being summed with the luma signal; this limits the chroma resolution slightly.

In order for the receiver to demodulate C and recover U and V, it needs to know precisely the frequency and phase of the subcarrier. The "color burst" is a 8–10 cycle sample of $\sin(\omega T)$ injected for this purpose.

---

[6] The sine $\sin(\omega T)$ term generates a pure single wave at frequency F_{sc}. The cosine $\cos(\omega T)$ term generates a wave at the same location but shifted by 90°. The resultant signal C can be demodulated with U and V recovered.

It is a beautiful technique. See [Jack] and [Poynton] for more details on both composite and component signals and interfacing.

Composite video may be viewed as an early form of video compression. By combining luma and chroma in clever ways, the bandwidth required to transport and store video is reduced significantly. The composite formulation makes acceptable compromises in image quality and has stood the test of time.

11.5.6   The S_Video Signal

The final signal to discuss is the analog S_Video signal sometimes called Y/C or YC. This is just signals Y' and C carried on separate wires. Because there are never any Y'/C mixing effects as may occur in a pure composite signal, R'G'B' can be recovered with higher fidelity. The burst is carried on the C signal. S_Video is rarely used in professional settings but is a popular SD consumer format.

11.5.7   Analog and Digital Broadcast Standards

Both analog and digital TV broadcast standards are in wide use. All of the video standards reviewed in the previous sections define baseband signals. These are not directly transmittable without further modification. Figure 11.8 shows the step of adding sound and other ancillary information to form a complete NTSC or PAL baseband signal. For analog broadcasts, the complete signal is upconverted to an RF channel frequency for ultimate reception by a TV. The input to this process may be a composite analog or digital component signal for added quality. Audio modulation uses FM and has a subcarrier of 4.5 MHz for NTSC. At the receiver, the RF signal is deconstructed and out plops R, G, B, and sound ready for viewing.

Three analog TV transmission systems span the world and they are NTSC, PAL, and SECAM (see Glossary). Each has variations with the color burst frequency and total baseband bandwidth being key variables. NTSC/M, J and PAL/B, D, G, H, I, M, N, and various SECAM systems are used worldwide and are adopted on a per country basis. See [Jack] for a complete list of systems and adopted countries.

Before 1953, NTSC only defined B&W visuals with a temporal rate of exactly 30 frames/s. When NTSC color was introduced, the committee had a conundrum to handle. If any nonlinearity arose in the signal chain, color spectra information, centered approximately at 3.58 MHz (F_{sc}), and the sound-modulated spectra, centered on 4.5 MHz, may interfere. The resulting intermodulation distortion would be apparent as visual and/or aural artifacts. The problem was avoided by changing the temporal frame rate. This is an overly simplified explanation, but the end result was to apply a scaling factor of 1000/1001 to the B&W frame rate. This resulted in a new frame rate of ~29.97 and a corresponding field rate of ~59.94. No big deal it seems. However, this change introduced a timing discrepancy that is a pain to deal with, as the wall clock is now slightly faster then the field rate.

The 1000/1001 factor is awkwardly felt when a video signal or file is referenced by time code. Time code assigns a frame number to each video frame, but a ~29.97 FPS rate yields a noninteger number of frames per second. A frame location based on a wall clock requires some time code gymnastics to locate it in the sequence. See Section 11.9 for more information on time code.

Digital Broadcast Standards

Analog TV broadcast systems are slowly being replaced with digital transmission systems worldwide. Figure 11.8 shows an SDI signal source feeding a digital broadcast system. There are three systems in general use. In Europe, Digital Video Broadcasting (DVB) standards began development in 1993 and are now implemented by 55+ countries over terrestrial, satellite, and cable. In the United States, the Advanced Television Systems Committee (ATSC) produced their defining documents in 1995, which is the basis of the terrestrial DTV system. In 2005, 1500+ U.S. stations were transmitting using DTV formats. In Japan, the Integrated Services Digital Broadcasting (ISDB) system began life in 1999 and supports terrestrial, satellite, and cable. All three systems offer a selection of SD and HD video resolutions, use MPEG-2 compression, have six-channel surround sound, support non-AV data streams, and use advanced modulation methods to squeeze the most bits per allocated channel bandwidth. The MPEG Transport Stream (TS) is the basic data carrier for all these systems. The TS is a multiplexing structure that packages A + V + data into a single bit stream ready for transmission. The TS method has found wide use. Many codecs have a mapping into the TS structure, including the popular H.264 method.

The typical transmitted maximum compressed HD data rate is ~20 Mb/s for 1080i/60 programming, although smaller values are common as broadcasters trade off image quality for extra bandwidth to send other programming or data streams. The main AV program source to the encoding and transmission system is usually SDI or HD-SDI signals. No longer are composite signals used or desired. The new standards create a digital pipe to the viewer and the broadcaster can use it in a wide variety of ways. The Web is filled with information on digital broadcast standards. See www.atsc.org or www.dvb.org for more information.

11.5.8   Professional Signal Formats—Some Conclusions

How should we rank these signal formats in terms of quality? Well, the purest is R′G′B′ but due to its high bandwidth requirements, it is only used for very high-end AV applications. The SD/HD Y′CrCb format is the workhorse of most facilities. It provides excellent quality; all components are separate, 4:2:2 resolution, 10 bits per component and all digital. Component video values are easily stored in a file. Plus, audio channels may be multiplexed into the SDI stream, creating an ideal carrier for AV essence. All analog and composite formats are fading out. There are other formats for sure and some are specific to consumer use and others for very high-end HD use. Knowledge of the ones covered in this section will allow you to springboard to other formats with ease.

Figure 11.11 outlines a general selection of common interface standards across analog, digital, and AV/IT systems. Although R′G′B′ is also transported for high-end applications, it is not shown on the diagram. Most digital facilities use SDI links and AES/EBU links to carry AV signals. The next two sections review these two important links. Together with LAN/WAN they make up the lion's share of transport means in a converged AV/IT system.

 In terms of video quality and transport convenience, digital trumps analog, component formats trump composite, and serial links trump parallel links.

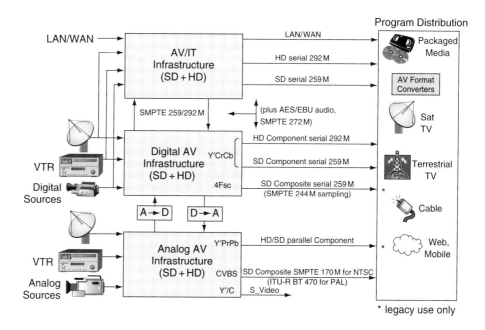

FIGURE   Common professional AV interface standards.

11.11

11.6   SDI REVIEW—THE UBIQUITOUS AV DIGITAL LINK

The Serial Digital Interface (SMPTE 259 M for SD, 292 M for HD) link has revolutionized the digital AV facility. It has largely replaced the older analog composite link and digital parallel links so it is worth considering this link for a moment to fully appreciate its power within the digital facility. SDI supports component video (Y'CrCb) SD and HD formats (supporting a variety of frame rate standards). The typical SD line bit rate is 270 Mb/s (with support from 143 to 360 Mb/s depending on the data format carriage) and is designed for point-to-point, unidirectional connections (see Appendix G).

SDI is not routable in the LAN/IP sense; however, an entire industry has been created to *circuit switch* SDI signals using video routers. Due to nondisplayable areas in the raster scan, the active image data payload is less than the link rate of 270 Mb/s. For example, the actual

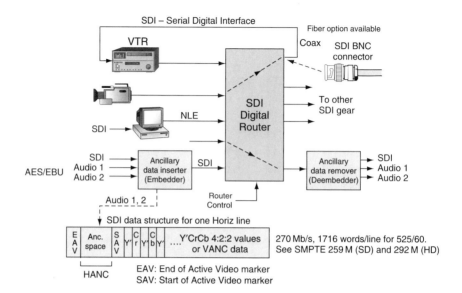

Basic SDI use and framing data structure.

active picture data payload of a 525 lines, 10 bits/pixel, 4:2:2 component signal is ~207.2 Mb/s, not counting the vertical and horizontal
blanking areas. Figure 11.12 shows the basic framing structure of an
SDI signal and an example of SDI link routing. Routers range in size
from a basic 8 × 1 to mammoth 512 × 512 I/O and larger. About 57
Mb/s out of the total of 270 is available to carry nonvideo payloads,
including audio. These nonvideo data are carried in both horizontal
ancillary (HANC) and vertical ancillary (VANC) blanking areas. In a
nonpicture line, data between SAV and EAV markers carry ancillary
VANC data.

Examples of payloads that SDI can carry are as follow.

◆ SD video with embedded digital audio. One channel of video and eight
embedded uncompressed stereo pairs (16 audio channels) are a supported payload.
◆ Ancillary data carried in HANC and VANC areas. SMPTE has standardized several schemes for HANC and VANC nonvideo data carriage.

♦ Carriage of compressed formats in the SDTI-CP wrapper. SDTI-CP (Serial Digital Transport Interface—Content Package) is a means to carry compressed formats such as MPEG and DV over SDI links. This method was popularized by Sony's IMX digital MPEG VTR and Panasonic's DVCPro VTRs. See SMPTE standards 326M and 331M for more information.

♦ HD-SDI (SMPTE 292M) uses a line bit rate 5.5 times higher than that of 259M (270Mb/s typical), clocking in at 1.485 Gb/s to carry uncompressed HD video, embedded audio, and ancillary data.

There is no H/V timing waveform as with the analog luma or composite video signal. Rather, timing is marked using SAV, EAV words, and other sync words. These markers may be used to help create H/V timing as needed. Most professional AV/IT systems will be composed of a mix of SDI, HD-SDI, AES/EBU audio, and LAN/WAN links. The workhorse for audio is the AES/EBU link discussed next.

11.6.1 The AES/EBU Audio Link

The AES/EBU audio standard defines the data structures and physical serial link to stream professional digital audio. It came about as a result of collaboration between the AES and the EBU and was later adopted by ANSI. The default AES/EBU uncompressed sample rate is 48 kHz, although 44.1 and 96 kHz are also supported. An audio sample accuracy of 24 bits/sample (per channel) is supported, but not all equipment will use the full 24 bits. Most devices use 16 or 20 bits per sample. A full frame is 32 bits, but 8 bits of this are dedicated to nonaudio user bits and synchronization.

A shielded, twisted-pair cable with XLR connectors on both ends is used to transfer two channels of audio and other data using a line data rate of about 3 Mb/s for 48-kHz sampling. There is also a version that uses coax cable with BNC connectors. Both versions are in wide use. The link also supports a raw data mode for custom payloads. One example of this is the transport of compressed AC3 5.1 and Dolby-E audio formats. The AES/EBU data structure may be embedded into an SDI stream for the convenience of carrying up to 16 audio channels and video on one cable (see Figure 11.12).

11.6.2   The Proteus Clip Server Example

Announcing the new—drum roll please—Proteus clip server; the newest IT-friendly video server with the ability to record (one channel in) and playback (two channels out) AV files using networked storage. Okay, Figure 11.13 is fictional, but it exemplifies an AV/IT device with a respectable quota of rear panel I/O connectors. A little inspection reveals SDI video I/O (BNC connectors), AES/EBU audio I/O (XLR connector version), time code signal in, a Gen Lock input, an analog signal output using YPrPb ports, composite monitoring ports, and a LAN connection for access to storage/files, management processes, device control, and other network-related functions.

The Gen Lock input signal (sometimes called *video reference*) is a super clean video source with black active video or possibly color bars. The Proteus server extracts the H/V timing information from the Gen Lock signal and uses this to perfectly align all outputs with the same H/V timing. Most AV facilities use a common Gen Lock signal distributed to all

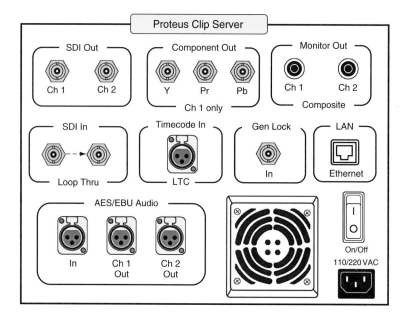

FIGURE   The Proteus clip server: rear panel view.

11.13

devices. This assures that all video signals are H/V synced. Alignment is needed to assure clean switching and proper mixing of video signals. Imagine cross fading between two video signals each with different H/V timing; the resultant hodgepodge is illegal video. Sometimes it is unavoidable that video signals are out of sync. The services of a "frame sync" are used to align signals to a master video reference (see Appendix B).

Remember too that SDI signals may carry embedded audio channels on both inputs and outputs. Also, the SDI-In signal has a loop thru port. The input signal is repeated to the second port for routing convenience.

11.7   VIDEO SIGNAL PROCESSING AND ITS APPLICATIONS

Video is a signal with 3D spatiotemporal resolutions and has traditionally been processed using hardware means. With the advent of real time software processing, hardware is playing a smaller roll but still finds a place, especially for HD rates. Image handling may be split into two camps: raw image generation and image processing. The first is about the creation and synthesis of original images, whereas the second is about the processing of existing images. Of course, audio signal processing is also of value and widely used, but it will not be disussed here. Image processing is a weighty subject, but let us peek at a few of the more common operations.

1. Two- and three-dimensional effects, video keying, compositing operations, and video parameter adjustments
2. Interlaced to progressive conversion—deinterlacing
3. Standards conversion (converting from one set of H, V, T spatiotemporal samples to another set)
4. Linear and nonlinear filtering (e.g., low-pass filtering)
5. Motion analysis, tracking (track an object across frames, used by MPEG)
6. Feature detection (find an object in a frame)
7. Noise reduction (reduce the noise across video time, 3D filtering)
8. Compressed domain processing (image manipulation using compressed values)

These operators are used by many video devices in everyday use. The first three deserve special mention. Item number one is the workhorse of the video delivery chain. Graphics products from a number of vendors can overlay moving 2D and 3D fonts onto live video, squeeze back images, composite animated images, transition to other sources, and more. Video editors apply 2D/3D effects of all manner during program editing. Real time software-based processing has reached amazing levels for both SD and some HD effects operators. Video parameter adjustments of color, contrast, and brightness are run of the mill for most devices.

Video keying adds a bit of magic to the nightly TV news weather report. A "key" is a video signal used to "cut a hole" in a second video to allow for insertion of a third video signal (the fill) into that hole. Keying places the weather map (the fill) behind the presenter who stands in front of a blue/green screen. The solid color background is used to create the key signal. Keying without edge effects is a science, and video processing techniques are required for quality results.

Interlace to Progressive Conversion—Deinterlacing

Recall that an interlaced image is composed of two woven fields, with the second one being time shifted compared to the first. Each field has half the spatial resolution of the complete frame as a first-order approximation. If the scene has object motion, the second field's object will be displaced. Figure 11.3 shows the "tearing" between fields due to object displacement. Fortunately, the brain perceives an interlaced picture with a common amount of interfield image motion just fine. However, to print a single interlaced frame without obvious tearing artifacts or to convert between scanning formats, it is often necessary to translate the image to a progressive one. This process is referred to as deinterlacing, as the woven nature of interlace is, in effect, unwoven. Ideally, the resulting progressive video imagery should have no interlaced artifact echoes. Unfortunately, this is rarely the case.

So what methods are used to unweave an interlaced image? A poor man's converter may brute force replicate or average select lines, fields, or frames to create the new image. These are not sophisticated techniques and often yield poor results. For example, Figure 11.14 (top) shows an

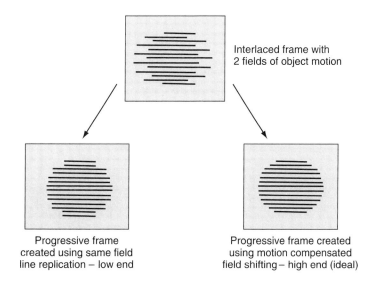

Interlaced frame with
2 fields of object motion

Progressive frame
created using same field
line replication – low end

Progressive frame created
using motion compensated
field shifting – high end (ideal)

FIGURE

11.14

Interlaced to progressive conversion examples.

interlaced image frame with field tearing. The bottom left image in Figure 11.14 is a converted progressive image using simple same-field line doubling. It is obvious that the spatial resolution has been cut in half.

At the high end of performance, motion-compensated deinterlacing measures the field-to-field motion and then aligns pixels between the two video fields to maximize the vertical frame resolution. Figure 11.14 (lower right) illustrates an ideally deinterlaced image. There are countless variations on these themes for eking out the best conversion quality, but none guarantee perfect conversion under all circumstances. See [Biswas] for a good summary of the methods.

Standards Conversion

The news department just received a breaking story in the PAL video format. It needs to be broadcast immediately over an NTSC system. Unfortunately, the two scanning standards are incompatible. Converting from one H/V/T scanning format to a second H/V/T format is a particularly vexing problem for video engineers (item #3 in list given earlier). Translating the 25-frame PAL story to a 30-frame NTSC video sequence requires advanced video processing. This operation is sometimes referred to as a "standards conversion" because there is conversion between two different video-scanning standards. The PAL/NTSC conversion requires 5 new frames be manufactured per second along with per frame H/V resizing. Where will these new frames come from? Select lines, fields, or frames may be replicated or judiciously averaged to create the new 30-frame per second video. Using motion tracking with line interpolation, new frames may be created with image positioning averaged between adjacent frames.

Reviewing Table 11.1, we see 10 different standards (plus the 1000/1001 rate variations) for a total of 15 distinct types. There are 210 different combinations of bidirectional conversions just for this short list. Yes, image-processing algorithms and implementation are becoming more important as scanning standards proliferate worldwide. In widespread use are SD-to-HD upconversion and HD-to-SD downconversion products. Several vendors offer standards converter products.

Compressed Domain Processing

Before leaving the theme of video processing, let us look at item #8 in the list given earlier; the hot topic of compressed domain processing (CDP). Video compression is covered in the next section, but the basic idea is to squeeze out any image redundancy, thereby reducing the bit rate. It is not uncommon for facilities to record, store, and play out raw MPEG streams. However, working natively with MPEG and manipulating its core images are not easy. For example, the classic way for a TV station to add a flood watch warning message to the bottom of an MPEG broadcast video is to decode the MPEG source, composite the warning message, and then recode the new picture to MPEG. This flow adds another generation of encoding and introduces an image quality hit—often unacceptable. With CDP, there is no or very little quality hit in order to add the message. It is inserted directly into the MPEG data stream using complex algorithms that modify only the new overlay portion of the compressed image.

This is an overly simplified explanation for sure, but the bottom line is CDP is a powerful way to enhance MPEG streams at cable head ends and other pass-through locations. Several vendors are offering products with graphical insert (e.g., a logo) functions. See, for example, the Terayon BP 5100 product. Predictably, video squeeze backs and other operations will be available in a matter of time. Watch this space!

Well, that is the 1000 foot view of some common video processing applications and tricks. Moving on, if there is any one technology that has revolutionized AV, it is compression. The next section outlines the main methods used to substantially reduce AV file and stream bit rates.

11.8   AV BIT RATE REDUCTION TECHNIQUES

The data structures in a digital AV system are many and varied. In addition to uncompressed video, there are several forms of scaled and compressed video. The following four categories help define the space.

1. Uncompressed AV signals
2. Scaled uncompressed video in H/V/T dimensions, luma decimation, chroma decimation—lossy
3. Lossless compressed AV
4. Lossy compressed AV

Uncompressed video is a data hog from a bandwidth and storage perspective. For example, top end, raw digital cinema resolution is ~4K × 2K pixels, 24 FPS, yielding ~7 Gb/s data rate. A standard definition 4:4:4 R′G′B′ signal has an active picture area bit rate of ~311 Mb/s. It is no wonder that researchers are always looking for ways to reduce the bit rate yet maintain image quality. Methods #2, 3, and 4 in the list are bit rate reduction methods and are broadly rated against image quality in Figure 11.15. To better understand Figure 11.15, the term "lossy" needs to be defined.

Lossy, in contrast to lossless, is used to describe bit rate reduction methods that remove image structure in such a way that it can never be recovered. This may sound evil but it is a good trick if the amount of image degradation is acceptable for business or artistic purposes. The lower left quadrant of Figure 11.15 rates quality versus bit reduction for method #2 given earlier. Chroma decimation is generally kind to the image and was discussed in Section 11.5.4. If luma decimation is used, it

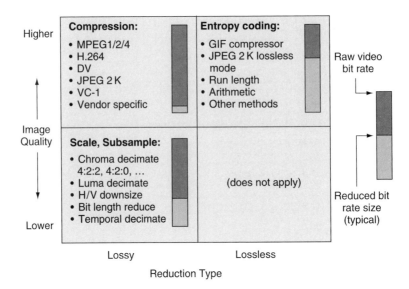

Video data rate reduction examples.

is much easier to notice artifacts. H/V scaling is done to reduce overall image size. For example, scaling an image to H/2 × V/2 saves an additional factor of 4 in bit rate but the image size is also cut by 4. Another trick is to brute force reduce the Y′CrCb bit length per component, say from 10 to 8 bits. This causes some visual banding artifacts in areas of low contrast. The last knob to tweak is frame rate. Reducing it saves a proportional amount of bits; keep going and the image gets the jitters.

The bit rate meter for this method shows a typical 3:1 savings for a modest application of scaling and decimation with virtually no loss of visual quality. Although these methods reduce bit rate, they are not classed as video compression methods. True compression techniques rely on mathematical cleverness, not just brute force pixel dropping.

The next trick in the bit rate reduction tool box is shown in the upper right quadrant of Figure 11.15. Lossless encoding squeezes out image redundancies, without sacrificing any quality. This class of rate reduction is called entropy coding after the idea that bit orderliness (low entropy) can be detected and coded with fewer bits. A good example of this is the common GIF still-image file compressor. It is based on the famous LZW (Lempel–Ziv–Welch) algorithm. GIF is not ideal for video but is the basis for similar methods that are applied to video. JPEG 2000 (JPEG2K) has a lossless mode supporting up to 12 bits/pixel encoding, resulting in outstanding quality. Run length coding is employed by MPEG encoders and other compressors to condense strings of repeating digits. Arithmetic coding is used by the H.264 video compressor and others to further pinch down the data rate by locating and squeezing out longer term value orderliness. Most lossless coders achieve bit savings in the 25–50% range, but the results are strongly content dependent.

There is no guarantee that a pure lossless encoder will find redundancies so the worst case reduction factor may be zero. For example, losslessly coding a video of pure noise results in a bigger file due to coding overhead. As a result, in practice stand-alone lossless video coders are not common. However, lossless techniques are used liberally by traditional lossy video compressors (the upper left quadrant of Figure 11.15). A lossy compressor uses lossless techniques to gain a smidgen more of overall efficiency.

The real winner in bit rate reduction is true video compression (upper left quadrant of Figure 11.15). It has the potential to squeeze out a factor of ~100 with passable image quality. Consumer satellite and digital cable systems compress some SD channels to ~2.5 Mb/s and exceed the 100:1 ratio of savings. Web video compression ratios reach >1000:1 but the quality loss is obvious. To get these big ratios, compressors use a combination of scaling, decimation, and lossy encoding.

However, some studio quality codecs compress by factors as small as 3–6 with virtually lossless quality. A 20:1 reduction factor yields a ~15 Mb/s SD signal, which provides excellent quality for many TV station and AV facility operations. Video compression is discussed in Section 11.8.1, but first some notes on audio bit rate reduction.

Audio Bit Rate Reduction Techniques

The four quadrants of Figure 11.15 have corresponding examples for audio bit rate reduction. Uncompressed audio formats are commonly based on the 16/20/24 bit AES/EBU (3.072 Mb/s per stereo pair, including overhead bits) format or BWAV format.

The EBU's Broadcast WAV format is a professional version of the ubiquitous WAV sound file format but contains additional time stamp and sync information. Lossless audio encoding is supported by the MPEG4 ALS standard but it is not commonly used. One form of audio scaling reduces the upper end frequency limit, which enables a lower digital sample rate with a consequent bit rate reduction. This is a widespread practice in nonprofessional settings. Finally, audio compression is used in all forms of commercial distribution and some production. [Bosi] gives a good overview of audio encoding and associated standards, including MP3, AAC, AC3, and other household names. These are distribution formats for the most part. Dolby-E is used in professional settings where quality is paramount. However, let us concentrate on video compression for the remainder of the discussion.

11.8.1   Video Compression Overview

When it comes to compression, one man's redundancy is another man's visual artifact so the debate will always continue as to how much and what kind of compression are needed to preserve the original material. There are three general classes of compression usage. At the top end are the program producers. Many in this class want the best possible quality and usually compress very lightly (slight bit rate reduction) or not at all. Long-term archive formats are often at high quality levels. The next class relates to content distribution. In this area, program producers distribute materials to other partners and users. For example, network TV evening newscasts are sent to local affiliates using satellite means and compressed video. The level of compression needs to be kept reasonably high and is often referred to as mezzanine compression. Typically, HD MPEG2 programming sent at mezzanine rates range from 35- to 65-Mb/s encoded bit rates. The third class is end-user consumption quality. This ranges from Web video at ~250 Kb/s to SD-DVD at <10 Mb/s to HDTV at 15–20 Mb/s to digital cinema at <250 Mb/s.

Figure 11.16 shows the landscape of the most common (there are many more) video compression formats in use. Why so many? Well, some are proprietary whereas others are standardized. Some are designed for SD only, some for HD only, and some are both. A few are defined as a video tape and compression format and some are improvements in a

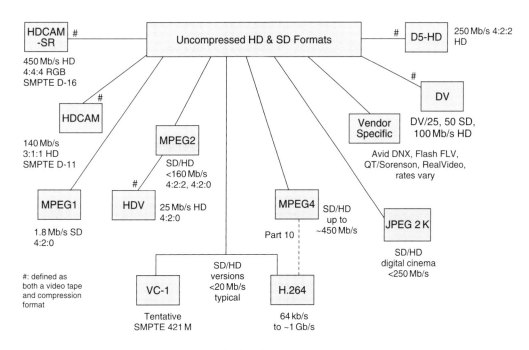

FIGURE   Popular lossy–compressed video formats.

11.16

long line of formats. For example, MPEG1 begat MPEG2, which begat MPEG4, which begat MPEG4 part 10 (same as H.264, ITU-T spec, also called the AVC, Advanced Video Codec). In Figure 11.16, the approximate maximum compressed data rate is given alongside each format box; the values are only a general guide. As a common rule, the compressors accept 8 bits of video component in the $Y'CrCb$ format. However, several of the HD formats support 10-bit encoding. The fidelity range extensions (FRExt) of H.264 support encoding rates up to ~1 Gb/s for very high-end cinema productions. Most encoders apply some form of chroma and/or luma decimation before the actual compression begins. The compressors in Figure 11.16 are video-only formats for the most part. Audio encoding is treated separately.

Of special note are the nearly quality-equivalent codecs H.264 and VC-1 (Microsoft's WM9 technology, tentatively SMPTE 421M). These two formats are destined to run neck and neck for the next few years as users decide on the successor(s) to the venerable MPEG2 format. They are both MPEG-like formats and rely on many of MPEG's methods, but with new tweaks to squeeze even more quality per compressed bit. They are the most versatile compression formats ever invented, seeing that both perform at very low bit rates with excellent quality, support SD and HD, and may be streamed over networks.

H.264 and VC-1 encoding methods are a factor of 1.5 to 3 times better in bit usage compared to standard MPEG2 at lower bit rate ranges (.01–20 Mb/s for SD/HD). There are meaningful bandwidth and storage benefits to making the switch to these codecs. Regardless of the exact improvement ratio, these formats yield more quality per compressed bit compared to others in general use.

Figure 11.17 compares legacy MPEG2 against H.264 coding efficiency for the same SD source material [Sullivan]. This test demonstrates the superiority of H.264 for both bandwidth and storage usage. Here we see an improvement of 2.75:1 for H.264, although this ratio is a function of source material; it is not a constant. Expect to see satellite TV, cable, and telco operators (over DSL) using VC-1 and H.264 in their next generation of program delivery.

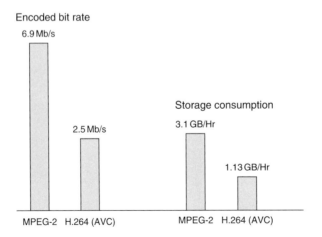

FIGURE

11.17

Comparing codec efficiencies.

SD source video encoded for nearly identical viewing quality.

11.8.2   Summary of Lossy Video Compression Techniques

In general, there are two main classes of lossy compression: *intraframe* and *interframe* coding. Intraframe coding processes each frame of video as stand alone and independent from past or future frames. This allows single frames to be edited, spliced, manipulated, and accessed without reference to adjacent frames. It is often used for production and video tape (e.g., DV) formats. However, interframe coding relies on exploiting temporal redundancies between frames to reduce the overall bit rate. Coding frame #*N* is done more efficiently using information from neighboring frames. Utilizing frame redundancies can squeeze a factor of two to three better compression compared to intra-only coding. For this reason, the DVD video format and ATSC/DVB transmission systems rely on intraframe coding compression. As might be imagined, editing and splicing interframes are thorny problems due to their interdependencies. Think of interformats as offering more quality per bit than intraformats.

Figure 11.18 illustrates a snapshot of common commercial video formats segregated according to type. This is a representative of common formats in use, but not all methods are listed. Intraformats are sometimes called *I frame only*, signifying that only intraframes are coded.

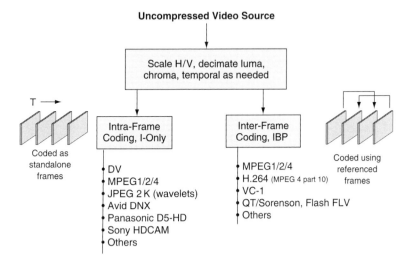

FIGURE
11.18   Snapshot of compression methods and coding formats.

Interformats are sometimes called **IBP or long GOP** (group of pictures), indicating the temporal association of the compression. The IBP and GOP concepts are described in short order. Note that some I frame-only formats such as JPEG 2000 and DV only use the intramode, whereas others such as MPEG are designed for either mode. In general, interformat compressors can also work in intra mode when required. JPEG2K is unique because it has modes for both still picture and video compression. When a JPEG format codes video, it is sometimes called Motion-JPEG.

Intraframe Compression Techniques

Squeezing out image redundancies begs the question, "What is an image redundancy?" Researchers use principles from *visual psychophysics* to design compressors. They learn which image structures are discardable (redundant) and which are not without sacrificing quality. Despite it's rather zen-sounding name, visual psychophysics is hardcore science. It examines the eye/brain ability to detect contrast, brightness, and color and to make judgments about motion, size, distance, and depth. A good compressor reduces the bit rate with corresponding small losses—undetectable ideally—in quality.

Of all the parameters, reducing high frequency detail and chroma decimation reap the most bit savings while maintaining image integrity. These techniques remove the spatial redundancy from the image. Scaling luma or reducing frame rates is usually bad business and quality drops off suddenly. Figure 11.19 outlines the processes (ignore the second, temporal step for the moment) needed to compress an intraframe video sequence. Each process contributes a portion of the overall compressed bit savings. The order of compression is as follows.

- Decimate chroma and luma in some cases. This provides a lossy bit savings of 50% for 4:2:0 scaling.
- Remove high-frequency spatial detail using a filter-like operator and quantize the result. This step saves as much as needed. Pushing this lossy step too far results in obvious visual artifacts.
- Lossless entropy coding. This step saves an additional 30% on average.

For the middle step, two methods take the lead: transform based (discrete cosine transform or DCT) and wavelet based. Both are filter-like

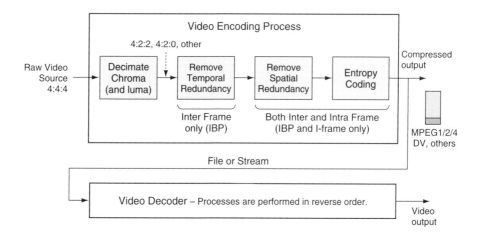

FIGURE   The basic encoding and decoding processes.

11.19

operations for reducing or eliminating higher frequency image terms, thus shrinking the encoded bit rate. High-frequency terms arise due to lots of image structure. For example, a close-up image of a plot of grass has significantly more high-frequency terms than say an image of a blue wall. The DCT-based filter is used by nearly all modern video compressors. JPEG2K is one major exception; it uses the wavelet method. Mountains have been written about spatial compressing methods. For good overviews see [Bhaskaran], [Symes], or [Watkinson].

Snapshot

The DCT in action: The DCT is a mathematical device used to transform small pieces of the image domain into an approximation of their frequency domain representation. Once transformed, high-frequency spatial terms can be zeroed out. Plus, other significant spectral lines are quantized to reduce their bit consumption—these steps are lossy. The DCT is tiled across an image frame repeatedly until all its parts have been processed. The resulting terms are entropy encoded and become the "compressed image bit stream." At the decoder, an inverse DCT is preformed and the image domain is restored, albeit with some loss of resolution.

Intraframe methods encode each video frame in isolation with no regard to neighboring frames. Most video sequences have significant frame-to-frame redundancies, and intramethods do not take advantage of this; enter interframe encoding.

Interframe Compression Techniques

Interframe compression exploits the similarities between adjacent frames, known as *temporal redundancy,* to further squeeze out the bits. Consider the talking head of a newscaster; how much does the head move from one video frame to the next? The idea is to track image motion from frame to frame and use this information to code more intelligently.

In a nutshell, the encoder tracks the motion of a block of pixels between frames using *motion estimation* and settles on the best match it can find. The new location is coded with motion vectors. The tracked pixel block will almost always have some residual prediction errors from the ideal and these are computed (*motion compensation*). The encoder's motion vectors and compressed prediction errors (lossy step) are packaged into the final compressed file or stream.

The decoder uses the received motion vectors and prediction errors and recreates the moved pixel block exactly—minus the loss when the error terms were compressed. Review Figure 11.19 and note the "remove temporal redundancy" step for interframe coding.

Various algorithms have been invented to track *pixel group* motion—not necessarily discernible objects. This step is one of the most computationally intensive for an encoding process. This form of encoding is sometimes referred to as IBP or long GOP encoding (see Figure 11.20). A GOP is a sequence of related pictures, usually from 12 to 15 frames in length for SD materials. Here, the I frame is a stand-alone anchor intraframe. It is coded without reference to any neighboring frames. The B frame is predicted bidirectionally from one or two of its I or P neighbors. A B frame has fewer coded bits than an I frame. The P frame is a forword predicted frame from the last anchor frame (I or P) and has more bits than a B frame but fewer than an

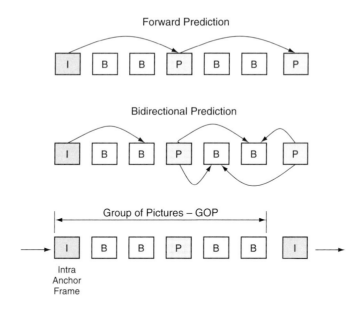

FIGURE   Interframe sequencing examples.

11.20

I frame.[7] Note that a B or P frame is not the poorer cousin of an I frame. In effect, all frames carry approximately equal image quality due to the clever use of motion estimation and compensation.

Most MPEG encoders use interframe techniques but they can also be configured to encode using *only* intraframe methods. Users trade off better compression efficiency against easy editing, splicing, and frame manipulation when choosing between IBP and I-only formats. Researchers are constantly looking for ways to improve compression efficiency, and the future looks bright for yet another round of codecs. In fact, initial work has begun on the tentative H.265 compressor, which holds out the promise of another ~50% bit rate reduction within 4–5 years.

---

[7] These are general IBP bit rate allocations and may differ depending on image content.

11.9   VIDEO TIME CODE BASICS

Last but not least is the concept of time code. This "code" is used to link each frame of video to a time value. The common home VCR and DVD use displayed time code to show the progress of a program. The format for professional time code is HH:MM:SS:FF, where H is the hours value (00 to 23), M is the minutes value, S is the seconds value, and F is the frame value (00 to 29 for 525i). A time code of 01:12:30:15 indicates the position of the video at 1 h, 12 min, 30 s, and 15 frames. If the first frame of the video is marked 00:00:00:00, then 01:12:30:15 is the actual running time to this point. A time code rollover example is 01:33:58:29 is followed by 01:33:59:00.

Accurate AV timing is the lifeblood for most media facilities. For example, time code is indispensable when queuing up a VTR or video server to a given start point. NLEs use time code to locate and annotate edit points. At a TV station, program and commercial playback is strictly controlled by a playout schedule tied to time code values for every second of the day. SMPTE 12M defines two types of time code: linear (also called longitudinal) time code (LTC) and vertical interval time code (VITC). LTC is a simple digital stream representing the current time code value along with some additional bits. Historically, the LTC low-bit rate format is carried by a spare audio track on the video tape. VITC is a scheme in which time code bits are carried in the vertical blanking interval of the video. This convenient scheme allows the time code to always travel with the video signal and is readable even when the video is in pause mode. In both cases, the time code display format is the same.

Although LTC and VITC were designed with video tape in mind, non-tape-based devices (video servers) often support one or both formats. Time code is carried throughout a facility using an audio cable with XLR connectors. Many vendors offer time code generators that source LTC referenced to a GPS clock. As a result, it is possible to frame accurately sync videos from different parts of a campus or venue and guarantee they are referenced to a common time code value.

Drop Frame Time Code

With 25 FPS video (625i) there is an integer number of frames per second. However, the 525i frame rate is ~29.97 FPS (see Section 11.5.7) and there is not an integer number of frames per second. Standard time code runs exactly 30 frames per second for 525i video. A time code rate of 30 frames per second instead of ~29.97 creates a 3.6-s error (an extra 108 video frames) every 60 min. This is light years in video time so we need a way to correct for this. One way to effectively slow down the 30 FPS time code signal is by skipping one time code value every 33.3333 s. This amounts to dropping 108 code points per hour. Now, the 30 FPS time code signal *appears* to run at ~29.97 FPS. In reality, this is accomplished by dropping frame code numbers 00:00 and 00:01 at the beginning of every minute except for every 10th min.

Importantly, no actual video frames are dropped, only the time code sequence is modified. If all this is confusing, at least remember that there are two forms of time code: *drop frame* and *nondrop frame*. In the 525i/29.97 world, drop frame is popular, whereas in the 625i/25 world, nondrop frame is popular. With 25 FPS material there is no need to play tricks with the time code values.

11.10   IT'S A WRAP—SOME FINAL WORDS

With this brief overview, you should be conversant with the basics of AV technology. These themes form the quilt that touches most aspects of professional AV systems. A key thesis in this book is leveraging IT to move AV systems to new heights of performance, reliability, and flexibility. By applying the lessons learned in this chapter, plus lessons from the others, you should be well equipped to understand, evaluate, and forecast trends in the new world of converged AV/IT systems.

REFERENCES

[**Bhaskaran**] Vasudev Bhaskaran et al., *Image and Video Compression Standards*, 2nd edition, 1997, Kluwer Press.
[**Biswas**] Mainak Biswas, Truong Nguyen, *A novel de-interlacing technique based on phase plane correlation motion estimation*, ISCAS, May 2003, http://videoprocessing.ucsd.edu/~mainak/pdf_files/asilomar.pdf.
[**Bosi**] Marina Bosi, Richard E. Goldberg, Leonardo Chiariglione; *Introduction to Digital Audio Coding and Standards*, 2002, Kluwer Press.

[**Jack**] Keith Jack, *Video Demystified, A Handbook for the Digital Engineer*, 3rd edition, Newnes, 2001.

[**Marpe**] Detlev Marpe et al, *Performance evaluation of Motion-JPEG2000 in comparison with H.264/AVC operated in pure intra coding mode*, Proceedings of SPIE—Vol. 5266, February 2004, pp. 129–137.

[**Poynton**] Charles Poynton, *Digital Video and HDTV, Algorithms and Interfaces*, Morgan Kaufmann, 2003.

[**Sullivan**] Gary J. Sullivan et al., *The H.264/AVC Advanced Video Coding Standard: Overview and Introduction to the Fidelity Range Extension*. SPIE Conference on Applications of Digital Image Processing XXVII. August, 2004.

[**Symes**] Peter Symes, *Digital Video Compression*, McGraw Hill/TAB, October 2003.

[**Watkinson**] John Watkinson, *The MPEG Handbook*, Focal Press, 2nd edition, November 1, 2004.

[**Wiegand**] Thomas Wiegand, Gary J. Sullivan, Gisle Bjontegaard, and Ajay Luthra, *Overview of the H.264/AVC Video Coding Standard*, IEEE Transactions on Circuits and Systems for Video Technology 2003.

Fast Shortcuts for Computing 2^N

There are 10 kinds of people in this world: those who understand binary math and those who do not. Many of us live in a binary world despite our base ten arithmetic system. Often we need to convert a 2^N notation to its decimal equivalent. Quick, what is the maximum addressable file size given a 32-bit number system? Well, that is 2^{32} and with a little calculator math we come up with 4,294,967,296 elements or approximately 4.3 billion. Is there a faster way to calculate the value? If we apply a few tricks we can quickly approximate the value to within 7.5% worst case. This is good enough for many practical uses.

The basic idea is to split the exponent (N) into two parts $n1$ and $n2$, such that $n1 + n2 = N$. Let $n1$ equal the tens value of N. So if $N = 24$, then $n1 = 20$ and $n2 = 4$. Now the trick for speedy computation is to approximate the value of 2^{n1} as a round number. We can do this because $2^{10} = 1024$ and $2^{20} = 1,048,576$ for example. So let us approximate 2^{10} to be 1000 and 2^{20} to be 1,000,000 (1 million or 10^6) and 2^{30} to be 1 billion. The max error is only 7.5% and often less.

To compute 2^{24} we set $n1 = 20$ and $n2 = 4$. The approximated value is 10^6 times 2^4, which is 16 million using $2^N = 2^{n1} * 2^{n2}$ where $2^{n1} = 1$ million for this example. The exact value is 16,777,216 so our approximation is within 5%. Of course the 2^{n2} values should be exact but there are only 9 of them to memorize. Most of us likely already know these values (2, 4, 8, 16, 32, 64, 128, 256, 512), especially if we smiled after reading the first sentence of this appendix. Table A.1 shows some other examples. Happy approximating!

N	2^N	Approx.
2	4	—
4	16	—
10	1024	1000 = 1 K
12	4096	4 * 1000
20	1,048,576	1 K * 1 K = 1 M
24	16.7 M	1 K * 1 K * 16 = 16 M
30	1.1 B	1 K * 1 K * 1 K = 1 B
32	4.3 B	1 K * 1 K * 1 K * 4 = 4 B

$$2^N = 2^{(n1 + n2)} = 2^{n1} * 2^{n2}$$

For this table, $K = 10^3$, $M = 10^6$ and $B = 10^9$

TABLE

A.1

B
Achieving Frame Accuracy in a Non-frame Accurate World

Keeping video signals synchronized is a time-honored process. Ideally, all routed video signals in a facility are raster time-aligned horizontally and vertically and with a known frame time code. The basic method used to synchronize a target video signal is to apply a correcting time shift and thereby align it with a provided master reference signal. In most cases, the vertical and horizontal timing of the target signal is altered to agree with the provided video house reference. There is usually a one or more frame delay (input to output delay of corrector) to accomplish the time alignment.

It is not difficult to imagine how this process works. The input signal needing correction is fed into a "frame synchronizer" (stand alone box or internal device process). It is written to a digital frame memory (sometimes called an elastic buffer) at the input rate and timing. Next, a separate process reads from the same memory to create a new signal for output. The output timing is aligned to the provided master reference signal. As long as the input data rate and output data are equal *on average*, then the buffer will not overflow or underflow. There is a clean separation of the two processes and any output H/V timing relation may be produced independent of the input signal timing.

Frame syncs are applied to many real world problems. For example, a received satellite video feed will not naturally be time aligned with a facility's internal timing reference so the received signal must be frame synced to align it. Incidentally, most video facilities have a video reference signal that is distributed to all AV gear. By using the reference signal, all device AV I/O can be aligned to the master reference signal. In some cases, the input frame rate and output frame rate are not precisely equal. Over time (sometimes many hours or days) the frame sync needs to duplicate or drop a frame to keep the buffer from underflowing or overflowing. If this is only done on occasion, then the frame jumps are rarely noticed. With GPS worldwide timing, frame buffers rarely exceed their limits. Also, the audio associated with an aligned video must be delayed or resampled for lip-sync agreement. An infrequent audio click may be detected due to the frame drop/add operation.

When signals are streamed across digital networks, they will invariably drift in time due to the introduced delay and jitter and may need to be frame corrected at some point in the workflow. Frame synchronizing is an important process in the real world of A/V systems.

Grid, Cluster, Utility, and Symmetric Multiprocessing Computing

Grids leverage underutilized CPU power from machines connected to the Internet (or a private network) to run various applications. *Clusters* are a formal collection of CPU resources (servers normally) connected to a private network for use in computing. At the most fundamental level, when two or more dedicated computers are used together to solve a problem, it is considered a cluster. *Utility computing* hides the complexity of resource (computers, networks, storage, etc.) management and provides what business wants: utilization on demand. Finally, *symmetric multiprocessing* (SMP) harnesses the power of N CPUs running in parallel. All of these techniques may be applied to AV computational problems. The following sections review the four methods.

GRID COMPUTING

Grid computing is a distributed environment composed of many (up to millions) heterogeneous computers (nodes), each sharing a small burden of the computational load. The power of the Internet enables thousands of cooperating PCs to be connected in a mesh of impressive computational power. By some estimates, most desktop PCs are busy only 5% of the time so why not put these underutilized resources to better use? Even some servers are idle for a portion of each day so a grid assembles and manages unused storage and CPU power on networked machines to run applications. The node application is run in the background and does not interfere with the primary user applications on the machine.

The potential of massive parallel CPU capacity is very attractive to a number of industries. In addition to pure scientific needs, bio-med, financial, oil exploration, and others are finding grids to be of value. If the computational solution is written with a grid in mind, it will run N times faster when N nodes are working in parallel on average. Figure C.1 shows trends ranging across local to enterprise to global grid computing. www.grid.org reports that 2.5 million computers from 200 countries

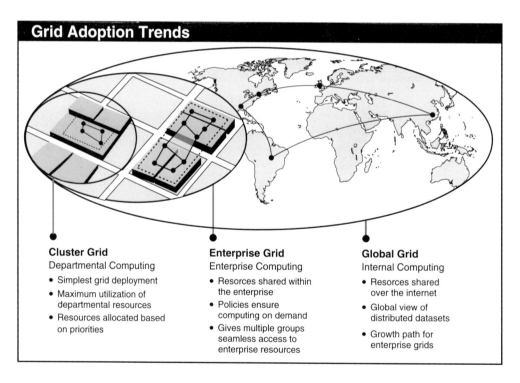

Grid Adoption Trends

Cluster Grid
Departmental Computing
- Simplest grid deployment
- Maximum utilization of departmental resources
- Resources allocated based on priorities

Enterprise Grid
Enterprise Computing
- Resorces shared within the enterprise
- Policies ensure computing on demand
- Gives multiple groups seamless access to enterprise resources

Global Grid
Internal Computing
- Resorces shared over the internet
- Global view of distributed datasets
- Growth path for enterprise grids

FIGURE   Grid computing environments.

C.1   Concept: Sun.

are now tied into one grid for the purposes of cancer research, searching for extraterrestrial life (SETI project at setiathome.ssl.berkeley.edu), and other noble causes. For local or enterprise grids, it is possible to define a QoS for the computing power. In a global sense, a guaranteed QoS is problematic, as most of the Internet-connected nodes are voluntary citizens.

Currently, there are very few commercial AV uses of a grid. One pioneer in this area is AXYZ Animation (www.axyzfx.com). They have a software package that partitions animation rendering projects onto a well-controlled local grid with excellent success. Some users of their product operate dual CPU machines as nodes. With the second processor dedicated to the grid, animators do not notice any impact on system performance as they do their normal work. As grids become more accepted, other AV operations may migrate to the grid.

GRID COMPUTING AND THE RIEMANN ZETA FUNCTION

One particularly interesting use of grid computing is related to finding the complex zeros of the Riemann zeta function. In 1859, Bernhard Riemann wrote a mathematical paper showing a formula for all the prime numbers less than N, the so-called prime number theorem (PNT). In this paper he asserted that all the zeros of the zeta function have a real part of $\frac{1}{2}$. This is the Riemann Conjecture. Since then, mathematicians have attempted to prove this but without success. It is one of the most difficult problems facing mathematicians today. There is a $1 million prize on the block if you can prove the conjecture (see www.claymath.org/millennium). Sebastian Wedeniwski of IBM used a grid configuration of ~11,600 nodes to find the first trillion complex zeros of the zeta function (www.zetagrid.net). Results show all zeros have a real part of $\frac{1}{2}$. This is not a proof of the Riemann Conjecture, but it provides tantalizing data to the affirmative.

To learn more about Riemann, the zeta function, complex zeros, the PNT, loads of interesting stories, and the quest to solve one of the greatest unsolved problems in mathematics, pick up a copy of the very entertaining book *Prime Obsession* by John Derbyshire. He treats the problem as a mystery and leads the reader through beautiful gardens of advanced, yet accessible, math to illuminate it.

CLUSTER[1] COMPUTING

A cluster is a common term meaning independent computers combined into a unified system through software and networking. Clusters are typically used for high-availability (HA) or high-performance computing (HPC) to provide greater computational power than a single computer can provide. The Beowulf project began in 1994 as an experiment to duplicate the power of a supercomputer with commodity hardware and software (Linux).

Today, Beowulf cluster technology is mature and used worldwide for serious computational needs. The commodity hardware can be any of a number of mass-market, stand-alone compute nodes. This ranges from two networked computers sharing a file system to 1024 nodes connected via a high-speed, low-latency network. Performance is improved proportionally by adding machines to the cluster.

Class I clusters are built entirely using commodity hardware and software using standard technology such as SCSI/ATA and Ethernet. They are typically less expensive than class II clusters, which may use specialized hardware to achieve higher performance. As Chapter 3B discussed, NAS clusters are very practical for A/V applications. Also, for high-end rendering and film effects work, a cluster is "without parallel." Clusters are in daily use for computing the world's most demanding scientific simulations.

Orion Multisystems (www.orionmultisystems.com) has created a stand-alone cluster workstation, a novelty among racks of servers that do the same job. Think of it as a "personal cluster." They package from 12 to 96 CPUs in one workstation. The 96 CPU version peaks at 300 gigaflops/s. This type of device may be used to convert file formats in real time among other A/V applications.

---

[1] Some of the material in this section is paraphrased from the Beowulf Web site, www.beowulf.org.

UTILITY COMPUTING

Next, there is *utility computing*. In theory, utility computing gives companies greater utilization of data center resources more cost effectively. It is based on flexible computing, storage, and network capacity that react automatically to changes in computing needs. The data center of the future should be self-configuring, self-monitoring, and self-healing. An engine room of resources is turned into a computing utility the way an electric power plant is used today: plug it in and use it without worries of where it came from or who manages its allocation and reliability.

However, some industry experts like to use other analogies. Tony Siress (Sun Microsystems) maintains that transportation is a good analogy, considering how businesses employ a combination of owned, leased, and rented cars to meet their changing transit needs. Taxi cabs are a good example of a fully outsourced piece of infrastructure, and they are the right approach in some situations. Utility computing is being sponsored by HP, IBM, and Sun and each has various initiatives in place. It is not mature and, to some pundits, it is an idea looking for a market. The jury is out for this approach at the moment. See www.utilitycomputing.com for more information.

SMP COMPUTING

The final method in our list to increase performance uses N tightly coupled CPUs. This is sometimes called symmetric multiprocessing. Commercial systems support 4 or 8 CPUs commonly, although 64 or more are possible. The programming model for an SMP system relies on dividing a large program into small threads spread out among the N CPUs. The CPUs share a common memory so a computational speed up of N may occur under a best-case scenario. Linux and Windows support SMP as do other OSs.

D | How Much Information Exists?

How much information exists? First, let us comprehend an exabyte's worth of data. Table D.1[1] provides some clues.

HOW MUCH INFORMATION EXISTS?

Since 2000, researchers at the University of California, Berkeley, have continued to estimate each year how much information exists on the planet Earth. An executive summary of their report, "How Much Information? 2003" is available at the Web site www.sims.berkeley.edu/research/projects/how-much-info-2003/execsum.htm. Table D.2 provides just a few highlights (all in per-year units):

The research firm IDC predicts that HDD shipments worldwide in 2009 will be 630 million units. With an average of 100 GB per HDD, this amounts to 63 Exabytes.

---

[1] Table D.1 was derived from some work by Roy Williams of Caltech. A Kilobyte (1024 bytes) is rounded to 1000 bytes.

Kilobyte (KB)	1000 bytes $- 10^3$ bytes 2 Kilobytes: A typewritten page 100 Kilobytes: A low-resolution photo
Megabyte (MB)	$1,000,000$ bytes $- 10^6$ bytes 2 Megabytes: A high-resolution photo 5 Megabytes: The complete works of Shakespeare 100 Megabytes: 1 meter of shelved books
Gigabyte (GB)	$1,000,000,000$ bytes $- 10^9$ bytes 1 Gigabyte: a pickup truck filled with books 100 Gigabytes: A library floor of academic journals
Terabyte (TB)	$1,000,000,000,000$ bytes $- 10^{12}$ bytes 2 Terabytes: An academic research library 10 Terabytes: The print collections of the U.S. Library of Congress 400 Terabytes: National Climactic Data Center (NOAA) database
Petabyte (PB)	$1,000,000,000,000,000$ bytes $- 10^{15}$ bytes 2 Petabytes: All U.S. academic research libraries 20 Petabytes: Production of hard-disc drives in 1995 200 Petabytes: All printed material
Exabyte (EB)	$1,000,000,000,000,000,000$ bytes $- 10^{18}$ bytes 2 Exabytes: Total volume of information generated in 1999

TABLE

D.1

How Big Is an Exabyte?

Information object	How many bytes
How much e-mail information per year	11,265 Terabytes
How much radio information	788 Terabytes
How much TV information	14,150 Terabytes
How much telephone information	576,000 Terabytes
How much postal information	150,000 Terabytes
How much office document information	195 Terabytes

TABLE

D.2

How Much Information?

E | 8B/10B Line Coding

When transmitting digital data across a LAN, WAN, or other link it is important to design the link with the following features.

1. No average DC term (DC-free) when data are viewed over several bytes. So, only AC components are present. DC cannot pass through optical fiber.
2. Allows for clock and bit recovery from received data stream.
3. Minimum frequency spectrum shape for greater cable reach.

Transmitting raw uncoded user data bit streams will not meet any of these requirements. Why? It is likely for long strings of ones or zeros to occur so conditions 1 and 2 are not met. Also, some data sequences have very high frequency components. The following describes two different ways to meet the three conditions just given.

◆ Use a block code. One example encodes 8-bit user data as 10-bit valued code words. In its most basic form, 256, 8-bit, user values are mapped into 256, 10-bit, code words. This coding type, used by Fibre Channel, is called 8B/10B, although there are other popular ones, such as 8B/14B (used by the common CD) and 64B/66B (10 gigabit Ethernet). Using 8B/10B requires a 25% higher line bit rate due to the overhead of the code words. Each of the 256 code words has an equal number of ones and zeros for all but four cases, but a DC-free balance is maintained over several code words. Sometimes payload rates are quoted (as with GigE) and sometimes line bit rates are quoted (as with Fibre Channel). So, buyer beware. IBM patented this coding concept in 1984.

◆ Use a scrambler to randomize and statistically balance data. This does not expand the message as 8B/10B does so it is more efficient. However, it does not guarantee a perfect DC-free balance, although blocks of reasonable size will be "nearly" balanced to high probability. Condition 3 is not strictly met but scrambling does generate a predictable spectrum shape.

Both methods are in wide use. The common SDI link (SMPTE 259M) uses the scrambling method. Some pathological data patterns have been known to cause a poorly designed receiver to lose clock recovery and generate bands of colors instead of the payload image. Scrambling does not always eliminate certain problem sequences that 8B/10B, for example, can deal with effectively.

F | Digital Hierarchies

There are two main classes of telecoms-based digital links in worldwide use for transporting telephone and data signals. One system is called plesiochronous digital hierarchy (PDH) and is based on multiplexing numerous individual channels into higher rate channels. The PDH is not synchronous but "nearly synchronous." The second link type depends on synchronous communications. The United States and Canada rely on SONET whereas the rest of the world uses the SDH. SONET stands for Synchronous Optical NETwork, and SDH is an acronym for Synchronous Digital Hierarchy. The ITU adopted SONET, with small variations, as the basis for the SDH. The SONET/SDH standards define a hierarchy of interface rates that permit different line rates to be multiplexed as with the PDH method.

The PDH uses clocks of different accuracies, whereas SONET transmits using a highly stable reference-clocking source for the entire SONET network. Both use different framing methods, line rates, line coding, and timing. Despite the many differences, there are common features to both systems.

◆ Each has a defined hierarchy of data rates (see later) for multiplexing lower rate signals of the same type.

◆ Each can carry telephone data payloads in multiples of DS0 (digital signal 0) at 64,000 bits/s.

◆ Many telecoms carriers offer PDH (T1, T3) and SONET/SDH (OC-3, OC-12) links as WAN access connectivity to their network.

◆ There are a variety of data packaging methods defined: IP packets over either, ATM over SONET/SDH, MPEG TS over either, and others.

The underlying technology of the PDH and SDH is complex and is not covered here. Table F.1 outlines the common naming and hierarchical relationships of the two methods.

North America, Europe, and Japan have chosen different basic PDH line rates, but the other aspects are identical. The J terminology is a colloquial naming scheme for Japan as E is for Europe and T for North America. The physical links are copper based for T1/T3 and E1/E3 but are usually optical for higher rates. Rates beyond T3/E3/J3 are not in common use for WANs. Table F.1 reviews PDH link naming and rates in use worldwide.

Line Speed	DS0's	North America	Europe	Japan
64 Kbps	1	—	—	—
1.544 Mbit/s	24	T-1	—	J-1
2.048 Mbit/s	32	—	E-1	—
6.312 Mbit/s	96	T-2	—	J-2
7.786 Mbit/s	120	—	—	—
8.448 Mbit/s	128	—	E-2	—
32.064 Mbit/s	480	—	—	J-3
34.368 Mbit/s	512	—	E-3	—
44.736 Mbit/s	672	T-3	—	—
97.728 Mbit/s	1440	—	—	J-4
139.264 Mbit/s	2016	—	—	—
139.268 Mbit/s	2048	—	E4	—
274.176 Mbit/s	4032	T-4	—	—
400.352 Mbit/s	5760	T-5	—	—
565.148 Mbit/s	8192	—	E-5	J-5

TABLE   PDH Naming and Rate Relationships

F.1

Optical carrier	Line data rate	User data rate	SONET	SDH
OC-1	51.84 Mbit/s	49.536	STS-1	—
OC-3	155.52 Mbit/s	148.608	STS-3	STM-1
OC-9	466.56 Mbit/s	445.824	STS-9	STM-3
OC-12	622.08 Mbit/s	594.824	STS-12	STM-4
OC-18	933.12 Mbit/s	891.648	STS-18	STM-6
OC-24	1244.16 Mbit/s	1188.864	STS-24	STM-8
OC-36	1866.24 Mbit/s	1783.296	STS-36	STM-12
OC-48	2488.32 Mbit/s	2377.728	STS-48	STM-16
OC-192	9953.28 Mbit/s	9510.912	STS-192	STM-64
OC-768	40 Gbit/s	—	STS-768	STM-256
OC-3072	160 Gbit/s	—	STS-3072	STM-1024

TABLE

F.2

SONET and SDH Relationships

OPTICAL CARRIERS IN SONET AND THE SDH

In SONET and the SDH the optical standard is typically known by an OC-x number where x is a multiple of the OC-1 rate of 51.84 Mbps. While the optical system is common, there are small differences in framing and bit rates between SDH and SONET. North America uses a STS-x (synchronous transport signal) format for frames (packets), whereas Europe uses a STM-x (synchronous transport module) format. Table F.2 lists the various SONET/SDH relationships.

CONCLUSION

The PDH and SONET/SDH systems are the backbone of the telecoms industry. Many telecom carriers offer A/V-friendly WAN services over T3/E3 and higher rates. IP data packaged over either method is a common offering. These methods plus pure Ethernet connectivity will continue to be the foundation of WAN technology worldwide.

270 Million—A Magic Number in Digital Video

The SDI link carries uncompressed SD video at 270-Mb/s line rates. Interestingly, the SDI link can synchronously carry a digitally sampled 625/25 line structure signal (used in the PAL system) or the 525/29.97003 line structure signal (used in NTSC systems) at the same line rate of 270 Mb/s. How is this possible as the two TV systems have apparently unrelated sampling rates? History records that the 525 and 625 analog systems were developed independently of each other. However, the two digital systems have a common sampling rate of 270 Mb/s. Let us see why.

In the 625 line system the horizontal line rate is $625 \times 50/2 = 15{,}625$ lines per second (LPS, units in hertz). In the 525 line system the LPS rate is $525 \times 60/2 \times 1000/1001 = 15{,}734.2657734$. Do the two line rates have a common relationship? By examining these two values, we get the following factorizations.

- $5^6 = 15{,}625$ (PAL)
- $(7 \times 25 \times 3) \times 30 \times (125 \times 8)/(7 \times 11 \times 13) = 15{,}734.265\ldots$ (NTSC)

Dividing the second value by the first yields an exact integer ratio of $144/143$. This relationship was not planned by the respective PAL/NTSC system designers, yet is of great benefit to us. Now, $144 \times 15{,}625\,\mathrm{Hz} = 143 \times 15{,}734.265\,\mathrm{Hz} = 2.25\,\mathrm{MHz}$ and this is the lowest common frequency that both line rates can be derived from. How may this value be used? All digitally sampled systems have a corresponding sample clock. This clock needs to be high enough (meets the Nyquist sample rate rules) to faithfully represent any analog video signal in digital form yet not be so high as to waste bandwidth and storage space. Given the bandwidth of SD video signals, a factor of 6 was deemed ideal, yielding a system sample clock of $6 \times 2.25\,\mathrm{MHz} = 13.5\,\mathrm{MHz}$. This is the basic sampling rate of SD digital video.

It turns out that each image RGB pixel set can be represented by a color difference component format. This digital format is referred to as Y′CrCb (luma, and two chroma samples). Y′CrCb is derived from RGB pixels via mathematical operations, albeit with some loss of image resolution. The SDI data structure format (component video mode) carries the Y′CrCb signal with 4:2:2 sampling. There is *one* Y′ value and *one* chroma (either Cr or Cb) value per RGB sample set on average.[1] SDI supports 10-bit samples so the luma/chroma sequence requires 2×10 bits. The overall SDI line rate is $13.5\,\mathrm{MHz} \times 20$ bits $= 270\,\mathrm{Mb/s}$. This rate is usable for both 625 and 525 line TV systems. So indeed, 270,000,000 is a magic number in SD digital video systems.

One more point of interest. The ratio 144/143 between the 525 and the 625 systems is also a measure of the spatial/temporal information content difference between the two systems. One has more spatial resolution (625/25), whereas the other has more temporal resolution (525/29.97). As humans, we value both spatial and temporal quality when viewing a moving image. There are of course countless levels of nuance when evaluating image attributes, but at a high level it is apparent that the two system's "image quality" differs by only .7% if the spatial and temporal resolutions are weighted equally.

---

[1] If this all sounds confusing, see Chapter 11 for more information on the Y′CrCb and 4:2:2 formats and their use in video systems.

H | A Novel AV Storage System

In high-end broadcast and postproduction environments, real time, high availability storage systems offer significant workflow advantages. This appendix reviews a new storage system architecture[1] designed specifically for the needs of AV. The design blurs the lines between NAS and SAN systems. It addresses a number of key needs, including support for a large number of real time editing clients and I/O channels, high data availability, hot-swap components, heterogeneous clients (Windows and MacOS), and wide range scalability in data rates and storage capacity.

Commercially available, enterprise-class NAS and SAN systems are hard pressed to meet these functional requirements. A NAS, in which client data pass through a single NAS server, does not scale easily and suffers from intrinsic data rate and latency constraints. Fibre Channel-based SAN topologies are also problematic and have limited client attach flexibility and scalability. Finally, commercially available clustered file systems are not designed to support data requests with real time QoS requirements.

---

[1] This material summarizes the Avid Unity ISIS storage architecture. General storage system technologies are discussed in Chapters 3A and 3B.

ARCHITECTURAL OVERVIEW

To overcome these deficiencies, an entirely new networked file system and storage infrastructure was developed. The file system is unique in several ways. Every editing client and I/O channel requires consistent, glitch-free, AV data streams delivered to/from storage. The file system arbitrates data transfer deadlines between clients and storage, ensuring clients complete transfers to storage within a prescribed time window. Without such functionality, a client's internal buffers would either overflow or starve. Further, the file system enables storage configurations to be modified dynamically, allowing system administrators to reassign, add, or remove storage from user groups without interrupting client operations.

To deliver the required performance and scalability, the file system is implemented as a clustered file system with intelligence distributed among the file system metadata managers (the system directors), the AV clients, and intelligent storage blade servers. AV clients access low data rate file metadata from the directors and access bulk file data via an Ethernet iSCSI-like connection to the storage blades. The director is mirrored offering an NSPOF design.

The storage infrastructure uses one or more blade chassis each containing up to 16 intelligent storage blades (see Appendix K). Each blade contains two disks (250- or 500-GB capacity each), a CPU, and dual gigabit Ethernet ports to connect to the back plane. Further, two independent Ethernet switch blades are integral components to each chassis, enabling clients to directly attach to the storage as well as interconnect multiple blade chassis. For the 24×7 world of broadcast, switch blades and power supplies are redundant and support hot swap. Figure H.1 illustrates a typical configuration of a small number of blade chassis and several real time clients.

User data are protected using a redundant array of independent nodes (RAIN) rather then RAID methods. When a client writes data to a storage blade, the blade is responsible for making a redundant copy on other blades. If any blade fails, the system director notifies all blades of the failure. A new copy of any lost blade data is made immediately. The data replication process occurs in parallel across all the blades, resulting in exceedingly short rebuild times and improving overall reliability.

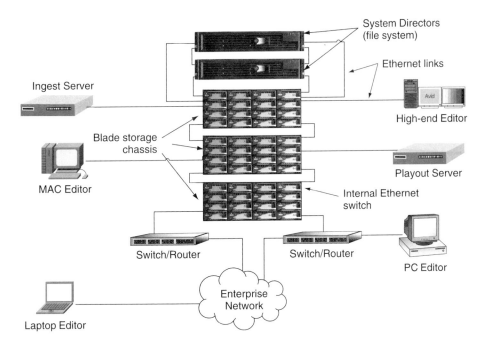

Sample unity ISIS™ configuration.

SUMMARY

The methods discussed in this appendix illustrate a new approach to AV real time storage. The combination of Ethernet-based storage access, an intelligent file system director, and distributed storage creates a system designed specifically for AV use. The system uses NSPOF design principles and clever use of blades to create a highly reliable and scalable real time storage system.

APPENDIX

Is It Rabbits Multiplying or Is It Streaming?

Inventors have dreamed up all manner of methods to stream content. One novel approach is based on a mesh of peer-to-peer connections. The idea centers on distributing the master stream from the source to only a few clients and not the entire population, as is normally the case. Each client (e.g., a PC viewing or listening station) functions as a normal client but in addition provides a ministream server that other clients may draw on. The ministream server may source two to six or more streams depending on the available link connection bandwidth. When deployed for home use over DSL or a cable modem, audio streaming bandwidths are low enough to allow the scheme to work well.

The aggregate connection bandwidth grows exponentially with the number of clients. With only 6 clients at the head of the client population (clients A.1 to A.6 in Figure I.1), 36 second level clients may be fed. This assumes that each client sources 6 streams. With 36 second-level clients, 216 others may be sourced, which in turn can source others. Yes, it is like rabbits multiplying. On first impression, it may seem that the system is a house of cards—if one client falters then many others downstream will be deprived of a stream. However, each client is constantly monitoring its own active input and one or more other source streams for data integrity. If the active stream falters, then an alternate is switched to in real time as needed. It is a delicate balancing act but it works quite well even as member clients drop and join the mesh.

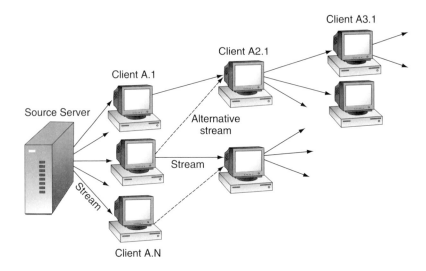

FIGURE   Architecture of a peer-to-peer RT streaming network.

I.1

One vendor of this technology is Abacast (www.abacast.com) and they have several marquee clients using their solution. The beauty of this architecture is that the entire client population shares a little of the burden to distribute streams. Meanwhile, the main source server only feeds a few tens of streams even though a total population of 100 K or more clients may be actively attached to the mesh. Long live the rabbits. See Chapter 4 for more information on P2P architectures.

How to Evaluate a Video Server

The mobile (Alexander Calder, 1898–1976) hangs in midair, suspended from a single point. Let us use the mobile as a guideline for evaluating broadcast products, particularly the video server.

Figure J.1 shows an example of a mobile illustrating the values of a video server. All of the elements represent either product features (right side) or the vendor's values (left side). The left side represents the extrinsic (outside the product) value of a product, and the right side represents the intrinsic (inside the product) value of a product. The combination of the extrinsic plus intrinsic values is the total value of a product and should equate the product's price.

The left side of the mobile illustrates a vendor's vision, product track record, financial stability, and service/support offerings. The right side notes aspects that are specific to the server's internal features. The discussion to follow focuses on these technical, intrinsic values and leaves the extrinsic vendor analysis to your better judgment.

There are five main intrinsic categories to consider; they are noted on the right side of the mobile and in Figure J.2. The topics are (1) the three planes, (2) architectures, (3) storage subsystems, (4) scalability, and (5) reliability. Next, let us examine the values associated with the three-plane model first.

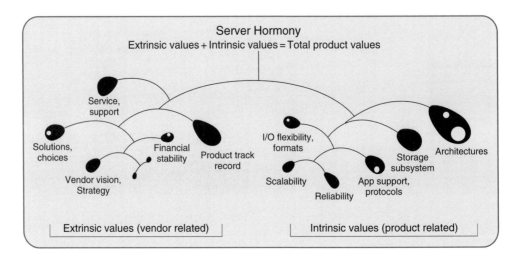

FIGURE   Server harmony.

J.1

THE THREE PLANES

Traditional IT devices have been designed using the three-plane model (see Chapter 7). This model is ideal for describing the *data, control,* and *management* aspects of a device. Each plane offers specific functionality as shown in Figure J.2.

The SDI interface on a server is a *data plane* component. File transfer using Ethernet is also a data plane component. It is worth mentioning the need for file exchange interoperability. For this to work smoothly, the file types and associated metadata must be standardized. MXF is becoming the standard of choice for this plane.

The AV *control plane* mainly uses proprietary command sets (Sony VTR Protocol, VDCP, etc.) over RS422 links. This is changing with most new protocols being IP based. However, machine control over standard

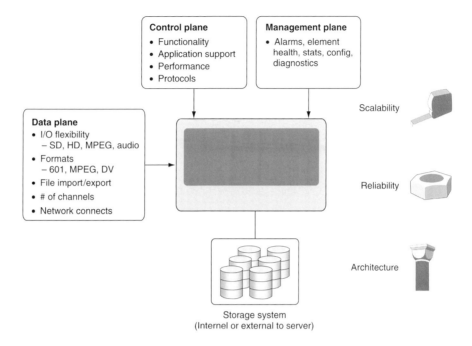

A servers' intrinsic value.

LANs also uses proprietary methods in 2005. Frankly, there are precious few true AV control standards, so ask what is provided during your evaluation.

Industry wide, the ***management plane*** is the least mature of the three. Today, in some cases, this plane is completely absent from AV devices. What is the purpose of this plane? It is a portal into a device to configure and monitor all aspects of its operations. Broadcast equipment suppliers are starting to include basic IT-based monitoring methods. See Chapter 9 for a summary of these concepts.

THE THREE ARCHITECTURES

Video servers are founded on three architectures.

1. Stand-alone server. Sufficient internal storage for all streaming AV/O needs. Of course external storage may be added to augment the internal. Video I/O ranges from 2 to 8 for most cases.

2. Networked node; file-linked. Server node with small internal storage, loaded (or unloaded) using the Just in Time File Transfer model (JITFT). This is mainly useful when the workflow is file centric. Typically, a single node supports 2 to 8 video I/O.

3. Networked node; storage-linked. Server nodes connect to external storage using SAN, NAS, or other methods. Typically, a single node supports 2 to 16 video I/O but nodes may be ganged for larger aggregate I/O using the services of an optional clustered file system (CFS).

In brief, *stand-alone* servers are restricted because they have limited networked storage access. The *file-linked* method relies on some external controller (automation) to move AV files to/from the server I/O node. The *storage-linked* method connects I/O nodes to external storage. This is a flexible architecture and allows nodes to share a common storage pool. Hybrid combinations of all three exist.

STORAGE SUBSYSTEMS

Storage may be divided into internal and external types. Internal storage is normally one or more hard disc drives configured as a JBOD (Just a Bunch of Discs) or a RAIDed configuration.

External storage comes in three main forms: DAS, SAN, and NAS attached. These are discussed in detail in Chapter 3B. When selecting a server, ask lots of questions about storage performance (under failure mode especially), reliability, hot and cold upgrade methods, product lifetime, and expected future disc upgrades.

SCALABILITY

So, you purchased a 2×4 (2 in, 4 out) server 6 months ago. Today your boss asks if the server can be upgraded to a 2×8. Can it be? What factors affect scalability?

For a small number of required I/O ports and storage capacity, the stand-alone server is the most practical. Its upgradeability is limited. File-linked systems are infinitely scaleable, as each node connects to a general-purpose IP network. The master source of media files is some off-line repository that has its own scalability and reliability requirements. As a result, the problem of scalability is moved, not eliminated.

Storage-linked systems are also scalable, but ask about the maximum number of nodes and total I/O. Most practical systems of this genre support <100 AV I/O ports.

RELIABILITY ISSUES

Several factors affect the reliability of a server system. The following aspects are key.

- Software complexity and maturity.
- Security against network hazards—viruses, worms, etc.
- Storage protection strategy.
- Redundant components, hot upgrades: fans, power supplies, I/O, etc.
- Redundant nodes: $N + N$ (true mirror) or $N + 1$ strategies. $N + 1$ provides for a spare node to take over when any one of the N fails. Ask the vendor about how the spare node is activated. This is not trivial and is the key to a smooth failover. Chapter 5 reviews failover modes.

Look for these basic things: the track record of the server, flexibility of the design, and maturity of the solution, including automation control. When in doubt over a manufacturer's claims, decide based on these fundamentals.

SUMMARY

The mobile illustration of the balanced server is useful for evaluating products of all types. Do not overlook any of the elements that make up the mobile and you may indeed find the "perfect server" for your needs.

K[1] | Blade Servers

Blade servers first emerged in 2001 and, after a rocky start, are finally gaining momentum. From server consolidation initiatives to grid computing projects, they are gradually moving into data centers, displacing regular single and dual CPU servers.

TECHNOLOGY OVERVIEW

A blade server plugs into the back or midplane of a chassis, like books slide into a bookshelf, sharing power, fans, floppy drives, and switches with other blade servers. The blades are literally servers on a card, containing processors, memory, integrated network controllers, an optional Fibre Channel HBA, and other I/O ports. Each blade typically comes with one or two local ATA or SCSI drives. For additional storage, blade servers connect to a storage pool facilitated by a NAS, Fibre Channel, or iSCSI SAN.

A high level of scale is achievable with blade servers by simply adding books to the shelf. Blade management is a key feature offered by vendors. HP (OpenView) and others are extending their server

---

[1] The majority of the text was provided by Jacob Gsoedl, IT Director of a F500 company.

management software to manage and provision blades. While chassis and blades are becoming commodity items, software is the big differentiator and should be at the top of the evaluation list when looking at blade server offerings.

THE PLAYERS

To no one's surprise, HP, IBM, Dell, Sun, and Intel have embraced and are offering blade server technology. According to market researcher IDC, IBM captured 44% of the blade server market in 2004, followed by HP with 32%. The lack of blade server standards has put smaller and lesser known players at a disadvantage.

In an attempt to seed the blade world, IBM introduced an open specification. Smaller companies can use this spec and create "IBM compatible" blade servers. Does this sound familiar? If IBM's spec becomes a de facto standard, then the IBM blade server will be the "PC of the server world."

BLADE SERVER MERITS AND CHALLENGES

Server and storage consolidation are an essential part of any IT cost reduction, and blade servers increasingly play an important role in it. Blade servers allow putting more processing power in less rack space, simplifying cabling, and reducing power consumption. Components such as the chassis, power supply, and fans can be shared across a mix of blades and blade generations, resulting in tangible savings and investment protection.

In combination with good management software, a blade server infrastructure is simpler to maintain and offers improved flexibility, manageability, and modular scalability by simply adding blades. The ability of system management software to dynamically assign blades and virtual machines to applications will give an additional boost to blade servers, bringing us ever closer to "on-demand" computing.

OUTLOOK

The overall trend is toward higher density and more manageable systems and, as a result, blade servers will be favored over larger form factor servers. Depending on the research study, forecasts for blade server sales for 2008 range from $2.5 to $9 billion, compared to $583 in million in 2003. Larger form factor servers will find a place where more expansion, additional redundancy options, higher processing power, more cooling, and in-box disk storage are required. As a result, the two server types will carve out individual market segments and will coexist for years to come.

A Glossary of AV/IT Terms

3:2 pull down—The process of converting 24-frame-per-second film to 60 (59.94 actually) fields/s video by repeating one film frame as three video fields and then the next film frame as two fields. The actual order is 2, 3 so 2:3 is more accurate but the principle is the same.

4:2:2 (4:4:4, 4:1:1, 4:2:0)—Common designations for pixel sampling relationships in a digital component video format. The first term relates to the luma (Y') sampling rate and the other two relate to the chroma (Cr and Cb) sampling rates. See Chapter 11 to decipher the hidden codes.

480i—Shorthand for a 480 active line, SD interlaced scanning standard usually with 720 horizontal pixels at various frame rates. 480p is the progressive version. Total lines are 525. NTSC is based on this scanning structure.

576i—Shorthand for a 576 active line, SD interlaced scanning standard usually with 720 horizontal pixels at various frame rates. Total lines are 625. PAL is based on this scanning structure.

720p—Shorthand for a 720 active line, HD progressive scanning standard with 1280 horizontal pixels at various frame rates. Total lines are 750.

1080i—Shorthand for a 1080 active line, HD interlaced scanning standard with 1920 horizontal pixels at various frame rates. 1080p is the progressive version. Total lines are 1125.

AAF—Advanced Authoring Format. A format for annotating the composition of an AV edit project. The AAF Association is responsible for its development.

Active picture area—This is the production area of the raster scan. For 525/NTSC systems there are 480 active lines and 576 for 625/PAL systems. The *safe picture* is a slightly reduced area that is likely viewable on most TVs.

AES—Audio Engineering Society. This group sets standards and recommendations for audio technology.

AES/EBU audio—The joint-effort standard for packaging digital audio up to 24 bits/sample onto a serial link. There is also a mapping for compressed audio.

Alpha—The measure of a pixel's opacity. A pixel with the maximum alpha value is solid, one with a value of zero is transparent, and one with an intermediate value is translucent.

ASI—Asynchronous Serial Interface. This is a 270-Mb/s serial link used most often to carry MPEG Transport Streams. MPEG data can be a single program of AV or many multiplexed programs. Most MPEG streams have data rates less than 100 Mb/s. DVB defines this spec.

Aspect ratio—The ratio of a display's horizontal versus vertical size expressed as H:V or H × V. 4 × 3 and 16 × 9 are common.

ATA—Advanced technology attachment. A parallel link for connecting disc drives and other devices inside a PC or other product. Initially developed for low-end device attachments. See Chapter 3B.

ATM—Asynchronous Transfer Mode. A WAN service based on layer 2 switching. ATM cells carry upper layer payloads such as TCP/IP.

ATSC—Advanced Television Systems Committee. This group defined the digital terrestrial broadcast standard in use for North America and elsewhere. It is based on MPEG encoding and supports SD and HD resolutions.

Automation—The process of controlling AV system operations with a hands-off scheduler. Facility routers, servers, VTRs, compositors, mixers, codecs, processors, and more are controlled by automation logic.

AV (or A/V)—Audio/visual or audio/video. A generic term for describing audio, video, graphics, animations, and associated technology.

AVC—Advanced video codec. This term describes the compression format also referred to as MPEG4 part 10 and separately as H.264.

AVI—Audio video interleaved. An AV wrapper or container format for multiplexing AV essence. It is not a compression format.

BWAV—The EBU's broadcast audio WAV format.

CCIE—Cisco certified Internet work expert.

CFS—Clustered file system. A file system shared in common by more than one client or server. A CFS provides users with a shared or common view of all stored files, usually from one large pool. A CFS is a networkable service either configured as stand alone or distributed among the nodes. In the latter case, a CFS is sometimes called a distributed file system (DFS).

Chroma—A value that conveys a color signal independent from the luma component.

CIF—Common intermediate format. This is a spatial resolution image format of 352 (H) × 288 (V) pixels, 4:2:0. See QCIF. CIF also has a secondary meaning: common image format. This second use is defined by MPEG as either 720 × 480 or 720 × 576. Beware of this acronym. See also SIF.

CIFS—Common Internet File System. A Microsoft developed remote file-sharing protocol. NAS servers often support this. See NFS.

CIM—Common Information Model. This is a model for describing managed information.

CIMOM—CIM Object Manager. This is a software component for accessing data elements in the CIM schema.

Closed captioning (CC)—Textual captioning on a TV screen for the hearing impaired. CC data are carried on unseen line 21 using NTSC. Standard EIA-608 defines CC data structures for analog transmission, and EIA-708 defines CC for digital transmission systems. Teletext subtitling is a similar system used in PAL countries.

Color burst—A burst of 8–10 cycles of subcarrier inserted into a composite video signal after the H_Sync pulse. It is used to synchronize the receiver's video color decoder circuitry.

Colorimetry—The science of defining and measuring color and color appearance.

Component video—A method of signal representation that maintains the original image elements separately rather than combined (encoded) as a single, composite signal. Video signal sets such as R'G'B' and Y'CrCb are component video signals.

Composite video—A standardized way to combine luma, chroma, and timing information into one signal. The NTSC and PAL standards define the methods to create a composite video signal. See Chapter 11.

Content—In the context of AV media, content = essence + metadata.

CORBA—Common Object Request Broker Architecture. See Chapter 4.

CoS—Class of service. An indicator of performance or feature set associated with a flow of information. A CoS may be set to prioritize an AV flow.

COTS—Commercial off-the-shelf. Products that can be purchased and integrated with little or no customization, thus facilitating customer infrastructure expansion and reducing costs. They are generic and not designed specifically to meet AV requirements for the most part.

CVBS—Composite video burst and sync. Shorthand to describe a composite video signal.

D1, D2, . . . D16—Various SMPTE-standardized video tape formats with D4, 8, and 13 not defined.

DAS—Direct attached storage. Storage that is local and dedicated to a device. Chapter 3B covers this in detail. Sometimes called direct access storage device (DASD).

DCML—Data Center Markup Language. A model that describes a data center environment.

DES—Data Encryption Standard. An international standard for encryption and decryption. The same key is used for both.

DHCP—Dynamic Host Configuration Protocol. A method to automatically assign an IP address to a newly attached network client. A DHCP server doles out IP addresses from a pool.

Diffserv—Differentiated services. A method defined by the IETF to segregate user data flows per class of service and associated QoS.

DNS—Domain Name Server. This is a network service that translates between a named address (as in www.ebay.com) and its IP address (66.135.208.89). The DNS may select an IP address from a pool, thereby performing a type of load balancing.

DRM—Digital rights management. The processes and techniques to secure and control the use of digital content by users.

DV—Digital Video. This is a video compression format and tape format. It is in common use for news gathering, consumer cameras, and editing. The nominal video rate is 25 Mb/s, but 50 and 100 are also standardized. See also HDV.

DVB—Digital Video Broadcasting. This is a European family of standards for digital transmission over terrestrial, cable, and satellite. DVB standards are implemented by 55+ countries. It supports SD and HD resolutions.

EBU—European Broadcasting Union. A television broadcast users' group dedicated to education, setting policy, and recommendations for its members. Based in Geneva.

EDL—Edit decision list. A text file for annotating the composition of an edit project. See AAF.

Embedded audio—The process of carrying audio and video on the same link; usually SDI as defined by SMPTE 259M or 292M.

Essence—Basic, low-level AV data structures such as MPEG, DV, or WAV data. It is distinguished from "content" that normally has metadata and other non-AV elements associated with it. An MXF file packages essence elements.

FCP—Fibre Channel Protocol. This is a mapping protocol for carrying the SCSI command set over the Fibre Channel link.

FEC—Forward error correction. A method to correct for faulty transmitted data by applying error correction at the receiver. FEC needs overhead bits and can only correct for a maximum number of bad bits per sent payload.

Fibre Channel (FC)—This is a serial link for moving data to/from a storage element or system. It may be optical or even copper based despite the name. Fibre (British spelling) is used instead of fiber to distinguish it from other optical fiber links. One-, 2- and 4-Gb/s links are defined.

Field—With interlaced video, two fields are used to create a full frame. The first complete field (odd lines of the frame) is followed by the second field (even lines of the frame) in time. In practice, the lines are numbered consecutively across fields.

FPS—Frames per second.

Frame—Essentially this is one complete picture. An interlaced frame is composed of two fields (two complete interlaced scans of the monitor screen). A frame consists of 525 interlaced horizontal lines in NSTC and 625 in PAL. A progressive frame is a sequential scan of lines without any interleaving.

Frame accurate—Actions on a video signal at a desired frame position.

Gamma—The exponent value applied to a linear-light signal to obtain an R′, G′, or B′ signal. For example, $R' = R^{.45}$ is a gamma corrected red-valued video signal. The .45 is the gamma value. The apostrophe indicates a gamma-corrected variable. See Chapter 11.

Gen Lock—See video reference.

GOLF—Group of linked files. A directory of associated files that are part of the same program material.

GOP—Group of pictures. In MPEG, a GOP is a collection of sequential pictures (frames) bound by temporal associations. A short GOP is one I frame. The long GOP format is normally a 12 to 15 length IBP sequence for SD. See IBP.

H.264—This is a video compression format also defined as MPEG 4 part 10. It offers superior compression compared to the older MPEG 2 methods.

HA—High availability. The ability of a device/system to withstand hardware or software failures. HA is achieved by using forms of element duplication. See Chapter 5.

HANC—Horizontal ANCillary data field. Both 292M and 259M SDI links contain ancillary data space in the horizontal and vertical dimensions. HANC is included in the portion of each scanning line outside the active picture area and may be used to carry embedded audio. The vertical ANCillary data space (VANC) corresponds to the analog vertical blanking interval. It encompasses much bigger chunks of data space than HANC. Metadata may be embedded in the VANC data space.

HBA—Host bus adaptor. An interface card that plugs into a computer's bus and provides network connectivity.

HD—High-definition video resolution. See Chapter 11.

HDD—Hard disc drive.

HDV—High-definition video. This is an AV tape and compression format using MPEG at 25 Mb/s for 1080i and ~19 Mb/s for 720p. The tape cartridge is the same as used for standard definition DV.

Horizontal sync—The portion of the video signal that triggers the receiver to start the next left-to-right raster scan.

HSM—Hierarchical Storage Management. The process of automatically moving/storing data to the lowest-cost devices commensurate with upper layer application needs.

HTTP—Hyper Text Transfer Protocol. A protocol used to carry data between a client and a server over the Web. HTTPS is an encrypted version of HTTP. See SSL.

IBP Pictures—Intraframe, Bidirectionally predicted, Predicted. This is MPEG shorthand for three different compressed video frame types. The I picture is a standalone compressed picture frame. The B picture is predicted from one or two of its I or P neighbors. The P picture is predicted from the previous I or P picture.

IETF—Internet Engineering Task Force. The body responsible for many of the Internet's standards.

IFS—Installable file system. This is a client or server software component that redirects local file system calls to another internal or external file system (a CFS).

IKE—Internet Key Exchange. IKE establishes a shared security policy and authenticates keys for services that require keys such as IPSec.

ILM—Information Lifecycle Management.

InfiniBand—A switched-fabric I/O technology that ties together servers, storage devices, and network devices

Interlace scan—A display image that is composed of time and spatially offset interleaved image fields. Two fields create a frame. Compare to progressive scan. See Chapter 11.

Interoperability—The capability to communicate and transfer data among various functional units without format or connectivity problems.

IP—Internet Protocol. The Internet Protocol, defined by RFC 791, is the network layer for the TCP/IP protocol suite. It is a connectionless, best-effort packet-switching protocol. This is most often referred to as IPV4. See Chapter 6.

IPSec—IP Security. A security protocol that provides for confidentiality and authentication of individual IP packets.

IPV6—A version upgrade of IPV4, including improved address space, quality of service, and data security.

iSCSI—SCSI commands over an IP-based link. It finds application in SAN environments and is a replacement technology for Fibre Channel. See Chapter 3B.

iSNS—Internet Storage Naming Service. The iSNS protocol is designed to facilitate the automated discovery, management, and configuration of iSCSI and Fibre Channel devices on a TCP/IP network.

IT—Information technology. Related to technologies for the creation, storage, processing, consumption, and management of digital information.

J2EE—Java 2 Enterprise Edition. A Java-based, runtime platform for developing, deploying, and managing multitier, server centric applications on an enterprise-wide scale. Java 2 Standard Edition (J2SE) is a reduced form of the J2EE model.

JITFT—Just in time file transfer. A concept of file exchange where the delivered file arrives at its destination "just in time" by some comfortable margin to be used for editing, playout, format conversion, or some other operation.

Key—See video key.

LAN—Local Area Network. A data network covering a limited area. See Chapter 6.

Long GOP—See GOP.

LTC—Linear (longitudinal) time code. The SMPTE 12M time code standard historically recorded onto the audio track of a VTR or audio recorder. See VITC.

Luma—A video signal related to the monochrome or lightness component of a scene. Often tagged as Y′.

LUN—Logical unit number. A LUN addresses a fixed amount of storage from a pool. The SCSI protocol uses LUNs to address portions of total storage.

MAM—Media Asset Management. These are the technologies used to index, catalog, search, browse, retrieve, manage, and archive specific media content objects. Also, more generally referred to as digital asset management when there are no time-based data types but mainly text and graphics.

MAN—Metro Area Network. See Chapter 6.

Metadata—Literally defined as structured data about data. Metadata is descriptive information about an object or resource.

MIB—Management Information Base. See Chapter 9.

MOS Protocol—Media Object Server Protocol. A protocol for managing the rundown list and associated operations per story for a news broadcast. See www.mosprotocol.com.

MPEG—Motion Picture Experts Group. This is an ISO/IEC standards body responsible for developing AV compression formats (MPEG 1, 2, 4) and other

AV-related standards (MPEG 7, 21). MPEG 2 is used universally as a distribution format for digital cable, satellite, over-the-air, and SD-DVD.

MPLS—MultiProtocol Label Switching. See Chapter 6.

MSCE—Microsoft certified systems engineer.

MSO—Multiple system operator. A cable industry term describing a company that operates more than one cable TV system

MXF—Material eXchange format. A file wrapper or container format for AV professional use. MXF encapsulates audio + video + metadata elements in a time-aligned manner. It also supports streaming. See Chapter 7 for more information.

NAS—Networked attached storage. Typically, a data server on a network that provides file storage. See Chapter 3B.

NAT—Network address translation. This is a method that maps a local area network private IP address to/from a globally unique IP address. The method conserves the precious, global IP address space.

.NET—This is Microsoft's programming framework for creating applications and services using combinations of servers and clients of all types. It relies on XML and Web services to implement solutions.

NFS—Network file system. A standardized protocol for networked file sharing. NAS file servers often support this. See CIFS.

NLE—Nonlinear editor. The computer-assisted editing of AV materials without the need to assemble them in a linear sequence. The visual equivalent of word processing. Tape-based editing is considered linear editing.

NRCS—News room computer system. A set of software applications for managing the editorial aspects of a news story

NRT—Nonreal time. See RT.

NSPOF—No single point of failure. A system that tolerates a single component failure using fast bypass techniques. Performance should always be specified under a single failure mode.

NTSC—National Television Systems Committee. It describes the SD system of color analog TV used mainly in North America, Japan, and parts of South America. NTSC uses 525 lines per frame and 29.97 frames (59.94 fields) per second.

OOP—Object-oriented programming.

PAL—Phase alternate line. The name of the SD analog color television system used mainly in Europe, China, Malaysia, Australia, New Zealand, the Middle East, and parts of Africa. It uses 25 frames per second and 625 lines per frame.

POTS—Plain old telephone service.

Progressive scan—An image that is scanned sequentially from top to bottom to create a single frame. Compare to interlace scan.

PSTN—Public Switched Telephone Network.

QCIF—Quarter common intermediate format. This is a spatial resolution image format of 176 (H) $\times$ 144 (V) pixels, 4:2:0. See CIF.

QoS—Quality of service. A guarantee of predictable metrics for the data rate, latency, jitter, and loss for a network connection. It can also apply to other services with corresponding QoS metrics for that service. For example, typical QoS metrics of a storage system are transaction latency, R/W access rate, and availability.

RAID—Redundant array of independent (or inexpensive) discs. A method to improve the reliability of an array of discs. See Chapter 5.

RDMA—Remote direct memory access. A method to move block data between two memory systems where one is local and one remote.

RFC—Request for comment. A specification developed by the IETF. The document series, begun in 1969, describes the Internet suite of protocols. Not all RFCs describe Internet standards but many do. Other bodies also contribute to the standards pool.

RFP—Request for proposal.

RGB—Red, green, and blue primary linear-light components. The exact color interpretation depends on the colorimetry scheme used.

R′G′B′—Red, green, and blue primary nonlinear light components. The prime symbol denotes a gamma-corrected value. See gamma.

RPC—Remote procedure call. A protocol for connecting to and running individual processes on remote computers across a network. The client/server model may use RPC-style message passing.

RT—Real time. An activity that occurs in "AV real time" such as live-streamed video/audio or AV device control.

RTP—Real Time Protocol. The IETF standard RFC 1889 for streaming AV usually across IP/UDP networks. Most Web-based AV streaming uses RTP. Professional IP-based video carriage often relies on RTP. Most AV data types (MPEG, MP3 audio, others) have a mapping for carriage using RTP.

Samba—Samba is an open-source implementation of Microsoft's CIFS protocol for file and printer sharing. For example, a Linux computer using Samba appears as a Windows-networked file system.

SAN—Storage area network. This is technology for sharing a pool of storage with many independent servers/clients. See Chapter 3B for more details.

SAS—Serial-attached SCSI. This a serial version of the venerable parallel SCSI link.

SATA—Serial ATA. The serialized form of the common ATA interface. SATA and SAS connectivity have converged; see Chapter 3A.

SCSI—Small Computer System Interface. The standard parallel interface for disc drives and other devices for high-end use. The SCSI command layer is used in Fibre Channel and other serial links; see Chapter 3A.

SD—Standard definition video resolution. See Chapter 11.

SDI—Serial Digital Interface. A serial coaxial link used to move AV digital data from point to point in a professional video system. The nominal line rate is 270 Mb/s for SD video. It is defined by SMPTE 259M for SD and 292M for HD. See Appendix G.

SDTI—Serial Digital Transport Interface (SMPTE 305M). This link uses SMPTE 259M (SDI) as an agnostic payload carrier. There are several defined data mappings onto the SDTI link with compressed payloads (MPEG, DV) being the most common.

SECAM—A French acronym describing an analog color television system. It is closely related to PAL in line structure and rates.

SI—System's integrator.

SIF—Source input format. A 4:2:0, 352×288 (25 FPS) or 352×240 (29.97 FPS) image.

SLA—Service level agreement. A service contract between a customer and a LAN/WAN/MAN service provider that specifies the working QoS and reliability a customer should expect.

SMB—Server message block. The foundation protocol for Microsoft Windows file-server access, also described as the common Internet file system (CIFS). See Samba.

SMEF—Standard Media Exchange Framework. A BBC-developed XML schema for describing MAM metadata.

SMI—Storage Management Initiative. A project of the Storage Networking Industry Association (SNIA) to develop and standardize storage management methods.

SMIL—Synchronized Multimedia Integration Language. A method for creating a synchronized presentation composed of independent multimedia objects.

SMP—Symmetric multiprocessing. See Appendix C.

SMPTE—Society of Motion Picture and Television Engineers. A professional engineering society tasked with developing educational forums and technical standards for motion pictures and television.

SNMP—Simple Network Management Protocol. See Chapter 9.

SOA—Service-oriented architecture. An architecture of distributed services available over a network. Consumers (clients) call networked (using middleware) service providers (servers) to perform some well-defined task. Both the .NET and J2EE frameworks are founded on SOA principles. See Web services.

SOAP—Simple Object Access Protocol. SOAP is a lightweight protocol for the exchange of information in a decentralized, distributed environment. It is XML based and consists of three parts: an envelope that defines the message and how to process it, a set of encoding rules for expressing the application related data types, and a convention for representing remote calls and responses.

SONET—Synchronous Optical Network. See Appendix F for more information.

SPOF—Single point of failure. Compare to NSPOF.

SQL—Structured Query Language. A standard language for querying and modifying relational databases.

SSL—Secure Sockets Layer. This is a method of encrypting networked data using a public key. HTTPS uses SSL.

S_Video—A base-band analog video format where the chroma and luma signals are carried separately to improve fidelity.

TCO—Total cost of ownership. This metric combines all the costs of a device from capital outlay to ongoing operational costs.

TCP—Transmission Control Protocol. It provides payload multiplexing and end-to-end reliability for data transfers across a network. TCP packets are carried by IP packets. This is a layer 4, connection-based protocol. See Chapter 6.

Timecode or time code—A number of the form HH:MM:SS:FF (hours, minutes, seconds, frames) that defines the frame sequence in a video file/stream or film. For 29.97 frames/s systems, FF spans from 00 to 29, whereas for 25 frames/s systems, FF spans from 00 to 24. An example is 11:49:59:24, which is immediately followed by 11:50:00:00 one frame later. See Chapter 11.

TLAN—Transparent LAN. This is a MAN that is Ethernet based end to end.

TOE—TCP offload engine. A hardware accelerator that offloads TCP/IP stack processing from the main device CPU.

Traffic system—A software application for managing the precise scheduling of programming, commercials, and live events throughout a TV station broadcast day. The output of a traffic system is the on-air, second-by-second schedule.

TS—Transport Stream. This is an MPEG systems layer spec for carrying compressed audio, video, and user data. Some non-MPEG compression formats also have mappings into the TS wrapper.

UDDI—Universal Description, Discovery, and Integration protocol. UDDI is a specification for maintaining standardized directories of information about Web services, their capabilities, location, and requirements.

UDP—User Datagram Protocol. It provides payload multiplexing and error detection (not correction) for end-to-end data transfers over IP. This is a layer 4, connectionless-based protocol. Compare to TCP. See Chapter 6.

UMID—Unique Material ID. A SMPTE standard, the UMID is an identifier for picture, audio, and data essence that is globally unique.

VANC—Vertical ANCillary data field. See HANC.

VBI—Vertical blanking interval. For NTSC, all the horizontal lines from 7 to 21 (field one) and from 270 to 284 (field two). These lines may carry nonvisual information such as time code, teletext, test signals, and closed caption text. For PAL, VBI spans lines 7–21 and 319–333.

VC-1—Video coding 1. This is a shorthand descriptor of the tentative SMPTE 421M standard of Microsoft's WM9 video codec.

VDCP—Video Disc Control Protocol. This is commonly used to control video server operations.

Vertical sync—The portion of the video signal that triggers the receiver to start the vertical retrace, thereby bringing the raster in position to start the top line.

Video key—A video signal used to "cut a hole" in a second video signal to allow for insertion of a third video signal (the fill) into that hole.

Video reference—Typically, this is an analog composite or SDI video signal with a black image active area. It is also called "black burst." It is distributed throughout a facility to any element that needs a common horizontal and vertical timing reference.

VITC—Vertical internal time code. A time code data structure described by SMPTE 12M and encoded in one or more lines of the VBI. See LTC.

VLAN—Virtual LAN. A logical, not physical, group of networked devices. VLANs enable administrators to segment their networks (department or region) without physically rearranging the devices or network connections. VLANs are segmented at layer 2 in the protocol stack.

VPN—Virtual private network. A secure, end-to-end, private data tunnel across the public Internet.

W3C—World Wide Web Consortium. A vendor-neutral industry body that develops standards for the Web. Popular W3C standards include HTML, HTTP, XML, SOAP, Web services, and others.

WAFS—Wide area file services. WAFS products accelerate data transfers across WANs using caching and protocol emulation techniques.

WAN—Wide Area Network. A network that connects computers or systems over a large geographic area. See Chapter 6.

WBEM—Web-based Enterprise Management initiative. See Chapter 9.

Web service—A self-describing, self-contained unit of programming logic that provides functionality (the service) through a network connection. Applications access Web services using SOAP/XML without concern for how the Web service is implemented. Do not confuse Web services with the classic Web server; they rely on completely different software models.

WMI—Windows Management Instrumentation. See Chapter 9.

WSDL—Web Services Description Language. WSDL defines a Web service's functionality and data types. It is expressed using XML.

XML—eXtensible Markup Language. A data language for structured information exchange. Values are associated with tags, enabling the definition, validation, and interpretation of data elements between applications and systems.

Y'CrCb—Digital component signal set for uncompressed SD and HD video. See Chapter 11.

Y'PrPb—Analog component signal set for uncompressed SD and HD video. See Chapter 11.

Index

Page numbers with "t" denote tables; those with "f" denote figures

---

[1] Numerals (i.e. 625) are indexed under their first digit (i.e. six).